Statistics and Data Analysis for Social Science

Eric J. Krieg

BUFFALO STATE COLLEGE

Allyn & Bacon

Boston   Columbus   Indianapolis   New York   San Francisco   Upper Saddle River
Amsterdam   Cape Town   Dubai   London   Madrid   Milan   Munich   Paris   Montreal   Toronto
Delhi   Mexico City   Sao Paulo   Sydney   Hong Kong   Seoul   Singapore   Taipei   Tokyo

Editor-in-Chief for Sociology and Social Work: Dickson Musslewhite
Project Manager: Lauren Macey
Editorial Assistant: Brittany Diego
Executive Marketing Manager: Kelly May
Marketing Assistant: Janeli Bitor
Senior Production Project Manager: Pat Torelli
Manufacturing Buyer: Debbie Rossi
Cover Administrator and Designer: Joel Gendron
Editorial Production and Composition Service: Laserwords
Photo Researcher: Katharine Cebik
Digital Media Editor: Thomas Scalzo

Credits appear on page 397, which constitutes an extension of the copyright page.

Cataloging-in-Publication data on file with the Library of Congress

10 9 8 7 6 5 4 3 2 1 RRD-OH 15 14 13 12 11

Allyn & Bacon
is an imprint of

www.pearsonhighered.com

ISBN 10: 0-205-72827-8
ISBN 13: 978-0-205-72827-5

To Pix, Anza, and Maria

Brief Contents

Contents

CHAPTER 3
Measures of Central Tendency   67

CHAPTER 4
Measures of Dispersion   103

CHAPTER 5
Probability and the Normal Curve   135

Preface

To the Instructor

When I began teaching statistics courses in 1994, I was surprised to see how good students were at getting correct answers. Students who claimed to be terrible at math had no problem calculating a wide range of statistics, including measures of central tendency, dispersion, association, and confidence intervals. However, students often had no idea why a particular statistic is calculated or what it tells us about the world. For example, knowing how to mathematically calculate a one-way chi-square is not the same as knowing why anyone would bother to do it. Consequently, their understanding of statistics resided in the realm of "how to" and not in the realm of "why." They did not know what the answers were telling them.

Since I began teaching statistics and data analysis in the early 1990s, I have struggled to find the right text. In the world of teaching and learning, problems often arise because of what is left out of books. As a whole, statistics teachers are guilty of teaching a partial curriculum—one that emphasizes quantity and breadth over quality and depth. It is of no use to students to know how to calculate 30 different statistics if they don't know when to use them or what they mean. Too often, statistics books for undergraduates have a tendency to present too many statistics in too complex a manner, thereby generating too much confusion. In response, I began formatting my class notes so they would be suitable for handouts. The notes eventually took the form of a short workbook intended to supplement a textbook. Over the years a number of teaching assistants made contributions to the workbook and eventually it became more comprehensive. Slowly students began to use it as a replacement for the texts that I assigned and now *Statistics and Data Analysis for Social Science* constitutes a text in and of itself. It is intended to overcome some of the problems that often arise in introductory statistics courses by presenting statistics in a more user-friendly and applied way that connects statistical concepts to real world examples.

A few of the ways in which this book attempts to overcome problems with many other texts are: (1) the number of statistical concepts presented is reduced to those that are most common, (2) the complexity of statistical calculations is reduced to what is necessary for understanding statistical concepts, (3) chapters are organized around "real world" applications/examples which act as references around which questions and discussions are organized, and (4) practice problems are included during incremental steps within the chapter, and at the end of each chapter, with selected answers provided.

Many of the techniques and methods for computing statistics in other texts differ slightly from the techniques demonstrated in *Statistics and Data Analysis for Social Science*. I have tried to present the most understandable approaches, which is not to say that these are the only or the best techniques, just that they are ones I have used successfully. I have attempted to summarize the major concepts in as straightforward a manner as possible. This text is not intended to be comprehensive. Statistical concepts that do not have a direct bearing on a student's investigation of the social world are not included. The style of presentation stems from students who first took the course and later assisted me in teaching the course. Together, we feel that the ideas presented here constitute material that is most central to quantitative analysis in the social sciences, and applicable to our everyday lives.

The order in which statistical concepts are presented in this text provides a logical sequence, allowing students to build their statistical knowledge on top of what they learned in the previous chapter. I like to think of this progression as walking up a flight of stairs—getting to the top of the staircase in one huge step is impossible; however, by taking it step-by-step, it is easy. Each chapter is a step in our staircase. My hope is that this will expand students' imaginations in regard to the ways that these statistical "tools" can be used to make sense of our world and, maybe, to make the world a better place.

Making Sense of Our Social World

Each chapter is written around a particular social problem that is used as an example for the application of statistical concepts. Wherever possible, examples are used so that students can get an idea of why a particular statistic, or group of statistics, is/are used. The social problem discussions are followed by examples of how to calculate the statistic. In my experience, students who know how to calculate a chi-square, for example, tend to have a better understanding of the situations in which a chi-square can and cannot be used. They also seem to have a clearer grasp of what a chi-square tells us about our data.

Applications come from many different areas of the social world, and include:

- Suicide rates and gender (chapter 1)
- Standardized testing in schools (chapter 1)
- Love Canal toxic waste disaster (chapter 2)
- Superfund sites, by state (chapter 2)
- Self-reported health and highest degree obtained (chapter 3)
- Fuel efficiency of different types of cars (chapter 3)
- Hours of television viewing (chapter 4)
- Educational attainment and race (chapter 4)
- Family wealth and life chances (chapter 5)
- Casino odds (chapter 5)
- Views on global warming and political party affiliation (chapter 6)
- How college students spend leisure money (chapter 6)
- Attitudes towards abortion rights (chapter 7)
- International literacy and fertility rates (chapter 7)
- Feelings about the Bible, by race (chapter 8)
- Socioeconomic status and happiness in marriage (chapter 8)
- Smoking on campus (chapter 9)
- Racial disparities in exposure to ecological hazards (chapter 9)
- Poverty in American families (chapter 10)
- SAT performance and success in college (chapter 10)

Pedagogical Features

A variety of pedagogical features is used to enhance the learning in each chapter.

Chapter Opening Examples

Each chapter opens with an example from the world around us, to motivate the chapter material and show the role of statistics in everyday life.

Formula Tables

At the beginning of each chapter, a table summarizes key formulas and symbols used in that chapter. For easy student reference, these formulas and symbols are also listed on the inside front and back covers of the text.

Now You Try It Exercises

After a statistical concept is introduced, the student is given a few practice exercises to reinforce understanding. Answers to these exercises are provided at the end of the chapter. For example:

- In chapter 3, after providing examples of how the mean, median, and mode are computed, the text introduces a Now You Try It exercise, giving raw data on the number of course credits taken by twenty college students. This exercise asks the student to compute the mean, median, and mode from the data, and the student can check the answer in the end-of-chapter material to see if he or she has understood the problem.
- In chapter 6, after examples on finding different confidence intervals for the standard error of the mean, a Now You Try It exercise asks the student to find the 95%, 99%, 90%, and 80% confidence intervals for the average number of "friends" logged by a sample of Facebook users. Correct answers appear at the end of the chapter.

Statistical Uses and Misuses

These boxes encourage students to be informed consumers of statistical information, by giving real examples of how statistics can inform or deceive. *Statistical Uses and Misuses* include:

- The media's use of percentages (chapter 2),
- Measures of central tendency, and what "average" can mean (chapter 3), and
- The use of probability in government risk management (chapter 6).

Eye on the Applied

These boxes take an important concept from the chapter and provide a case study example. Students see how statistics can reveal that the world is not always as it appears at first glance. Some case studies explored are:

- Describing and Summarizing Data: Blues and R&B Music (chapter 2),
- Public Education as Equalizer or Divider?: Performance of Magnate (or Magnet) Schools (chapter 4), and
- The Toxic Waste Trade in Your Community (chapter 8).

Integrating Technology

Optional technology examples demonstrate how technology facilitates the generation and interpretation of statistics. *Integrating Technology* boxes stem from the text's philosophy that statistical software can be one of the tools in a social scientist's toolbox. Some uses of technology detailed in these boxes are:

- Using SPSS or Excel to sort data in ascending or descending order (chapter 4),
- Exploring an online applet that demonstrates the concept of randomness in the normal curve (chapter 5),
- Creating a cross-tabulation table using SPSS for Windows (chapter 7), and
- How a cluster bar chart, created in SPSS, can visually represent the relationships between variables (chapter 8).

Other Special Pedagogical Features

In addition to the features described on previous pages, definitions of Key Terms are included in marginal boxes throughout the chapter and Key Terms are listed, with page numbers, at the end of each chapter. Chapter Exercises and Computer Exercises are included at the end of each chapter so that students can practice calculating and interpreting the statistics themselves. Answers to odd-numbered exercises are found at the end of the text.

Technology Inclusion

Statistics and Data Analysis for Social Science supports the optional use of technology in the introductory statistics for social science course. *Integrating Technology* boxes and the optional end-of-chapter *Computer Exercises* are resources for the instructor who wishes to use a statistical software package for exploration or computation. Although there are many statistical programs and calculators that are effective tools for the beginning student, SPSS for Windows is used in many of the technology examples in the text. SPSS output is to show what data "looks like," in support of the text's emphasis on the visual and graphical presentation of data. A Getting Started guide for SPSS is included as Appendix C, and stepped instruction for SPSS, with text-specific examples, is available in the separate SPSS Manual.

It is my hope that this book can take some of the fear out of statistics. In my experience, students tend to view statistics as an unnecessary burden that they are forced to complete. Unfortunately, it is often one of the last courses they take for their social science major. Delaying statistics to the end of their undergraduate careers robs students of the opportunity to apply useful dimensions of knowledge and critical thinking skills to their studies. Not much that we do in social science departments prepares students for statistics; therefore, we should start thinking of statistics as a "foundation" course that sharpens the analytic capabilities of students as they begin to move into upper division courses. *Statistics and Data Analysis for Social Science* is written in that spirit.

Acknowledgments

I extend my sincere thanks for the suggestions made by the following reviewers of the manuscript for this text:

Michael Abel, Brigham Young University, Idaho

Dusten Hollist, University of Montana, Missoula

Veena Kulkarni, Arkansas State University

Shannon Monnat, University of Nevada, Las Vegas

Christopher Sedelmaier, University of New Haven

Nancy Shields, University of Missouri, St. Louis

Berna Torr, California State University, Fullerton

Bethany Van Vleet, Arizona State University

Junmin Wang, University of Memphis

Aaryn Ward, Louisiana State University

Loretta Winters, California State University, Northridge

Joseph Whitmeyer, University of North Carolina, Charlotte

In addition to the comments made by these reviewers, I am indebted to Sandra Zirkes from Bowling Green State University for the feedback received. Although I am responsible for the final words on the printed page, her suggestions were of tremendous value.

I would like to thank Pearson Sales Representative, Lori Stucchio, and Executive Editor, Jeff Lasser, for encouraging me to write my manuscript, and the following team for bringing the project to fruition: Dickson Musslewhite, Editor-in-Chief; Lauren Macey, Project Manager; Jenn Albanese, Freelance Editor; and Pat Torelli, Senior Production Project Manager. Many thanks, as well, go to Patty Donovan of Laserwords.

Eric "Luke" Krieg
Buffalo State College

A Note from the Publisher on the Supplements

Instructor's Supplements

Unless otherwise noted, instructor's supplements are available at no charge to adopters—in printed or duplicated formats, as well as electronically through Pearson Higher Education's Instructor's Resource Center (www.pearsonhighered.com/irc).

Instructor's Manual and Solutions Manual

The Instructor's Manual provides helpful tools for instructors, including learning objectives, chapter summaries, key terms, discussion topics, and fully worked out answers to every question in the textbook. (0205731317)

Test Bank

The Test Bank includes multiple choice, true/false, and short answer questions to test students' comprehension of the material and ability to work out questions. (0205731309)

MyTest Computerized Test Bank

Pearson MyTest is a powerful assessment generation program that helps instructors easily create and print quizzes and exams. Questions and tests are authored online, allowing ultimate flexibility and the ability to efficiently create and print assessments anytime, anywhere! (0205734707)

PowerPoint Presentation

These PowerPoint slides combine lecture outlines with figures and tables from the text to help instructors present statistical principles in a stimulating way. Each chapter of the textbook has ten to fifteen slides that convey the key concepts on that chapter. (0205731295)

SPSS® Technology Manual

This technology manual provides support for using SPSS® with this textbook. It includes a quick start guide, stepped instruction, screenshots, to demonstrate the use of SPSS® with examples taken directly from the text. (0205206328)

Online Course Management MySocLab

MySocLab is a learning and assessment tool that enables instructors to access student performance and adapt course content—without investing additional time or resources. MySocLab is designed with instructor flexibility in mind—you decide the extent of integration into your course—from independent self-assessment to total course management.

New features in MySocLab include:

- Social Explorer—the premier interactive demographics Web site.
- **MySocLibrary**—with over 100 classic and contemporary primary source readings.
- **MyClassPrep**—New from Pearson, MyClassPrep makes lecture preparation simpler and less time consuming. It collects the very best class presentation resources—art and figures from our leading texts, videos, lecture activities, classroom activities, demonstrations, and much more—in one convenient online destination. You may search through MyClassPrep's extensive database of tools by content topic (arranged by standard topics within the sociology curriculum) or by content type (video, audio, simulation, Word documents, etc.). You can select resources appropriate to your lecture, many of which can be downloaded directly. Or you may build your own folder of resources and present from within MyClassPrep.

About the Author

Eric J. Krieg lives in Buffalo, NY and is an Associate Professor of Sociology at Buffalo State College. His teaching includes introduction to sociology, environment, social problems, research methods, theory, and statistics. His research interests include environmental justice, food and agriculture, community, and health. He has researched and published numerous journal articles on toxic wastes in Massachusetts, Vermont, and Buffalo, NY.

Upon publication of this text, Krieg begins a sabbatical in Santiago, Chile, where he and his family will live for six months. During this time, he will be researching the Chilean dairy industry, food chains, and developing a service-learning abroad course for undergraduates.

Concepts, Variables, and Measurement

CHAPTER

1

Introduction

What we consider to be real or not real is often a matter of personal experience and social standing. For example, one person might argue that racism does not exist in the United States because laws protect against racial discrimination. Another person might argue that racism does exist because he or she has experienced it firsthand, growing up in a community of color. Which claim is correct? While it is true that many laws do protect against

1

Life chances A phrase that Max Weber used in his analysis of social class to refer to differences in the likelihood of people from different class backgrounds having access to similar resources. Differential access to resources can lead to different opportunities (chances) in life.

acts of racial discrimination, it is also true that many communities of color have underfunded schools that limit their students' *life chances*.

In fact, 2000 Census data from the state of New York show that per capita income among whites is $27,244, and among blacks it is only $15,498. The difference reflects historical and institutionalized forms of discrimination (access to loans, education, jobs, and other pathways to upward mobility), not individual deficiencies. Thus while one person may be correct stating that racism does not exist because laws protect against it, another person might also be correct in stating that racism does exist due to structural barriers to personal success.

Unlike a rock analyzed by geologists, it is impossible to go outside, pick up some racism, and bring it back inside to analyze. Yet we know it exists by looking for examples in our own lives or in academic literature. In his book *Sundown Towns* (2005), sociologist James Loewen documents the existence of hundreds of towns across the United States that banned blacks from being within the town limits between sunset and sunrise. Similarly, sociologist Robert Bullard (1994) documents the tendency for communities of color to bear a disproportionate burden of ecological hazards relative to white communities.

The question may not be *Does racism exist?* Instead, the question may be *Depending on how you define it, does racism exist?* It is therefore extremely important to be very careful in how we define concepts, particularly if we are going to use those concepts to collect and statistically analyze data from the world around us.

Table 1.1 contains some important terms and definitions that are used in this chapter.

This chapter focuses on some of the most important underlying ideas behind statistics. It lays a foundation upon which we can move forward into actual statistical analyses. It is divided into three main sections: Concepts, Variables, and Measurement. Concepts are ideas that we hope to be able to effectively operationalize into variables. Variables are characteristics of people, or other units of analysis, that vary from case to case. Measurement refers to the considerations that we must take into account when creating variables.

TABLE 1.1

TERM	DEFINITION
Variable	Anything that varies from case to case *or* a logical set of attributes
Attribute	A characteristic of a variable
Conceptualization	The process of defining what is meant by a variable
Operationalization	The process of creating an actual measure for a variable
Level of measurement	Levels of measurement include nominal, ordinal, and interval/ratio
Nominal variable	A variable for which the attributes cannot be ranked from high to low
Ordinal variable	A variable for which the attributes can be ranked from high to low, but do not take numeric form
Interval/ratio variable	A variable for which the attributes can be ranked from high to low because they take numeric form
Mutually exclusive	A condition that exists when a case fits into one and only one attribute of a variable
Collectively exhaustive	A condition that exists when attributes of a variable exhaust all the possible values that cases may have
Validity	The degree to which a measure reflects the idea it was intended to measure
Reliability	The degree to which a measure yields consistent results across samples

Concepts

Concept An idea that we think represents something in the real world.

The Earth is Round and not the Center of the Universe? Imagine yourself in a world where many people believe that the world is flat and that if ships sail too far toward the horizon, they will drop off the edge of the Earth. Other people believe that the Earth is round and located at the center of the universe because the stars, Moon, and Sun appear to circle the Earth. Without evidence, how do we determine who is right?

One day, a group of sailors who had left years earlier on an expedition return, claiming that they have sailed *around* the world (Figure 1.1). Of course, if one believes that the Earth is flat, this claim is preposterous. For others, it reinforces the belief that the stars, Moon, and Sun circle the Earth. It also raises the possibility that the Earth is spinning and that it may not be the center of the universe. The movement of the stars may only give the illusion of the Earth being the center of the universe. These are dangerous claims that challenge fundamental belief systems and some people were persecuted and killed for such beliefs.

Over the years, evidence builds to support the claim that by sailing continuously in one direction, for example, west, a ship can actually end up where it began. If the only way that a line can end up where it began is by going around, then the ships must have sailed around the world. This finding presents a serious challenge to the dominant

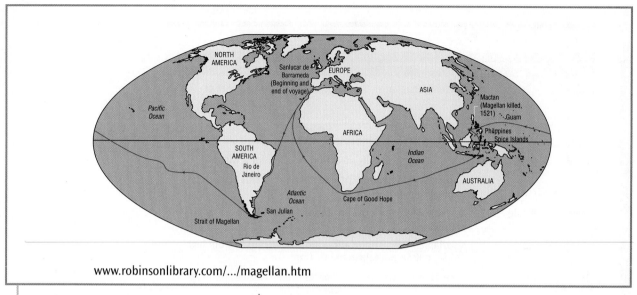

www.robinsonlibrary.com/.../magellan.htm

Figure 1.1 Magellan's Route Around the World

understanding of the world and eventually leads to new ideas regarding gravity, the laws of motion, astronomy, and even religion.

Why is it that ships sailing toward the horizon do not lift off the round Earth and sail off into space? Something must keep them "stuck" to the Earth—but what? Gravity. Gravity must keep ships attached to the round Earth and prevents them from leaving the Earth's surface and sailing off into space. The idea of gravity existed for about 1,000 years before Sir Isaac Newton published *Principia*, but he is generally credited with developing some of the models that many scientists still use today.

Has anyone ever seen gravity? Has anyone ever touched gravity? No, of course not. Gravity exists at the conceptual level. Today, we believe that all objects are somehow attracted to one another because of gravity. We use these ideas to predict the motion of planets, the trajectory of comets, and the presence of black holes. It is an idea that works well and can explain a lot of physics. Yet, if we could jump forward in time, we might be surprised to find that another concept has come to replace our current concept of gravity.

In this example, gravity is a human construct that was a long time in the making; it is a concept or an idea that we use to help us make sense of the way the world works. Concepts are ideas that we think represent reality.Like our understanding of the earth and gravity, social science is based on the creation and analysis of concepts. Racism, sexism, inequality, love, and hate are all examples of concepts. They do not exist in the sense that we can pick them up, weigh them, or put them under a microscope; however, we know that they exist because we live them every day. Such is the stuff of sociological analysis.

Scientific Revolutions

In his groundbreaking book *The Structure of Scientific Revolutions* (1962), philosopher Thomas S. Kuhn referred to the shift from believing that the world is flat to believing the world is round as a scientific revolution. Scientific revolutions occur when old understandings of the way the world works are replaced with new explanations. Kuhn argues that people tend to think of science as a slow accumulation of knowledge over time. This gradual accumulation of knowledge is incorporated into increasingly sophisticated models of how the world works that are then used to pursue a more informed knowledge of reality. Many people believe that this scientific "progress" is the way to find the truth that lies behind our misunderstandings of the universe.

Kuhn argues that the search for "truth" is misguided. He and many others argue that we never find the truth, but we do develop better and more sophisticated understandings of the world around us. For example, when the "flat earth" theory is challenged to the point of not working, a scientific revolution takes place in which old interpretations of the world are replaced with new. Given our relatively limited investigations into these topics, why should we expect that our new model will be the final one?

While the world around us exists physically, and many of our ideas about how it works seem to work quite well, our understanding of it is based on imperfect models and, often, flawed interpretations. In other words, the concepts developed to make sense of our surroundings often have shortcomings. Nevertheless, scientists use the best models available to them at the time until a new model is developed that does a better job. We refer to scientific eras when a single model of the world dominates other possible understandings as times of "normal science." The problem with these times is that anomalies tend to arise. Anomalies are scientific findings that cannot be explained by the dominant model(s) of the time.

Anomalies Phenomena that are not explained by existing models of understanding.

Take the example of learning that the world is not flat. A ship sailing around the world is an anomaly because it never should have happened if the world is flat. The ships should have fallen off the edge of the world, not returned to their point of origin. The events do not fit the current model of the Earth and they challenge us to find a new model with which to understand the world, and reconsider our current astronomy.

A couple of anomalies, however, do not always necessitate the overhaul of a system of logic and beliefs. It may be that those proclaiming the anomaly are persecuted for their beliefs, or that the anomaly itself was a misinterpretation of events. How many anomalies it takes to necessitate a change in the current paradigm is often a question of politics and power more than it is a question of legitimacy (particularly when religious beliefs are challenged). Let's just say that when enough evidence is accumulated to offer support for the claim that the world is not flat, a scientific revolution takes place in which old understandings are jettisoned for new models that work "better." On the following page is a box titled *Now You Try It*. These boxes are located throughout each chapter and are intended to provide readers with opportunities to check their understanding of the concepts as they are presented. The answers to the *Now You Try It* exercises are located at the end of each chapter. We now turn our attention to a sociological concept that seems to be withstanding the test of time.

Now You Try It

Here is an exercise that may help you realize just how much we take the world for granted. Have you ever stopped to wonder about the location of the moon in the night sky? The answer to the question posed below can be had in a couple of ways: quickly (by looking at the end of this chapter) or slowly (by gathering data over the next several days).

Most people know where the sun rises and where it sets. The sun rises in the east and sets in the west. But most people do not know where the moon rises and sets; or where Saturn rises and sets; or any heavenly body for that matter. So where does the moon rise and where does it set? Can you offer a logical explanation for your answer?

Answer at the end of the chapter.

Emile Durkheim, Structural Strain, Suicide, and Anomie

In 1912 Emile Durkheim (1858–1917) became the first person to ever hold the official title of "sociologist" at a university (at the Sorbonne in Paris). Although he studied and wrote on a number of sociological topics, including the division of labor, religion, education, and social control, he is probably most well known for his studies of suicide. An astute statistician, Durkheim poured over thousands of government documents to try and make sense of suicide, a normal part of all societies. What intrigued him, however, was that suicide rates change over time. Ultimately, he concluded that in times of great uncertainty, or what we might think of as times of normlessness, suicide rates go up. He called this state of normlessness *anomie*.

> **Anomie** A societal condition in which the normative standards of behavior are unclear.

Durkheim's concept of anomie is one example of a sociological concept that has withstood the test of time, a concept that he used to help better understand changes in suicide rates. And it appears that Durkheim's concept may be just as applicable today as it was in the early part of the 20th century when he developed it.

Sociologists have studied suicide for about a century. We know that the suicide rate in the United States is about 11, meaning that in any given year 11 people out of every 100,000 people will take their own lives. Another 600,000 will be admitted to emergency rooms for self-inflicted injuries (Centers for Disease Control, 2009). Of these roughly 33,000 people, males between the ages of 16 and 26 and males over the age of 70 are two of the demographic groups most likely to commit suicide. Why males? Why males of these age ranges? Explaining why requires the use of concepts.

As you can see from Table 1.2, the suicide rate is significantly higher for men than it is for women, a trend that holds true in every state. This raises interesting questions regarding differences in how males and females think about suicide and how they act on those ideas.

Durkheim is often noted for his contributions to our understanding of the conditions in which suicide is more likely to occur. He referred to certain characteristics of groups or communities as "social facts." In other words, he believed that social forces exist externally from individuals and these forces "push" and "pull" our actions into predictable patterns, including patterns pertaining to rates of suicide.

TABLE 1.2 *USA State Suicide Rates and Rankings by Gender, 2005*

2005 Rank	NATION - BOTH SEXES COMBINED State	Crude Rate	2005 Rank	MEN State	Crude Rate	2005 Rank	WOMEN State	Crude Rate
1	Montana	22.0	1	Montana	36.2	1	Wyoming	9.2
2	Nevada	19.9	2	Nevada	30.9	2	Nevada	8.5
3	Alaska	19.8	3	Alaska	30.4	3	Alaska	8.4
4	New Mexico	17.8	4	New Mexico	28.9	4	Montana	7.9
5	Wyoming	17.7	5	Colorado	27.0	5	Colorado	7.2
6	Colorado	17.2	5	North Dakota	27.0	6	New Mexico	6.9
7	Idaho	16.0	7	South Dakota	26.9	7	Arizona	6.7
8	Arizona	15.9	8	Idaho	26.8	8	Oklahoma	6.6
9	South Dakota	15.6	9	Wyoming	26.0	9	Oregon	6.4
10	Oregon	15.4	10	Arizona	25.0	9	Florida	6.4
11	Oklahoma	14.7	11	Oregon	24.5	11	Arkansas	6.1
12	North Dakota	14.5	12	Tennessee	24.0	12	Vermont	5.7
13	Arkansas	14.4	13	West Virginia	23.8	13	North Carolina	5.5
13	Tennessee	14.4	14	Oklahoma	23.1	14	Kentucky	5.3
15	West Virginia	14.1	14	Arkansas	23.1	14	Washington	5.3
16	Utah	14.0	16	Utah	22.9	16	Tennessee	5.2
17	Kentucky	13.6	17	Maine	22.5	16	Iowa	5.2
18	Maine	13.3	18	Kentucky	22.2	16	Hawaii	5.2
19	Florida	13.2	19	Kansas	22.0	19	Utah	5.0
19	Kansas	13.2	20	Mississippi	21.1	20	Idaho	4.9
21	Washington	13.1	21	Washington	20.9	20	South Carolina	4.9
22	Missouri	12.5	22	Missouri	20.8	22	Virginia	4.8
22	Vermont	12.5	23	New Hampshire	20.7	22	West Virginia	4.8
22	Mississippi	12.5	24	Florida	20.3	24	Missouri	4.7
25	New Hampshire	12.4	25	Indiana	20.2	25	Nebraska	4.6
26	South Carolina	12.0	26	Alabama	19.9	25	Louisiana	4.6
27	Indiana	11.9	27	Ohio	19.7		Total	4.5
28	Alabama	11.8	28	Vermont	19.6	27	Michigan	4.5
29	Ohio	11.7	29	South Carolina	19.5	27	Kansas	4.5
30	North Carolina	11.6	30	Pennsylvania	19.2	27	Maine	4.5
30	Wisconsin	11.6	31	Wisconsin	19.0	30	Mississippi	4.4
32	Pennsylvania	11.5	32	Virginia	18.3	30	New Hampshire	4.4
32	Virginia	11.5	33	Louisiana	18.2	30	South Dakota	4.4
34	Iowa	11.2	34	North Carolina	18.1	30	Wisconsin	4.4

(Continued)

2005	NATION - BOTH SEXES COMBINED		2005	MEN		2005	WOMEN	
Rank	State	Crude Rate	Rank	State	Crude Rate	Rank	State	Crude Rate
34	Louisiana	11.2		Total	17.8	34	Texas	4.3
	Total	11.0	35	Michigan	17.6	34	Pennsylvania	4.3
36	Michigan	11.0	36	Iowa	17.4	36	Alabama	4.1
37	Minnesota	10.7	36	Minnesota	17.4	36	California	4.1
38	Nebraska	10.6	38	Delaware	16.9	36	Ohio	4.1
38	Texas	10.6	38	Texas	16.9	39	Minnesota	4.0
40	Georgia	10.1	40	Nebraska	16.8	40	Georgia	3.9
41	Delaware	9.9	41	Georgia	16.6	41	Indiana	3.8
42	California	8.9	42	Maryland	14.1	41	Rhode Island	3.8
43	Illinois	8.5	43	Illinois	13.8	43	Massachusetts	3.6
44	Maryland	8.4	44	California	13.7	43	Connecticut	3.6
44	Connecticut	8.4	45	Connecticut	13.6	45	Illinois	3.4
44	Hawaii	8.4	46	Hawaii	11.6	46	Delaware	3.2
47	Massachusetts	7.5	46	Massachusetts	11.6	46	Maryland	3.2
48	Rhode Island	6.6	48	New York	10.4	48	District of Columbia	2.9
49	New Jersey	6.2	49	New Jersey	9.9	49	New Jersey	2.6
49	New York	6.2	50	Rhode Island	9.6	50	New York	2.2
51	District of Columbia	5.7	51	District of Columbia	8.8	51	North Dakota	1.9

Data Source: CDC's WISQARS website "Fatal Injury Reports," http://www.cdc.gov/ncipc/wisqars/; downloaded 24 January 2008 "Crude rate" refers to rates per 100,000 population. Prepared by John L. McIntosh, Ph.D., Indiana University South Bend for posting by the *American Association of Suicidology* (www.suicidology.org) - January 2008.

Suicide exists in all societies (to varying degrees), but the number of suicides per 100,000 people (the suicide rate) is likely to vary depending on social conditions. To test this idea, Durkheim analyzed historical data on the number of suicides from one year to the next. Among other trends, he found that males were more likely to commit suicide than females and that Protestants were more likely to commit suicide than Catholics. Why?

Durkheim was fortunate to be a contemporary of other well-known sociologists, namely Karl Marx (1818–1883) and Max Weber (1864–1920). This allowed him to combine his own ideas with those of his contemporaries, and in particular, ideas about the workings of capitalism and the impact that capitalism may have on people.

Durkheim theorized that all people are inherently social beings and that humans need one another to (1) survive materially and (2) set limits on our worldly desires. He argues that without a society to set normative standards for the accumulation of wealth and other worldly possessions, the capacity for humans to constantly want "more" is endless. This is important because, as Max Weber showed in his famous book *The Protestant Ethic and the Spirit of Capitalism*, the confluence of the Protestant ethic (hard work, frugal living, and reinvestment as a way to accumulate wealth to demonstrate one's worth to God) and the spirit of capitalism (an ever-expanding economy with seemingly limitless capacity for growth) created the very conditions in which vast quantities of material wealth can be generated.

Anomie Then.   Analyzing how suicide rates vary over time and from one society to the next, Durkheim (1897/1951) concluded that people were more likely to commit suicide during times of uncertainty, for example, during economic depression. Out of this finding he developed his concept of anomie. Anomie is a condition in society that increases when the established rules and regulations of society become blurred or no longer seem to apply. An example of this is a questioning of the belief in free market economies during times of economic crisis.

When rules become less clear, or in the absence of rules, people are more likely to suffer as their society is increasingly characterized by a state of pathological anomie (unhealthy or extreme levels of anomie). It is during these times that Durkheim detected increased rates of suicide.

At particular risk of suicide during times of economic slowdown are males and Protestants. Higher societal expectations for economic success among males can result in greater levels of anomie among men during economic recessions because males are more likely to experience declining social status. Similarly, because the accumulation of wealth has greater religious significance to Protestants than to Catholics (according to Weber), economic downturns can create the belief of less favorable outcomes in the afterlife (going to heaven) and generate greater levels of anomie. Therefore, we can predict and explain higher suicide rates among males and Protestants during times of economic decline. And Durkheim's concept of anomie remains particularly useful for explaining the high rate of suicide among young men today.

Anomie Now.   A recent article in *Newsweek* magazine based on the work of sociologist Michael Kimmel (who recently published a book titled *Guyland* [2008]) notes that American males between the ages of 16 and 26 have one of the highest rates of suicide in the country. It is interesting that this rate seems to coincide in an era of extended juvenile behavior for this group. Twenty-something men in the late 1990s and early 2000s are much more likely to be extending their college party lifestyle for an additional decade or more than are any of their historical counterparts. The rise in suicide rates and the delay of life course changes may both be explained sociologically.

A 30-plus year contraction in wages, limited opportunities for upward mobility, and declining labor force status relative to females have created the conditions in which male college graduates face one of the toughest job markets in history. It may be that as the relative social status of males declines young males entering the workforce are more likely to be confronted with the question of what it means to be male. Thus the social context in which anomie rises begins to emerge. As the societal norms of "maleness" are increasingly blurred by the economic downturn, suicide rates are likely to increase.

Some sociologists have noted that mass media corporations are capitalizing on the newfound status of young males by promoting a culture that endorses partying, lack of responsibility, and objectification of women (Kimmel, 2008). These young males appear to be victims of the strain that results from high societal goals for achievement (high income, material wealth) without the means (strong job markets, expanding economy) to reach them. Consequently, they are more likely to turn to media portrayals of what it means to be male as cues for their own behavior and worldviews.

To summarize, Durkheim, like all scientists (chemists, physicists, biologists, botanists, psychologists, sociologists, and others), looked for patterns. Upon identifying a pattern, the goal is to explain it. To explain changes in suicide rates, Durkheim developed the concept of anomie.

New models of the way the world works enable us to make sense of our surroundings, but these models are often based on highly abstract ideas like anomie. While this is not necessarily a problem, it does require scientists to remain relatively open-minded about the possibility of flaws in their models. Identifying and explaining patterns among variables is a difficult and often abstract process.

Why Statistics?

How does statistics contribute to our understanding of the world? Why should students take an entire course on statistics? These are good questions for which there are some good and some not-so-good answers. The not-so-good answers tend to go something like this: "It is required for the degree." "I had to take it, so should you." "You can't be a good social scientist without statistics." Actually, you can be a very good social scientist without statistics, but you can be even better with some basic statistical tools at your disposal. This brings us to the good answers to the question, *Why statistics?*

Statistics Numeric representations of reality that facilitate our ability to describe, communicate, predict, and act.

For better or worse, we live in a world of statistics, statistical reasoning, and decisions made on the basis of statistics. In the most basic sense, statistics are numerical representations of reality. Often they are valid representations, other times they are not so valid. Statistics are used to describe conditions (such as average income), communicate more effectively (baseball fans understand the meaning of a .300 hitter), predict outcomes (such as the likelihood of a baseball player getting a hit), and develop policy (such as whether a drop of 3,000 points in the Dow Jones Industrial warrants a financial bailout package). In this sense, statistical knowledge at the individual level provides deeper insight into the kind(s) of forces that make the world what it is.

In his widely acclaimed book *Damned Lies and Statistics: Untangling Numbers from the Media, Politicians, and Activists* (2001), sociologist Joel Best argues that there are several kinds of statistics "consumers" in the world: the Awestruck, the Naive, the Cynical, and the Critical. Best defines the Awestruck as those who fail to think critically about statistics and are likely to believe what they hear about a statistic (p. 162). The Naive consist of those who are "basically accepting" of statistics because they tend to feel that most people, including statisticians, are sincere (pp. 162–163). The Cynical are those who tend to reject statistics on the basis that they amount to nothing more than sophisticated lies that are generated out of particular interests (p.164). Finally, Best discusses the Critical consumers. These are people who understand that every statistic is a complex way of conveying information. They tend to know something about statistics and they tend to know what kinds of questions to ask to clarify confusion or misleading statements (pp. 166–167).

The purpose of taking a statistics course is not to learn how to calculate a bunch of different statistics, although you will be asked to do that. Instead, the purpose of such a course is to increase the range of analytical tools that we have to approach and live in the world with which we are confronted. It is to learn to think critically and reflectively about what others tell us about the world so that we can come to our own, well-informed conclusions. In this sense, statistical literacy is really no different from other types of literacy (language, computer, financial) or skills (driving, cooking, home repair) that we need to navigate our daily routines.

The goal of this book is to provide you with an introduction to some of the most important statistical concepts (central tendency, dispersion, probability, and association). Real-world examples and data are used as much as possible to try and convey the manners in which these tools and skills can be applied. Examples with step-by-step calculations are included. Finally, the book is based on the belief that by working through a few calculations, students are more likely to grasp the concepts and be able to apply them more effectively.

Variables

Conceptual Definitions of Variables

Scientific analysis tends to consist of making sense of (1) describing how cases are distributed and (2) describing how variables interact with one another. For the most part, very few constants exist in science and really none exist in the social sciences. Everything varies from case to case. As we move from one person to the next, sex, age, hair color, education, and food preferences all vary. This is true when we compare individuals; and it is true when we compare families, communities, cultures, and any other *unit of analysis*. Scientists in general, but particularly social scientists, work with what are called *variables*. Two common ways of thinking about variables are (1) anything that varies from case to case and (2) logical groupings of *attributes*.

> *Units of analysis* are scientists' objects of analysis, or who or what is being studied.
>
> A variable is defined here as anything that varies from one case to the next. For example, the sex of a respondent in a survey might vary between males and females. Variables are the building blocks of scientific research.
>
> *Attributes* are defined here as a set of logical characteristics for a variable. Logical groupings of attributes constitute variables. For example, the attributes *male* and *female* constitute the variable Sex of Respondent.

In social science, variables can measure ideas or physical attributes. Physical attributes are easy to comprehend. For example, we might want to describe the members of a college sports team. The players' height, weight, age, and sex are all easily described variables. We might then want to describe their overall academic success. To do this we might check their SAT scores, their overall GPA, or whether they have made the Dean's List. But do any of these really give us a true reflection of their level of academic success? Maybe, but some ideas are harder to measure than others.

Units of analysis The who or what that data describe. Tend to consist of individuals or groups/places (towns, schools, teams, etc.).

Variable Anything that may vary from one case to the next (sex, height, level of education, etc.).

Attributes A logical set of characteristics for a variable.

For example, take the concept of *hate*. Hate exists only at the conceptual level. It is not a physical reality, though it has very real consequences. We might see examples of actions that we feel are motivated by *hate*, such as gay-bashing, shouting racial slurs, or genocide; but we still cannot pick up the hate, put it on a scale, and measure it. We must first define exactly what we mean by *hate* before we can find ways to measure it. After we have measured it in some methodologically valid and reliable manner, we can describe its characteristics statistically. The following excerpt is from the Federal Bureau of Investigation Uniform Crime Report and describes what that organization considers to be a hate crime.

The FBI collects data regarding criminal offenses that are motivated, in whole or in part, by the offender's bias against a race, religion, sexual orientation, ethnicity/national origin, or disability and are committed against persons, property, or society. Because motivation is subjective, it is difficult to know with certainty whether a crime resulted from the offender's bias. Moreover, the presence of bias alone does not necessarily mean that a crime can be considered a hate crime. If law enforcement investigation reveals sufficient evidence to lead a reasonable and prudent person to conclude that the offender's *actions* were motivated, in whole or in part, by his or her bias, then the incident should be reported as a hate crime. (http://www.fbi.gov/ucr/hc2006/methodology.html, September 18, 2008)

As this shows, it is very difficult to determine a motivation and therefore it is very difficult to classify crimes as hate crimes. It is likely that racism, sexism, and other kinds of bias are responsible for a far greater number of crimes than are documented by the FBI.

In Durkheim's analysis of suicide, the unit of analysis is societies (which he defined very loosely) while anomie and suicide are variables (because they vary across time and place). The level of anomie in any given society changes over time. And the level of anomie tends to vary from one society to the next. Anomie, like hate, is not something that can be seen with the naked eye; yet it seems to be a reality because it makes sense logically and it is supported by historical data. "Seeing" anomie requires abstract thought and theoretical understanding. And as you may have already guessed, debates over how to measure concepts like anomie, that may or may not exist in reality, are common.

Hypothesis A prediction about the distribution of a variable or the association between two variables.

Independent variable The variable that is controlled or held constant in a hypothesis.

Dependent variable The variable that is influenced by changes in the independent variable.

Direction of effect The part of a hypothesis that predicts whether two variables are positively or negatively associated.

Independent and Dependent Variables

Statistical association is discussed in much greater detail in Chapter 8; however, it is briefly introduced here. The idea behind statistical association is that we are working with two (or more) variables; one is called the independent variable and the other is called the dependent variable. We predict (or hypothesize) that a change in one variable, for example education, is associated with a change in another variable, income. When we say that education and income are associated, we are hypothesizing (making an educated guess or an informed prediction). To use more scientific language, we *hypothesize* that education and income are positively associated. The positive wording refers to the direction of effect. This means that we predict that increases in education are accompanied by increases in income. A negative direction of effect would exist when increases in education are accompanied by decreases in income.

In this example, education is the independent variable and income is the dependent variable. In other words, our assumption is that a respondent's income is, at least partially, a result of how much education they have. A good way to remember which variable is independent and which is dependent is to phrase the hypothesis in an "*if . . . then . . .* " format. For example, *if education increases, then income increases.* In this format, the independent variable always follows the *if* and the dependent variable always follows the *then.*

It is important to note that an association between two variables does not mean that changes in the independent variable *caused* changes in the dependent variable. Scientists use the phrase *Association does not imply causation* to emphasize this fact. Just because people with higher levels of education may have higher incomes, it does not mean that their education caused them to have higher income. To effectively argue that two variables are associated, three criteria must be met:

1. The cause must precede the effect. This means that we would have to show that education came before higher income as opposed to higher income preceding greater levels of education. This could be very difficult because people with higher incomes can afford greater levels of education.
2. Changes in the dependent variable must be the result of change in the independent variable and not some preceding or intervening variable. In other words, it is possible that higher levels of income could be the result of any number of factors, one of which may be education.
3. The association must be present "often enough." This means that we may find cases in which education and income are not associated; however, a few cases do not threaten the overall trend. The question then becomes *How often must the prediction hold true?* This is a tricky question and represents a point at which science often becomes political and the subject of debate.

Operational Definitions of Concepts

In thinking about concepts and variables, it is useful to think chronologically. Defining what we mean by an idea must precede devising ways to measure our ideas. Describing or defining an idea that we think represents something in the real world is a process called conceptualization. Devising ways to measure the ideas we have conceptualized is called operationalization.

When we take an idea, a concept, and define what exactly we mean by it, we are conceptualizing. For example, when we take the concept of income and conceptualize it, we might refer to the amount of money a person makes at a given job in a given year. Or we might refer to the amount of money they make at their job added to the amount of money they earn from investments. Either technique is a valid way to conceptualize income.

When we take an idea, a concept, and devise a measure by which to compare one case to the next, we are operationalizing a variable. For example, we could operationalize the concept of sex as consisting of two attributes: male and female. In this sense, the term variable could be defined as a logical set of attributes. As in the example above we might conceptualize income to refer to the amount of money a person makes at their job in a given year; but this leaves several possibilities open. We might refer to the actual dollar amount ($32,515), or we might refer to a range of income ($0–19,999; $20,000–29,999; $30,000–39,999; etc.). In other words, there

Conceptualization The process of defining what we mean by a concept.

Operationalization The process of developing a variable that measures a concept.

is no right or wrong way to operationalize concepts into variables (it depends more on what you want to know).

Conceptualization is the process of describing what we mean by an idea.

Operationalization is the process of devising a specific measure for a variable that we have conceptualized.

Most social scientists probably believe that anything can be measured (alienation, class conflict, anomie), but only recently do they have access to the kinds of technological resources to gather, analyze, and communicate data that we now have at our disposal. Social scientists claim that anything can be measured, even concepts (ideas with no "real" existence). So why couldn't we measure something as abstract as Marx's concept of alienation or Durkheim's concept of anomie?

Alienation. Karl Marx argued that capitalism is a mode of economic production based on conflict between two classes of people: capital (aka the bourgeoisie) and labor (aka the proletariat). Class membership is determined by one's relationship to the means of production. Capital owns the means of production and labor does not. At work, members of the labor class sell their ability to do work (their labor power) to capital in exchange for a wage rate. Marx claims that this has the effect of alienating people from their labor because individuals no longer control their labor nor do they control the products of their labor.

Logically, this makes sense; however, can we measure alienation in some way to offer empirical evidence that it actually exists? As in the case of Durkheim's *anomie*, Marx's *alienation* exists at the conceptual level. Can you think of ways to operationalize alienation?

You may not care very much about what you do for work as long as you make enough money. On the other hand, you might prefer to sacrifice some income for work that gives you a great deal of satisfaction, meaning work that is less alienating. From this we might surmise that someone who likes the type of work they do is less alienated from their labor than someone who does not like the type of work they do.

Although we cannot pick up alienation and put it on a scale to see how much of it a person experiences, we can ask people whether or not they are likely to stay at a job for the income, or to sacrifice some income for a job that they like. Those who indicate that they would be willing to take less pay but have a job that they like would be those experiencing greater levels of alienation. In this way, we have taken the concept of alienation and operationalized it as a variable.

Would you be willing to take a pay cut to have a job that you enjoy more than your current job?

Yes

No

One problem that arises with this variable is that it has a class bias embedded within it. In other words, people who don't make enough money to make ends meet are much more likely to answer "No." Therefore, we could only compare the responses from those respondents of relatively similar class standing. We could argue that those who answer "Yes" are experiencing greater levels of alienation from their work than those who answer "No."

Several factors must be considered when operationalizing a variable. Two of these are that the variable must be (1) *collectively exhaustive* and (2) *mutually exclusive*.

Collectively Exhaustive. We cannot say that a variable is operationalized correctly unless the attributes of that variable are collectively exhaustive. Attributes are collectively exhaustive when an attribute exists for every possible case.

Alienation A condition in which people suffer from a "disconnection" between themselves and their work, and disconnection from one another.

Collectively exhaustive A necessary condition for variables that is met when the attributes of a variable include every possible response.

EXAMPLE 1

Attitude Toward the Quality of City Parks

Suppose we are conducting a study of city parks and we want to find out how people of different racial backgrounds feel about the quality of parks in different neighborhoods. We might only have enough resources to sample 100 respondents. In our random sample we expect our sample to break down as follows:

TABLE 1.3   *Which of the Following Would You Classify Yourself As?*

White	50%
African American	35%
Native American	5%
Asian	5%
Latino	5%
Total	100%

It is entirely possible, however, that we have a respondent from Cape Verde who does not feel that any of our categories of race are applicable to him or her. How do we handle cases like this?

Statistically, 100 respondents could be an insufficient number of respondents upon which to claim that we have statistically significant results, particularly if we operationalize the variable in a way that allows some attributes to contain very small numbers of respondents, such as one Cape Verdean. Therefore, instead of having an attribute for each ethnicity, we might operationalize our variable as: White, African American, and Other. Our data might then look like Table 1.4.

This attribute of "Other" allows us to make the variable collectively exhaustive, leaving no one out. It does, however, have the effect of "glossing" over potentially important subtleties in the data by failing to differentiate Native Americans, Asians, Latinos, and Cape Verdeans.

If we are concerned about being able to generate statistically significant results to Native Americans, Asians, or Hispanics, we must then sample a larger number of respondents. Then we can change the attribute "Other" to "Native American, Asian, Latino, Cape Verdean, and Other."

TABLE 1.4   *Which of the Following Would You Classify Yourself As?*

White	50%
African American	35%
Other	15%
Total	100%

Mutually Exclusive. We cannot say that a variable has been operationalized correctly unless the attributes of that variable are mutually exclusive. Attributes are mutually exclusive when the attributes do not overlap each other. For example, we might ask people to tell us what their annual pre-tax income is by placing an X on the appropriate line.

As you can see in Table 1.5, there is a problem with the variable on the left. What if you make $10,000, $40,000, or $60,000? Which line do you place an X on? The problem is that the variable to the left is not operationalized such that the attributes are mutually exclusive. The variable to the right is operationalized such that the attributes are mutually exclusive.

Mutually exclusive A necessary condition for variables that is met when each case can be applied to only one attribute of a variable.

Table 1.6 has two problems. Can you explain what is wrong with it? First, the attributes are not collectively exhaustive. It is possible, and likely, that in our sample we will find a respondent who makes more than $80,000 per year. There is no attribute in our variable for such a respondent to indicate this to us.

The second problem deals with mutual exclusivity. As you can see, a person making $10,000, $40,000, or $60,000 could respond to either of two attributes. It is vital that statisticians be aware of the sources of their data to avoid these kinds of problems. A common saying in statistics is "garbage in, garbage out." This means that if the data used to generate statistics are methodologically sound, then the statistics generated by that data are not representative of reality.

Remember that all variables must be operationalized such that the attributes are both collectively exhaustive and mutually exclusive. When variables do not meet these two requirements, data must be considered unreliable and invalid. Consequently, the statistics generated from such data must be considered suspect and nonrepresentative of the concepts they are intended to represent.

TABLE 1.5 *Pre-tax Income (2005)*

___ $0–10,000	___ Less than $10,000
___ $10,000–40,000	___ $10,000–39,999
___ $40,000–60,000	___ $40,000–59,999
___ $60,000 and higher	___ $60,000 and higher

TABLE 1.6 *Pre-tax Income (2005)*

___ $0–20,000

___ $20,000–40,000

___ $40,000–60,000

___ $60,000–80,000

Measurement

Levels of Measurement

Now that we have seen how social scientists are able to measure practically anything, provided the concept is operationalized in a valid and reliable manner, we can discuss *levels of measurement*. As with most tasks in life there is more than one way to skin a cat (whatever that means) and, as you might have guessed, there is more than one way to operationalize a variable.

For example, if I ask you if you like chocolate, you could answer *yes* or *no*. If I ask you how much you like chocolate, you could answer from the following list: *not at all*, *a little*, or *a lot*. Or I could have you indicate on a scale of 1 to 100 how much you like chocolate. A fundamental difference exists between these ways of measuring. One elicits responses that cannot be ranked from high to low and the others elicit responses that can be ranked from high to low. In the case of the 1–100 ranking, we can even count how far from 0 a person likes chocolate.

These are the three levels of measurement: nominal, ordinal, and interval/ratio. All variables can be categorized into one of these three levels, though sometimes the differences are not so clear. It is extremely important to understand the different levels of measurement and how to identify the level at which a variable is operationalized. The statistics that can be used to describe a variable depend on the level at which the variable is operationalized. In other words, if a variable is operationalized at the nominal level, only certain statistics can be used. For example, as we will see in the next chapter, measures of central tendency (mean, median, and mode) are statistics used to describe where cases tend to cluster in a distribution. In the case of a nominal variable, only the mode can be used; however, in the case of an ordinal variable, both the mode and the median can be used. The following briefly describes each level of measurement and explains how they differ.

Nominal. Nominal variables have attributes that cannot be ranked from high to low. The attributes are nothing more than different categorical responses. For example, male or female are attributes of the variable of gender. Male is not more or less than female and female is not more or less than male. Similarly, we have the example of *religiosity*.

> **Levels of measurement** The degree of mathematical precision that can be applied to a variable. The three levels of measurement are referred to as nominal, ordinal, and interval/ratio.

> **Nominal** Variables operationalized at the nominal level have attributes that cannot be rank-ordered.

EXAMPLE 2

Religiosity

Suppose we ask 100 people whether Jesus (or any other religious figure) is part of their religiosity and get the results in Table 1.7.

TABLE 1.7 *Is Jesus Part of Your Religiosity?*

Yes	50%
No	50%

TABLE 1.8   *How Strong Is Your Belief in Jesus?*

Not Strong	33%
Somewhat Strong	34%
Very Strong	33%
Total	100%

This does not mean that the people who answered "yes" are more religious. People who answer "yes" are not more or less religious than the people who answered "no"; it is just that some people have Jesus as part of their religiosity and some people do not. Therefore, the attributes cannot be ranked from high to low or more to less. They simply indicate a difference between two groups of people: those for whom Jesus is part of their religiosity and those for whom Jesus is not part of their religiosity.

Ordinal.   Ordinal variables have attributes that can be ranked from high to low, but the "distances" between the attributes can't be measured. For example, consider a questionnaire that asks you how much you like a particular flavor of ice cream. Your choices are *a lot*, *somewhat*, and *a little*. A person indicating they like the flavor a lot obviously likes it more than someone who likes it a little. Yet we cannot measure exactly how much more the first person likes it.

In the religiosity example we see the same kind of logic. Suppose our data yield the results in Table 1.8.

Some peoples' belief in Jesus is "not strong," others is "somewhat strong," and others is "very strong." Therefore we know that a person who answers "very strong" has a stronger belief in Jesus than someone who answers "not strong." But how much stronger is it? We don't know because we have no way of measuring the "distance" between "not strong" and "very strong." We can rank-order our respondents from high to low in their belief in Jesus by placing them into one of the three attributes, but we have no way of addressing the question of how much stronger is one respondent's belief than the next.

Ordinal Variables operationalized at the ordinal level have attributes that can be rank-ordered, but those attributes do not reflect actual numeric values.

Interval/ratio Variables with attributes based on real or relative numeric values (meaning the attributes can be rank-ordered and used to conduct mathematical calculations).

Interval/Ratio.   Interval/ratio variables have attributes that can be both ranked and measured. Attributes take the form of specific numbers, often with specified units of analysis. For example, the number of tackles that a football player has in a game varies from player to player. One player may have five tackles and another player has seven. The second one has more, *and* we know exactly how many more.

The same logic holds true for our measure of religiosity. When we ask respondents to tell us how many times they attend religious services in a month, they answer with a numeric amount. If one respondent attends religious services eight times a month and another attends one time each month, we know that the difference is seven. Respondents who attend more often are considered more religious, and therefore the first respondent might be considered to have eight times the religiosity as the second respondent. Not only do we know that the first respondent attends religious services more often, we know exactly how many more times.

Interval and ratio variables differ, but are treated the same statistically—that is why they are lumped into the same category. The difference between interval and ratio variables is that ratio variables have a true zero-point while interval variables have an arbitrary zero-point. For example, if I ask you how many skateboards you own and you say zero, then you own no skateboards. This is a ratio variable with a true zero. If I ask you how you rate the mayor on a scale of –10 to +10 and you say 4, then you have some approval of the mayor. Had you answered 0 you have still indicated some approval, but not as much as someone who answered 4.

The 0 on the scale of –10 to +10 is an arbitrary zero. The same is true for a temperature of 0 degrees. On the Fahrenheit scale, 0 degrees represents an arbitrary zero. It is an arbitrary point on a thermometer that happens to be 32 degrees below the temperature at which water freezes. On the Celsius scale, 0 degrees happens to be the temperature at which water freezes. This is an arbitrary point (why wouldn't we consider zero to be the point at which some other liquid freezes?). On neither the Fahrenheit nor the Celsius scale does 0 degrees represent the absence of heat.

Regardless of the level at which variables are operationalized, the attributes of all variables must be both **mutually exclusive** and **collectively exhaustive.**

Below is an example using a question that is often used for course and instructor evaluations. As this example shows, any concept can be operationalized in a number of ways. In the first technique, we have a yes or no question (a **nominal** variable). In the second, we incorporate the concept of degree (an **ordinal** variable). And in the third, we incorporate the concept of degree in a measurable manner (an **interval/ratio** variable). Each of these represents a different level of measurement.

EXAMPLE 3

Operationalizing Course Challenge
Variables can be conceptualized and operationalized in any number of ways.

> **Nominal:** Did you find the course challenging? Yes   No
> **Ordinal:** How challenging was the course? Not at all   Somewhat   Very
> **Interval/Ratio:** In a range from 0 to 100, how challenging was this course? ___

When gathering data, it is generally a good idea to collect the data at the highest level possible. For example, suppose you are doing research (a survey) on Grade Point Averages. You could ask respondents to circle which category their GPA falls within, as the box below shows. Or you could have respondents simply write down their GPA.

EXAMPLE 4

Surveying Student Grade Point Averages

TABLE 1.9 *GPA*

0.00–1.00

1.01–2.00

2.01–3.00

3.01–4.00

What is your GPA? _____

The advantage to having them write down their GPA, say it is 3.22, is that it allows you to see exactly what each respondent's GPA is. In other words, if you use the box above, you "gloss over" what could be important aspects of the data. For example, it could be that an important "cutoff" point in the data is 2.25, not 2.00; but by operationalizing it as in the box, this important trend might never be detected. Additionally, if you ask respondents to indicate their GPA, you can always go back to it and categorize it according to any grouping you desire.

Integrating Technology

Recoding Data

Statistical software programs allow researchers to *manipulate* data. Despite the negative connotation associated with the word *manipulate*, there is nothing ethically questionable about data manipulation. The term refers to the process of sorting cases, selecting particular cases, and other similar processes that allow for more detailed and effective statistical analysis of data. One common type of data manipulation is called "recoding."

When data are collected and entered into a computerized database, they contain numeric codes. For example, Male = 1 and Female = 2. In the case of nominal and ordinal variables the codes do not reflect actual value; they simply allow us to enter 1s and 2s into a database instead of typing out Male and Female. In the case of ratio (and often interval) variables, however, codes do reflect real values. For example, the number of years of education someone has might be 16. In this case, the number 16 is entered into the database.

Suppose we wanted to compare two different groups defined on the basis of whether or not they completed 12 years of education so that we could compare their income levels. By manipulating the data, we can quickly and easily create two groups of respondents – one group with less than 12 years of education and one with 12 or more years of education. We can assign a value of 1 to all respondents with less than 12 years of education and a value of 2 to all respondents with 12 or more years of education. In doing so, we essentially created a new variable by taking an interval/ratio variable and turning it into an ordinal variable. We know that every respondent in the second group has more years of education than any respondent in the first group, but we do not know the exact difference between any two respondents. This is *recoding*.

Data can only be recoded from higher-order levels of measurement to lower-order levels of measurement. In other words, we can recode interval/ratio variables into ordinal or nominal variables; and we can recode ordinal variables into ordinal variables with fewer attributes or into nominal variables. We cannot, however, recode in the other direction—nominal to ordinal or ordinal to interval/ratio. It is therefore important to try and collect data at the highest level of measurement possible because it provides a greater range of analytical possibilities later.

Take the example of attitude toward gun control. As Table 1.10 shows, gun control can be operationalized as a nominal, ordinal, or interval/ratio variable.

TABLE 1.10 *Gun Control as a Nominal, Ordinal, and Interval/Ratio Variable*

NOMINAL	ORDINAL	RATIO
Does your state have strict gun control laws?	How important of an issue is gun control to you?	On a scale of 0 to 10, how important is gun control to you?
Yes	Very important	Respondent indicates a number.
No	Somewhat important	
	Not important	

Graphical Representation of Data (What Data "Look" Like)

As we move from interval/ratio, to ordinal, to nominal levels of measurement, more and more information is lost and the range of statistical techniques that can be applied to the data diminishes. Therefore, it is usually a good idea to collect data at the highest level possible, for example, at the interval/ratio level, and then consider recoding it into ordinal or nominal later. This, of course, is a methodological consideration as much as it is a statistical consideration. While it is usually possible to recode downward (interval/ratio to ordinal to nominal), it is never possible to recode upward (nominal to ordinal to interval/ratio). The three charts below show how responses can be presented graphically.

Pie Charts.   The chart in Figure 1.2 is called a pie chart. Pie charts are common ways of presenting data for nominal or ordinal variables. Remember that the attributes of nominal variables cannot be ranked from high to low. In this example, an argument could be made that if all the respondents were from the same state, the attributes could be ranked in some kind of high to low ordering. Often, what seem like clear-cut differences between nominal and ordinal variables turn out to have many more "shades of gray" than first appear.

Pie chart Often used with nominal and ordinal variables, pie charts consist of a circle cut into "pie slices" that add up to 100%. Each pie slice represents an attribute for the variable.

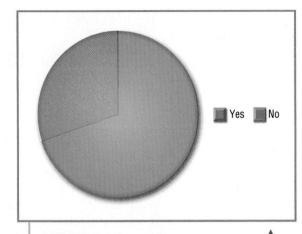

Figure 1.2 **Does Your State Have Strict Gun Control Laws?**

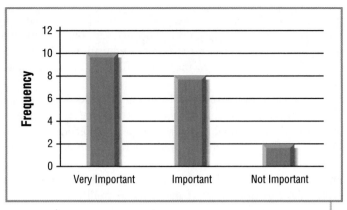

Figure 1.3 **How Important Is Gun Control to You? (*N* = 20)**

Bar chart Often used with nominal and ordinal variables, a series of bars represent the different attributes of a variable. The height of each bar reflects either frequencies or percentages for each attribute.

Histogram Used with interval/ratio variables to represent the frequency of each attribute for a variable. Similar to a bar chart.

Bar Charts. The chart in Figure 1.3 is called a bar chart. Bar charts are often used for ordinal variables because they show trends in a variable. As this chart shows, respondents are more likely to feel that gun control is important or very important than not important.

Histograms. Finally, the chart in Figure 1.4 is called a histogram. Histograms are generally used to represent interval/ratio data. The height of each bar in the histogram is proportionate to the number of respondents for each response. Unlike bar charts, histograms show all of the data for all responses without groupings and are used to show patterns for interval/ratio variables.

Just as some types of charts are more or less appropriate for visual representations of data, the same is true for statistics. Remember that statistics are nothing more than numeric representations of data that allow us to describe, summarize, and communicate information. Therefore, data collected at different levels of measurement (nominal, ordinal, interval/ratio) are appropriate for different types of statistics. In Chapter 2, we turn our attention to a group of statistics called measures of central tendency. As you may have already guessed, the statistics that can be used to describe a variable depend on whether the variable is operationalized at the nominal, ordinal, or interval/ratio level.

Figure 1.4 **On a Scale of 1 to 10, How Important Is Gun Control to You? (N = 50)**

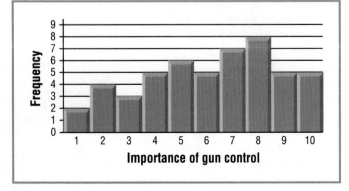

Validity and Reliability

An old saying about statistics goes "garbage in, garbage out." There is a lot of truth to this statement and it raises the issue that sound methodological decision making is the foundation for meaningful statistical analysis. In other words, if we are not careful in how we collect our data and measure our concepts, how can we have any faith in the statistics that come out of that data? Two terms are of particular importance: validity and reliability.

Validity refers to whether we are measuring what we think we are measuring. Does a variable actually reflect the concept that we think it is?

Reliability refers to the likelihood that a particular measure yields consistent results over time. Is a questionnaire item worded in such a way that respondents interpret it in similar ways?

Suppose a researcher wants to develop a questionnaire item to measure the class standing of a group of college students. When discussing class standing, most people probably think of an individual's relative position in the social structure on the basis of wealth, income, or power. Although *class standing* is not a difficult concept to grasp, it is a difficult concept to operationalize. Here are a couple questions that the researcher might ask:

What was your income last year (in dollars)?

What was your income last week (in dollars)?

Each of these questions does a pretty good job of measuring income, but problems arise with each of them. Are students who made higher amounts of income last year really of higher class standing than those who made lower amounts? Maybe; but it is also possible that some students might not need any income at all because they have a lot of money in the bank. Or perhaps they have very low, or no, income because they receive a check from their parents every other week. In this sense the questions are not valid because there is a good chance that we are not measuring what we think we are measuring.

Now consider the following questions:

Would you say that you live in a working-class, middle-class, or upper-class neighborhood?

Are you financially secure?

Each of these questions does a pretty good job of measuring respondents' subjective class identification, but they, too, have problems. For example, the first question forces respondents to choose from one of three attributes. Often people are reluctant to admit, or do not know, that they are more upper class than middle class. Americans like to fit in. Therefore, it is likely that a vast majority of respondents will answer middle class. If we were to add one more attribute to the number of choices that respondents have, we might find that patterns emerge in the data that cannot be detected with only three attributes. Greater levels of precision, however, do not necessarily increase reliability.

The second question is not reliable because each respondent may read it in a completely different way. For example, respondent A might read the question after having just found out that she needs to buy $700 in books for the upcoming semester. Feelings of financial security may have disappeared in the course of an afternoon upon hearing this news. In this sense, the measure could yield different results depending on the day-to-day finances of respondents instead of on their overall long-range financial position.

When trying to measure difficult concepts like class standing, it is often best to use a variety of measures that can be analyzed independently or combined into a single overall (or composite) measure. For example, many sociologists use a combination of income, education, and occupation to determine respondents' overall socioeconomic status. It is important to remember that measures can be valid without being reliable; and, likewise, measures can be reliable without being valid. The goal is to strive for high levels of both validity and reliability to avoid the problem of "garbage in, garbage out."

Validity The degree to which a variable measures what we think it is measuring.

Reliability The degree to which a measure yields consistent results.

Eye on the Applied

Taking the Trash out of Standardized Testing

As is the case of all scientific inquiry, good social science research is dependent on high quality data. This means that data should be both valid and reliable. If a measure of a concept is valid, we are really measuring what we believe to be measuring. Often this is not the case and the consequences of invalid data can be summarized as "garbage in, garbage out."

The No Child Left Behind Act gained widespread support across the nation and has the goal of ensuring that elementary, middle, and high school students achieve minimum levels of education as set by federal and state governments. Standardized tests are used to assess students' abilities. The percent of students who pass these tests is then used as an indicator of schools' ability to educate their students. In this manner, standardized tests provide data that are used to assess both individual students and entire schools, or even school districts.

Standardized testing is believed to assess the cognitive abilities of students and, therefore, act as an indicator of how good a job schools are doing; however, it may not. For example, in many urban high schools, English is not the first language for many students. This can generate lower test scores for non-English-speaking students. Suppose a history course focuses on the transition from agricultural to industrial economies. The students understand the ideas and can write about them, but on the standardized test, the term "agrarian" is more likely to be misinterpreted by students for whom English is not their first language. In this way, the standardized test is biased and not valid because it measures English proficiency, not knowledge of history. It is therefore debatable whether the schools are failing students or whether the standardized tests are failing the schools.

A second and more likely problem with standardized testing is the assumption that schools with higher percentages of students who pass the exams are better schools. Is a high school in which 87% of the students pass a standardized test a better school than one in which 77% of the students pass? Are the students really learning more? Perhaps they are just learning different content, some of which is assessed on standardized tests and some of which is not.

One trend that most educators agree on is that if you teach only the material that will appear on a test, more of the students will pass that test. Is the school in which 87% of the students pass teaching only the material that will be on the test? If so, then the outcome of standardized testing is to reduce overall learning to a narrowly defined curriculum of items that appear on tests.

In the world of education reform and standardized testing, it is useful not only to understand how to interpret statistics but also to understand the social conditions (political and otherwise) in which those statistics were generated.

Individual Data

Every year, the National Opinion Research Center (NORC) at the University of Chicago conducts its annual General Social Survey (GSS). NORC has conducted this survey every year since 1972 and many of the questionnaire items have remained unchanged. This allows researchers to conduct *longitudinal* analyses (comparing changes in responses over time).

In the 2006 GSS, NORC sampled 4,510 individuals. Not every respondent was asked every question. This means that responses from as few as 2,000 people are used to generalize to the entire population of the United States. Incredible as this may seem, the consistency of these statistics over time indicate that the data gathered is both valid and reliable. Needless to say, NORC researchers must be very diligent in their survey research methodology to ensure that the data are of high quality.

The GSS survey data is known as individual-level data because all of the variables represent characteristics of the individuals that were sampled (sex, race, income level, political party affiliation, occupational prestige score, and their attitudes toward hundreds of different social issues).

Below are three examples of some of the GSS variables and how they are operationalized. The data in these tables represent all the responses from 1972 to 2006. As you can see in Table 1.11, the variable sex is operationalized as 1 = Male and 2 = Female. The numeric codes (1 and 2) are used in many statistical software programs and allow data entry to be done by entering numeric codes rather than typing out "Male" and "Female." You can see that since 1972, this questionnaire item has been administered to 51,020 respondents and 22,439 of these respondents, 44.0%, have indicated that they are male. Another 28,581 have indicated that they are female.

Tables 1.11, 1.12, and 1.13 are known as frequency tables. Table 1.12 shows data on respondents' highest degree, an ordinal variable, and Table 1.13 shows data on respondents' years of education, an interval/ratio variable. As Table 1.13 shows, interval/ratio variables do not have labels for their codes because the attributes are already in numeric form. Frequency tables are discussed in greater detail in the next chapter.

TABLE 1.11 *Example of a Nominal Variable from the GSS*

SEX	RESPONDENT'S SEX			

Text of this Question or Item

23. Code respondent's sex

% Valid	% All	N	Value	Label
44.0	44.0	22,439	1	MALE
56.0	56.0	28,581	2	FEMALE
100.0	100.0	51,020		Total

Properties

Data type: Numeric

Missing-data code: 0

Record/column: 1/108

TABLE 1.12   *Example of an Ordinal Variable from the GSS*

DEGREE			RS HIGHEST DEGREE	
% Valid	**% All**	**N**	**Value**	**Label**
23.2	23.1	11,777	**0**	LT HIGH SCHOOL
51.7	51.6	26,307	**1**	HIGH SCHOOL
5.1	5.1	2,601	**2**	JUNIOR COLLEGE
13.6	13.6	6,918	**3**	BACHELOR
6.4	6.4	3,253	**4**	GRADUATE
	0.1	29	**8**	DK
	0.3	135	**9**	NA
100.0	100.0	51,020		Total

Properties
Data type: Numeric
Missing-data codes: 7, 8, 9
Record/column: 1/104

TABLE 1.13   *Example of an Interval/Ratio Variable from the GSS*

EDUCATION			HIGHEST YEAR OF SCHOOL COMPLETED	
% Valid	**% All**	**N**	**Value**	**Label**
0.3	0.3	137	**0**	
0.1	0.1	38	**1**	
0.3	0.3	132	**2**	
0.4	0.4	223	**3**	
0.6	0.5	280	**4**	
0.7	0.7	371	**5**	
1.3	1.3	666	**6**	
1.6	1.6	811	**7**	
4.9	4.8	2,470	**8**	
3.5	3.5	1,765	**9**	
4.8	4.8	2,451	**10**	
6.0	6.0	3,065	**11**	
31.1	31.0	15,814	**12**	
8.3	8.3	4,235	**13**	
10.7	10.6	5,422	**14**	
4.3	4.3	2,211	**15**	
11.8	11.8	6,025	**16**	

EDUCATION			HIGHEST YEAR OF SCHOOL COMPLETED	
% Valid	**% All**	**N**	**Value**	**Label**
2.9	2.9	1,482	**17**	
3.3	3.3	1,660	**18**	
1.3	1.3	648	**19**	
1.9	1.9	962	**20**	
	0.1	64	**98**	DK
	0.2	88	**99**	NA
100.0	100.0	51,020		Total

Properties

Data type: Numeric

Missing-data codes: 97, 98, 99

Record/columns: 1/96-97

Ecological Data

The U.S. Bureau of the Census conducts a national census every 10 years. Census questionnaires come in both long and short form, with most people answering on the short form. Although data are collected from individuals, no data in the census can be analyzed at the level of the individual. Instead, data are tallied by region of the country, state, county, minor civil division, census tracts, block groups, blocks, and other levels of analysis. In this way, census data allow researchers to compare characteristics of states, counties, cities, and so on, without having any knowledge on specific individuals who provided the data. In fact, to protect the identity of people, many census variables are not available at the census tract, block group, or block level.

For example, suppose that you and your family immigrate to the United States from the Dominican Republic and indicate on the census form that you are Dominican. It is likely, in most communities, that you are one of very few Dominican families. Therefore, if data on ethnicity were made available at the block or block group level, other people, using census data, would be able to learn more about your income level, your family makeup, and a host of other data that should be kept private. In other words, if data are made available at too "local" a level, you could be "outed" without your approval. It is therefore important that census data be made available in ways that maintain the anonymity of those who provided it.

Census data are collected and put into databases in interval/ratio form. For example, suppose we are interested in studying population in the state of Vermont. Communities could be defined as counties, towns and cities, zip codes, or block groups. Suppose we decide to analyze population by county and subsequently divide the state into its 14 counties. The table below shows each of the 13 counties, their total population, and their farm population. We can use these data to calculate the percent of each county's population that lives on farms without revealing who those individuals are.

As Table 1.14 shows, Vermont's two biggest farm populations are located in Addison and Franklin counties. We do not know, however, where these counties are located or where they lie in relation to other counties with significant farm populations.

TABLE 1.14 *Demographic Characteristics of Vermont Counties (N = 14)*

COUNTY	POPULATION	FARM POPULATION	PERCENT FARM POPULATION
Addison	35,974	1,429	4.0
Bennington	36,994	327	.9
Caledonia	29,702	824	2.8
Chittenden	146,571	1,027	.7
Essex	6,459	118	1.8
Franklin	45,417	1,821	4.0
Grand Isle	6,901	200	2.9
Lamoille	23,233	514	2.2
Orange	28,266	1,136	4.0
Orleans	26,277	1,031	3.9
Rutland	63,400	807	1.3
Washington	58,039	688	1.2
Windham	44,216	534	1.2
Windsor	57,418	746	1.3
Total	608,827	11,202	

Figure 1.5 **Vermont Farm Population by County, 2000**

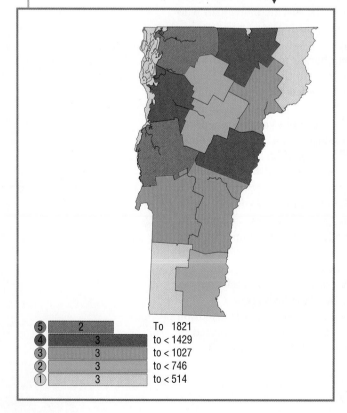

⑤	2	To 1821
④	3	to < 1429
③	3	to < 1027
②	3	to < 746
①	3	to < 514

It is possible, with a variety of different software packages, to map census data to create visual representations that allow researchers to see geographic patterns in data that might not otherwise be noticed. For example, the map in Figure 1.5 shows that Vermont's farm population is heavily concentrated in two counties, and you can see that these two counties are located in the western part of the state in what is called the Champlain Valley.

When data are represented in both table and graphic formats, we are able to understand it more easily and use it more effectively.

Statistical Uses and Misuses

The Individualistic Fallacy

When working with data representing individuals, it is important not to fall victim to the *individualistic fallacy*. This is a mistake that occurs when researchers infer characteristics of members of a group based on information they obtained from one person in that group. It can be thought of as over-generalizing.

Consider this example: You go to visit a friend in Boston over spring break. While staying at this friend's house, you overhear a number of conversations and complaints regarding problems with high taxes. When you get home you mention to some other friends that Bostonians are in support of lower taxes. The problem is that you have taken a small (unscientific) sample of Bostonians who are all part of the same group of acquaintances and used their opinions to generalize the whole city of Boston.

The individualistic fallacy can be thought of as generalizing from the individual (or small group) to larger groups.

The Ecological Fallacy

Another term to be considered is called the *ecological fallacy*. The ecological fallacy is a type of error in which characteristics of an area or a region are believed to be the characteristics of the people in that region. An example is as follows: *The state of Oklahoma has one of the largest Native American populations (as a percent of the total population) of all the states. It is also a state that ranks very high in per capita alcohol consumption. Therefore, Native Americans are heavy drinkers.*

It is important, however, to consider other possibilities. Oklahoma is home to a significant number of Indian reservations. Often, these reservations are home to casinos where a significant amount of alcohol consumption takes place by those that gamble. Therefore, it may not be the Native Americans who are consuming all the alcohol. As you can see, the ecological fallacy has the potential to foster and perpetuate stereotypes.

In sum, the ecological fallacy is a mistake that is made when we impose characteristics of a group upon individuals in that group.

EXAMPLE 5 (INDIVIDUAL-LEVEL DATA):

Operationalizing Studiousness

We begin with the concept of *studiousness*. Studious can refer to many different ideas: attending class regularly, studying outside of class time, or doing all of the assigned readings. Suppose that we define it as the number of hours a person spends studying outside of class each week. We can measure this concept on a questionnaire in many different ways.

Consider the following:

Nominal: Do you study in the library? Yes   No
Ordinal: How often do you study in the library? Never   Sometimes   Often
Interval/Ratio: How many hours do you spend studying in the library each week? _____

Individualistic fallacy A type of error that occurs when the characteristics of an individual are imposed upon all of the members of a group to which that individual belongs.

Ecological fallacy A type of error that results from drawing conclusions about individuals from characteristics of a group.

Our conceptual definition of studiousness is the effort that one puts into being a student. Our operational definition of studiousness is done in three different ways. Each has its own advantages and limitations. It is always possible that our operational definitions have little to do with the actual concept with which we began. When our operational definition fails to measure the concept with which we began, we say the variable is lacking *validity*.

For example, if we asked our respondents how many hours they went to the library each week, we could have an invalid measure. It is possible that some students go to the library only to take naps. In this case, a significant number of hours in the library would not indicate greater levels of studiousness. Or it may be that some students indicate that they never go to the library. Does this mean they are not studious? It may be that they have a home office or other place where they do their studying.

If this is the case, it means that our measure only measures part of the concept we intend it to measure. It may be that a student does not use the library at school because they have a better place to study. Or it may mean that they study in other places because they are not afforded the opportunity to study in the library. In either case, we cannot safely conclude that a student who does not study in the library very often is not studious. In this sense, our indicator lacks what is called *content validity* in that it only measures part of what we want it to measure.

Ultimately, social scientists can measure anything, but only with varying degrees of validity and reliability. *Validity* refers to the question "Are we measuring what we think we are measuring?" *Reliability* refers to the question "Can we expect consistent results if our measure is repeated?" In other words, do all our respondents understand the question the same way?

Validity refers to the ability of a measure to accurately reflect the concept it is intended to measure. Reliability refers to the ability of a measure to collect similar data each time it is applied. The following are examples of variables operationalized at different levels.

1. The number of hours you spend studying each day (0, 1, 2, 3, 4, 5, . . .). Ratio
2. How often you would say you study (none, some, a lot). Ordinal
3. Your favorite subject in school. Nominal
4. The frequency of skipping classes (never, sometimes, often). Ordinal
5. The number of classes you skipped last semester (0, 1, 2, 3, 4, ...) Ratio
6. The number of study group meetings you had last semester (0–1, 2–3, 4–5, 6+)

Don't be fooled by #6. Grouped data take the form of ordinal variables.

EXAMPLE 6 (ECOLOGICAL DATA):

Toxic Hazards and Other Locally Unwanted Land Uses

Locally unwanted land uses (or LULUs, as they are often referred to) can take many forms, ranging from toxic waste sites to wind farms. Toxic waste sites in particular pose a wide range of threats to both environmental and human health and include, among others, Superfund sites, state-level hazardous sites, industrial emissions, landfills, incinerators, waste-to-energy plants, tire piles, and trash transfer stations.

A colleague of mine, Daniel Faber from Northeastern University in Boston, and I spent a number of years developing variables to assess the relative contamination of one community to the next. We found that by using only one or two indicators of ecological hazards, say state-level hazardous sites and landfills, our indicator suffered from a lack of content validity. In other words, we were only measuring a portion of the total hazards and could not compare the relative contamination levels in one town to the next.

Ultimately we came up with a composite measure that included 17 different types of ecological hazards. Each type of hazard was awarded a certain number of "points" and when the points were tallied for each community, they represented what we call each community's Ecological Hazard Points, or EHPs. EHP is a ratio variable that in 2005 ranged from 0 in some small remote towns in Massachusetts to about 3,500 in the city of Boston.

Because each community is a different size, we then divided the number of EHPs by the number of square miles of land in each community to get EHP/sq. mile. This allowed us to compare the relative risks that each community faced.

After developing this variable, we were able to test whether lower-income communities and those with significant nonwhite populations were most likely to have high ecological hazard scores. Not surprisingly, they were. To arrive at this conclusion, we divided all the communities into four groups based on the percentage of the total population that was nonwhite. In other words, we began with a ratio variable and recoded it into an ordinal variable.

1. Percent of population that is nonwhite (0, 1, 2, 3, 4 . . . 100) Ratio
2. Percent of population that is nonwhite (0–4.9%, 5–14.9%, 15–24.9%, 25% and greater) Ordinal
3. Number of EHPs/sq. mile in community (0, 1, 2, 3, 4 . . . 127) Ratio
4. Number of EHPs/sq. mile in community (0–5, 6–10, 11– 15, 16 or more) Ordinal

The chart in Figure 1.6 shows the relationship between Environmental Hazard Points per square mile with the percentage of nonwhite population. In this chart, EHP is operationalized as an interval/ratio variable and race is operationalized as an ordinal variable. As you can see, the number of environmental hazard points increases as the percentage of the population that is nonwhite increases.

The chart in Figure 1.7 shows the relationship between EHPs *per square mile* with the percentage of nonwhite population (variables operationalized at the ratio level). A "best fit line" has been added to the chart to more clearly show the trend in the data. As in the previous chart, the trend shows a positive association between the two variables—as the percentage of the nonwhite population increases, so does the intensity of ecological hazards.

Figure 1.6 **Environmental Hazard Points by Race**

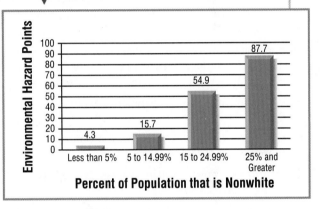

Figure 1.7 **Environmental Hazard Points Per Square Mile by Race**

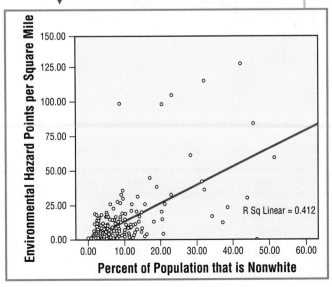

Chapter Summary

This chapter focuses on three main ideas: concepts, variables, and measurement. Concepts are ideas that we have about the world around us; variables are characteristics that vary from case to case; and measurement refers to the ways that we choose to assess the characteristics that vary from case to case. Because concepts are ideas based on what we know, we should expect them to change over time. As Thomas Kuhn argues in his book, *The Structure of Scientific Revolutions*, ideas about the world often change rapidly. Consequently, the ways that we conceptualize and operationalize variables also change over time. Measurement can be done at the nominal, ordinal, and interval/ratio levels. In all three types, the attributes of variables must be collectively exhaustive and mutually exclusive. Two types of data that social scientists work with are individual data and ecological data. While individual data describes characteristics of individuals, ecological data describes characteristics of groups or regions.

Exercises

1. Suppose we conceptualize academic achievement to mean how well a person does in school. Operationalize this concept in two ways.

2. Suppose you want to operationalize racism at the individual level (the degree of racist opinions a person holds). Operationalize this concept in two ways.

3. Come up with a way to operationalize proficiency in Spanish.

4. In your own words, explain what is meant by the term *mutually exclusive*.

5. In your own words, explain what is meant by the term *collectively exhaustive*.

6. Explain the difference between conceptualization and operationalization.

7. What is the problem with the variable below?

THE NUMBER OF BOOKS YOU READ LAST SUMMER
0–2 books
2–4 books
4–6 books
6 or more books

8. What is the problem with the variable below?

THE NUMBER OF BOOKS YOU READ LAST SUMMER
1–2 books
3–5 books
6 or more books

At what level are each of the following variables operationalized?

9. *Age* (1, 2, 3 . . .)

10. *Sex* (male, female, other)

11. *Class standing* (freshman, sophomore, junior, senior, other)

12. *Marital status* (married, single, divorced, widowed, other)

13. *Median Household Income* (annual household income in dollars)

14. How much you like the food on campus (a lot, some, a little, other)

15. The number of toxic waste sites in your community (0, 1, 2, 3, . . .)

16. The number of toxic waste sites in your community (0, 1–5, 6–10, 11+)

17. *Your GPA* (below average, average, above average)

18. Explain why it is best to collect data at the highest level of measurement possible.

Computer Exercises

Go to the National Opinion Research Center's 2006 General Social Survey Codebook at http://sda.berkeley.edu/D3/GSS08/Doc/gs06.htm. Use the information provided in the sequential list of variables to determine whether they are operationalized at the nominal, ordinal, or interval/ratio level.

Variable Name

19. ABANY	24. AGE	29. MUSICALS	34. PAIDSEX
20. ACQGAY	25. BIBLE	30. MYFAITH	35. POLVIEWS
21. ACTLIT	26. BLKJOBS	31. NATBORN	36. RACE
22. ADULTS	27. CARSGEN	32. NUMDAYS	37. SEX
23. ADVFAM	28. CONCONG	33. PAEDUC	38. TRUST

Now You Try It Answer

1: All heavenly bodies rise in the east and fall in the west. This is a function of the rotation of the Earth on its axes. If you have a globe and a flashlight, you can shine the light on the globe, imagining the light is sunlight, and spin the globe to better understand this.

Key Terms

Alienation, 14
Anomalies, 5
Anomie, 6
Attributes, 11
Bar chart, 22
Collectively exhaustive, 14
Concept, 3
Conceptualization, 13
Dependent variable, 12
Direction of effect, 12

Ecological fallacy, 29
Histogram, 22
Hypothesis, 12
Independent variable, 12
Individualistic fallacy, 29
Interval/ratio, 18
Levels of measurement, 17
Life chances, 2
Mutually exclusive, 16
Nominal, 17

Operationalization, 13
Ordinal, 18
Pie chart, 21
Reliability, 23
Statistics, 10
Units of analysis, 11
Validity, 23
Variable, 11

Works Cited

Best, J. (2001). *Damned Lies and Statistics: Untangling Numbers from the Media, Politicians, and Activists.* Berkeley: University of California Press.

Bullard, R. D. (1994). *Unequal Protection: Environmental Justice and Communities of Color.* San Francisco: Sierra Club Books.

Centers for Diseases Control and Prevention. (2009, May 15). *FastStats.* Atlanta, GA: Autho. Retrieved September 18, 2008, from http://www.cdc.gov/nchs/faststats/suicide.htm

Durkheim, E. (1951). *Suicide: A Study in Sociology* (J. A. Spaulding & G. Simpson, Trans.; G. Simpson, Ed.). New York: Free Press. (Original work published 1897)

Faber, D. R., & Krieg, E. J. (2005). *Unequal Exposure to Ecological Hazards 2005: Environmental Injustices in the Commonwealth of Massachusetts.* Boston: Philanthropy and Environmental Justice Research Project, Northeastern University.

Kimmel, M. (2008). *Guyland: The Perilous World Where Boys Become Men.* New York: HarperCollins.

Kuhn, T. (1962). *The Structure of Scientific Revolutions.* Chicago: University of Chicago Press.

Loewen, J. (2005). *Sundown Towns: A Hidden Dimension of American Racism.* New York: New Press.

Marx, K. (1998). *Capital* (D. McLelland, Ed.). New York: Oxford University Press.

Newton, I. S. (1848). *Principia.* New York: D. Adee.

Weber, M. (2004). *The Protestant Ethic and the Spirit of Capitalism.* New York: Routledge.

Frequency Tables

Introduction

It is said that most communication is nonverbal and that a picture contains a thousand words. It can also be said that a table might contain nearly as many words as a picture. Scientists of all fields make extensive use of tables because they are excellent tools with which to communicate large amounts of information in very concise ways. Therefore, it is important to know not only how to read tables but how to create them. In this chapter, we will learn how to read and how to construct frequency tables. Another type of table called a *cross-tabulation table*, is discussed in greater detail in Chapter 8.

Data Characteristics that can be empirically observed and measured.

Frequency The number of times an event or value occurs.

Frequency table A table for a single variable that indicates the number of cases for each attribute of the variable.

Cross-tabulation table A table that consists of two frequency tables, one in the rows and the other in the columns.

This chapter also marks the point at which *Now You Try It* exercises are included. You will see these appear in strategic places throughout this and the following chapters. They are intended to provide students with opportunities to test their comprehension of the main concepts that are presented in the chapter. Answers to the *Now You Try It* exercises are found at the end of each chapter.

Before we begin, Table 2.1 contains a few important symbols and formulas that are used.

TABLE 2.1 *Symbols and Formulas*

SYMBOL	MEANING OF SYMBOL	FORMULA
N	The number of cases in a table	
F	The frequency of cases for a particular attribute	
Cf	The cumulative frequency of cases for a group of attributes	Σf
P	The sample proportion	$P = \dfrac{f}{N}$
π	The population proportion	$\pi = \dfrac{f}{N}$
$\%$	Percent	$\% = \dfrac{f}{N}(100)$
$c\%$	Cumulative percent	$c\% = \dfrac{cf}{N}(100)$
Ratio	The relative frequency of cases across different populations	$Ratio = \dfrac{f_1}{f_2}$

Toxic Waste and "Superfund"

In 1980, President Ronald Reagan signed into law the Comprehensive Environmental Response, Compensation, and Liability Act (CERCLA), otherwise known as "Superfund." It is considered by many to be the most ambitious piece of environmental legislation ever written and, among other goals, was intended to help fund the cleanup of the nation's worst hazardous waste sites.

The passage of Superfund came about when national news coverage of a neighborhood in Niagara Falls, New York, alerted the public to the possibility of toxic wastes being present in their communities. This neighborhood, Love Canal, is a typical blue-collar working-class community that in many ways could be considered "Anywhere USA." As sociologist Andrew Szasz (1994) argues, mass media brought the issue into the homes of nearly all Americans. The news coverage was the result of the work of a citizen organization, the Niagara Falls Homeowners Association (NFHA), led by a woman named Lois Gibbs. Gibbs and some of her neighbors felt that their community contained unusually high numbers of miscarriages, stillbirths (babies born dead), and children with birth defects. Watching community activism unfold to reveal the extent of the toxic threat, millions of Americans were left

Figure 2.1 Love Canal Neighborhood Before and After the Toxic Waste Disaster

with the feeling that if the Love Canal community was contaminated, almost any community could be contaminated.

Eventually, the federal government was persuaded to offer the residents of Love Canal a "buyout" option in which homeowners would be offered a "fair" market value for their home. Most residents accepted the buyout as a way to escape the toxic threats to their health; however, many noted that while their home ownership investments were saved, their community was ripped apart and lost.

Although many other communities around the country are well known for their fight to protect themselves (Times Beach, Missouri, and Warren County, North Carolina), Love Canal is credited as a landmark case that spurred the passage of CERCLA in 1980. Superfund, as CERCLA is commonly referred to, consists of a legal and financial plan to clean up the nation's most contaminated toxic sites and deter companies from illegally dumping waste.

The "fund" in Superfund was originally a $1.6 billion trust fund to be used (1) for litigation against responsible parties and (2) for cleanup efforts when responsible parties could not be identified. In addition to holding polluters responsible for their wastes, Superfund imposes $10,000 per-day fines against responsible parties that do not come forward to claim their responsibility. To help ensure that they do come forward, Superfund can hold multiple parties responsible. Overall, the attempt was to make it no longer pay to pollute.

It is debatable how successful these efforts have proven. Certainly, a great deal more cleanup has been done with Superfund than would have been achieved without it. And because of the Superfund Amendment and Reauthorization Act of 1986 that added an additional $5.8 billion to the Superfund, citizens now have the rights and the tools to find out what chemicals are being used and disposed of in their communities.

Approximately 1,200–1,300 active Superfund sites are scattered across the country, with tens of millions of Americans living within a few miles of them. Hundreds of other Superfund sites have been cleaned up. Despite this alarming number of hazards, it is likely that tens or hundreds of thousands of other, less dangerous sites exist across the country.

In fact, by the late 1980s, a number of scientific studies revealed that toxic waste sites are far more common than people previously believed. Superfund sites are but one type of hazard and scientific investigations soon showed that other, less dangerous sites were quite common in most communities. Leaking underground storage tanks, toxic spills, industrial emissions, waste transfer stations, and a variety of other ecological hazards pose a greater risk to overall public health than do Superfund sites listed on the Environmental Protection Agency's *National Priority List* (NPL). Nevertheless, as of May 2, 2008, the NPL contained 1,641 sites in the United States, Guam, Puerto Rico, U.S. Virgin Islands, Trust Territories, American Samoa, and the Northern Mariana Islands.

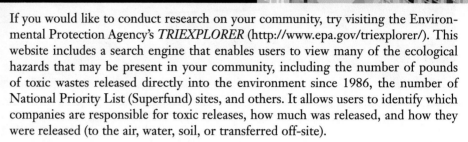

Integrating Technology

If you would like to conduct research on your community, try visiting the Environmental Protection Agency's *TRIEXPLORER* (http://www.epa.gov/triexplorer/). This website includes a search engine that enables users to view many of the ecological hazards that may be present in your community, including the number of pounds of toxic wastes released directly into the environment since 1986, the number of National Priority List (Superfund) sites, and others. It allows users to identify which companies are responsible for toxic releases, how much was released, and how they were released (to the air, water, soil, or transferred off-site).

Individual and Ecological Data

Individual data Data that represents characteristics of individuals (people, houses, cars, dogs, etc.).

Ecological data Data that represents characteristics of groups (towns, cities, counties, etc.).

Now is a good time to recap the difference between individual data and ecological data. Individual data is representative of a single person. For example, if we conducted a sample of college students our unit of analysis is individual students. Ecological data, on the other hand, is representative of groups or areas. For example, the number of police cars in each town is a characteristic of the towns we are studying, not the individuals in the towns. The data generated in the U.S. Census is probably one of the best examples of ecological data. Data from the census can be used to generate thousands of statistics at the national, state, county, town, and even block levels; however, it is impossible to use census data to learn anything about any one individual. In this sense, census data is ecological data because it is representative of geographic areas and not of individuals.

Frequency Tables

Frequency tables allow us to organize large quantities of data so that they can be described and communicated with others easily by summarizing the distribution of cases across the attributes of a single variable. Typically, frequency tables include more than just the frequencies of cases; they also include a variety of percentages. This chapter introduces readers to the role that frequencies, proportions, percentages, and cumulative percentages play in the use of tables. We look at how Superfund sites are classified and how they are geographically distributed nationwide by state. Before doing so, however, we first analyze some data that is representative of individuals (as opposed to Superfund sites or states).

Before we begin our discussion, let's take a moment to see what a frequency table actually looks like. Table 2.2 is a frequency table for the variable SEX. SEX is operationalized as Male or Female. As you can see, the table provides a great deal of information, including the frequency of males ($f = 2,003$) and the frequency of females ($f = 2,507$). Together, these add up to the number of respondents ($N = 4,510$).

Often, some respondents are unwilling or unable to provide data. In these cases, they are often counted as "missing data." They are typically shown in the frequency column below the total. Table 2.2, a graphic representation of which is shown in

TABLE 2.2 *Respondent's Sex*

		FREQUENCY	PERCENT	VALID PERCENT	CUMULATIVE PERCENT
Valid	MALE	2003	44.4	44.4	44.4
	FEMALE	2507	55.6	55.6	100.0
	Total	4510	100.0	100.0	

Figure 2.2, does not have any missing values in it, but tables discussed later in the chapter do. It is important to realize that missing data are not included in any statistics.

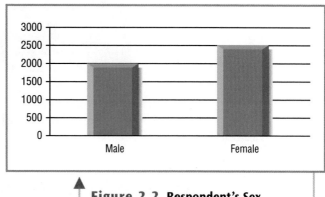

Figure 2.2 **Respondent's Sex**

Proportions, Percentages, and Ratios

Proportions. It is important to understand the basics behind proportions and percentages before working with frequency tables. Proportions and percentages allow us to describe groups of cases, and allow us to make comparisons across populations.

EXAMPLE 1

Satisfaction with Social Life
Suppose we sample 500 males and 600 females. Of the 500 males, 375 are satisfied with their social life. Of the 600 females, 425 are satisfied with their social life.

Based on these numbers, it is difficult to determine whether males or females tend to be more satisfied with their social life. Proportions and percentages allow us to overcome this problem. We can mathematically represent 375 out of 500 males being satisfied with their social life with the following formula:

Proportion A way to standardize the frequency of cases so that comparisons can be made across populations.

$$P = \frac{f}{N}$$

In this formula, f is equal to the number of males who indicate they are satisfied with their social life and N is equal to the total number of males who answered the question. Therefore:

$$P = \frac{375 \; satisfied}{500 \; total} = \frac{375}{500} = .750$$

Therefore, the proportion (*P*) of males who are satisfied with their social life is .750.

Using the same formula for females, we find that:

$$P = \frac{f}{N} = \frac{425 \; satisfied}{600 \; total} = \frac{425}{600} = .708$$

Based on this we can compare the proportion of males who are satisfied to the proportion of females who are satisfied and draw a conclusion as to which group is most likely to be satisfied with their social life. In this case, the answer is males because they have a higher proportion.

All proportions range between a low of 0 and a high of 1.0. This is because the value of the denominator in the proportion equation is always greater than or equal to the value of the numerator. In the calculation of a proportion, the numerator is never larger than the denominator.

Percentage A way to standardize the frequency of cases as the number of responses per 100 cases.

Percentages. Percentages are extremely easy to calculate once you know how to calculate proportions. To determine a percentage, first, calculate a proportion and, second, multiply the proportion by 100. That's it! The formula for a percentage is shown below:

$$\% = \frac{f}{N}(100)$$

Using our example above, we can calculate the percent of males who are satisfied with their social life as follows:

$$\% = \frac{f}{N}(100) = \frac{375}{500}(100) = .75(100) = 75.0$$

That is, 75% of males are satisfied with their social life.

Similarly, for females:

$$\% = \frac{f}{N}(100) = \frac{425}{600}(100) = .708(100) = 70.8$$

As with proportions, we can now compare males to females. While 75.0% of males are satisfied with their social life, only 70.8% of females are satisfied.

Ratios. A ratio is another important statistical tool that allows us to communicate more easily. Using our example above, suppose someone asked us "How many females are in your sample for each male?" In other words, they want to know the ratio of females to males. We could say that for each 600 females we have 500 males, but this is not easy to understand. The solution is fairly simple using the formula below:

> **Ratio** A way to compare the relative frequency of cases across populations.

$$Ratio = \frac{f_1}{f_2}$$

In this case, f_1 is equal to the number of females and f_2 is equal to the number of males. Essentially, we are standardizing the number of males as 1 by putting the frequency for males in the denominator of our equation.

$$Ratio = \frac{f_1}{f_2} = \frac{600}{500} = 1.2$$

This tells us that for each male, there are 1.2 females.

A way to remember which frequency goes in the numerator and which goes in the denominator is to use the phrasing of the question being asked. For example, if we want to know the ratio of females to males, we put the frequency for males in the denominator. If we want to know the ratio of males to females, we put the frequency of females in the denominator. Essentially, whichever variable follows the word *to* in our question is the one that goes in the denominator.

Now You Try It 1

Suppose we want to know about students' attitudes toward a ban on tobacco use on campus. We decide to survey 500 students, 355 of whom live on-campus and 145 of whom live off-campus. Of those who live on-campus, 276 indicate that they approve of a tobacco ban and of those who live off-campus, 92 approve of a tobacco ban.

Use this information to answer the following questions.

1. What proportion of all students approve of a tobacco ban?
2. What percent of on-campus students approve of a tobacco ban?
3. What percent of off-campus students approve of a tobacco ban?
4. What is the ratio of on-campus to off-campus students?

*Answers at end of chapter.

EXAMPLE 2

Public Opinion on Environmental Spending
How do people in the United States view the environment? Do they feel we are doing enough to protect it? These questions are easy to ask but difficult to answer.

Americans have an interesting relationship with their environments. Generally, the U.S. population subscribes to a view of nature known as "Western dualism." As the word "dualism" implies, it is really two views of nature that are held simultaneously. On the

Value labels Descriptive labels for the attributes of a variable.

Frequency A column in a frequency table that shows the number of times a particular attribute occurs.

Percent A column in a frequency table that standardizes frequencies by expressing them as the number of times an attribute occurs per 100 cases. Based on all cases.

Valid percent A column in a frequency table that standardizes frequencies by expressing them as the number of times an attribute occurs per 100 cases. Based on only those cases that provided data.

Cumulative percent A column in a frequency table that shows the percent of cases above or below a certain point or attribute.

one hand, we tend to think of nature as an object—something that is "out there," separate from us, and to be used to make our lives better (think of burning coal for electricity). On the other hand, we tend to think of nature as an extension of ourselves—a part of who we are that should be protected for its own sake. Although most of us probably lean toward one or the other of these two views, it is likely that we have a little of both in us.

Data from the 2006 General Social Survey shed light on which of these two views tends to dominate the American mindset. They represent varying opinions on whether we are spending too little, about right, or too much on improving environmental protections (Figure 2.3). We might claim that those claiming that we spend too little to protect the environment tend to feel that nature has intrinsic value and those claiming that we spend too much tend to objectify nature.

Table 2.3 provides us with a great deal of information on the variable itself and the distribution of cases. As you can probably tell, the variable is ordinal because the attributes can be rank-ordered from high to low (from "too little" to "too much"). The table consists of a series of five columns: (1) Value Labels, (2) Frequencies, (3) Percents, (4) Valid Percents, and (5) Cumulative Percents.

Table 2.3 also tells us that the sample consisted of 4,510 respondents; however, it is important to note that 3,064 of those respondents are classified as "missing." This means that, for whatever reasons, either the question did not apply to them (NAP) or they did not provide an answer to the question (DK). After removing the 3,064 missing cases (3,026 NAP cases and 38 DK cases), we are left with 1,446 cases. Therefore, we really have two values of *N*, but for all intents and purposes missing cases are almost always excluded from the analysis. Consequently, *N* = 1,446.

The Frequency column in the table tells us that 992 respondents indicated that they feel the government is spending too little on protecting the environment. The Percent column tells us that these 992 respondents make up 22.0% of the 4,510 included in the sample. The Valid Percent column tells us that these 992 respondents make up 68.6% of the 1,446 respondents who provided data. Each row in the table is read the same way.

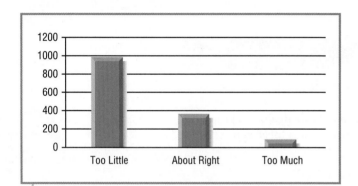

Figure 2.3 Improving Protecting Environment

TABLE 2.3 *Improving Protecting Environment*

		FREQUENCY	PERCENT	VALID PERCENT	CUMULATIVE PERCENT
Valid	TOO LITTLE	992	22.0	68.6	68.6
	ABOUT RIGHT	365	8.1	25.2	93.8
	TOO MUCH	89	2.0	6.2	100.0
	Total	1446	32.1	100.0	
Missing	NAP	3026	67.1		
	DK	38	.8		
	Total	3064	67.9		
Total		4510	100.0		

The last column in the table, the Cumulative Percent column, is read slightly differently. For example, the table tells us that 365 respondents felt that we are spending about the right amount on environmental protection, which happens to be 25.2% of respondents who provided data. The 93.8% in the Cumulative Percent column is based on the total number of respondents who felt that we are spending either too little or about right. In other words, the 93.8% is calculated by adding the 992 who answered too little with the 365 who answered about right. This means that 1,357 respondents answered either too little or about right and these 1,357 respondents comprise 93.8% of the 1,446 valid responses.

It is interesting that despite 68.6% of the American public claiming that we spend too little on environmental protection, we have such a staggering array and degree of environmental problems that have yet to be solved. We now take a look at some Superfund data to see how it can be organized into frequency tables and how to calculate the various percent column values.

Superfund Sites: Frequency Table for a Nominal Variable

Our unit of analysis is the waste site and all Superfund waste sites are listed on what is called the *National Priorities List*. Not all of the sites on the list are currently active. Some sites are listed as *active/final* while others are listed as *deleted* or *proposed*. The difference is that not all sites have undergone sufficient evaluation by the Environmental Protection Agency (EPA) to qualify for the Superfund Program. Those that are still under review are considered *proposed* sites. Those that are either cleaned or are not deemed dangerous enough to meet Superfund requirements are considered *deleted*. And those that are deemed worthy of Superfund actions are considered *active/final*.

Table 2.4 was taken from the website *scorecard.org* on November 12, 2008, and ranks each state by the number of Superfund sites that were considered either "active/final" or "proposed" between 1993 and 2004. You can use the website to help assess the level of toxic contamination in your community.

Table 2.4 lists only sites that are either final or proposed and does not include all Superfund sites. A more complete list also includes those that are listed as *deleted*. Generally, deleted sites are those that have been cleaned up. Including deleted sites gives us a better sense of the total hazards that a state has faced over time.

Using data collected directly from the Environmental Protection Agency website on November 13, 2008, we see that each of the 1,650 sites falls into one and only

TABLE 2.4 *Superfund Sites by State*

RANK	STATE	NUMBER OF SUPERFUND SITES
1.	NEW JERSEY	116
2.	CALIFORNIA	98
3.	PENNSYLVANIA	95
4.	NEW YORK	93
5.	MICHIGAN	69
6.	FLORIDA	52
7.	WASHINGTON	47
8.	ILLINOIS	45
	TEXAS	45
9.	WISCONSIN	40
10.	OHIO	35
11.	MASSACHUSETTS	32
12.	INDIANA	30
	VIRGINIA	30
13.	NORTH CAROLINA	29
14.	MISSOURI	27
15.	SOUTH CAROLINA	25
16.	MINNESOTA	24
17.	NEW HAMPSHIRE	20
18.	MARYLAND	19
	UTAH	19
19.	COLORADO	18
20.	CONNECTICUT	16
	GEORGIA	16
	LOUISIANA	16
21.	ALABAMA	15
	DELAWARE	15
	MONTANA	15
22.	IOWA	14
	KENTUCKY	14
23.	KANSAS	13
	NEW MEXICO	13
	TENNESSEE	13
24.	MAINE	12
	OREGON	12
	RHODE ISLAND	12
25.	ARKANSAS	11
	NEBRASKA	11

RANK	STATE	NUMBER OF SUPERFUND SITES
	OKLAHOMA	11
26.	PUERTO RICO	10
	VERMONT	10
27.	ARIZONA	9
	IDAHO	9
	WEST VIRGINIA	9
28.	ALASKA	6
29.	MISSISSIPPI	5
30.	HAWAII	3
31.	GUAM	2
	SOUTH DAKOTA	2
	VIRGIN ISLANDS	2
	WYOMING	2
32.	DISTRICT OF COLUMBIA	1
	NEVADA	1

There is limited information about many potentially significant sources of contamination. Scorecard's profiles of hazardous waste sites are limited to active/final and proposed sites on the National Priority List and are derived from multiple sources dating from 1993 to 2004.

one of these three attributes. Therefore, the variable is operationalized in a way that its attributes are both collectively exhaustive and mutually exclusive. By counting the number of sites in each attribute, we can quickly and easily describe the distribution of Superfund sites in Table 2.5.

As you can see in the bar chart in Figure 2.4, the height of each bar corresponds to its frequency (or valid percent). Bar charts are good ways of displaying data at the nominal or ordinal levels. The data labels at the top of each bar can represent frequencies, percentages, or both depending on what you would like to display. In this case, they show frequencies. The same data are shown in the form of a pie chart in Figure 2.5. The relative size of each pie slice represents either the number of cases or the valid percent of cases.

TABLE 2.5 *National Priority List Status*

		FREQUENCY	PERCENT	VALID PERCENT	CUMULATIVE PERCENT
Valid	Deleted	330	20.0	20.0	20.0
	Active/Final	1257	76.2	76.2	96.2
	Proposed	63	3.8	3.8	100.0
	Total	1650	100.0	100.0	

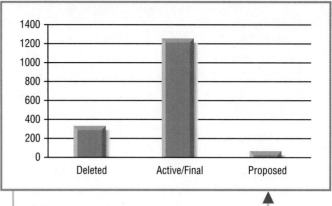

Figure 2.4 **National Priority List Status**

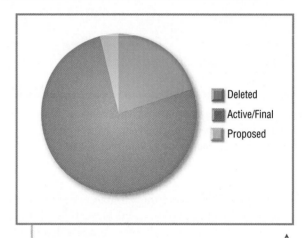

Figure 2.5 **National Priority List Status**

Site Status is operationalized as a nominal variable because the attributes cannot be rank-ordered from high to low. It is often tempting to think of some nominal variables as ordinal variables. In the case of "Site Status," for example, some might claim that we can rank the attributes because active/final sites pose a greater threat than do deleted or proposed sites. Two problems arise with this kind of logic. First, a proposed site could actually pose a much greater threat than an active/final site. Second, the variable is not intended to assess the risk posed by a site; it is only intended to describe how the EPA has classified the site. If we wanted to rank sites according to the threats that they pose, we would have to create new variables with new attributes based on new concepts and measurements. As it is, no ranking can be done and the variable must be treated as nominal.

The frequency table provides a significant amount of information. First, it tells us how many cases are included in the table, N. In this case, N is equal to 1,650. Second, it tells us the frequency of each attribute (hence the name "frequency table"). For example, of the 1,650 sites, 330 are labeled Deleted from the list. Likewise, it tells us that 1,257 sites are Active/Final and 63 are Proposed. Third, it tells us the percent of the time that each attribute occurs. For example, the 330 Deleted sites constitute 20.0% of the 1,650 total sites. We now look at how the percent, valid percent, and cumulative percent are computed.

EXAMPLE 3

Calculating Proportions and Percents Using Superfund Site Data

Before we can calculate a percent, we must first calculate a proportion. Proportions are always expressed in decimal form and range between 0 and 1.0. Proportions can be turned into percentages by multiplying them by 100 (essentially just moving the decimal two places to the right). The formulas for proportion (P), percent (%), and cumulative percent (c%) are shown below. It should be noted that the percent and valid percent are not always the same, as they are in the case of "Site Status." They are based on different values of N. The percent is always based on the total number of cases in the table whereas the valid percent is based on only those cases that actually provide data. It is almost always preferable to use the valid percent and not the percent.

Formula for calculating the proportion: $P = \dfrac{f}{N}$

Formula for calculating the percent: $\% = \dfrac{f}{N}(100)$

Formula for calculating the cumulative percent: $c\% = \dfrac{cf}{N}(100)$

We begin by calculating proportions for each of the three attributes. These are computed by taking the frequency of sites for a particular attribute and dividing by the total number of cases.

$$P = \frac{330}{1650} = .200 \qquad .200\,(100) = 20.0\%$$

$$P = \frac{1257}{1650} = .762 \qquad .762\,(100) = 76.2\%$$

$$P = \frac{63}{1650} = .038 \qquad .038\,(100) = 3.8\%$$

By dividing the number of cases in each attribute (f) by the total number of cases in the table (N), we obtain a proportion. By multiplying the proportion by 100, we obtain a percent. For example, the proportion of cases that are deleted is .200 and the percent of cases that are deleted is 20.0%.

You can see that next to the Percent column in Table 2.5 is a Valid Percent column. In this particular table, the two columns are the same; however, this is not always the case. Oftentimes, frequency tables contain what are called "missing" cases. An example of a table with missing cases is presented later.

The final column in the frequency table is called the Cumulative Percent column. Cumulative Percent columns offer a running total of the Frequency column. For example, you can see that the first cumulative percent value is 20.0%. The next is 96.2%. This value is based on a cumulative frequency (cf) and is obtained by adding the frequency for deleted to the frequency for active, dividing by N, and multiplying by 100. For example:

$$c\% = \frac{330 + 1257}{1650}(100) = 96.2\%$$

This means that 96.2% of all Superfund sites are either Deleted or Active/Final.

Now You Try It 2

Suppose you are doing a study of student integration into social life on campus and want to find out what percent of students live on campus. Using a survey research method, you ask students about their sex, class standing, and what percent of their time they spend on campus. You then test out your questionnaire on a group of students in a dining hall and find the following:

RESPONDENT #	SEX	CLASS STANDING	TIME ON CAMPUS
1	Male	Freshman	90
2	Male	Junior	75
3	Female	Junior	60
4	Female	Sophomore	85
5	Female	Freshman	95
6	Male	Senior	50
7	Female	Junior	70
8	Female	Senior	60
9	Male	Sophomore	90
10	Female	Junior	70

Using the data from the test of your questionnaire, construct a frequency table for the variable Sex. Be sure to include value labels, frequencies, percents, valid percents, and cumulative percents. It is also standard procedure to include a title with each table.

*Answers at end of chapter.

Frequency Table for an Ordinal Variable

For this example the NPL sites are organized into four groups based on the number of sites in each state. Our unit of analysis is no longer the waste site. The unit of analysis is now the state because we are looking at characteristics of states, not characteristics of waste sites. Therefore, the data presented here is ecological data. Territories were removed from the data and only the 50 U.S. states and the District of Columbia are included. This reduces the overall number of cases to 51, so that $N = 51$. It also reduced the number of sites in these states from 1,650 to 1,616 because some geographic regions have been left out of the analysis.

EXAMPLE 4

Analyzing Superfund Site Data by State

The states are now organized into four groups (attributes) based on the number of waste sites. The first group of states consists of those that contain anywhere from 0 to 15 Superfund sites. The second group of states consists of those that contain anywhere from 16 to 30

TABLE 2.6 *Frequency of Superfund Sites*

		FREQUENCY	PERCENT	VALID PERCENT	CUMULATIVE PERCENT
Valid	0–15 sites	18	35.3	35.3	35.3
	16–30 sites	16	31.4	31.4	66.7
	31–45 sites	7	13.7	13.7	80.4
	46 or more sites	10	19.6	19.6	100.0
	Total	51	100.0	100.0	

Superfund sites. The third group of states consists of those that contain anywhere from 31 to 45 Superfund sites. The final group of states consists of those that contain 46 or more sites. Table 2.6 shows the distribution and Figure 2.6 shows the distribution in the form of a bar chart.

Table 2.6 indicates that 18 states have between 0 and 15 sites; 16 states have between 16 and 30 sites; 7 states have between 31 and 45 sites; and 10 states have 46 or more sites. The attributes are mutually exclusive and collectively exhaustive. As you can see, all of the columns in the frequency table are the same as they were for the previous one. They are the same for all frequency tables generated by SPSS for Windows.

This variable is ordinal, although it is easy to be fooled into thinking that it is interval/ratio because the attributes are represented as ranges of numbers. Here is the justification. When looking at the attributes, it is possible to say that those states with 31–45 sites have more than those states with 16–30 sites. On the other hand, we cannot tell exactly how many more sites a state with "16–30" sites contains relative to a state with "0–15" sites. It could be one additional site or it could be 30 additional sites. Or it could be anything in between. The point is we just don't know; nor can we tell from the table. Therefore, we can only say that a particular state has more or less than another state, thereby making the variable ordinal. Because we are unable to determine the exact difference in the frequency of sites between the two states, the variable must be ordinal.

This is called grouped data and it is important to realize that just because the table has numbers for the attributes, it does not make it an interval/ratio variable.

All of the percentages are calculated using the same methods and formulas that were used to calculate them in the previous table using the formula for percentage (%).

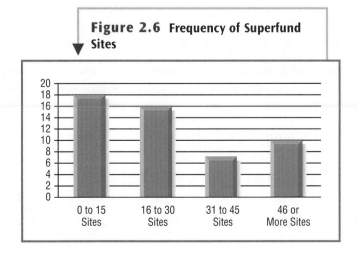

Figure 2.6 Frequency of Superfund Sites

$$\% = \frac{f}{N}(100)$$

0–15 sites: $\% = \frac{18}{51}(100) = 35.3$ Therefore, 35.3% of all states contain 0–15 Superfund sites.

16–30 sites: $\% = \frac{16}{51}(100) = 31.4$ Therefore, 31.4% of all states contain 16–30 Superfund sites.

31–45 sites: $\% = \frac{7}{51}(100) = 13.7$ Therefore, 13.7% of all states contain 31–45 Superfund sites.

46 or more sites: $\% = \frac{10}{51}(100) = 19.6$ Therefore, 19.6% of all states contain 46 or more Superfund sites.

The Cumulative Percent column is more applicable for tables with ordinal variables. Cumulative percents are calculated using the following formula:

$$c\% = \frac{cf}{N}(100)$$

0–15 sites: $c\% = \frac{18}{51}(100) = 35.3$ Therefore, 35.3% of all states contain 0–15 Superfund sites.

0–30 sites: $c\% = \frac{18 + 16}{51}(100) = 66.7$ Therefore, 66.7% of all states contain 0–30 Superfund sites.

0–45 sites: $c\% = \frac{18 + 16 + 7}{51}(100) = 80.4$ Therefore, 80.4% of all states contain 0–45 Superfund sites.

0–46 or more sites: $c\% = \frac{18 + 16 + 7 + 10}{51}(100) = 100.0$ Therefore, 35.3% of all states contain 0–46 or more Superfund sites.

Now You Try It 3

Using the preliminary data from your study of integration into campus social life, construct a frequency table for the variable Class Standing. Be sure to include value labels, frequencies, percents, valid percents, and cumulative percents.

RESPONDENT #	SEX	CLASS STANDING	TIME ON CAMPUS
1	Male	Freshman	90
2	Male	Junior	75
3	Female	Junior	60
4	Female	Sophomore	85
5	Female	Freshman	95
6	Male	Senior	50

RESPONDENT #	SEX	CLASS STANDING	TIME ON CAMPUS
7	Female	Junior	70
8	Female	Senior	60
9	Male	Sophomore	90
10	Female	Junior	70

*Answers at end of chapter.

Frequency Table for an Interval/Ratio Variable

For this example the NPL sites are organized by states and the District of Columbia (hence $N = 51$ instead of 50). Unlike the last example the states are not grouped into categories on the basis of how many sites they contain. Yet we use the same formula for percent (%) and cumulative percent that we used for the previous tables.

$$\% = \frac{f}{N}(100)$$

$$c\% = \frac{cf}{N}(100)$$

EXAMPLE 5

Looking at Interval/Ratio Variables in Superfund Site Data

Table 2.7 indicates that two states have one Superfund site, one state has one site, and so on.

For one Superfund site: $\% = \dfrac{2\ states}{51}(100) = 3.9$ Therefore, 3.9% of all states have one Superfund site.

For two Superfund sites: $\% = \dfrac{1\ state}{51}(100) = 2.0$ Therefore, 2.0% of all states have two Superfund sites.

For three Superfund sites: $\% = \dfrac{1\ state}{51}(100) = 2.0$ Therefore, 2.0% of all states have three Superfund sites.

This process is repeated for each row in the table, so that each row consists of a value, frequency, percent, valid percent, and cumulative percent. Cumulative percents are now discussed.

The Cumulative Percent column is particularly useful for tables with interval/ratio variables. For example, if we want to know how many states have less than five Superfund sites, we look at the first column of Table 2.7 and identify those rows in the table that indicate 0–4 sites. When we move across the table, we find that the cumulative percent for four sites is 11.8%. This means that 11.8% of all states have four or fewer Superfund sites.

The Cumulative Percent column is best thought of as a running total of the Valid Percent column. It is important to realize, however, that the calculation of cumulative percents cannot be accomplished by adding up the valid percents. The reason for this is that it is possible that the rounding error in each valid percent equation could be

TABLE 2.7 *Frequency of Superfund Sites*

		FREQUENCY	PERCENT	VALID PERCENT	CUMULATIVE PERCENT
Valid	1	2	3.9	3.9	3.9
	2	1	2.0	2.0	5.9
	3	1	2.0	2.0	7.8
	4	2	3.9	3.9	11.8
	8	1	2.0	2.0	13.7
	9	1	2.0	2.0	15.7
	11	1	2.0	2.0	17.6
	12	2	3.9	3.9	21.6
	13	2	3.9	3.9	25.5
	14	3	5.9	5.9	31.4
	15	2	3.9	3.9	35.3
	16	2	3.9	3.9	39.2
	17	1	2.0	2.0	41.2
	18	2	3.9	3.9	45.1
	20	4	7.8	7.8	52.9
	21	1	2.0	2.0	54.9
	22	2	3.9	3.9	58.8
	23	3	5.9	5.9	64.7
	29	1	2.0	2.0	66.7
	33	1	2.0	2.0	68.6
	34	2	3.9	3.9	72.5
	36	1	2.0	2.0	74.5
	40	1	2.0	2.0	76.5
	44	1	2.0	2.0	78.4
	45	1	2.0	2.0	80.4
	46	1	2.0	2.0	82.4
	51	1	2.0	2.0	84.3
	59	1	2.0	2.0	86.3
	65	1	2.0	2.0	88.2
	72	1	2.0	2.0	90.2
	84	1	2.0	2.0	92.2
	107	1	2.0	2.0	94.1
	110	1	2.0	2.0	96.1
	123	1	2.0	2.0	98.0
	140	1	2.0	2.0	100.0
	Total	51	100.0	100.0	

compounded when they are summed. The way to get around the possibility of compounded rounding error is to base the cumulative percent on cumulative frequencies. Using our example of states with 0–4 Superfund sites, we find that two states have 0 sites, one state has one site, one state has two sites, and two states have four sites. Therefore:

$$c\% = \frac{2 + 1 + 1 + 2 \; states}{51}(100) = 11.8 \quad \text{Therefore, 11.8\% of all states have four or fewer Superfund sites.}$$

If we want to calculate how many states have 12 or fewer sites, our equation is as follows:

$$c\% = \frac{2 + 1 + 1 + 2 + 1 + 1 + 1 + 2 \; states}{51}(100) = 21.6 \quad \text{Therefore, 21.6\% of all states have twelve or fewer Superfund sites.}$$

Now You Try It 4

Using the preliminary data from your study of integration into campus social life, construct a frequency table for the variable Time on Campus. Be sure to include value labels (in this case the actual values), frequencies, percents, valid percents, and cumulative percents.

RESPONDENT #	SEX	CLASS STANDING	TIME ON CAMPUS
1	Male	Freshman	90
2	Male	Junior	75
3	Female	Junior	60
4	Female	Sophomore	85
5	Female	Freshman	95
6	Male	Senior	50
7	Female	Junior	70
8	Female	Senior	60
9	Male	Sophomore	90
10	Female	Junior	70

*Answers at end of chapter.

Constructing Frequency Tables from Raw Data

Constructing frequency tables is a relatively simple process, but it requires careful attention to detail. Imagine that you walk into a typical classroom on a college campus and ask each student to tell you his or her age. You get the following results:

17, 18, 18, 19, 19, 19, 19, 20, 20, 20, 20, 20, 20, 20, 21, 21, 21, 22, 24, 25

The following sections demonstrate how these data are organized into a frequency table.

The Frequency Column. Taking these 20 cases of raw data and organizing them into a frequency table begins with making a table with two columns, one that lists the attributes of our variable (the ages that respondents indicated) and one that lists the frequency (f) that each age occurred (Table 2.8).

The Percent Column. To calculate the Percent column, we divide each frequency by N to obtain the proportion. Then we multiply the proportion by 100 to obtain the percent.

$$17: \quad \% = \frac{1}{20}(100) = 5.0\%$$

$$18: \quad \% = \frac{2}{20}(100) = 10.0\%$$

$$19: \quad \% = \frac{4}{20}(100) = 20.0\%$$

$$20: \quad \% = \frac{7}{20}(100) = 35.0\%$$

$$21: \quad \% = \frac{3}{20}(100) = 15.0\%$$

TABLE 2.8 *Age of Respondent*

	FREQUENCY (f)
17	1
18	2
19	4
20	7
21	3
22	1
24	1
25	1
Total (*N*)	20

TABLE 2.9 *Age of Respondent*

	FREQUENCY	PERCENT
17	1	5.0
18	2	10.0
19	4	20.0
20	7	35.0
21	3	15.0
22	1	5.0
24	1	5.0
25	1	5.0
Total	20	100.0

$$22: \quad \% = \frac{1}{20}(100) = 5.0\%$$

$$24: \quad \% = \frac{1}{20}(100) = 5.0\%$$

$$25: \quad \% = \frac{1}{20}(100) = 5.0\%$$

We can then add the percentages to the Percent column in Table 2.9.

The Cumulative Percent Column. Finally, we can create a Cumulative Percent column ($c\%$) using cumulative frequencies (cf). Remember, Cumulative Percent columns summarize data up to a given point in a frequency table. For example, we may want to know what percent of respondents are younger than 20. To calculate this, we need to find out how many respondents are younger than 20 (which, in this case, is another way of asking for the cumulative frequency for 17, 18, and 19-year-olds). We do this as follows:

$$c\% = \frac{cf}{N}(100)$$

$$17: \quad c\% = \frac{1}{20}(100) = 5.0\%$$

$$18: \quad c\% = \frac{1 + 2}{20}(100) = 15.0\%$$

$$19: \quad c\% = \frac{1 + 2 + 4}{20}(100) = 35.0\%$$

$$20: \quad c\% = \frac{1 + 2 + 4 + 7}{20}(100) = 70.0\%$$

$$21: \quad c\% = \frac{1 + 2 + 4 + 7 + 3}{20}(100) = 85.0\%$$

$$22: \quad c\% = \frac{1 + 2 + 4 + 7 + 3 + 1}{20}(100) = 90.0\%$$

$$24: \quad c\% = \frac{1 + 2 + 4 + 7 + 3 + 1 + 1}{20}(100) = 95.0\%$$

$$25: \quad c\% = \frac{1 + 2 + 4 + 7 + 3 + 1 + 1 + 1}{20}(100) = 100.0\%$$

These values can now be added as another column in Table 2.10.

Getting back to our earlier question, because there are one 17-year old, two 18-year olds, and four 19-year olds, the cumulative frequency is $1 + 2 + 4 = 7$. Therefore, the cumulative percent for 19 year-olds is 35.0%. We can now state that 35.0% of our sample is less than 20 years old.

Integrating Technology

In its annual *Human Development Report*, the United Nations gathers tremendous amounts of data from countries all over the world and makes these data available to the public via the Internet. Data can be viewed online or downloaded into Microsoft Excel files (which can then be saved in a variety of formats that most statistics software programs can read). These include data on literacy rates, health care, carbon dioxide emissions, gender discrimination, vital statistics (births, deaths), and income inequality, among many others.

Follow this link for the most recent report: http://hdr.undp.org/en/

One interesting exercise is to sort countries from lowest to highest by different variables to see what other countries have similar characteristics. While we in the United States tend to compare the U.S. to many western European countries, you may be surprised to see that in terms of income inequality, the U.S. is much more similar to many less developed and "third world" nations.

TABLE 2.10 *Age of Respondent*

	FREQUENCY	PERCENT	CUMULATIVE PERCENT
17	1	5.0	5.0
18	2	10.0	15.0
19	4	20.0	35.0
20	7	35.0	70.0
21	3	15.0	85.0
22	1	5.0	90.0
24	1	5.0	95.0
25	1	5.0	100.0
Total	20	100.0	

EXAMPLE 6

Student Satisfaction with the College Environment

Here is another example. Now suppose that for a class project, you are asked to survey students on their overall satisfaction with the overall quality of their college environment. You sample 500 students, asking them if they are "very satisfied," "somewhat satisfied," or "not satisfied." You are now faced with the task of sifting through 500 sheets of paper with your respondents' responses in an attempt to figure out how they tend to feel about their college experience. This is a good time to consider constructing a frequency table.

To construct a frequency table, you must tally the responses for each of the three attributes. Suppose you find that 342 respondents are "very satisfied," 116 are "somewhat satisfied," and 42 are "not satisfied." You can now summarize your responses in a table format like the one in Table 2.11.

The next task is to display these data in the form of percents instead of frequencies. For example, if someone asked how satisfied students are with their college experience, you could answer that 342 out of 500 are very satisfied. This kind of answer, however, is not easy to interpret. It makes more sense to state our response as a percentage because it summarizes our findings by putting them into a format that is easy to understand and communicate.

As we did earlier, percentages for all of our responses are calculated using the formula

$$\% = \frac{f}{N}(100)$$

where f is equal to the frequency of a given attribute and N is the number of cases.

$$\text{Very satisfied:} \quad \% = \frac{342}{500}(100) = 68.4$$

$$\text{Somewhat satisfied:} \quad \% = \frac{116}{500}(100) = 23.2$$

$$\text{Not satisfied:} \quad \% = \frac{42}{500}(100) = 8.4$$

TABLE 2.11 *How Satisfied are You with Your College Experience?*

	FREQUENCY (f)
Very satisfied	342
Somewhat satisfied	116
Not satisfied	42
Total	500

Often the percentages that we calculate do not add up to 100.0% like they do in this case. This is due to rounding error. With our percentages added, it looks like Table 2.12.

Finally, we can calculate the cumulative percent ($c\%$). Remember that cumulative percents are like running totals as we move down the list of attributes. For example, if we count all the respondents who are "very satisfied," we are up to 68.4% of all respondents.

$$c\% = \frac{342}{500}(100) = 68.4$$

If we want to include all the respondents who are either "very satisfied" or "somewhat satisfied," we have to add up the frequencies for each of the two attributes.

$$c\% = \frac{342 + 116}{500}(100) = 91.6$$

We can now state that 91.6% of all respondents are either "Very Satisfied" or "Somewhat Satisfied" with their college experience.

TABLE 2.12 *How Satisfied are You with Your College Experience?*

	FREQUENCY (f)	PERCENT (%)
Very satisfied	342	68.4
Somewhat satisfied	116	23.2
Not satisfied	42	8.4
Total	500	100.0

TABLE 2.13 *How Satisfied are You with Your College Experience?*

	FREQUENCY (f)	PERCENT (%)	CUMULATIVE % ($c\%$)
Very satisfied	342	68.4	68.4
Somewhat satisfied	116	23.2	91.6
Not satisfied	42	8.4	100.0
Total	500	100.0	

TABLE 2.14 *How Satisfied Are You with Your College Experience?*

		FREQUENCY	PERCENT	VALID PERCENT	CUMULATIVE PERCENT
Valid	Very satisfied	342	68.4	68.4	68.4
	Somewhat satisfied	116	23.2	23.2	91.6
	Not satisfied	42	8.4	8.4	100.0
	Total	500	100.0	100.0	

And if we want to include all the respondents who answered either "very satisfied," "somewhat satisfied," or "not satisfied" (which is everyone in the table), our equation looks like this:

$$c\% = \frac{342 + 116 + 42}{500}(100) = 100.0$$

Of course this is 100% of all the cases. It is tempting for many students to calculate the cumulative percent ($c\%$) by adding percentages from the Percent column, for example, $68.4 + 23.2\%$. However, this is risky because of the potential for rounding error in each percent to add up to a more significant rounding error when we combine the percentages. When the Cumulative Percent column is added, it looks like Table 2.13.

It is common for social scientists to use statistical software packages to enter and analyze their data. A common one is called SPSS for Windows. SPSS stands for "Statistical Program for the Social Sciences." It is used to generate many of the tables and charts presented in this book. Table 2.14 is based on the same data as the one above and was generated using SPSS for Windows.

The table is neat, orderly, and easily interpreted. Best of all, many statistical software packages automatically generate these tables with just a few clicks of the mouse. The chart in Figure 2.7 provides the same information as the table, but does so in a way that emphasizes the trend that most students are very satisfied.

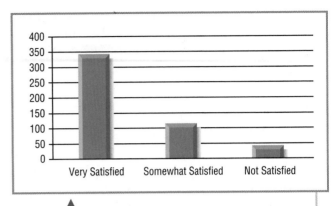

Figure 2.7 How Satisfied Are You with Your College Experience?

Statistical Uses and Misuses

Beware of "mindblowing" statistics! Newspapers, magazines, and other media outlets often report on rapid change in society. For example, we may read in the local paper that our community's murder rate has jumped by 50% relative to a year ago. This may or may not be cause for concern. If the number of murders at this time last year was two, then a 50% increase means that our community has had three murders this year. An increase from two to three is not much of an increase (at least in most cities) and to report that as a 50% increase, while statistically true, is to mislead the consumers of these statistics by making them think the problem is bigger than it really is.

Another problem that can arise with percentages is related to the social and geographic specificity of statistics. Often, statistics that are intended to represent an entire society really only represent a portion of the population. For example, we may read that the number of murders so far this year is double the number of murders from this time last year. This does not, however, mean that everyone is at twice the risk of being murdered. It may be that a vast majority of all murders take place in cities with populations of 250,000 or more. (I should state that this is only a hypothetical example and that I do not actually know where most murders take place.) It is therefore possible that the overall increase in urban murders is rising, and causing the nationwide murder rate to rise, while other types of communities are actually seeing declines in the murder rate.

The same could be true with any kind of social phenomena: child abductions, runaways, rapes, etc. It is important to know what kinds of questions to ask when we hear these "mind-blowing" statistics. What are the frequencies upon which these statistics are based? To what populations can these statistics be generalized? And maybe most importantly, who has an interest in reporting these kinds of statistics?

TABLE 2.15 *Ever Work as Long as One Year?*

		FREQUENCY	PERCENT	VALID PERCENT	CUMULATIVE PERCENT
Valid	YES	1330	29.5	87.7	87.7
	NO	187	4.1	12.3	100.0
	Total	1517	33.6	100.0	
Missing	NAP	2988	66.3		
	NA	5	.1		
	Total	2993	66.4		
Total		4510	100.0		

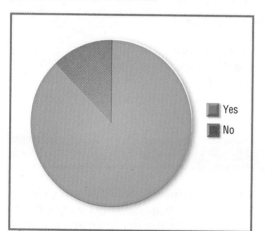

Figure 2.8 **Ever Work as Long as One Year?**

> **Missing cases** Cases in a frequency table that, for whatever reason, do not provide data.

Frequency Tables and Missing Cases. As you can see by comparing these two tables, the one generated by SPSS for Windows provides an additional column, the "Valid Percent" column. The difference between "Percent" and "Valid Percent" is important. While Percent columns are based on the total number of cases in the data, Valid Percent columns are based on only the cases that provided data for the variable being analyzed. In other words, the value of N is often different for percent and valid percent. In the previous example, they are the same because all 500 respondents provided data; however, as Table 2.15 shows, this is not always the case. Figure 2.8 shows the data from Table 2.15 in the form of a pie chart. Notice that missing cases are not included in the pie chart and would only detract from the pattern in the data.

Table 2.15 is based on data from the 2006 General Social Survey. As you can see, the values of the "Percent" column differ a great deal from the values in the "Valid Percent" column. In fact, it is the difference between claiming that 29.5% of the sample has ever worked as long as a year and claiming that 87.7% of the sample has ever worked as long as a year—a significant discrepancy to say the least! The Percent column values are based on an N of 4,510 (the total number of people included in the sample). All of these cases are included even though 2,993 of them did not provide any data. The formula for this percent is:

$$\% = \frac{1330}{4510}(100) = 29.5$$

The Valid Percent column values are based on an N of 1,517, which includes only those respondents who provided data for the table. The formula for the valid percent is:

$$Valid \% = \frac{1330}{1517}(100) = 87.7$$

It is preferable to use the Valid Percent over the Percent because missing cases really don't tell us anything. Would you feel comfortable claiming that 29.5% of the sample has ever worked as long as one year when 2,993 (66.4%) of those people did not provide any data at all? Of course not! That is why we use the valid percent.

You can see that Table 2.15 indicates that 2,993 cases are missing. Cases may be missing for a variety of reasons. For example, in this table, 2,988 respondents indicated that the question was not applicable (NAP) to them (we don't know why) and that another 5 respondents did not answer (NA) the question (again, we do not know why).

Table 2.16 is a frequency table for a variable that describes respondents' political views. The first column lists the attributes of the variable "Think of Self as Liberal or Conservative." The frequency column shows the number of respondents who answered "extremely liberal," "liberal," and so on. The percent column shows the percentage out of all 1,500 respondents who were presented with the questionnaire. The Valid Percent column shows only the percent of responses based on the number of valid responses ($N = 1,443$). In other words, 1,500 respondents were included in the study, yet only 1,443 respondents provided valid responses. Of the 57 respondents who did not provide data, 48 did not know what to answer (DK) and nine indicated that the questionnaire item was not applicable to them (NA). Because these 57 respondents provide no data, it is a good idea to leave them out of the analysis. Finally, the Cumulative Percent column, which is based on only those valid cases providing data, represents a "running total" of the data from one row to the next.

Generally, missing cases are left out of all analyses. Many students see this as problematic, but it is important to remember that the data is *missing*. For whatever reason, a respondent chose not to give us that information or the question did not apply to them. Therefore, it is common practice to exclude missing cases. The Valid Percent and Cumulative Percent columns in the frequency table are calculated on

TABLE 2.16 *Think of Self as Liberal or Conservative*

		FREQUENCY	PERCENT	VALID PERCENT	CUMULATIVE PERCENT
Valid	Extremely liberal	30	2.0	2.1	2.1
	Liberal	163	10.9	11.3	13.4
	Slightly liberal	193	12.9	13.4	26.7
	Moderate	527	35.1	36.5	63.3
	Slightly conservative	248	16.5	17.2	80.5
	Conservative	241	16.1	16.7	97.2
	Extremely conservative	41	2.7	2.8	100.0
	Total	1443	96.2	100.0	
Missing	DK	48	3.2		
	NA	9	.6		
	Total	57	3.8		
Total		1500	100.0		

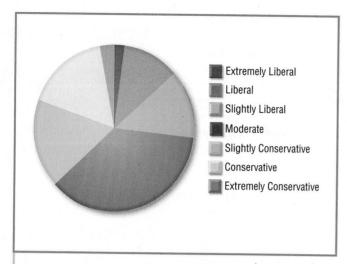

	Extremely Liberal
	Liberal
	Slightly Liberal
	Moderate
	Slightly Conservative
	Conservative
	Extremely Conservative

Figure 2.9 **Think of Self as Liberal or Conservative**

the basis of no missing cases. In Table 2.16, you can see that the response "extremely liberal" has a percent of 2.0 and a valid percent of 2.1. We see that 30 respondents are extremely liberal. This represents 2.0% of the 1500 respondents polled and 2.1% of the 1,443 respondents who answered the question. The difference is this: The percent is based on 1,500 cases and the valid percent is based on 1,443 cases. If you feel that it is important to include missing cases, read the Percent column instead of the Valid Percent column. A graphic representation (in this case it is a pie chart) of Table 2.16 is shown in Figure 2.9.

Eye on the Applied

Describing and Summarizing Data

Frequency tables may be the most commonly used method of summarizing and communicating large amounts of data. They are much more common than you might think. A quick test of this can be done using a *USA Today* newspaper or a *Time* or *Newsweek* magazine. Take a few minutes and flip through one of these publications, making note of the number of pie charts and bar graphs you see. Each pie chart and bar graph is based on a frequency table. A wide array of computer software programs allow users to quickly change the format in which data is presented from a table, which is understood by those trained to read tables, to graphic forms, which most people can easily understand. The example below shows the same data in three different formats.

Blues and R&B Music

		FREQUENCY	PERCENT	VALID PERCENT	CUMULATIVE PERCENT
Valid	Like It	823	54.9	57.4	57.4
	Mixed Feelings	348	23.2	24.3	81.7
	Dislike It	263	17.5	18.3	100.0
	Total	1434	95.6	100.0	
Missing	System	66	4.4		
Total		1500	100.0		

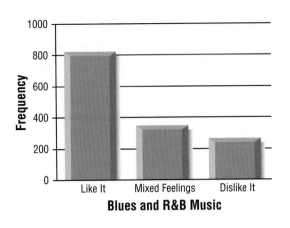

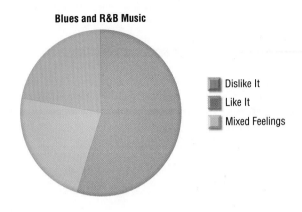

As you can see, a significant amount of data is lost when presented in graphic form as opposed to a table.

Chapter Summary

This chapter is all about how to organize data so that we can more easily summarize results, identify trends, and communicate results with other scientists. Two of the most popular ways to summarize data are in frequency tables and cross-tabulation tables. Frequency tables show the distribution of cases across the attributes of a single variable whereas cross-tabulation tables show the distribution of cases across two variables. These tables make extensive use of both frequencies and percentages (percent, valid percent, cumulative percent, column percent, row percent, and total percent).

In addition to tables, this chapter also emphasizes the presentation of data in more visual forms such as charts (pie charts, bar charts). As a general rule, pie charts are used for nominal variables, bar charts are used for either nominal or ordinal variables.

Exercises

Use the table below to answer the following questions:

Religious Preference

		FREQUENCY	PERCENT	VALID PERCENT	CUMULATIVE PERCENT
Valid	Protestant	953	63.5	63.9	63.9
	Catholic	333	22.2	22.3	86.2
	Jewish	31	2.1	2.1	88.3
	None	140	9.3	9.4	97.7
	Other	35	2.3	2.3	100.0
	Total	1492	99.5	100.0	
Missing	DK	1	.1		
	NA	7	.5		
	Total	8	.5		
Total		1500	100.0		

1. How many respondents provided data for the table?
2. How many respondents did not provide data?
3. What percent of respondents is Protestant?
4. How many of the respondents are Protestant?
5. Is the variable nominal, ordinal, or interval/ratio?
6. What proportion of respondents is Catholic?
7. What proportion of respondents is Jewish?

Use the table below to answer the following questions:

How Do You Get to Class?

Car	37
Public transportation	18
Walk	28
Bike	12
Other	20
Total	115

8. How many respondents provided data for this table?
9. What percent of respondents walk to class?
10. What percent of respondents either bike or walk?
11. What percent of respondents do not take public transportation?

Use the frequencies in the table below to fill in the percent, valid percent, and cumulative percent columns. Then use the table to answer the following questions.

Think of Self as Liberal or Conservative

		FREQUENCY	PERCENT	VALID PERCENT	CUMULATIVE PERCENT
Valid	Extremely Liberal	139			
	Liberal	524			
	Slightly Liberal	517			
	Moderate	1683			
	Slightly Conservative	618			
	Conservative	685			
	Extremely Conservative	167			
	Total	4333			
Missing	DK	154			
	NA	23			
	Total	177			
Total		4510	100.0		

12. Is this variable nominal, ordinal, or interval/ratio?
13. How many respondents provided data for this table?
14. What percent of respondents consider themselves moderate (always use valid percent)?

15. What percent of respondents consider themselves more liberal than moderate?
16. What percent of respondents are either slightly conservative or slightly liberal?

Computer Exercises

Construct a frequency table using the data below. Then use the table to answer the following questions.

How Often Do You Use the Library?

Daily	Several times a week	Weekly	Daily	Several times a week
Several times a week	Daily	Several times a week	Monthly	Never
Weekly	Daily	Never	Several times a week	Several times a week
Daily	Several times a week	Several times a week	Several times a week	Daily
Never	Weekly	Several times a week	Monthly	Weekly

17. Is this variable nominal, ordinal, or interval/ratio?
18. How many attributes does this variable have?
19. What is *N* equal to?
20. How many respondents use the library on a daily basis?
21. What percent of respondents use the library several times a week?
22. What percent of respondents use the library more often than monthly?

Answer the following questions using the GSS2006 data provided.

23. How many respondents are married?
24. What proportion of respondents are married?
25. What percent of respondents are divorced?
26. Of males, what proportion are separated?
27. Of females, what percent are widowed?
28. What is the ratio of married to unmarried respondents?

Key Terms

Cross-tabulation table, 36
Cumulative percent, 42
Data, 36
Ecological data, 38
Frequency, 36, 42

Frequency table, 36
Individual data, 38
Missing cases, 60
Percent, 42
Percentage, 40

Proportion, 39
Ratio, 41
Valid percent, 42
Value labels, 42

Now You Try It Answers

1: 1. .736   2. 77.7%   3. 63.4%   4. 2.4

2:

Sex of Respondent

		FREQUENCY	PERCENT	VALID PERCENT	CUMULATIVE PERCENT
Valid	Male	4	40.0	40.0	40.0
	Female	6	60.0	60.0	100.0
	Total	10	100.0	100.0	

3:

Class Standing of Respondent

		FREQUENCY	PERCENT	VALID PERCENT	CUMULATIVE PERCENT
Valid	Freshman	2	20.0	20.0	20.0
	Sophomore	2	20.0	20.0	40.0
	Junior	4	40.0	40.0	80.0
	Senior	2	20.0	20.0	100.0
	Total	10	100.0	100.0	

4:

Percent of Time R Spends on Campus

		FREQUENCY	PERCENT	VALID PERCENT	CUMULATIVE PERCENT
Valid	50	1	10.0	10.0	10.0
	60	2	20.0	20.0	30.0
	70	2	20.0	20.0	50.0
	75	1	10.0	10.0	60.0
	85	1	10.0	10.0	70.0
	90	2	20.0	20.0	90.0
	95	1	10.0	10.0	100.0
	Total	10	100.0	100.0	

Works Cited

Szasz, A. (1994). *Ecopopulism: Toxic Waste and the Movement for Environmental Justice*. Minneapolis: University of Minnesota Press.

U.S. Environmental Protection Agency. (2010, May 10). *National Priorities List*. Retrieved September 18, 2009, from http://www.epa.gov/superfund/sitesnpl/

CHAPTER

3

Measures of Central Tendency

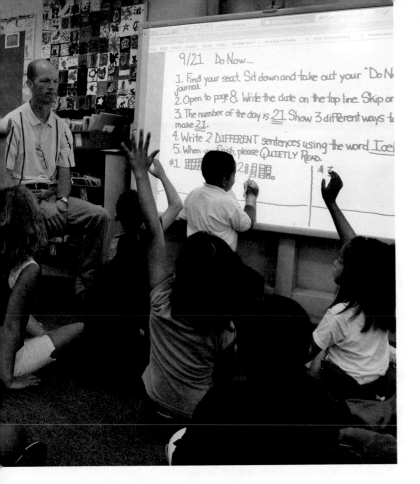

Introduction

How much income does the typical American take home each year? Are SAT math scores higher since the implementation of "No Child Left Behind"? Is the typical level of education higher for males than for females? These kinds of questions are addressed using a group of statistics known as *measures of central tendency*. The most commonly known of these is the mean, or average. Others include the mode and the median. They tell us what is

Measures of central tendency A group of statistics that indicate where cases tend to cluster in a distribution or what is typical in a distribution. The most common measures of central tendency are the mode, median, and mean.

typical of a distribution of cases. In other words, they tell us where most cases in a distribution are located.

In this chapter we learn the three most commonly used measures of central tendency: the mode, the median, and the mean (Table 3.1). Pay particular attention to the circumstances in which each one is used, what each of them tells us, and how each one is interpreted. You also learn how to calculate each of these measures using raw data and grouped data (data in frequency tables).

TABLE 3.1 *Symbols and Formulas*

TERM/SYMBOL	MEANING OF SYMBOL	FORMULA
Measures of central tendency	A group of statistics (mode, median, and mean) that are used to describe where cases tend to fall in a distribution. They tell us what is typical in a distribution.	
Mode (Mo)	The most frequently occurring value or attribute	
Median (Md)	The value of the middle case in a rank-ordered distribution	
Mean ($\bar{X}$)	The mathematical average for sample data	$\bar{X} = \dfrac{\Sigma X}{N}$
Mean (μ)	The mathematical average for population data	$\mu = \dfrac{\Sigma X}{N}$
Position of the median	Formula used to determine which case number (in a rank-ordered distribution of cases) is the median	$\dfrac{N + 1}{2}$
Outliers	Cases with very high or very low values	

Averages and Energy Consumption

Average A statistic that represents what is typical in a distribution.

Averages are one of the most commonly used statistics that we encounter on a daily basis. Averages are used to analyze the weather, gas mileage in our cars, stock market performance, and our weekly expenditures. Like all statistics, averages allow us to summarize, describe, and predict events in our daily lives.

Surprisingly, the mathematical average is just one of three commonly used measures of central tendency that describe what is typical about some data. In statistics, the mathematical average is referred to as the mean. The other two commonly used measures of central tendency are the mode and the median. Each of these three measures (mean, median, and mode) can tell us what is typical about a distribution of cases; taken together, they tell us even more. Each represents a unique description of the values around which cases tend to cluster (hence the name "central tendency").

Averages can be found in all walks of life, but are particularly common in the world of sports. For example, a person watching a professional football game is likely to encounter the following averages: yards gained per game, yards allowed per game, yards per play, yards per carry, yards per throw, yards per catch, yards per kickoff return, yards per punt return, and hang time of punts. Statistically, these are referred to as means, but we tend to call them averages. And these are just the obvious averages.

Other "hidden" averages that we often do not think of as averages include the following: winning percentage, pass completion percentage, and field goal percentage. Baseball, basketball, hockey, and other sports provide viewers with a plethora of statistical averages that consumers can use to reify their sports viewing experience by using them to draft fantasy teams, bet on events, and talk sports with friends. Like all statistics, we tend to use these averages to summarize, describe, and predict the outcome of sporting events and individual performances. In fact, sports may be the social institution most responsible for single-handedly popularizing statistics among the American public. This chapter discusses these three statistics—mode, median, and mean—and it will demonstrate the advantages and drawbacks of each using a variety of examples.

The distribution of cases across the attributes of any variable can be described using a variety of statistics. The three most commonly used measures of central tendency are the mode, median, and mean. Each is based on a distinct logic, but all three are used for the same general purpose: They tell us where in a distribution the cases tend to cluster.

The mode, median, and mean cannot be used interchangeably. Each tells us something different about a distribution. The mode tells us which attribute has the greatest frequency. The median tells us the value of the case that divides the distribution into two equal-sized parts, one part containing cases with greater values and the other part containing cases with lesser values. The mean tells us the arithmetic average of the cases.

It is important to understand that certain measures of central tendency apply to only certain types of variables. When working with nominal variables, only the mode can be used. When working with ordinal variables, only the mode and the median can be used. When working with interval/ratio variables, all three can be used. See Table 3.2.

On October 12, 2006, the U.S. Census Bureau announced that the population of the United States would reach 300 million people on the morning of October 17, 2006 at about 7:46 a.m. (EDT). Of course nobody really knows for sure when the population reached this historic milestone, but at some point during mid-October 2006, it is highly likely that somebody became the 300 millionth live American. As only the fourth country in the history of the world to reach this milestone, it puts the United States in the same company as China, India, and the former USSR.

TABLE 3.2 *When to Use the Mode, Median, and Mean*

	NOMINAL	ORDINAL	INTERVAL/RATIO
Mode	✓	✓	✓
Median	NA	✓	✓
Mean	NA	NA	✓

Population has been a popular topic for social analysts, city planners, and environmentalists for thousands of years. As world population grew into the 19th century, the work of the Reverend Thomas Malthus (1766–1834) took on greater significance. Malthus (1798/1993) argued that because population grows exponentially while food production grows linearly, the day will come when hunger and starvation become unavoidable aspects of life on Earth. He also argued that a series of preventive checks, such as delayed marriage and abstinence, would help to avoid or at least minimize the problems associated with food shortages. While some analysts still adhere to variations on Malthus's ideas, others claim that nutrition and starvation have economic, political, and technological dimensions that Malthus did not consider.

Nevertheless, in the current model of development, with population growth come increases in energy consumption. History shows that the more people we have, the more energy we consume. The question is, How big of an increase in energy consumption accompanies the increases in population growth? A comparison of countries helps answer this question. According to the U.S. Energy Information Administration (2003), the U.S. population, which was then just under 300 million people, consumed a total of 104.3 EJ of energy. ("EJ" stands for exajoule, or 10^{18} joules of energy.) By comparison, China, with a population of 1.3 billion people, consumed 47.9 EJ and India, with 1.1 billion, consumed 14.8 EJ. To put all these numbers in perspective, while the population of the United States is only 23% that of China, we consume more than twice the total amount of energy that China consumes. That means that, at 2003 consumption levels, China's population could increase to nearly 3 billion people before it consumes as much energy as the United States. Similarly, while the U.S. population is only 27% that of India, we consume over seven times the total amount of energy.

On a per capita basis, this means that, on average, each American was consuming 99,623 kWh per year whereas each Chinese resident was, on average, consuming 10,221 kWh (10.2% of an American) and each Indian resident was, on average, consuming 3,859

kWh (less than 4% of an American). These kinds of statistics put population growth in perspective by differentiating between qualitatively different types of populations. Averages make them understandable. For example, on average, a single baby born in the United States uses as much energy as about 10 Chinese babies and 25 Indian babies. As biologist Paul Ehrlich (Ehrlich & Ehrlich, 2008) notes, data on consumption tell us a lot about the kind of society in which we live. With a dwindling supply of nonrenewable fuels (fossil fuels), the world may be able to accommodate many more people; however, it may not be able to accommodate too many more Americans.

Definitions of Mode, Median, and Mean

Mode The most frequently occurring value in a distribution.

Mode. The mode is the value or number that occurs most often. In a frequency distribution, the attribute with the greatest frequency is the mode. It is possible to have more than one mode in a distribution. A distribution with two modes is called a bimodal distribution. Likewise, a distribution with three modes is a trimodal distribution. The mode can be used to describe nominal, ordinal, and interval/ratio variables.

Median. The median is the value of the middle case in a rank-ordered distribution and divides the number of cases with higher and lower values into two equally sized groups. For example, using the numbers 4, 5, and 6, the median is 5 because it is in the middle. In a frequency distribution with an even number of cases, say we are using the numbers 4, 5, 6, and 7, the median is the value between 5 and 6, or 5.5. In small datasets like these, it is easy to identify the middle.

In larger datasets, such as those with hundreds or thousands of cases, it is much more difficult to determine the midpoint. A simple formula can help. To determine the number of the case that falls in the middle of a rank-ordered distribution of cases (meaning they are in order from lowest to highest), use the formula $\frac{N+1}{2}$. In our example, using the values 4, 5, and 6, our N is equal to 3. Using $\frac{N+1}{2}$ we find that $\frac{3+1}{2} = 2$. The answer 2 tells us that we need to count over two cases in our rank-ordered distribution of cases. The second case has a value of 5 so the median is 5. *Note:* When finding the median, always remember to first rank the cases in order from lowest to highest. Also remember that the median is not equal to the result of the formula $\frac{N+1}{2}$. This only tells us which case number to go to in order to find the value of the median. The median is equal to the value of the middle case.

$$\text{Position of the median} = \frac{N+1}{2}$$

The median is a very popular measure of central tendency when working with ecological data representative of towns, states, and other geopolitical units. For example, when describing the typical income of a city, such as Buffalo, it is often better to use median household income than to use average household income. Doing so helps to control for the effect of outliers (discussed below).

Mean. The mean is the mathematical average. It is equal to the sum (Σ) of the values of all cases divided by the number of cases (N). The formula for the mean is:

$$\overline{X} = \frac{\Sigma X}{N}$$

The mean is the most sophisticated of all the measures of central tendency, because it incorporates the most information in its calculation; but it is also a relatively "unstable" measure. The symbol for the mean is $\overline{X}$ and is pronounced "x bar." The mean can be greatly influenced by cases with extremely low or extremely high values. These very high or very low values are called outliers. Outliers have the effect of pulling the mean toward them and skewing the data. Skew occurs when outliers pull the mean far from the other two measures of central tendency.

> **Median** The value of the middle case in a rank-ordered distribution.

> **Mean** The mathematical average. It is calculated by summing all of the values of the cases in a distribution and dividing by the total number of cases.

> **Skew** The degree to which a normal distribution is distorted due to the effect of outliers.

Calculating Measures of Central Tendency with Raw Data

Public transportation is considered a good way to reduce the cost of owning an automobile and an effective means by which to reduce the amount of carbon dioxide emissions in the atmosphere. Suppose that we are interested in learning more about the ability of improvements in public transportation to reduce the amount of driving that people in a particular neighborhood do. It is first necessary to find out how often people in this neighborhood use the bus; so we begin by sampling 15 residents on how many times they have boarded a city bus in the past two weeks. (Obviously we would want to sample

TABLE 3.3 *Number of Bus Rides*

RIDER #	# BUS TRIPS
1	5
2	3
3	10
4	5
5	8
6	6
7	5
8	4
9	0
10	2
11	14
12	5
13	7
14	4
15	3

more than 15, but this is for demonstration purposes.) Our sample yields the data shown in Table 3.3.

To begin our analysis, the cases (values for number of bus trips) are first rank-ordered from lowest to highest values:

0 2 3 3 4 4 5 5 5 5 6 7 8 10 14

The mode is defined as the value that occurs most frequently. It is the simplest measure of central tendency to calculate because all we have to do is count the number of times each value occurs. Four respondents indicated that they boarded city buses five times in the past two weeks. Because no value has a frequency greater than 4, the mode for this data is 5. It is important to remember that the mode is not equal to the frequency of five bus rides in the last two weeks (which is 4); it is equal to five bus rides.

Mode = 5

The median is defined as the value of the case that divides a rank-ordered distribution in half. In datasets with a very small number of cases, such as our bus riding example, it is fairly simple to determine the middle case. If we select the middle case, there should be seven cases with higher values and seven cases with lower values. The middle cases, the seven below it, and the seven above it add up to 15 cases. But what do we do when we have hundreds, thousands, or even tens of thousands of cases? We need a way to determine which case is in the middle. We use the formula below to solve this problem:

$$\textit{Position of the median} = \frac{N + 1}{2}$$

We take the number of cases, add one, and divide by two. In this case, it means that our equation looks like this:

$$Position\ of\ the\ median = \frac{15 + 1}{2} = \frac{16}{2} = 8 \quad \text{The middle case is case number 8.}$$

0	2	3	3	4	4	5	**5**	5	5	6	7	8	10	14
Case #1	2	3	4	5	6	7	**8**	9	10	11	12	13	14	15

Looking back at our rank-ordered distribution of cases, we simply count (from right to left or from left to right) over to the eighth case. In this data, the value of the eighth case is equal to 5. Therefore, the median is equal to 5.

$$\textbf{Median} = \textbf{5}$$

The mean is equal to the arithmetic average of all the cases. To calculate the mean, we add the values of all the cases to determine the sum (Σ). Then we divide the sum by the number of cases (N). The formula for the mean looks like this:

$$\overline{X} = \frac{\Sigma X}{N}$$

In other words, this is the sum of the values of individual cases, divided by the number of cases. For our bus riding dataset, it looks like this:

$$\overline{X} = \frac{\Sigma(0, 2, 3, 3, 4, 4, 5, 5, 5, 5, 6\ 7, 8, 10, 14)}{N} = \frac{81}{15} = 5.4$$

$$\textbf{Mean} = \textbf{5.4}$$

As these results show, the mode and the median have the same value of 5. The mean, on the other hand, is slightly larger and has a value of 5.4. Looking at the rank-ordered distribution of cases, we can see that the cases above the median (14, 10, 8, 7, 6, 5, 5) tend to be of greater difference from the median than are the cases below the median (0, 2, 3, 3, 4, 4, 5). Because the degree of difference from the median is greater on the higher value side than it is on the lower value side, we know that the mean is going to be pulled toward the higher values.

Now You Try It 1

Now that you have seen a demonstration of how measures of central tendency are calculated using raw data, try to calculate them on your own using the data below. The data represent responses from 20 students who were asked "How many credits are you taking this semester?"

15	16	15	12	9	15	16	16	15	15	18	12	10	14	12	15	15	18	15	15

What is the value of the mode? The median? The mean?
*Answers are located at the end of the chapter.

Calculating Measures of Central Tendency with Grouped Data

Often, sociologists and other scientists do not work with raw data. Instead, they work with grouped data, such as frequency tables. Frequency tables actually make the calculation of the three measures of central tendency easier. Table 3.4 is generated using SPSS for Windows and is based on the same data that were used in the bus riding example.

Mode.   To find the mode using a frequency table, look in the Frequency column for the largest (f) value. In this example, that value is 4. Remember, this does not mean that the mode is equal to 4; instead, it means that four different respondents indicated that they took five bus rides in the past two weeks. The mode is **5**.

Median.   To find the median using a frequency table, we have two options available. The first is to determine the position of the middle case using the formula $\frac{N + 1}{2}$. After determining the middle case, we then use the Frequency column in the table to count the cases. For example, the middle case is equal to $\frac{15 + 1}{2}$ or 8. We then begin counting frequencies from the top of the table until we get to the eighth case. When we add up all of the respondents who took zero, one, two, three, or four bus rides we have six cases. When we include the four respondents who took five bus rides we are up to 10 cases. Therefore, the eighth case was one of the respondents who took five bus rides. The median is therefore equal to 5.

A second, simpler method to use to determine the median is the Cumulative Percent column. Remember that the Cumulative Percent column is a running percentage total based on the Frequency column, so rather than use the formula to find the middle case, we can look for the "50.0%" point in the Cumulative Percent column.

As evidenced by Table 3.4, the 50% mark must often be imagined rather than seen. For example, if we include all the respondents who rode the bus zero times, we have included 6.7% of the sample; if we include all the respondents who rode the bus either zero or one time, we have included 13.3% of the sample. If we continue this process

TABLE 3.4   *Number of Bus Rides in the Past Two Weeks*

		FREQUENCY	PERCENT	VALID PERCENT	CUMULATIVE PERCENT
Valid	0	1	6.7	6.7	6.7
	2	1	6.7	6.7	13.3
	3	2	13.3	13.3	26.7
	4	2	13.3	13.3	40.0
	5	4	26.7	26.7	66.7
	6	1	6.7	6.7	73.3
	7	1	6.7	6.7	80.0
	8	1	6.7	6.7	86.7
	10	1	6.7	6.7	93.3
	14	1	6.7	6.7	100.0
	Total	15	100.0	100.0	

until we include all of those who rode the bus zero, one, two, three, or four times, we have included 40.0% of the sample. Taking this one step further and including all those who rode the bus zero, one, two, three, four, or five times, we are up to 66.7% of the sample, well past the 50% mark. Therefore, we know that the median must fall somewhere beyond those who rode four times or less, but behind those who rode six times or less. In other words, the 50% mark has to fall between 40.0% and 66.7%. This means that the median falls in the group that rode the bus five times in the last two weeks. The median is **5.**

Mean. To find the mean using a frequency table, it is necessary to use the Value and Frequency columns to determine the total number of bus rides the 15 respondents have taken. For example, if two respondents rode the bus three times each, they rode a total of six times (2×3). Therefore, to determine the total number of bus rides taken (ΣX), we need only to multiply number of bus rides by the frequency of respondents for each row in the table.

For example, Table 3.5 shows that zero bus rides were taken by one respondent. Therefore, $0 \times 1 = 0$ bus rides. Similarly, two bus rides were taken by one respondent. Therefore, $2 \times 1 = 2$ bus rides. This process is repeated for each value of bus rides and the results are added to give us the sum total of bus rides (ΣX). After determining this, we divide the number of bus rides by the number of respondents to determine our average using the formula for the mean:

$$\overline{X} = \frac{\Sigma X}{N}$$

The following is a demonstration using the bus riding data.

Once we have determined the sum of bus rides, we only have to divide by N to calculate the mean, just as we did with the example using raw data. Therefore, the mean, $\overline{X} = \frac{\Sigma X}{N}$, is equal to $\frac{81}{15}$ or 5.4. The process of calculating the mean using a frequency table may seem cumbersome at first, but it can save a great deal of time, particularly when working with frequency tables that have hundreds or thousands of cases.

The mean is **5.4.**

TABLE 3.5 *Number of Bus Rides in the Past Two Weeks*

	RIDES	FREQUENCY	FREQUENCY OF BUS RIDES
Valid	0	1	$0 \times 1 = 0$
	2	1	$2 \times 1 = 2$
	3	2	$3 \times 2 = 6$
	4	2	$4 \times 2 = 8$
	5	4	$5 \times 4 = 20$
	6	1	$6 \times 1 = 6$
	7	1	$7 \times 1 = 7$
	8	1	$8 \times 1 = 8$
	10	1	$10 \times 1 = 10$
	14	1	$14 \times 1 = 14$
	Total	15	Sum of bus rides (ΣX) = 81

Statistical Uses and Misuses

In his now classic book *How to Lie with Statistics* (1954), Darrell Huff discusses the idea of the "well chosen average" (p. 27). As Huff notes, the term *average* can be used to refer to any one of the three different measures of central tendency discussed here; however, as has been shown in this chapter, each of these measures tells us something quite different. Using Huff's real estate example, it is often said buyers are better off with a low-cost house in a high-income neighborhood than a high-cost house in a low-income neighborhood. If a real estate agent tells you that your $150,000 house is the average cost of a home in your neighborhood, are they referring to the mean (the mathematical average), the median, or the mode? Unless you know what questions to ask, you may never find out until after you've bought the most expensive house on the block (the one house that is dragging the average home price up to $150,000 [i.e., the outlier]).

Similarly, in his book *Full House* (1997), Stephen J. Gould calls for further analysis of the median life expectancy for those diagnosed with often-fatal diseases. For example, when a person is diagnosed with a deadly disease, their doctor may tell them that the median life expectancy of someone with this disease is 2 years. In other words, they are being told that they have 2 years to live. According to Gould, this leaves out at least

one important consideration: how advanced was the disease when it was detected? The longer a disease goes undetected, the shorter the life expectancy of the person with the disease because of the lack of treatment; however, if the disease is detected in its early stages, then life expectancy is much longer.

As these two examples show, it is necessary to have a working knowledge of both the statistics (measures of central tendency) and the context (real estate, medical) in which the statistics are being used. Without this knowledge, people risk being misinformed, misled, and maybe even "hustled" by someone with something to gain from others' lack of statistical know-how!

Education and Central Tendency

Roughly a quarter of the United States population receives a four-year bachelor's degree or higher. In fact, according to the 2006 General Social Survey (National Opinion Research Center, 2006), 16.9% reported receiving a bachelor's degree and 8.9% reported receiving a graduate degree. Unbeknownst to many, upon receiving a bachelor's degree we become a member of the top 1% of the world's most educated people (formally educated). This says quite a lot about the degree of educational inequality nationally and globally.

Table 3.6 shows the distribution of education degrees in the United States in 2006. As the table and the corresponding chart below show, the most common degree that people tend to receive in this country is a high school degree ($f = 2,273$) and the second most common degree is a bachelor's degree ($f = 763$).

TABLE 3.6   *Respondent's Highest Degree*

		FREQUENCY	PERCENT	VALID PERCENT	CUMULATIVE PERCENT
Valid	LT HIGH SCHOOL	691	15.3	15.3	15.3
	HIGH SCHOOL	2273	50.4	50.4	65.8
	JUNIOR COLLEGE	377	8.4	8.4	74.1
	BACHELOR	763	16.9	16.9	91.1
	GRADUATE	403	8.9	8.9	100.0
	Total	4507	99.9	100.0	
Missing	NA	3	.1		
Total		4510	100.0		

Figure 3.1 provides a visual representation of this pattern. The highest frequency in a frequency table, which is also the tallest bar in the bar chart, represents an attribute around which cases tend to cluster. The attribute with the greatest frequency of cases is referred to as the mode.

Mode = High School

We can also see that the median is equal to "High School Degree" because the 50% mark in the Cumulative Percent column comes somewhere after the "LT High School" respondents and before the "Junior College" respondents.

Another way to calculate the median is to find the middle case and use the Frequency column of the table to determine in which attribute the middle case falls. For example, we know that $N = 4,507$. Therefore, using the formula for the position of the median, $\frac{N + 1}{2}$, we know which case is the middle case. $\frac{4507 + 1}{2} = 2,254$. Now we must find case 2,254.

If we add up all the respondents with "LT High School" we are up to 691 cases.

If we add up all the respondents with "LT High School" and "High School" we are up to 2,964 cases.

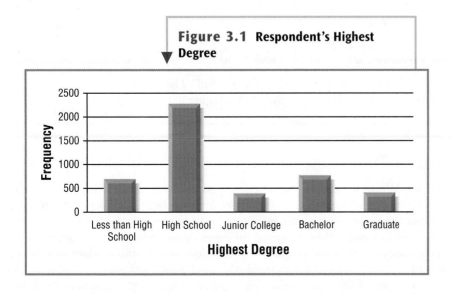

Figure 3.1 Respondent's Highest Degree

At this point we have surpassed the middle case number of 2,254. Therefore, the middle case is somewhere in the group labeled "High School." The median is "High School."

Median = High School

We can see that education is not distributed evenly across the population. It is likely that wealthier people are more likely to have higher degrees as are people whose parents went to college, who are white, and who are male. In a recent study published in the *American Sociological Review*, sociologists Claudia Buchman and Thomas DiPrete (2006, p. 515) note that in 1960, 65% of all bachelor's degrees were awarded to men. This held true until 1982 and since then, more bachelor's degrees have been awarded to women than to men. Today, women receive about 60% of all bachelor's degrees.

This interesting trend is exemplified in another GSS2006 variable, "Respondent's Highest Degree," which is operationalized at the ordinal level. Another variable, "Years of Education," is operationalized at the interval/ratio level. We use this variable to investigate the relationships between education and health.

Now You Try It 2

Now that you have seen a demonstration of how measures of central tendency are calculated using frequency tables, try to calculate them on your own using the data below. The table below shows data from 50 respondents who were asked how many brothers and sisters they have.

TABLE 3.7 *Number of Brothers and Sisters*

		FREQUENCY	PERCENT	VALID PERCENT	CUMULATIVE PERCENT
Valid	0	4	8.0	8.0	8.0
	1	15	30.0	30.0	38.0
	2	11	22.0	22.0	60.0
	3	8	16.0	16.0	76.0
	4	6	12.0	12.0	88.0
	5	6	12.0	12.0	100.0
	Total	50	100.0	100.0	

What is the value of the mode? The median? The mean?
*Answers are located at the end of the chapter.

Central Tendency, Education, and Your Health

Most people hope to live long, healthy lives. Epidemiological research shows that among other factors, social class is a major determinant of health and longevity (California Newsreel, 2008). In other words, people of upper-class standing are more likely to stay healthy and live longer than are people of lower class standing. Greater access to health care, healthier lifestyles, less dangerous working conditions, and healthier diets are just a few of the benefits that come with greater levels of wealth and income. Not surprisingly, education is one of the keys to achieving higher class standing. So just how much education does the typical resident of the United States have?

Each year the National Opinion Research Center (NORC) at the University of Chicago conducts its General Social Survey (GSS) in which thousands of Americans are interviewed on topics ranging from their age to their education to their opinions about government spending. One of the questionnaire items included each year is the number of years of education that each respondent has. More precisely, interviewers ask respondents something to the effect of, "What is the highest year of school you have completed?" The responses for the year 2006 are shown in Table 3.8.

This table indicates that of the 4,510 people sampled, only 4,499 provided data; therefore $N = 4,499$. Measures of central tendency tell us how many years of education these 4,499 respondents tend to have.

TABLE 3.8 *Highest Year of School Completed*

		FREQUENCY	PERCENT	VALID PERCENT	CUMULATIVE PERCENT
Valid	0	22	.5	.5	.5
	1	4	.1	.1	.6
	2	28	.6	.6	1.2
	3	13	.3	.3	1.5
	4	11	.2	.2	1.7
	5	23	.5	.5	2.2
	6	69	1.5	1.5	3.8
	7	32	.7	.7	4.5
	8	85	1.9	1.9	6.4
	9	127	2.8	2.8	9.2
	10	152	3.4	3.4	12.6
	11	215	4.8	4.8	17.4
	12	1204	26.7	26.8	44.1
	13	422	9.4	9.4	53.5
	14	628	13.9	14.0	67.5
	15	212	4.7	4.7	72.2
	16	687	15.2	15.3	87.4
	17	167	3.7	3.7	91.2
	18	208	4.6	4.6	95.8
	19	78	1.7	1.7	97.5
	20	112	2.5	2.5	100.0
	Total	4499	99.8	100.0	
Missing	DK	2	.0		
	NA	9	.2		
	Total	11	.2		
Total		4510	100.0		

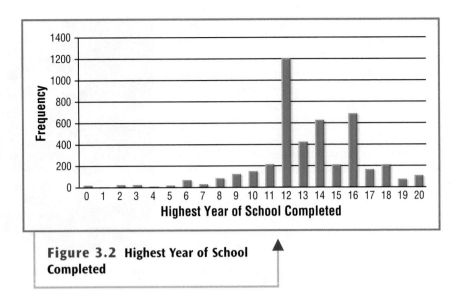

Figure 3.2 **Highest Year of School Completed**

Figure 3.2 represents this table in graphic form. It is useful because it gives us a visual representation of the data from the table and allows us to see trends that are not readily apparent in the table. Relatively few respondents have less than 8 or 9 years of education whereas a significant number cluster between 12 and 16 years of education. Those respondents with less than 6 years of education qualify as outliers and (1) lower the mean and (2) negatively skew the distribution.

As we can see, 1,204 respondents indicated that they have 12 years of education, most likely the equivalent of a high school degree. We also see that a large number of respondents have 14 years of education (a two-year college degree) and 16 years of education (a four-year college degree). Because no other attribute has a greater frequency than 12, the mode is equal to 12.

$$\text{Mode} = 12$$

Using the chart to determine the median is virtually impossible. For this we use the table. Remember, the median is the 50% mark, or the point at which half the cases fall above and half fall below. Using the equation $\frac{N+1}{2}$ we find that $\frac{4,499+1}{2} = 2,250$. In other words, case number 2,250 is the middle case in the distribution, so the number of years of education that case number 2,250 has is the median. Again, rather than adding all of the cases, we can use the Cumulative Percent column to locate the 50% mark in the distribution.

After including all respondents up to and including 12 years of education, we are only up to 44.1% of the sample; however, after including all respondents up to and including 13 years of education, we are up to 53.5% of the sample. Therefore, the middle case had to be a person with 13 years of education. Consequently, the median is equal to 13.

$$\text{Median} = 13$$

Calculating the mean is also done most easily with the table. First, we must determine the total number of years of education that all 4,499 respondents have obtained. Then we divide by the number of respondents. Table 3.9 shows these calculations.

TABLE 3.9 *Highest Year of School Completed*

		FREQUENCY	
Valid	0	22	$0 \times 22 = 0$
	1	4	$1 \times 4 = 4$
	2	28	$2 \times 28 = 56$
	3	13	$3 \times 13 = 39$
	4	11	$4 \times 11 = 44$
	5	23	$5 \times 23 = 115$
	6	69	$6 \times 69 = 414$
	7	32	$7 \times 32 = 224$
	8	85	$8 \times 85 = 680$
	9	127	$9 \times 127 = 1,143$
	10	152	$10 \times 152 = 1,520$
	11	215	$11 \times 215 = 2,365$
	12	1204	$12 \times 1,204 = 14,448$
	13	422	$13 \times 422 = 5,486$
	14	628	$14 \times 628 = 8,792$
	15	212	$15 \times 212 = 3,180$
	16	687	$16 \times 687 = 10,992$
	17	167	$17 \times 167 = 2,839$
	18	208	$18 \times 208 = 3,744$
	19	78	$19 \times 78 = 1,482$
	20	112	$20 \times 112 = 2,240$
	Total	$N = 4,499$	Sum $= 59,807$

Using the formula $\overline{X} = \frac{\Sigma X}{N}$ we find that $\frac{59,807}{4,499} = 13.3$. The mean number of years of education for respondents in this sample is 13.3. Therefore, if the sampling was done in a methodologically sound manner, we can predict that the average number of years of education for Americans is 13.3.

Mean = 13.3

To test the hypothesis that income is associated with health, we would have to gather additional data on our respondents' health status so that we could statistically determine whether those respondents with the highest levels of education are in fact those who tend to have higher levels of overall health. A variety of statistical tools called "measures of association" can be used to test our prediction; however, they are presented in a later chapter.

Table 3.10 shows that there is some connection between education and perception of personal health. For example, of those with LT High School, we see that only 13.5% of respondents consider their health to be Excellent. This is quite low compared to all other levels of education, including High School (25.7%), Junior College (28.8%), Bachelor (39.4%), and Graduate (41.8%). These results are shown in Figure 3.3.

TABLE 3.10 *Condition of Health by Highest Degree*

		LT HIGH SCHOOL	HIGH SCHOOL	JUNIOR COLLEGE	BACHELOR	GRADUATE	TOTAL
EXCELLENT	Count	72	465	80	229	130	976
	% within RS HIGHEST DEGREE	13.5%	25.7%	28.8%	39.4%	41.8%	27.8%
GOOD	Count	202	877	138	276	147	1640
	% within RS HIGHEST DEGREE	37.8%	48.5%	49.6%	47.5%	47.3%	46.7%
FAIR	Count	199	358	49	64	32	702
	% within RS HIGHEST DEGREE	37.2%	19.8%	17.6%	11.0%	10.3%	20.0%
POOR	Count	62	108	11	12	2	195
	% within RS HIGHEST DEGREE	11.6%	6.0%	4.0%	2.1%	.6%	5.6%
Total	Count	535	1808	278	581	311	3513
	% within RS HIGHEST DEGREE	100.0%	100.0%	100.0%	100.0%	100.0%	100.0%

We might also want to view this data when education is operationalized as an interval/ratio variable. In this example, education is operationalized as the number of years of education that a respondent indicates they have completed. In this example, the axes have been switched and Respondents' Health is now the categorical variable on the x-axis of the chart. The height of each bar indicates the mean number of years of education for each category of health.

Figure 3.3 Percent of Respondents Indicating They Are in Excellent Health by Highest Degree

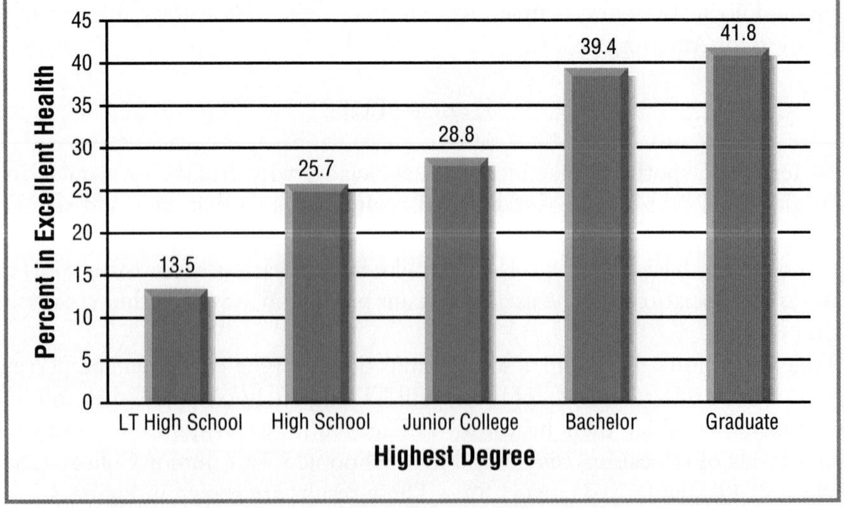

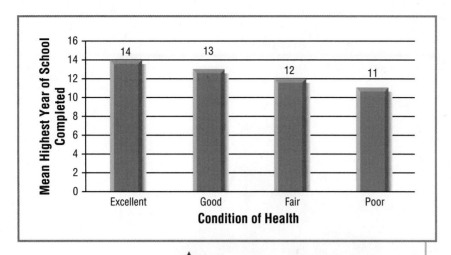

Figure 3.4 **Mean Highest Year of School Completed by Condition of Health**

As Figure 3.4 shows, those who feel they are in excellent health have an average of 14 years of education, those in good health have 13 years, those in fair health have 12 years, and those in poor health have 11 years. These relatively simple averages tell us that sociology and the study of inequality has a great deal to offer in the way of public health improvements. The social bases of health may be far more important than anyone previously thought.

Income and Central Tendency: The Effect of Outliers

Outliers are cases with values that far exceed the normal range of values in a distribution. They have the effect of skewing data (significantly pulling the distribution in one direction) and, in some cases, should even be removed from the data; however, their removal needs to be justified.

For example, suppose you live in a town with a population of 40 ($N = 40$), with 10 residents earning $25,000 per year, 20 residents earning $50,000 per year, and 10 residents earning $75,000 per year. This is an interval/ratio variable and all three measures of central tendency (mean, median, and mode) are equal to $50,000 per year. A frequency table and *histogram* with normal curve for these data are shown in Table 3.11 and Figure 3.5.

TABLE 3.11 *Income*

		FREQUENCY	PERCENT	VALID PERCENT	CUMULATIVE PERCENT
Valid	$25,000	10	25.0	25.0	25.0
	$50,000	20	50.0	50.0	75.0
	$75,000	10	25.0	25.0	100.0
	Total	40	100.0	100.0	

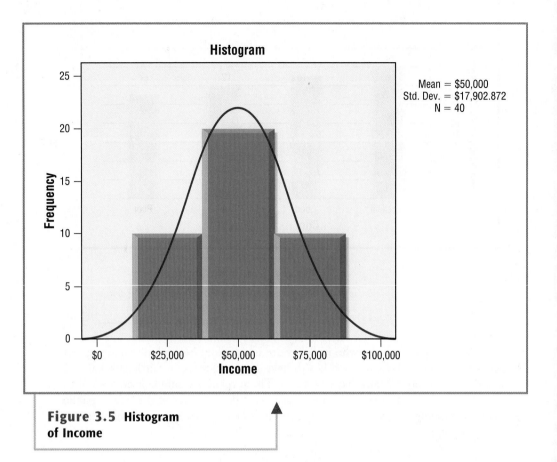

Figure 3.5 Histogram of Income

The chart shows a perfectly even distribution of cases around a mean of $50,000.

Now suppose that two wealthy computer software developers move in, each with an income of $200,000 per year. This brings the town population to 42 and has the effect of raising the mean income to $57,143. The mean income for the town rises dramatically, but is not representative of most people in the town. After all, 40 of the 42 residents still make an average of $50,000 per year. The wealthy computer software moguls are considered outliers, cases that have the effect of pulling the average toward the value of the outlier. Just like outliers with very high values can raise an average, so too can outliers with very low values lower an average. If a very poor person with an income of $1 per year moved into town in place of the person with very high income, it would have the effect of pulling the mean income for the town down. The effect that the two very high-salaried residents have on the town's income distribution is shown in the frequency table and histogram with normal curve in Table 3.12 and Figure 3.6.

Notice that in the first histogram, the normal curve line went to the bottom of the chart at about $100,000 and in the second histogram ($N = 42$) the normal curve line goes to the bottom of the chart at about $200,000. This has the effect of making the normal curve have a "tail" on the right-hand side and skewing it positively (toward larger values).

Unlike the mean, the median is unaffected by the outlier because the person with very high income represents only a single case or a very small number of cases. As the point at which half the cases fall below and half fall above, the addition of either a computer software mogul or a very poor person does not affect the median income of

Histogram A bar graph of an interval/ratio variable in which the height of each bar reflects the frequency of each value.

Outliers Cases with values either higher or lower relative to the typical pattern in a distribution.

TABLE 3.12 *Income*

		FREQUENCY	PERCENT	VALID PERCENT	CUMULATIVE PERCENT
Valid	$25,000	10	23.8	23.8	23.8
	$50,000	20	47.6	47.6	71.4
	$75,000	10	23.8	23.8	95.2
	$200,000	2	4.8	4.8	100.0
	Total	42	100.0	100.0	

the town at all. The median remains $50,000 per year. Often, particularly in the case of income data that is likely to contain outliers, it is more common to use the median than it is to use the mean. In these cases, the median gives us a better representation of the typical income of the community.

Like the median, the mode is not affected by the presence of outliers. More people make $50,000 than any other amount and the mode, therefore, remains at $50,000 per year.

Figure 3.6 Histogram of Income with Outliers in Data

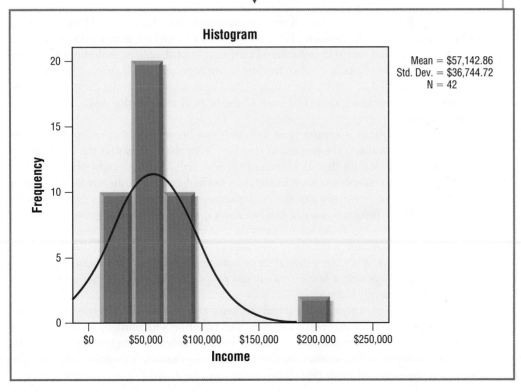

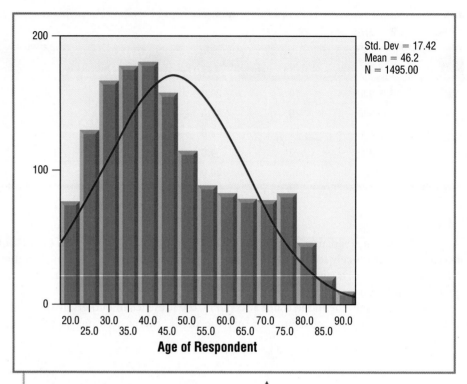

Figure 3.7 **Histogram of Age of Respondent**

Generally it is useful to use all three measures of central tendency when describing where cases fall in a distribution. Figure 3.7 shows a histogram with a normal curve of age. Some summary statistics are offered to the right of the chart, including *N* and the mean. We see that the tallest bar in the histogram represents 40.0 years. Therefore the mode, or the modal age, is 40. We also see that the peak of the normal curve is at an age higher than that of the mode. The peak of the normal curve is the mean. In this case, it is 46.2 years.

Because the mean is greater than the mode, we know that more cases with higher values (possibly outliers) are present in the data. This also means that the mean, being affected more by outliers than the mode or median, will fall to the right of the mode.

Because most distributions approximate a normal curve, but do not take the exact shape of a normal curve, we say that distributions are skewed. A distribution can be skewed positively (which is usually, but not always, to the right) or negatively (which is usually, but not always, to the left). Remember, *skew* is the result of *outliers*. Skew refers to the tail of a distribution. Outliers are cases in the distribution with either very high or very low values. They have the effect of pulling the mean toward them. Therefore, a distribution of age with a few extremely old people would have a higher average than without the extremely old people.

The mean is the measure of central tendency that is most affected by outliers. The median is generally not affected. Therefore, a distribution with outliers tends to be more skewed than a distribution without outliers. Often, outliers are excluded from statistical analyses because they distort the normal trends in the data so significantly that the resulting statistics no longer represent what is typical, or average, about a population.

TABLE 3.13 *Age of Respondent*

		AGE OF RESPONDENT				STATISTICS		
		FREQUENCY	PERCENT	VALID PERCENT	CUMULATIVE PERCENT		AGE OF RESPONDENT	
Valid	18	5	12.5	12.5	12.5	N	Valid	40
	19	17	42.5	42.5	55.0		Missing	0
	20	18	45.0	45.0	100.0	Mean		19.33
	Total	40	100.0	100.0		Median		19.00
						Mode		20

TABLE 3.14 *Age of Respondent*

		AGE OF RESPONDENT				STATISTICS		
		FREQUENCY	PERCENT	VALID PERCENT	CUMULATIVE PERCENT		AGE OF RESPONDENT	
Valid	18	5	12.5	12.5	12.5	N	Valid	40
	19	17	42.5	42.5	55.0		Missing	0
	20	17	42.5	42.5	97.5	Mean		21.83
	120	1	2.5	2.5	100.0	Median		18.00
	Total	40	100.0	100.0		Mode		19, 21

The examples below further demonstrate the effect of outliers. Table 3.13 represents a distribution of 40 respondents between the ages of 18 and 20. Table 3.14 represents those same respondents, except that a 20-year-old has been replaced with a respondent who is 120 years old, an outlier.

As you can see, the addition of the outlier has no effect on the median; it remains unchanged. The mean, however, does change.

In the table that contains the 120-year-old respondent, we see a significant increase in the mean. In fact, the mean increases from 19.33 to 21.83. We know that if we plotted a normal curve for each of these distributions that the distribution containing the 120-year-old respondent would be skewed positively to the right. This demonstrates the usefulness of having more than one measure of central tendency to describe how cases are distributed. Some examples of how to calculate measures of central tendency are now offered.

Eye on the Applied

The Technological Fix to Climate Change

Many people feel that by adopting new technologies, we can save both money and the environment by burning less fossil fuel. Some trend data from the Bureau of Transportation Statistics reveals that putting our faith in this "technological fix" may do more harm than good.

Between 1990 and 2002, average new vehicle fuel efficiency for passenger cars increased from 10.3 to 12.1 kilometers per liter, a 17% gain. The gain is even greater when switching from regular to the hybrid versions of new cars, indicating that technology can indeed stretch more distance out of a unit of gasoline. In fact, the average fuel-efficiency again for the hybrid versions of the 2007 Honda Accord, Honda Civic, and Ford Escape is 33%.

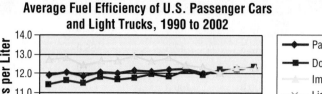

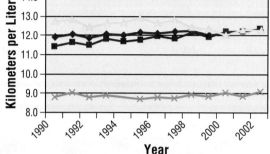

Average Fuel Efficiency of U.S. Passenger Cars and Light Trucks, 1990 to 2002

Source: U.S. Bureau of Transportation Statistics (2009)

Yet, U.S. Bureau of Transportation Statistics data show a steady increase in the total number of vehicle miles traveled. Americans increased their aggregate number of vehicle-miles traveled by 87% between 1980 and 2002. Between 1990 and 2002 the increase is 35%. Despite well-intentioned attempts on behalf of individuals to reduce their transportation fuel consumption by switching to hybrids, rising population and growing automobile culture create conditions that significantly boost aggregate levels of transportation fuel consumption. It would appear that an immediate and total conversion to hybrid vehicles would initially reduce the total amount of transportation fuels consumed to around those levels found in the early 1990s (hardly a benchmark era for sustainability).

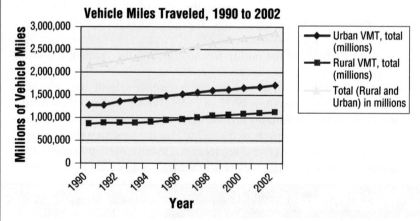

Vehicle Miles Traveled, 1990 to 2002

Source: U.S. Bureau of Transportation Statistics (2009)

The reality of these aggregate statistics is that we consume more than ever despite gains made in efficiency, just as we drive more than ever despite gains in fuel economy. It may be time to remove the phrase "miles per gallon" from the discourse on climate change. It may do more harm than good. This idea reflects sociologist Emile Durkheim's claim that the whole is greater than the sum of its parts. In other words, we can't rely on an analysis of individual drivers to solve climate change. Instead, we need to understand driving—a phenomenon that takes place at the societal level, not the individual level.

EXAMPLE 1

Calculating Measures of Central Tendency with Raw Data

Suppose that the following nine cases constitute our data.

$$4, 5, 8, 3, 2, 5, 4, 5, 5$$

Rank-ordering the cases from low to high results in: 2 3 4 4 5 5 5 5 8.

The Mode. There are more 5s than any other value. So the mode $= 5$.

The Median. Since there are nine cases, the position of the middle case is $\dfrac{N + 1}{2}$ or $\dfrac{9 + 1}{2} = 5$.

The median is equal to the value of case #5. If we count over four cases we see that the value of the fifth case is equal to 5. So the median $= 5$.

The Mean. The mean is obtained by summing the value of each case and dividing by the number of cases using the formula $\bar{X} = \dfrac{\Sigma X}{N}$.

Therefore, $\bar{X} = \dfrac{2 + 3 + 4 + 4 + 5 + 5 + 5 + 5 + 8}{9} = \dfrac{41}{9} = 4.6$.

So the mean $= 4.6$.

Integrating Technology

Statistical software programs help researchers not only speed up the process of data analysis, they also help to improve the quality of data quickly and easily. Often we want to analyze only a portion of our sample. SPSS for Windows and most other programs include a function that allows users to select only certain cases for analysis.

For example, suppose we are conducting a multicampus nationwide study of injuries associated with alcohol consumption. Our data may indicate that physical injury is two times as likely to occur among college students when alcohol was consumed. Being able to select out particular cases allows us to conduct the same type of analysis across different subgroups of our sample, thereby allowing us to compare males to females, student athletes to nonathletes, campus-based students to off-campus students. Or we could compare male student athletes who live on campus to female student athletes who live on campus. The ability to apply a common statistical analysis across different groups enables researchers to (1) statistically test hypotheses and (2) build better theoretical models of human behavior by specifying the social contexts in which alcohol-related injuries are most likely to occur.

A recent article in the *Journal of American College Health* (Yusko, Buckman, White, & Pandina, 2008) indicates that although student athletes consume alcohol less often than nonathletes, they are more likely to binge-drink when they do consume alcohol, perhaps as a result of attempting to "maximize" their relatively limited amount of party time. These trends are particularly true for male student athletes. This is just one example of a comparative study in which the data were analyzed using a statistical software package.

Statistical software programs provide the possibility of conducting such comparisons in as little as a few minutes or even seconds.

EXAMPLE 2

Calculating Measures of Central Tendency Using Raw Data

As global warming becomes an increasing threat to our way of life on this planet, I was curious to learn more about the most fuel-efficient cars on the market. Visiting the U.S. Department of Energy website *http://www.fueleconomy.gov,* I learned that the most fuel-efficient midsize cars, large cars, and midsize station wagons on the market for 2009 are the Toyota Prius, Nissan Versa, Hyundai Sonata, Honda Accord, Volkswagen Jetta Sportwagen, Kia Rondo, and Saab 9-5 Sport Combi. They are listed along with the city and highway gas mileage ratings in Table 3.15.

Table 3.15 tells us which cars to consider if we are looking for a fuel-efficient family sedan; however, it does not tell us how fuel efficiency has changed over time. In other words, we can use Table 3.15 to shop for the most fuel-efficient vehicle, but we need more data to determine whether our choices will make any difference over time.

TABLE 3.15 *MPG for Select Vehicles*

MAKE AND MODEL	CITY MPG	HIGHWAY MPG
Toyota Prius	48	45
Nissan Versa	26	31
Hyundai Sonata	22	32
Honda Accord	22	31
Volkswagen Jetta Sportwagen	30	41
Kia Rondo	20	27
Saab 9-5 Sport Combi	18	27

To investigate this a little further, I searched for all the family sedans that get over 20 miles per gallon (mpg) for 1994 and 2009. The results of this search are presented in Table 3.16.

TABLE 3.16 *Fuel Efficiency for Family Sedans (>20 mpg), 1994 and 2009*

1994			2009		
Make and Model	City	Highway	Make and Model	City	Highway
Mazda 626	23	31	Toyota Prius (Hybrid)	48	45
Honda Accord	22	29	Nissan Altima (Hybrid)	35	33
Chevrolet Corsica	22	28	Toyota Camry (Hybrid)	33	34
Buick Century	22	28	Chevrolet Malibu (Hybrid)	26	34
Oldsmobile Cutlass Ciera	22	28	Saturn Aura (Hybrid)	26	34
Oldsmobile Achieva	21	32	Hyundai Elantra	25	33
Pontiac Grand Am	21	32	Kia Spectra	24	32
Infiniti G20	21	29	Nissan Altima	23	32
Mitsubishi Galant	21	28	Saturn Aura	22	33
Dodge Spirit	21	27	Kia Optima	22	32
Plymouth Acclaim	21	27	Hyundai Sonata	22	32
Subaru Legacy	20	28	Honda Accord	22	31
Toyota Camry	20	27	Chevrolet Malibu	22	30
Hyundai Sonata	19	26	Toyota Camry	21	31
Chrysler LeBaron	19	25	Volkswagen Passat	21	31
Ford Taurus	18	27	Mazda 6	21	30
Mercury Sable	18	27	Chrysler Sebring	21	30
Eagle Vision	18	26	Dodge Avenger	21	30
			Ford Fusion	20	29
			Mercury Milan	20	29
			Mitsubishi Galant	20	27
			Subaru Legacy	20	27
			Nissan Maxima	19	26
			Nissan Altima	19	26
			Mercury Sable	18	28
			Hyundai Azera	18	26
			Buick Lacrosse/ Allure	17	28

Source: http://www.fueleconomy.gov/feg/byMPG.htm, December 17, 2008.

To calculate the three measures of central tendency, let's assume that we want to compare city driving conditions in 1994 to those of 2009.

Mode. For the model year 1994, the most frequently occurring value is 21 mpg $(f = 6)$. Therefore, the mode for 1994 is equal to 21 mpg.

For the model year 2009, the most frequently occurring values are 21 and 22. For each, $f = 6$. Because there are two modes, we call this a bimodal distribution. Comparing the mode from 1994 to 2009, we see very little difference in fuel efficiency (21 mpg compared to 21 or 22 mpg).

Median. As you can see, the city mpg is already ranked from high to low in Table 3.15. Therefore, we need only to determine the middle case using the following formula.

$$Position \ of \ the \ median = \frac{N + 1}{2}$$

Once we have determined the position of the median, we determine the value of the median by reading the mileage for that particular automobile. For the 1994 model year:

$$Position \ of \ the \ median = \frac{18 + 1}{2} = \frac{19}{2} = 9.5$$

When we count down 9.5 cases, we see that the median is right between the mileage for the Mitsubishi Galant (21 mpg) and the Dodge Spirit (also 21 mpg). Therefore, the median mpg for these 1994 family sedans is 21 mpg.

For the 2009 model year:

$$Position \ of \ the \ median = \frac{27 + 1}{2} = \frac{28}{2} = 14$$

Therefore, when we count down to the 14th case, we find that the median is equal to the mpg of the Toyota Camry. In this case, the city mpg of the 2009 Toyota Camry is 21. Therefore, the median mpg for these 2009 family sedans is 21 mpg.

So far, our comparison of modes and means offers little hope of finding overall increases in fuel efficiency between 1994 and 2009. A comparison of the medians, however, may tell a different story.

Mean. To determine the average miles per gallon using our formula for the mean $(\bar{X} = \frac{\Sigma X}{N})$, we must determine (1) the number of cases (N) and (2) the sum of all the different cars' mpg values (ΣX). For the model year 1994, $N = 18$ and $\Sigma x = 369$. Therefore, our formula for the mean is equal to:

$$\bar{X} = \frac{\begin{array}{c} 23 + 22 + 22 + 22 + 22 + 21 + 21 + 21 + 21 \\ + 21 + 21 + 20 + 20 + 19 + 19 + 18 + 18 + 18 \end{array}}{18}$$

$$= \frac{369}{18} = 20.5$$

This means that, on average, 1994 model year family sedans got 20.5 mpg.

Doing the same for the 2009 model year, we find that $N = 27$ and $\Sigma x = 626$. Therefore, our formula for the mean is equal to:

$$\bar{X} = \frac{\begin{array}{c} 48 + 35 + 33 + 26 + 26 + 25 + 24 + 23 + 22 + 22 + 22 + 22 + 22 \\ + 21 + 21 + 21 + 21 + 21 + 20 + 20 + 20 + 20 + 19 + 19 + 18 + 18 + 17 \end{array}}{27}$$

$$= \frac{626}{27} = 23.2$$

Therefore, between 1994 and 2009, the average mpg of family sedans increased from 20.5 to 23.2, a 2.7 mpg (13%) increase. A significant portion of this increase is the result of hybrid technology. In fact, when the hybrid cars are removed from the 2009 model year data, the average mpg is 20.8, a .3 mpg, or 1%, increase over 1994 levels. This modest increase may indicate that internal combustion engines may not be any more fuel efficient than they were 15 years ago and that gains in fuel efficiency are due mainly to a whole new type of engine—hybrid engines.

The statistics we have calculated here represent only city driving fuel efficiency. Using the data provided, we will now generate frequency tables and calculate these statistics for highway driving.

EXAMPLE 3

Calculating Measures of Central Tendency Using Grouped Data

Tables 3.17 and 3.18 represent the data for 1994 model year highway driving and 2009 model year highway driving.

The Mode. For cars built in 1994, you can see from the Frequency column in Table 3.17 that the two largest frequencies are equal to 5 ($f = 5$), cars that get 27 and 28 mpg on the highway. Therefore the distribution is bimodal and the modes are equal to 27 and 28.

For cars built in 2009, you can see from the Frequency column in Table 3.18 that the two largest frequencies are equal to 4 ($f = 4$), cars that get 30 and 32 mpg on the highway. Again, the distribution is bimodal. This means that the modes are equal to 30 and 32 mpg.

The Median. Using the Cumulative Percent column in Table 3.17, we see that the 1994 model year cars that get 27 mpg or less make up only 44.4% of the sample. Cars that

TABLE 3.17 *Highway MPG for 1994 Model Year*

		FREQUENCY	PERCENT	VALID PERCENT	CUMULATIVE PERCENT
Valid	25	1	5.6	5.6	5.6
	26	2	11.1	11.1	16.7
	27	5	27.8	27.8	44.4
	28	5	27.8	27.8	72.2
	29	2	11.1	11.1	83.3
	31	1	5.6	5.6	88.9
	32	2	11.1	11.1	100.0
	Total	18	100.0	100.0	

TABLE 3.18 *Highway MPG for 2009 Model Year*

		FREQUENCY	PERCENT	VALID PERCENT	CUMULATIVE PERCENT
Valid	26	3	11.1	11.1	11.1
	27	2	7.4	7.4	18.5
	28	2	7.4	7.4	25.9
	29	2	7.4	7.4	33.3
	30	4	14.8	14.8	48.1
	31	3	11.1	11.1	59.3
	32	4	14.8	14.8	74.1
	33	3	11.1	11.1	85.2
	34	3	11.1	11.1	96.3
	45	1	3.7	3.7	100.0
	Total	27	100.0	100.0	

get 28 mpg make up an additional 27.8% of the sample. Because the 50% mark in the frequency table comes somewhere between cars that get 27 mpg and cars that get 29 mpg, the median is equal to 28 mpg.

Using the Cumulative Percent column in Table 3.18, we see that 2009 model year cars that get 30 mpg or less make up 48.1% of the sample. Cars that get 31 mpg make up an additional 11.1%. Because the 50% mark in the frequency table comes somewhere between cars that get 30 mpg and cars that get 32 mpg, the median is equal to 31 mpg.

The Mean. To calculate the mean mpg for 1994 model year cars, we multiply the frequency of each mpg by the number of cars that get that many miles per gallon. For example, for 1994 only 1 car gets 25 mpg, so $1 \times 25 = 25$. Two cars get 26 mpg, so $2 \times 26 = 52$. The equations are in Table 3.19.

TABLE 3.19 *1994 Model Year*

FREQUENCY × MPG	$\sum X$
1 × 25 =	25
2 × 26 =	52
5 × 27 =	135
5 × 28 =	140
2 × 29 =	58
1 × 31 =	31
2 × 32 =	64
N = 18	505

TABLE 3.20 *2009 Model Year*

FREQUENCY × MPG	$\sum X$
3 × 26 =	78
2 × 27 =	54
2 × 28 =	56
2 × 29 =	58
4 × 30 =	120
3 × 31 =	93
4 × 32 =	128
3 × 33 =	99
3 × 34 =	102
1 × 45 =	45
N = 27	833

Using the formula for the mean:

$$\bar{X} = \frac{\Sigma X}{N} = \frac{505}{18} = 28.1 \text{ mpg}$$

This means that on average, the 18 cars analyzed for 1994 get 28.1 mpg on the highway.

For 2009, the equations are in Table 3.20.

Using the formula for the mean:

$$\bar{X} = \frac{\Sigma X}{N} = \frac{833}{27} = 30.9 \text{ mpg}$$

This means that on average, the 27 cars analyzed for 2009 get 30.9 mpg on the highway.

EXAMPLE 4

Calculating Measures of Central Tendency Using Grouped Data

TABLE 3.21 *Number of Children*

		NUMBER OF CHILDREN		
		FREQUENCY	PERCENT	VALID PERCENT	CUMULATIVE PERCENT
Valid	0	414	29.7	29.7	29.7
	1	242	17.3	17.3	47.0
	2	398	28.5	28.5	75.6
	3	226	16.2	16.2	91.8
	4	115	8.2	8.2	100.0
	Total	1395	100.0	100.0	

The Mode. In this example there are 414 respondents with zero children. There are more zeros than any other value, so the mode = 0.

The Median. To find the median, we can use two different methods. First, we can find the position of the middle case by taking $\frac{1395 + 1}{2}$, which gives a value of 698. If we begin adding cases as we move down the Frequency column, we find that after summing all of the 0s we have 414 cases. After summing all the 0s and 1s we have 656 cases, still not up to the middle case number of 698. If we sum all the 0s, 1s, and 2s we have 1,054 cases. Therefore, case number 698 came after the 1s, but before the end of the 2s. Therefore, the median is equal to 2.

The second method by which to calculate the median in this example is to locate the 50% mark in the Cumulative Percent column. The 50% mark represents case 698 (the middle case). Starting at the top of the Cumulative Percent column, imagine that the percentages from 0 to 100% are all listed. Move down the column until you come to the 50% mark. After including all the 0s, we are up to 29.7%. After including all the 0s and 1s, we are up to 47.0%. After including all the 0s, 1s, and 2s, we are up to 75.6%. Therefore, the 50% mark came after the 1s, but before the end of the 2s. Therefore, the median must be equal to 2.

The Mean. To calculate the mean, we must begin by determining the total number of children that the 1,395 respondents have. To do this we use the following technique: We have 414 cases with a value of 0 so,

$$414 \times 0 = 0$$

We have 242 cases with a value of 1 so,

$$242 \times 1 = 242$$

We do this for all the values as follows:

$$
\begin{array}{rcl}
414 \times 0 & = & 0 \\
242 \times 1 & = & 242 \\
398 \times 2 & = & 796 \\
226 \times 3 & = & 678 \\
115 \times 4 & = & 460 \\
\hline
\text{Total} & & 2{,}176
\end{array}
$$

We now know that our 1,395 respondents ($N = 1{,}395$) have a total of 2,176 children. We can now put these numbers into our formula for the mean:

$$\bar{X} = \frac{\Sigma X}{N}$$

$\bar{X} = \frac{\Sigma X}{N} = \frac{2176}{1395} = 1.6$. Therefore, on average, each one of our respondents has 1.6 children. Of course, it is not possible to have 1.6 children, but means are not always based on whole numbers.

Chapter Summary

This chapter focuses on measures of central tendency, statistics that are used to describe where cases tend to cluster in a distribution. The three most commonly used measures are the mode, the median, and the mean. While the mode can be used with nominal, ordinal, and interval/ratio variables, the median can only be used with ordinal and interval/ratio variables. The mean can only be used when working with interval/ratio variables. Therefore, each measure makes a unique contribution to our understanding of data.

It is important to be able to calculate all three measures of central tendency using both raw data and grouped data (frequency tables). It is also important to be able to understand how these measures can be used in graphic representations of data.

Exercises

Calculate the mode, median, and mean for the following raw data set:

$$3, 6, 2, 4, 3, 5, 4, 7, 4, 2$$

1. Mode
2. Median
3. Mean

Calculate the mode, median, and mean for the following raw data set:

$$9, 6, 5, 5, 10, 7, 3, 5, 6, 15, 8, 9, 10, 2, 3,$$
$$11, 4, 6, 7, 13, 10, 5, 6, 6, 3, 9, 12$$

4. Mode
5. Median
6. Mean

Calculate the mode, median, and mean for the following frequency tables. If a measure does not apply, indicate so by answering "not applicable."

Labor Force Status

		FREQUENCY	PERCENT	VALID PERCENT	CUMULATIVE PERCENT
Valid	WORKING FULL TIME	2321	51.5	51.5	51.5
	WORKING PART TIME	440	9.8	9.8	61.3
	TEMP NOT WORKING	84	1.9	1.9	63.1
	UNEMPL, LAID OFF	143	3.2	3.2	66.3
	RETIRED	712	15.8	15.8	82.1
	SCHOOL	139	3.1	3.1	85.2
	KEEPING HOUSE	490	10.9	10.9	96.1
	OTHER	177	3.9	3.9	100.0
	Total	4506	99.9	100.0	
Missing	NA	4	.1		
Total		4510	100.0		

7. Mode
8. Median
9. Mean

Age of Respondent

		FREQUENCY	PERCENT	VALID PERCENT	CUMULATIVE PERCENT
Valid	18	19	6.3	6.3	6.3
	19	47	15.5	15.5	21.8
	20	50	16.5	16.5	38.3
	21	52	17.2	17.2	55.4
	22	72	23.8	23.8	79.2
	23	63	20.8	20.8	100.0
	Total	303	100.0	100.0	

10. Mode
11. Median
12. Mean

Education Spending

		FREQUENCY	PERCENT	VALID PERCENT	CUMULATIVE PERCENT
Valid	TOO LITTLE	1111	24.6	74.7	74.7
	ABOUT RIGHT	281	6.2	18.9	93.6
	TOO MUCH	95	2.1	6.4	100.0
	Total	1487	33.0	100.0	
Missing	NAP	3002	66.6		
	DK	21	.5		
	Total	3023	67.0		
Total		4510	100.0		

13. Mode
14. Median
15. Mean
16. Explain what happens to the mode if we add an outlier with a very high value.
17. Explain what happens to the median if we add an outlier with a very high value.
18. Explain what happens to the mean if we add an outlier with a very high value.

Use the tables below to calculate all the measures of central tendency that apply. If a measure does not apply, indicate so by answering "not applicable."

Improving & Protecting Environment

		FREQUENCY	PERCENT	VALID PERCENT	CUMULATIVE PERCENT
Valid	TOO LITTLE	506	33.7	70.2	70.2
	ABOUT RIGHT	178	11.9	24.7	94.9
	TOO MUCH	37	2.5	5.1	100.0
	Total	721	48.1	100.0	
Missing	NAP	752	50.1		
	DK	22	1.5		
	NA	5	.3		
	Total	779	51.9		
Total		1500	100.0		

19. Mode

20. Median

21. Mean

Prays in Public School

		FREQUENCY	PERCENT	VALID PERCENT	CUMULATIVE PERCENT
Valid	YES, DEFINITELY	462	30.8	38.8	38.8
	YES, PROBABLY	297	19.8	24.9	63.7
	NO, PROBABLY	199	13.3	16.7	80.4
	NO, DEFINITELY	234	15.6	19.6	100.0
	Total	1192	79.5	100.0	
Missing	NAP	154	10.3		
	CAN'T CHOOSE	134	8.9		
	NA	20	1.3		
	Total	308	20.5		
Total		1500	100.0		

22. Mode

23. Median

24. Mean

Computer Exercises

Use the GSS2006 database to answer the following questions.

25. What is the modal age for all respondents?
26. What is the median age for all respondents?
27. What is the mean age for all respondents?

What is the mode, median, and mean for each of the following variables? If a measure does not apply, indicate so by writing NA in the space provided. Be sure to write numeric responses only for interval/ratio variables and text responses for nominal and ordinal variables.

VARIABLE	MODE	MEDIAN	MEAN
28. Wrkstat			
29. Prestg80			
30. Marital			
31. Sibs			
32. Vote00			
33. Gunlaw			
34. Health			
35. Satjob			
36. Sexeduc			
37. Sei			

Split the data by sex in order to answer the following questions. Be sure to indicate the values for each group.

QUESTION	MALES	FEMALES
38. What is the mean occupational prestige score (prstg80)?		
39. What is the modal response for abany?		
40. What is the median response for mothers' years of education (maeduc)?		
41. What is the modal response for fathers' highest degree (padeg)?		
42. What is the median response for socioeconomic index (sei)?		
43. What is the mean response for socioeconomic index (sei)?		
44. What is the average age at which respondents are first married (agewed)?		

Now You Try It Answers

1: Mode = 15, Median = 15, Mean = 14.4

2: Mode = 1, Median = 2, Mean = 2.3

Key Terms

Average, 68
Histogram, 84
Mean, 71
Measures of central tendency, 68

Median, 71
Mode, 70
Outliers, 84
Skew, 71

Works Cited

Buchman, C., & DiPrete, T. (2006). The Growing Female Advantage in College Completion: The Role of Family Background and Academic Achievement. *American Sociological Review* Volume 71, Number 4, 515-541.

California Newsreel. (2008). *Unnatural Causes: Is Inequality Making us Sick?* [Motion picture]. San Francisco: Author.

Ehrlich, P. R., & Ehrlich, A. H. (2008). *The Dominant Animal: Human Evolution and the Environment*. Washington, DC: Island Press.

Gould, S. J. (1997). *Full House: The Spread of Excellence from Plato to Darwin*. New York: Three Rivers Press.

Huff, D. (1954). *How to Lie with Statistics*. New York: Norton.

Malthus, T. (1993). *An Essay on the Principle of Population* (G. Gilbert, Ed.). Oxford , UK: Oxford University Press. (Original work published 1798)

National Opinion Research Center. (2006). *General Social Survey*. Chicago: Author.

U.S. Energy Information Administration. (2003).

U.S. Bureau of Transportation Statistics, Research and Administrative Technology Administration. (2009).

U.S. Census Bureau. Newsroom. http://www.census.gov/ newsroom/releases/archives/population/cb06-156 .html. Accessed on 11/11/2010.

Yusko, D. A., Buckman, J., White, H. R., & Pandina, R. J. (2008). Alcohol, Tobacco, Illicit Drugs, and Performance Enhancers: A Comparison of Use by College Student Athletes and Nonathletes. *Journal of American College Health*, Volume 57, Issue 3 281–289.

Measures of Dispersion

Introduction

According to the 2006 General Social Survey, Americans have completed an average of 13.29 years of education. Of course this does not mean that each and every American has exactly 13.29 years; some have more and some have less. The 2006 General Social Survey also tells us that 15.3% of the U.S. population has less than a high school degree and that 16.9% has a bachelor's degree; but these ordinal measures tell us very little about how cases are distributed around the average of 13.29 years. Do most

CHAPTER

4

103

Dispersion The degree to which cases are clustered around a particular value, usually the mean.

Americans have just about 13–14 years? Or are there lots of people with 10 years and lots of people with 16 years?

These are questions that measures of central tendency cannot help us to answer. They are questions that go beyond averages. In other words, once we know an average, we may want to know something more about the data it begins to describe. For example, the numbers 4, 5, and 6 have an average of 5. So do the numbers 3, 5, and 7. And so do the numbers 2, 5, and 8. You can see from these sets of numbers that an average of 5 can come from a group of tightly clustered numbers or from a group of widely dispersed numbers. Measures of dispersion tell us about the degree of clustering among cases in a data set. This degree of clustering is referred to as dispersion. The terms variability and dispersion are often used interchangeably, but the term dispersion will be used here. Table 4.1 presents relevant formulas and symbols for our discussion of dispersion.

TABLE 4.1 *Symbols and Formulas*

TERM/SYMBOL	MEANING OF SYMBOL	FORMULA
Measures of dispersion	A group of statistics (range, variance, standard deviation) that is used to describe how spread out cases are across a distribution. They tell us how tightly cases tend to cluster. Used with interval/ratio variables.	
Range	The distance between the case with the highest value and the case with the lowest value	$R = H - L$
Interquartile range	The distance from the third to the first quartile	$Q = Q_3 - Q_1$
Deviation	The distance that a particular case falls from the mean	$D_i = X - \bar{X}$
Mean deviation	The average distance that each case (measured as a positive value) falls from the mean	$D_t = \dfrac{\Sigma(|X - \bar{X}|)}{N}$
Sum of squares	The sum of squared deviations from the mean	$ss = \sum(X - \bar{X})^2$
Variance	A type of average. The average of the squared "distances" from the mean.	$s^2 = \dfrac{\Sigma(X - \bar{X})^2}{N}$
Standard deviation	A type of average equal to the square root of the variance. It is the square root of the average of the squared "distances" from the mean.	$s = \sqrt{\dfrac{\Sigma(X - \bar{X})^2}{N}}$

Many questions cannot be answered using measures of central tendency because measures of central tendency only tell us around what values cases tend to cluster. They do not tell us how tightly cases tend to cluster around those values. Therefore, we need a new group of statistics that describe the degree to which cases are clustered (or spread out). These statistics are known as measures of dispersion. Distributions can be described more completely when both measures of central tendency and measures of dispersion are used.

In this chapter we learn how to calculate and interpret five of the most commonly used measures of dispersion: the range, interquartile range, mean deviation, variance, and standard deviation. As in the case of measures of central tendency, it is important to understand what these measures tell us and what their limitations are. We learn how to calculate each of these with both raw and grouped data.

The Distribution of Education in the United States

The United States is a relatively highly educated country. According to data from the General Social Survey (National Opinion Research Center, 2006), Table 4.2, about 85% of Americans have at least a high school education and 34% of Americans have more than a high school education. This means that only about 15% of respondents have less than a high school degree. For these same respondents, 38% have fathers with less than a high school degree and 34% have mothers with less than a high school degree. Additionally, the mean number of years of education for all Americans is 13.29, compared to only 11.27 years for their mothers and 11.28 years for their fathers. This appears to

TABLE 4.2 *RS Highest Degree*

		FREQUENCY	PERCENT	VALID PERCENT	CUMULATIVE PERCENT
Valid	LT HIGH SCHOOL	691	15.3	15.3	15.3
	HIGH SCHOOL	2273	50.4	50.4	65.8
	JUNIOR COLLEGE	377	8.4	8.4	74.1
	BACHELOR	763	16.9	16.9	91.1
	GRADUATE	403	8.9	8.9	100.0
	Total	4507	99.9	100.0	
Missing	NA	3	.1		
Total		4510	100.0		

indicate that Americans are an increasingly educated population. The United Nations *Human Development Report* ranks the United States 13th in the world on the *Human Development Index* (2009). This relatively high ranking is due in part to a strong record of public education.

While the United States is one of the most highly educated countries in world, this education is not distributed evenly across the population. For example, when we look at the distribution of respondents' highest degree by race, we find that 13% of Whites have less than 12 years of education, however, 21.6% of Blacks and 36.5% of Others have less than 12 years of education. These patterns are shown in Table 4.3 and in Figure 4.1. Clearly, it is important to look closely at these data to describe the distribution of education in American society. Because averages and percentages are not capable of fully describing a distribution, it is important to have an additional set of tools at our disposal. The set of tools to which we now turn our attention is measures of dispersion. We begin our investigation of measures of dispersion with some hypothetical data to illuminate the concept of dispersion and how it relates to our example of education.

Measures of dispersion A group of statistics that describe how tightly or loosely cases in a distribution are clustered.

An Example of Two Communities. Imagine two counties, each with a population with an average of 12 years of education. In the first county, every citizen has 12 years of education; but in the second county half the population has 0 years of education and the other half has 24 years of education. Analyzing only the average may lead a researcher to believe that these are very similar counties; however, upon closer examination of how the average of 12 years is divided among the population, one would conclude that they are nothing alike. Without measures of dispersion, we know nothing about how widely education is distributed around the average years of education for a population.

Now suppose we have two groups of students, Group A and Group B, with six in each group ($N = 6$). Suppose Group A graduated from one college and Group B graduated from a different college. Five years after graduation, each group averages $50,000 in annual income. Therefore, for each group the mean is equal to $50,000.

TABLE 4.3 *Education by Race*

RACE OF RESPONDENT			FREQUENCY	PERCENT	VALID PERCENT	CUMULATIVE PERCENT
WHITE	Valid	Less than 12 Years	428	13.0	13.0	13.0
		12 Years	917	27.9	27.9	41.0
		More than 12 Years	1939	59.0	59.0	100.0
		Total	3284	100.0	100.0	
BLACK	Valid	Less than 12 Years	137	21.6	21.6	21.6
		12 Years	165	26.0	26.0	47.6
		More than 12 Years	332	52.4	52.4	100.0
		Total	634	100.0	100.0	
OTHER	Valid	Less than 12 Years	216	36.5	36.5	36.5
		12 Years	122	20.6	20.6	57.1
		More than 12 Years	254	42.9	42.9	100.0
		Total	592	100.0	100.0	

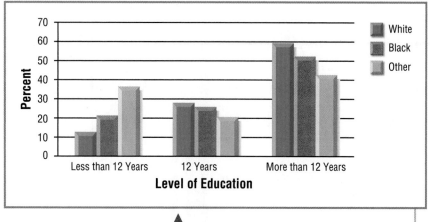

Figure 4.1 **Distribution of Education by Race**

This does not mean, however, that every person in each group is making $50,000, as shown in Figure 4.2.

Despite having the same mean, it is clear that these are two very different distributions with Group B being more tightly clustered around the mean than Group A. We can begin to describe this difference statistically using a histogram.

As noted at the beginning of this chapter, data from the 2006 General Social Survey indicate that Americans, on average, have about 13.29 years of education. Yet this is not true for all groups. For Whites, the mean is 13.66; for Blacks, the mean is 12.87; and for Others the mean is only 11.69, two years less than it is for Whites. Histograms generated in SPSS for Windows show this difference in Figures 4.3, 4.4, and 4.5.

Three statistics are presented in the upper right-hand corner of each chart: the mean, standard deviation, and number of cases. The groups are similar in that each contains respondents that have between 0 and 20 years of education; however, they are not identical distributions. You can see that the cases in the third chart (Others) are more spread out than they are for the first two charts. This is particularly true for the height of the bar at the lower end of the distribution, respondents with less than 8 years of education. This indicates a greater degree of dispersion among Others relative to the degree of dispersion among Whites and Blacks. This is confirmed by the value of the second statistic in each chart, the standard deviation (s).

As you can see, the standard deviation in years of education for Whites is 2.929 and for Blacks is 2.951. These are very similar values. For Others, however, the standard deviation is equal to 4.360. It is this significantly higher standard deviation that makes

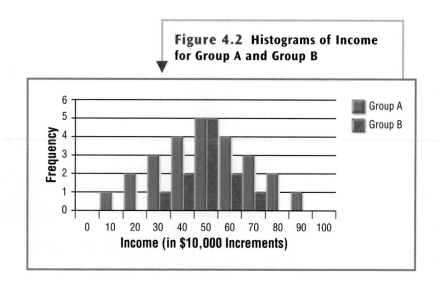

Figure 4.2 Histograms of Income for Group A and Group B

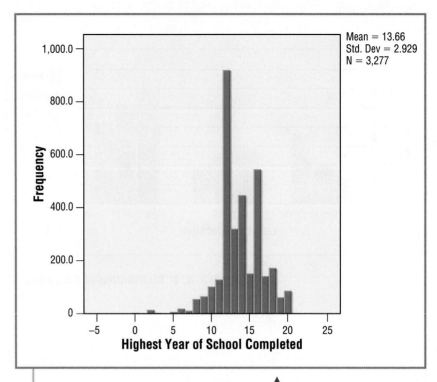

Figure 4.3 Race of Respondent: White

Figure 4.4 Race of Respondent: Black

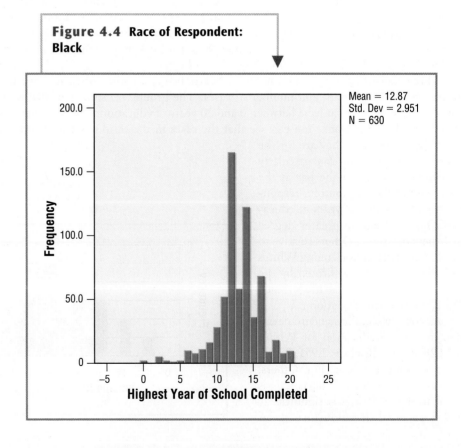

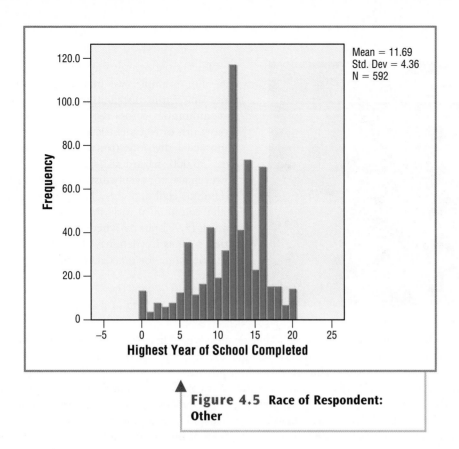

Figure 4.5 Race of Respondent: Other

the histogram for Others look different. The larger the standard deviation, the more widely distributed are cases around the mean. But let's not get ahead of ourselves! It is important to begin this discussion with an investigation into some other measures of dispersion before we get to the standard deviation. The range, interquartile range, mean deviation, variance, and standard deviation all help us to describe this difference. We now turn our attention to these five measures of dispersion, beginning with the range.

Range

The range is found by subtracting the lowest value in a set of data from the highest. The range offers a rough idea of how much variation there is in the categories of a variable.

Using the earlier example of college students in Groups A and B in Figure 4.2, the highest value in Group A is $90,000 and the lowest value is $10,000. Using the formula for the range, we see that:

Range The difference between the values of the highest and lowest cases in a distribution.

$$R = H - L$$
$$R = 90,000 - 10,000 = 80,000$$

The range is equal to $80,000 for Group A. For group B, we see that:

$$R = 70,000 - 30,000 = 40,000$$

The range is equal to $40,000 for Group B. Therefore, the respondents in Group A are more widely dispersed than are the respondents in Group B.

The range can also apply to ecological data. For example, we may want to know more about the distribution of waste sites in communities across the state. The Commonwealth of Massachusetts is home to 351 minor civil divisions (towns and cities) and over 30,000 hazardous sites. These sites, however, are not evenly distributed across the 351 minor civil divisions. The city of Boston is the community with the most ecological hazards (3,972 points) whereas other communities, such as Leyden, have 0 points. Therefore, the range for this data is equal to

$$R = H - L$$
$$R = 3972 - 0 = 3972$$

Overall, the range is a rather simplistic measure of dispersion that requires us to use only two cases in a distribution to determine its value, the one with the highest value and the one with the lowest value. In this way, it provides us with a rough idea of the degree of dispersion, but by virtue of omitting the values of all but two of the cases, a great deal of data is never put to use. Other measures of dispersion, such as the mean deviation, variance, and standard deviation, use more data and offer a more complete understanding of our data by using the values of more cases in their calculations.

Integrating Technology

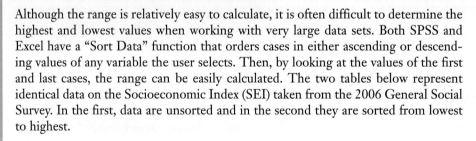

Although the range is relatively easy to calculate, it is often difficult to determine the highest and lowest values when working with very large data sets. Both SPSS and Excel have a "Sort Data" function that orders cases in either ascending or descending values of any variable the user selects. Then, by looking at the values of the first and last cases, the range can be easily calculated. The two tables below represent identical data on the Socioeconomic Index (SEI) taken from the 2006 General Social Survey. In the first, data are unsorted and in the second they are sorted from lowest to highest.

UNSORTED DATA	SORTED DATA
35.7	28.4
32.0	28.6
43.7	29.2
34.4	32.0
36.5	32.3
36.5	34.4

UNSORTED DATA	SORTED DATA
78.5	35.7
32.3	36.5
38.4	36.5
62.0	38.4
44.7	41.6
49.6	43.7
63.5	44.7
45.3	45.3
29.2	49.6
28.4	50.7
41.6	62.0
68.8	63.5
68.1	68.1
91.2	68.1
76.5	68.8
50.7	76.5
68.1	78.5
28.6	91.2

Once data have been sorted, it is much easier to calculate the range:

$$R = H - L$$

Because the range only uses two of the 24 values of data, a great deal of information is left out. As we will see, the mean deviation, variance, and standard deviation make use of all available data. Although they are more difficult to calculate, they give us a better overall picture of the distribution.

Interquartile Range

Another type of range is called the interquartile range. As you may have guessed, the interquartile range is based on dividing a distribution into quarters, four equal-sized parts known as quartiles. The difference between the value of the cases at the third and first quartiles is equal to the interquartile range. Literally, it is the range of values of the two middle quartiles.

> **Interquartile range** The difference between the values at the third and first quartiles in a distribution.

For example, suppose that we sample 20 individuals on the number of years of school they have completed and get the following results (ranked in order from lowest to highest).

8 10 10 10 12 12 12 12 12 12 12 14 14 16 16 16 16 17 18 20

If you recall from our discussion in Chapter 3, the median is equal to the value of the middle case. The formula for finding the middle case is $\frac{N+1}{2}$ or $(N + 1)(.5)$. Because two quartiles is equal to one half, the second quartile is the same thing as the median. Therefore, the data above the second quartile is equal to,

$$Q_2 = (20 + 1)(.5) = \textit{Value of case number } 10.5 = 12$$

When we count over 10.5 cases, we find that it falls between two values of 12. Therefore, $Q_2 = 12$, as shown below.

$$25\% \qquad 25\% \qquad 25\% \qquad 25\%$$

8 10 10 10 12 | 12 12 12 12 12 | 12 14 14 16 16 | 16 16 17 18 20

Low Score $\qquad\quad Q_1 \qquad\qquad Q_{2\ (median)} \qquad\qquad Q_3 \qquad\qquad$ High Score

We use a similar method to find the location of the first and third quartiles. For the first quartile, we use the formula $N + 1(.25)$ and for the third quartile we use the formula $N + 1(.75)$. Therefore, in our example we find that,

$$Q_1 = \textit{Value of case number } (20 + 1)(.25) = \textit{Value of case number } 5.25 = 12$$

and

$$Q_2 = \textit{Value of case number } (20 + 1)(.75) = \textit{Value of case number } 15.75 = 16$$

We can now calculate the interquartile range using the formula,

$$Q = Q_3 - Q_1 = 16 - 12 = 4$$

Box Plot A way to graphically demonstrate a distribution using the median, the 25th percentile, the 75th percentile, and the high and low values in a data set.

The interquartile range gives us a sense of the amount of dispersion across the middle part of a distribution. It does not, however, tell us much about dispersion that may be located in the tails of a distribution. SPSS for Windows can quickly create what are called *box plots*, charts like the one shown in Figure 4.6. You can see that the

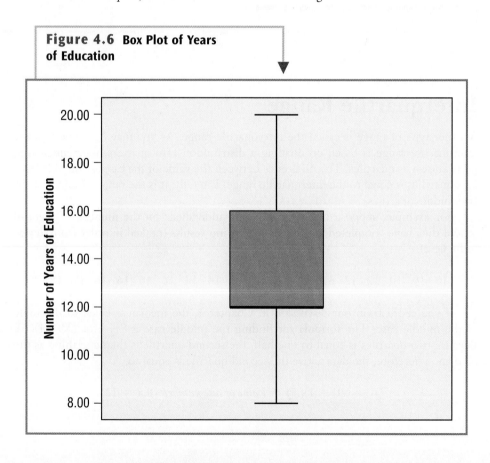

Figure 4.6 **Box Plot of Years of Education**

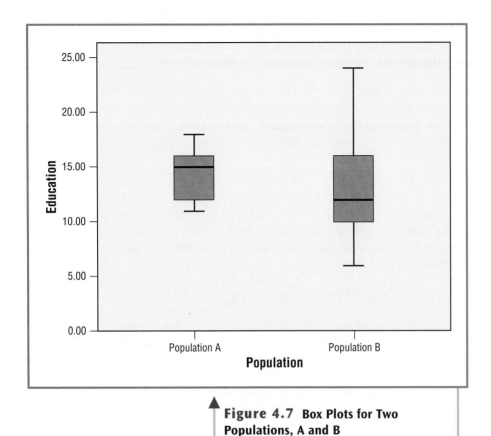

▲ **Figure 4.7** **Box Plots for Two Populations, A and B**

box plot contains a box in the center that ranges from values of 12 to 16. This box represents the interquartile range of our data. The chart also has lines that indicate the highest and lowest values of our data. The horizontal line, at the bottom of the box in this example, represents the median. Box plots are a good way to quickly assess the characteristics of a distribution and a good way to make comparisons between different groups. For example, use the box plots in Figures 4.6 and 4.7 to compare years of education between two populations.

As you can see from Figure 4.7, Population A has much less overall dispersion and a much smaller interquartile range than does Population B. The median is also significantly higher for Population A. Overall, while some people in Population B have very high levels of education (and very low levels of education) that far exceed anyone in Population A, as a group, Population A is more highly educated.

Mean Deviation

The mean deviation, as you might have guessed from its name, is a type of average. Although it is rarely used, a brief summary is offered here as a way to introduce concepts that are useful in understanding a much more commonly used measure of dispersion, the standard deviation. The mean deviation differs from the mean because it is based on the degree to which cases differ from the mean rather than the actual values of the cases. For example, if the average number of courses that students take is five and you

Mean deviation The mathematical average of deviations from the mean (measured in absolute values).

take four, you vary from the mean by a value of 1. This amount is called the deviation and can be calculated by taking the absolute value of the difference between the value of a particular case and the mean, using the following formula:

$$D_i = |X - \bar{X}|$$

When calculating the mean deviation, this is done for each case in the distribution. The values are then summed and divided by N to obtain the mean deviation.

$$D_t = \frac{\Sigma(|X - \bar{X}|)}{N}$$

It is necessary to use the absolute values of the deviations from the mean, otherwise, the values will add up to 0. Because absolute values are used, the mean deviation can also be called the mean absolute deviation. This mathematical certainty is a unique characteristic of the mean.

Mean Deviation Using Raw Data

If we take any group of numbers, suppose it is the number of courses that students at your school take, the average represents the point at which half of the total deviation falls above and half falls below. Therefore, if we sum the positive and negative deviations they will add to 0.

Consider this example: Suppose we ask six students how many courses they are currently enrolled in and we get the results shown below.

4
5
4
6
5
6

The values add to 30 and because $N = 6$, the mean is 5. If we subtract the mean from each value, we find:

$$4 - 5 = -1$$
$$5 - 5 = 0$$
$$4 - 5 = -1$$
$$6 - 5 = 1$$
$$5 - 5 = 0$$
$$\underline{6 - 5 = 1}$$
$$\text{Sum} = 0$$

This is the case for any group of numbers and requires us to use absolute values when calculating the mean deviation. When variations from the mean are put in absolute value (positive value), we find:

$$4 - 5 = -1 = 1$$
$$5 - 5 = 0 = 0$$
$$4 - 5 = -1 = 1$$
$$6 - 5 = 1 = 1$$
$$5 - 5 = 0 = 0$$
$$\underline{6 - 5 = 1 = 1}$$
$$\text{Sum} = 4$$

Using the formula for the mean deviation, we find:

$$D_t = \frac{\Sigma(\,|\,X - \overline{X}\,|\,)}{N} = \frac{4}{6} = .67$$

We can now say that the mean deviation is equal to .67. This means that, *on average*, cases deviate from the mean by .67. On average, students deviate from the mean number of courses by .67 courses.

Now You Try It 1

Use the two data sets below to calculate the range and mean deviation. In what way are the two groups similar? In what ways are they different?

Number of Class Meetings Missed in the Past Semester

Males	Females	
3	7	*Hint #1:* To calculate the range, begin by rank-ordering the cases from lowest to highest.
7	4	
9	9	*Hint #2:* When finding the mean deviation, remember to first calculate the mean. Then determine how much each case differs from the mean in absolute value.
12	8	
1	6	
8	8	
2	5	
14	9	

Variance and Standard Deviation

We are now ready to get back to our discussion of the standard deviation. While the mean deviation gives us an idea about the nature of dispersion in our data, it is not a widely used measure. Also based on the concept of deviations from the mean are two more commonly used measures, the variance and the standard deviation. These are practically the same measure. In fact, they are identical except that one is expressed in squared units while the other is expressed in standard units. To obtain the standard deviation (the most commonly used measure of dispersion), we need only to take the square root of the variance. Therefore, we now turn our attention first to the variance and then to the standard deviation.

Variance The mathematical average of the squared deviations from the mean.

Variance (s^2)

Like the mean deviation, the variance is an average based on deviations from the mean. And like the calculations for the mean deviation, it is necessary to make sure that the deviations from the mean are expressed as positive values. Otherwise, the sum of deviations from the mean will add up to 0. Rather than taking the absolute values of deviations from the mean, the variance squares the deviations from the mean. While this has the effect of turning all of these values into positive numbers, it also has the effect of altering the scale of their values. In other words, 3s become 9s, 9s become 81s, and so on.

In this sense, it is important to remember that the variance, (s^2), is always expressed in "squared units," while the standard deviation, (s), is expressed in standard units. The variance is determined by summing the squared deviations from the mean and dividing by N.

The formula for the variance is:

$$s^2 = \frac{\Sigma(X - \overline{X})^2}{N}$$

We now calculate the variance using data on television viewing hours per day for two groups: Group A and Group B.

EXAMPLE 1

Calculating the Variance Using Raw Data
Our data for Group A is:

$$3, 2, 4, 2, 4$$

Using the same technique that we used to determine deviations from the mean, we subtract the mean from each value $(X - \overline{X})$ in Table 4.4. The sum of these squared deviations from the mean is equal to the *sum of squares* and is denoted by the symbol *ss*.

TABLE 4.4

X	$X - \overline{X}$	$(X - \overline{X})^2$
3	$3 - 3 = 0$	0
2	$2 - 3 = -1$	1
4	$4 - 3 = 1$	1
2	$2 - 3 = -1$	1
4	$4 - 3 = 1$	1
		$ss = 4$

Because the deviations from the mean are all equal to either 0 or 1, the squared deviations from the mean are also equal to either 0 or 1. This means that for this particular example, the sum of squares is the same as the sum of absolute value deviations, but only because we are working with only 0s and 1s.

We can now put the sum of squares (the numerator) and N (the denominator) into the equation for the variance.

$$s^2 = \frac{\Sigma(X - \bar{X})^2}{N} = \frac{4}{5} = .8$$

So in this example the variance is equal to .8. We now calculate the variance for Group B.

For Group B the data is:

$$1, 0, 7, 6, 1$$

Using the same technique that we used to determine deviations from the mean, we subtract the mean from each value $(X - \bar{X})$ in Table 4.5. The sum of these squared deviations from the mean is equal to the *sum of squares* and is denoted by the symbol *ss*.

TABLE 4.5

X	$X - \bar{X}$	$(X - \bar{X})^2$
1	$1 - 3 = -2$	4
0	$0 - 3 = -3$	9
7	$7 - 3 = 4$	16
6	$6 - 3 = 3$	9
1	$1 - 3 = -2$	4
		$ss = 42$

We can now put the sum of squares and N into the equation for the variance.

$$s^2 = \frac{\Sigma(X - \bar{X})^2}{N} = \frac{42}{5} = 8.4$$

As you can see, 8.4 is an unusually large number, particularly since our data values only go up to a maximum of 7. This is a result of squaring the difference between the case values and the mean. In other words, our variance of 8.4 is expressed in a different unit of analysis than that of the data. To make the results more intelligible, we must remove the squaring effect by taking the square root of the variance. By doing so, we have calculated the standard deviation.

Standard Deviation (*s*)

Standard deviation The square root of the mathematical average of the sum of squared deviations from the mean. The square root of the variance.

The standard deviation is equal to the square root of the variance. Therefore, to calculate the standard deviation, it is necessary to first calculate the variance. Once we have calculated the variance, we simply take the square root and the result is the standard deviation.

EXAMPLE 2

Calculating the Standard Deviation Using the Variance

Therefore, for Group A, the variance (s^2) is equal to .8. By taking the square root of .8, we find that:

$$s = \sqrt{s^2} = \sqrt{.8} = .9$$

The standard deviation is equal to .9. This means that the cases differ from the mean of 3 hours of television viewing by an average of .9 hours (56 minutes).

For Group B, the variance (s^2) is equal to 8.4. By taking the square root of 8.4, we find that:

$$s = \sqrt{s^2} = \sqrt{8.4} = 2.9$$

The standard deviation is equal to 2.9. This means that each case differs from the mean of 3 hours of television viewing by an average of 2.9 hours (174 minutes).

It is important to remember that the variance and standard deviation are averages. They are averages of how much cases tend to differ from the mean. The variance is expressed in units of analysis that have been squared and the standard deviation is expressed in standard units (meaning nonsquared units) of analysis (hence the name *standard* deviation).

EXAMPLE 3

Calculating the Standard Deviation Using Raw Data

Suppose we are interested in learning more about intergenerational differences in education. Specifically, we want to know how much more or less formal education people have compared to their grandparents. To investigate, we gather data from 10 females, each of whom is 40 years old. First, we ask them how many years of formal education they have. Then we ask them how many years of formal education their grandmother had when she was 40 years old. The difference between the two is calculated as follows:

Respondent's Education – Respondent's Grandmother's Education = Change in Education

The result can be either positive (for cases in which the respondent has more years of education than did her grandmother) or negative (for cases in which the respondent has less years of education than did her grandmother). In this example, all respondents have as much or more education than did their grandmothers at the same age. Our data is presented below in Table 4.6.

TABLE 4.6

RESPONDENT #	RESPONDENT'S EDUCATION	RESPONDENT'S GRANDMOTHER'S EDUCATION	CHANGE IN EDUCATION
1	12	10	2
2	16	12	4
3	12	10	2
4	14	10	4
5	14	12	2
6	12	12	0
7	12	8	4
8	16	12	4
9	16	14	2
10	12	10	2

To begin, we calculate the means as follows:

$$\bar{X} = \frac{\Sigma X}{N} = \frac{2 + 4 + 2 + 4 + 2 + 0 + 4 + 4 + 2 + 2}{10} = \frac{26}{10} = 2.6$$

We now determine how much each case differs from the mean in Table 4.7.

TABLE 4.7

CHANGE IN EDUCATION (X)	DEVIATION FROM THE MEAN ($X - \bar{X}$)
2	$2 - 2.6 = -.6$
4	$4 - 2.6 = 1.4$
2	$2 - 2.6 = -.6$
4	$4 - 2.6 = 1.4$
2	$2 - 2.6 = -.6$
0	$0 - 2.6 = -2.6$
4	$4 - 2.6 = 1.4$
4	$4 - 2.6 = 1.4$
2	$2 - 2.6 = -.6$
2	$2 - 2.6 = -.6$

These values are then squared and summed to give us the *sum of squares* in Table 4.8.

TABLE 4.8

DEVIATION FROM THE MEAN ($X - \bar{X}$)	SQUARED DEVIATIONS FROM THE MEAN
−.6	.36
1.4	1.96
−.6	.36
1.4	1.96
−.6	.36
2.6	6.76
1.4	1.96
1.4	1.96
−.6	.36
−.6	.36
	Sum of Squares = 16.4

The next step is to obtain the variance by dividing the sum of squares by the number of cases. Therefore,

$$s^2 = \frac{ss}{N} = \frac{16.4}{10} = 1.6$$

The final step in our equation is to determine the standard deviation by taking the square root of the variance. Therefore,

$$s = \sqrt{s^2} = \sqrt{1.6} = 1.26$$

This tells us that the average deviation from the mean is 1.26 years of education. At first, this may appear to be a small value, but remember that we are looking at the average deviation in changes in intergenerational education. The average change in intergenerational education is 2.6 years with a standard deviation of 1.26 years.

A Note on Samples and Populations (N or $N - 1$?). You may have noticed that if you input these same data into SPSS for Windows, you will find that you do not get the same results. Instead, you get a variance of 1.82 and a standard deviation of 1.35. The reason for this is that the SPSS for Windows software does not use N in its calculation of these statistics. Instead, the variance and standard deviation are based on $N - 1$. The reason for this is that sample data and population data are treated differently. Up to this point, we have only discussed statistics in ways that assume that our data are perfectly reflective of the population from which they were drawn. Because this is seldom, if ever the case, statisticians have devised a set of tools to control for the differences between sample data and population data. One such tool is to use $N - 1$ in place of N. These differences are discussed in greater detail in Chapters 5 and 6.

At this point, you might want to check with your instructor to see if he or she wants you to use N or $N - 1$ in the denominator of these equations. Different instructors prefer different methods. It is also important to realize that the difference between using N and $N - 1$ diminishes as sample size increases and that significant differences are only seen when working with a small number of cases. The examples and practice problems in this chapter are based on using N in the calculations.

We now turn our attention to calculating measures of dispersion with grouped data.

Integrating Technology

A variety of data analysis programs offer users the ability to work with data quickly and easily. Histograms and normal curves offer visualizations of how cases are distributed. SPSS for Windows provides users with the ability to quickly generate histograms with normal curve distributions of data. For example, suppose we have two groups of respondents (one black and one white) and we want to compare their overall socioeconomic standing (in this case a measure based on occupation and prestige). SPSS for Windows allows us to quickly create different groups by "splitting" the database by race. We can then create a histogram with a normal curve for each group as shown below.

As you can see, the mean SEI score is 51.4 among Whites, 44.1 among Blacks, and 43.5 among Others. The difference between the bars and the normal curve is that the

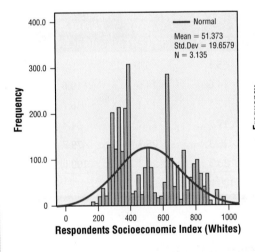

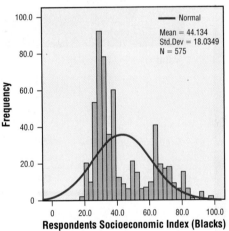

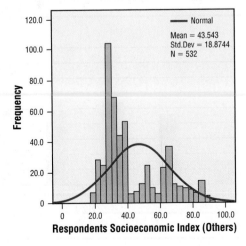

bars are our actual observations while the curve represents our predicted observations. As you can see, each group has a significant number of cases with low values, relatively few cases with "average" values, and slightly more cases than expected with high values. The difference between the bars and the curve indicate that SEI is not normally distributed. Identifying this discrepancy in the charts is relatively easy; however, without graphically presenting data, it is usually only possible to the very well-trained statistician.

The normal curve and its unique properties are discussed in greater detail later in this chapter.

EXAMPLE 4

Calculating Variance and Standard Deviation Using Grouped Data

Suppose we sample a group of students living in an off-campus housing facility to better understand the distribution of age. Our data yield the following frequency table in Table 4.9 and histogram in Figure 4.8.

TABLE 4.9 *Age of Respondent*

		FREQUENCY	PERCENT	VALID PERCENT	CUMULATIVE PERCENT
Valid	18	8	5.1	5.1	5.1
	19	23	14.6	14.6	19.6
	20	27	17.1	17.1	36.7
	21	28	17.7	17.7	54.4
	22	40	25.3	25.3	79.7
	23	32	20.3	20.3	100.0
	Total	158	100.0	100.0	

Figure 4.8 Age of Respondent

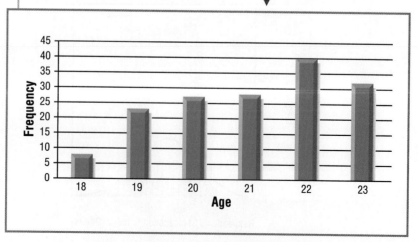

The mean age of the students is 21 years ($\bar{X} = 21$). As you can see from the first row (18-year-olds) in Table 4.10, our process for calculating the variance and standard deviation is essentially the same as when we work with raw data. To find the sum of squares using grouped data:

1. Find the difference between an 18-year-old's age and the mean.
2. Square that amount. At this point, we have found the squared difference between only one 18-year-old and the mean; but we have eight 18-year-olds.
3. Multiply the squared difference from the mean by the frequency for that age group. In this case we multiply 9 (the squared difference) by 8 (the frequency of 18-year-olds) to get 72.
4. Repeat steps 1–3 for each age group and add the results to get the sum of squares.
5. Divide the sum of squares by N to get the variance.
6. Take the square root of the variance to get the standard deviation.

To calculate the variance:

$$s^2 = \frac{\Sigma(X - \bar{X})^2}{N} = \frac{359}{158} = 2.3$$

To calculate the standard deviation:

$$s = \sqrt{\frac{\Sigma(X - \bar{X})^2}{N}} = \sqrt{\frac{359}{158}} = \sqrt{2.3} = 1.5$$

This tells us that while the mean age of the group of students is 21, the average deviation from the mean is 1.5 years.

TABLE 4.10

X	$X - \bar{X}$	$(X - \bar{X})^2$	$(X - \bar{X})^2 f$
18 ($f = 8$)	-3	9	9 * 8 = 72
19 ($f = 23$)	-2	4	4 * 23 = 92
20 ($f = 27$)	-1	1	1 * 27 = 27
21 ($f = 28$)	0	0	0 * 28 = 0
22 ($f = 40$)	1	1	1 * 40 = 40
23 ($f = 32$)	2	4	4 * 32 = 128
			Sum of Squares = 359

Now You Try It 2

Use the data below to calculate the mean, variance, and standard deviation. (*Hint:* You need to calculate the mean first.)

$$9 \quad 7 \quad 6 \quad 5 \quad 1 \quad 3 \quad 13 \quad 6 \quad 8 \quad 9 \quad 10$$

$$s^2 = \frac{\Sigma(X - \bar{X})^2}{N}$$

$$s = \sqrt{\frac{\Sigma(X - \bar{X})^2}{N}}$$

Statistical Uses and Misuses

Other Ways of Thinking about Dispersion: The GINI Coefficient

Corrado Gini (1864–1965) was an Italian statistician who wanted to find a way to measure the overall level of income inequality in society. Once this was accomplished, it would then be possible to apply the measure to different societies as a way to compare one country to another. Ultimately, he was able to develop a measure that was later named after him, the GINI Coefficient.

The GINI Coefficient is a number that ranges between 0 and 1.0. While it can be used to describe the overall distribution of virtually any variable, it is very often used to describe the overall distribution of income in a town, county, region, or country. The chart below helps us to interpret what the GINI Coefficient measures.

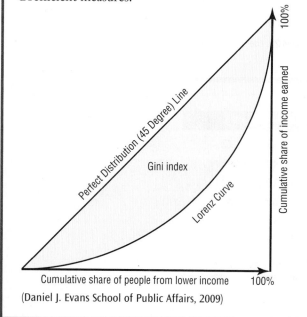

(Daniel J. Evans School of Public Affairs, 2009)

As you can see, the *x*-axis represents the percent of the population and the *y*-axis represents the percent of income. A perfectly even distribution of income would mean that 10% of the population received 10% of the income, 20% of the population received 20% of the income, and so on. This results in a straight line. Should 10% of the population receive only 1% of the income, the line begins to sag. The more sag in the line, the greater the degree of inequality of income distribution.

The actual GINI Coefficient is the proportion of area under the triangle that is between the sagging line and the even line.

The United Nations *Human Development Report* lists the GINI Coefficient for income for practically all of the nations of the world. It is interesting to note that many Americans may tend to believe that the GINI Coefficient in the United States (45.0) would be similar to western European nations such as the United Kingdom (34.0), France (28.0), and Germany (28.0); however, the nations with similar GINI Coefients are actually Kenya (44.5), Philippines (44.5), Cameroon (44.6), Cote d'Ivoire (44.6), Uruguay (45.2), Jamaica (45.5), Uganda (45.7), and Ecuador (46.0).

Remember that this does not mean the United States has similar income levels. Income in the U.S. is much higher than these countries. The way that income is distributed, however, is similar to these countries. In other words, when measured using the GINI Coefficient, income distribution in the United States represents that of developing nations (sometimes referred to as third world nations).

Now let's take a look at some toxic waste data from the Massachusetts study (Faber & Krieg, 2005) using towns that have somewhere between 25 and 50 waste sites. A frequency table of the results is shown in Table 4.11. The mean number of sites is 37.

We can calculate the sum of squares the same way we would if working with raw data. The only difference is that we multiply the squared difference between X and the mean by the number of times X occurs. In other words, we multiply it by the frequency of X. This is shown in Table 4.12.

Now that we have determined that the sum of squares is equal 4,485, we can divide it by N ($N = 76$) to get the variance.

$$S^2 = \frac{\Sigma(X - \bar{X})^2}{N} = \frac{4485}{76} = 59.0$$

TABLE 4.11 *Frequency of Sites*

SITES		FREQUENCY	PERCENT	VALID PERCENT	CUMULATIVE PERCENT
Valid	25	5	6.6	6.6	6.6
	26	3	3.9	3.9	10.5
	27	5	6.6	6.6	17.1
	28	1	1.3	1.3	18.4
	29	4	5.3	5.3	23.7
	30	2	2.6	2.6	26.3
	31	2	2.6	2.6	28.9
	32	1	1.3	1.3	30.3
	33	3	3.9	3.9	34.2
	34	2	2.6	2.6	36.8
	35	5	6.6	6.6	43.4
	36	1	1.3	1.3	44.7
	38	4	5.3	5.3	50.0
	39	2	2.6	2.6	52.6
	40	5	6.6	6.6	59.2
	41	4	5.3	5.3	64.5
	42	6	7.9	7.9	72.4
	43	2	2.6	2.6	75.0
	44	3	3.9	3.9	78.9
	45	4	5.3	5.3	84.2
	46	2	2.6	2.6	86.8
	47	1	1.3	1.3	88.2
	48	2	2.6	2.6	90.8
	49	6	7.9	7.9	98.7
	50	1	1.3	1.3	100.0
	Total	76	100.0	100.0	

By taking the square root of the variance, we get the standard deviation.

$$s = \sqrt{\frac{\Sigma(X - \overline{X})^2}{N}} = \sqrt{\frac{4485}{76}} = \sqrt{59.0} = 7.7$$

This tells us that, while the mean number of waste sites in these towns is 37, towns typically have within 7.7 sites of the mean. This is useful information, but it also begs the question of just what we mean by "typical." The standard deviation and the normal curve share some interesting properties that tell us just what is meant by "typical." We now shift our discussion to why the standard deviation is such an important statistical tool.

TABLE 4.12

X	f	$X - \bar{X}$	$(X - \bar{X})^2$	$(X - \bar{X})^2 f$
25	5	$25 - 37 = -12$	144	$144 * 5 = 720$
26	3	$26 - 37 = -11$	121	$121 * 3 = 363$
27	5	$27 - 37 = -10$	100	$100 * 5 = 500$
28	1	$28 - 37 = -9$	81	$81 * 1 = 81$
29	4	$29 - 37 = -8$	64	$64 * 4 = 256$
30	2	$30 - 37 = -7$	49	$49 * 2 = 98$
31	2	$31 - 37 = -6$	36	$36 * 2 = 72$
32	1	$32 - 37 = -5$	25	$25 * 1 = 25$
33	3	$33 - 37 = -4$	16	$16 * 3 = 48$
34	2	$34 - 37 = -3$	9	$9 * 2 = 18$
35	5	$35 - 37 = -2$	4	$4 * 5 = 20$
36	1	$36 - 37 = -1$	1	$1 * 1 = 1$
38	4	$38 - 37 = 1$	1	$1 * 4 = 4$
39	2	$39 - 37 = 2$	4	$4 * 2 = 8$
40	5	$40 - 37 = 3$	9	$9 * 5 = 45$
41	4	$41 - 37 = 4$	16	$16 * 4 = 64$
42	6	$42 - 37 = 5$	25	$25 * 6 = 150$
43	2	$43 - 37 = 6$	36	$36 * 2 = 72$
44	3	$44 - 37 = 7$	49	$49 * 3 = 147$
45	4	$45 - 37 = 8$	64	$64 * 4 = 256$
46	2	$46 - 37 = 9$	81	$81 * 2 = 162$
47	1	$47 - 37 = 10$	100	$100 * 1 = 100$
48	2	$48 - 37 = 11$	121	$121 * 2 = 242$
49	6	$49 - 37 = 12$	144	$144 * 6 = 864$
50	1	$50 - 37 = 13$	169	$169 * 1 = 169$
	N = 76			Sum of Squares = 4485

Eye on the Applied

Public Education as Equalizer or Divider?

A great deal of debate takes place over the question of whether public education reduces overall inequality or reinforces existing patterns of inequality. Famous Brazilian educator Paulo Freire was one of the leading figures in *critical pedagogy* until his death in 1997. His most famous book is *Pedagogy of the Oppressed* (1970), Freire argued that by taking the view of students as "empty vessels" into which knowledge should be poured, schools fail to teach students how to challenge existing forms of domination and instead teach them to conform to existing power structures. Today, many educators and sociologists claim that Freire was correct and that standardized testing at the federal and state levels serves the interests of those in power rather than serving as a tool to bring about a more egalitarian society.

Increasingly, standardized testing is used to determine whether public schools are meeting the needs of their students. In New York, all students must pass basic-level math skills or forgo their high school diploma. Aside from the obvious problem of determining which skills are deemed important (there is no art or music exam), is the problem of how average test scores are used to assess school performance.

Many cities have what are called "magnate schools" (also called magnet schools) where students must meet certain criteria to gain admission. Such schools cater to "gifted and talented" students. These are public schools funded by local residents, yet not all children may attend. Not only must students test into these schools, they must maintain a grade point average (GPA) high enough to remain in the schools.

Generally, standardized testing results are made available at the end of the school year. In the case of Buffalo, New York, students unable to maintain a high enough GPA to remain in the magnate schools are transferred into nonmagnate schools before the standardized tests are given. Ultimately, this means that magnate schools are more likely to have those students most likely to pass, while nonmagnate schools take on the task of educating students that the magnate schools kicked out. This kind of process has the effect of making magnate schools appear to be stronger educational institutions, when, in fact, they inflate their average test scores by expelling weaker students into other schools.

We can therefore predict that the average test score will be higher in magnate schools and that the standard deviation of scores in magnate schools will be smaller than that of nonmagnate schools. Even if the schools have identical averages, it is likely that the variation around the average will be greater for nonmagnate schools.

If statistical analyses offer support for these ideas, it would raise serious questions about whether public education increases or decreases overall levels of inequality. What do you think about Freire's ideas?

Standard Deviation and the Normal Curve

As you probably know, normal curves (also known as bell curves) are evenly distributed. This means that if we were to split a normal curve down the center, each half would be a mirror image of the other half. An example of a normal curve is shown in Figure 4.9.

Normal curve A bell-shaped symmetrical distribution.

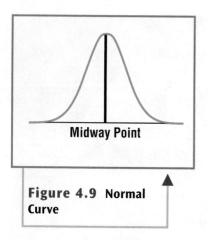

Figure 4.9 **Normal Curve**

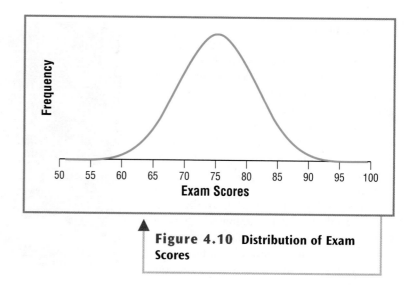

Figure 4.10 **Distribution of Exam Scores**

While a great many occurrences in the natural and social world tend to *approximate* normal curves (the age of students attending your school, the distribution of grade point averages, the amount of money you spend on books each semester, etc.), actual normal curves exist only as theoretical constructs. In other words, they exist only in theory, not in reality.

For example, suppose that a sociology professor gives students an exam. Because a C is considered average, we might expect the mean for the exam to be equal to a 75. Therefore, while very few students receive a 100, more students receive 90s, even more receive 80s, and the most common score would be a 75. Similarly, very few students would receive a 50, more would receive above a 50, even more receive 60s, and the most common score would be a 75. This is shown in Figure 4.10.

One of the unique properties of the normal curve is that all three measures of central tendency fall on the same value. In this example, the mean score is 75. This happens to be the point at which half the cases fall below and half above. Therefore, 75 is also the median exam score. And because 75 is the most frequently occurring exam score (the tallest point on the curve), it is also the mode.

This brings us to the explanation of why measures of dispersion are so important when it comes to describing a distribution. It is possible to have two distributions with identical measures of central tendency (say 75), but different values for their standard deviation. For example, suppose we have two groups of students that each took the SAT. Each group averages a combined score of 1100; but while one group has a standard deviation of 100, the other has a standard deviation of 50. The scores are shown in Figures 4.11 and 4.12.

As you can see from the charts above, each group averaged 1100 on the SAT;

Figure 4.11 **Group A: Distribution of SAT Scores (Mean = 1100, Std. Dev. = 100)**

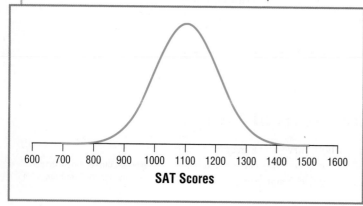

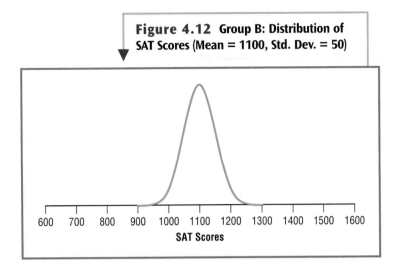

Figure 4.12 Group B: Distribution of SAT Scores (Mean = 1100, Std. Dev. = 50)

however, while one group is widely dispersed around the mean, the other group is more tightly clustered around the mean. As these charts demonstrate, it is necessary to have both measures of central tendency and measures of dispersion to more fully describe a distribution. While measures of central tendency tell us where cases tend to cluster (in this case around 1100), measures of dispersion tell us how spread out cases tend to be.

In addition to the highest point representing the mode, median, and mean, the normal curve has another important property. This time it is related to the standard deviation. For all normal curves, 68% of all cases fall within one standard deviation of the mean. This is true regardless of how clustered or how spread out the cases may be.

Using our examples of SAT scores, we see that $\overline{X} = 1100$ and $s = 100$. If 68% of all cases fall within one standard deviation of the mean, then 68% of all cases should fall within 100 points of 1100 points or 1100 $\pm$ 100. Therefore, for Group A, 68% of all

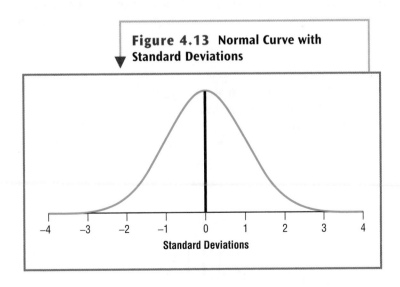

Figure 4.13 Normal Curve with Standard Deviations

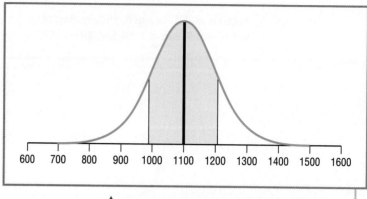

Figure 4.14 Group A: Percentage of Cases that Fall within 1 Standard Deviation (±) of the Mean

students received somewhere between 1000 and 1200 points on the SAT. When this is graphed it looks like Figure 4.14.

The shaded area to the left of the mean (1 standard deviation below the mean) constitutes roughly 34% of all cases and the shaded area to the right of the mean (1 standard deviation above the mean) constitutes roughly 34% of all cases. Together, the entire shaded area is equal to 68% of all cases. When we make a similar chart for Group B, it looks like Figure 4.15.

Each of the two charts contains a shaded area that goes from 1 standard deviation below the mean to one standard deviation above the mean. Each shaded area accounts for a total of 68% of the total area under the normal curve (68% of all cases). When we move to an additional standard deviation from the mean ($\pm 2s$), 95% of the total area under the curve (95% of cases) is included in the shaded area.

These unique properties of the normal curve are very important for the study of probability and make the standard deviation the most common of all measures of dispersion. In the next chapter, we begin discussing probability and further analyze the usefulness of the normal curve.

Figure 4.15 Group B: Percentage of Cases that Fall within 1 Standard Deviation (±) of the Mean

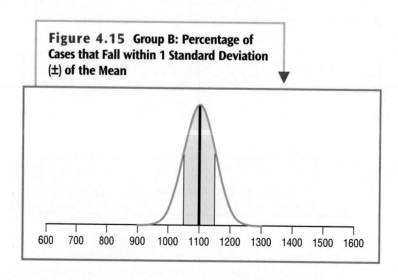

Now You Try It 3

Use the table below to calculate the variance and standard deviation. (*Hint:* The mean is equal to 2.9.)

Parking Tickets this Semester

		FREQUENCY	PERCENT	VALID PERCENT	CUMULATIVE PERCENT
Valid	1	2321	51.5	51.5	51.5
	2	440	9.8	9.8	61.3
	3	84	1.9	1.9	63.1
	4	143	3.2	3.2	66.3
	5	712	15.8	15.8	82.1
	6	139	3.1	3.1	85.2
	7	490	10.9	10.9	96.1
	8	177	3.9	3.9	100.0
	Total	4506	99.9	100.0	
Missing	NA	4	.1		
Total		4510	100.0		

Chapter Summary

This chapter focuses on measures of dispersion, statistics that are used to describe how cases in a distribution tend to be spread out. The three most commonly used measures of dispersion are the range, variance, and standard deviation. The variance and standard deviation are the most commonly used measures of dispersion and are interpreted in relation to the mean. The mean deviation is less common, but learning it plays an important role in understanding the overall concept of dispersion. All these measures are used only with interval/ratio measures.

While it is important to understand the differences between each of these, it is particularly important to understand how they differ from measures of central tendency.

Remember, measures of central tendency tell what is typical about the values of cases in a distribution and measures of dispersion tell us how tightly cases tend to cluster in a distribution. Describing distributions using both measures of central tendency and measures of dispersion allows us to achieve a far more complete understanding of our data. Histograms play an important role by offering visual displays of distributions and the normal curve is very important because it places our understanding of the standard deviation in the context of the theory of probability. We now turn to the theory of probability in Chapter 5.

Exercises

Use the data in the box below to calculate the mean, range, interquartile range, mean deviation, variance, and standard deviation. *Note:* For these exercises our calculations of the variance and standard deviation will use $N - 1$ in the denominator.

5	6	2	8	7	6	6	12	6	5	4	5

1. Mean: _____
2. Range: _____
3. Interquartile range: _____
4. Variance: _____
5. Standard deviation: _____

Find the range, interquartile range, variance, and standard deviation for the following sets of data:

Set A: 9, 6, 7, 4, 6, 4, 8, 7, 6, 3

6. Range: _____
7. Interquartile range: _____
8. Variance: _____
9. Standard deviation: _____

Set B: 9, 4, 18, 1, 16, 2, 17, 4, 15, 4

10. Range: _____
11. Interquartile range: _____
12. Variance: _____
13. Standard deviation: _____

Set C: 2, 30, 28, 5, 9, 20, 6, 11, 20, 9

14. Range: _____
15. Interquartile range: _____
16. Variance: _____
17. Standard deviation: _____

For the tables below, calculate the mode, median, mean, range, interquartile range, variance, and standard deviation.

18. Mode: _____
19. Median: _____
20. Mean: _____
21. Range: _____
22. Interquartile range: _____

Hours Per Day Watching TV

		FREQUENCY	PERCENT	VALID PERCENT	CUMULATIVE PERCENT
Valid	0	56	4.0	4.0	4.0
	1	311	22.0	22.0	25.9
	2	422	29.8	29.8	55.7
	3	282	19.9	19.9	75.6
	4	183	12.9	12.9	88.6
	5	95	6.7	6.7	95.3
	6	67	4.7	4.7	100.0
	Total	1416	100.0	100.0	

23. Variance: _____
24. Standard deviation: _____

Number of Brothers and Sisters

		FREQUENCY	PERCENT	VALID PERCENT	CUMULATIVE PERCENT
Valid	0	82	7.0	7.0	7.0
	1	238	20.3	20.3	27.2
	2	316	26.9	26.9	54.1
	3	264	22.5	22.5	76.6
	4	164	14.0	14.0	90.6
	5	111	9.4	9.4	100.0
	Total	1175	100.0	100.0	

25. Mode: _____
26. Median: _____
27. Mean: _____
28. Range: _____
29. Interquartile range: _____
30. Variance: _____
31. Standard deviation: _____

Age of Respondent

		FREQUENCY	PERCENT	VALID PERCENT	CUMULATIVE PERCENT
Valid	18	5	4.8	4.8	4.8
	19	17	16.2	16.2	21.0
	20	18	17.1	17.1	38.1
	21	22	21.0	21.0	59.0
	22	15	14.3	14.3	73.3
	23	28	26.7	26.7	100.0
	Total	105	100.0	100.0	

Age When First Married

		FREQUENCY	PERCENT	VALID PERCENT	CUMULATIVE PERCENT
Valid	16	32	4.8	4.8	4.8
	17	43	6.4	6.4	11.2
	18	118	17.6	17.6	28.8
	19	129	19.2	19.2	48.0
	20	121	18.0	18.0	66.0
	21	132	19.7	19.7	85.7
	22	96	14.3	14.3	100.0
	Total	671	100.0	100.0	

32. Mode: _____

33. Median: _____

34. Mean: _____

35. Range: _____

36. Interquartile range: _____

37. Variance: _____

38. Standard deviation: _____

39. Mode: _____

40. Median: _____

41. Mean: _____

42. Range: _____

43. Interquartile range: _____

44. Variance: _____

45. Standard deviation: _____

Use the chart below to answer the following questions.

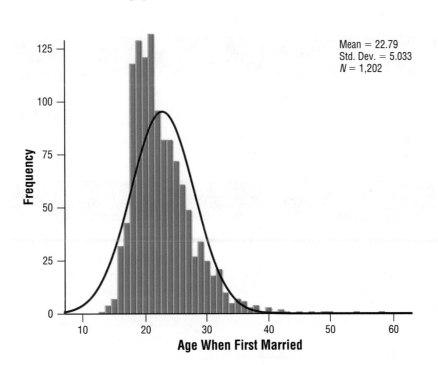

Mean = 22.79
Std. Dev. = 5.033
N = 1,202

46. What is the average age of respondents when they first married? _____

47. How many respondents provided data for this chart? _____

48. What is the variance equal to? _____

Computer Exercises

Use the GSS2006 database to answer the following questions. For some questions, you will need to know how to split the database into groups.

51. What is the standard deviation for age?

52. What is the standard deviation for age among males?

53. What is the standard deviation for age among females?

54. Which group is most dispersed around their respective average age: Whites, Blacks, or Others?

55. What is the range for the variable SEI (Socioeconomic Index)?

49. Based on the properties of the normal curve, we might predict that 68% of all respondents were married between the ages of _____ and _____.

50. Based on the properties of the normal curve, we might predict that 95% of all respondents were married between the ages of _____ and _____.

56. What is the standard deviation for SEI among males?

57. What is the standard deviation for SEI among females?

58. Based on our knowledge of the standard deviation we might predict that, among males, 68% of males will have SEI scores between _____ and _____.

59. Based on our knowledge of the standard deviation we might predict that, among females, 95% of females will have SEI scores between _____ and _____.

60. Using the mean and the standard deviation, compare the distribution of the number of years of education (EDUC) for males with that of females.

Now You Try It Answers

Answers to 1: Males: Range – 13 Mean deviation – 3.75
Females: Range – 5 Mean deviation – 1.5

Answers to 2: Mean – 7 Variance – 10.2 Standard deviation – 3.2
Answers to 3: Variance – 5.8 Standard deviation – 2.4

Key Terms

Box plot, 112
Dispersion, 104
Interquartile range, 111

Mean deviation, 113
Measures of dispersion, 106
Normal curve, 127

Range, 109
Standard deviation, 118
Variance, 115

Works Cited

Daniel J. Evans School of Public Affairs. (2009, April 12). *How to Generate a Lorenz Curve and GINI Coefficient.* Seattle: University of Washington. Retrieved April 14, 2009, from http://www.urbansim.org/docs/tutorials/lorenz-curve.pdf

Faber, D. R., & Krieg, E. J. (2005). *Unequal Exposure to Ecological Hazards 2005: Environmental Injustices in the Commonwealth of Massachusetts.* Boston: Philanthropy and Environmental Justice Research Project at Northeastern University.

Freire, P. (1970). *Pedagogy of the Oppressed.* New York: Herder & Herder.

National Opinion Research Center. (2006). *General Social Survey.* Chicago: Author.

United Nations. (2009). *Human Development Reports.* Retrieved May 18, 2010, from http://hdrstats.undp.org/en/indicators/167.html

CHAPTER

5

Probability and the Normal Curve

Introduction

America is often viewed as a "land of opportunity." Many consider it the place where anyone can grow up to be a rock star, movie star, sports hero, or even president. But what are the odds of something like that happening? The population of the United States is over 300 million people, one of whom is the president. So what is the probability that anyone can grow up to be the president? Probably not as good as your elementary school teachers would have you believe. Whatever it is, it is a very low probability.

Probability The likelihood that a particular event will occur.

We often don't think about the likelihood of particular events taking place because we cannot control them. We know automobile accidents take place every day, but we seldom think about it when we get in the car to go to the grocery store. How about the chance of staying healthy until a ripe old age? What is the probability of finishing high school? Of getting a bachelor's degree? A graduate degree? What are your chances of getting heart disease? Are males more or less likely to die of heart disease? These questions and ones like them are questions of probability. While we know that it may be possible for anyone to grow up to be president, we also know that it is not probable and that it will most likely not happen to us personally. After all, since 1980, only 5 out of more than 300 million people have actually become President of the United States.

Up to this point we have focused on descriptive statistics, the use of statistics to describe distributions. We now turn our attention to inferential statistics, the use of statistics to infer characteristics of a population from a sample. This was discussed briefly in Chapter 4 in a discussion on whether to use N or $N - 1$ in the formula for the standard deviation. We will revisit these considerations in Chapter 6; but for now attention is focused on answering questions related to the basic rules of probability. For example, what is the probability of your favorite baseball player getting a hit in his next at-bat? What is the probability of a football game having more than 50 points scored? Or the probability of having more than six days in July that exceed 90 degrees Fahrenheit?

In this chapter we learn the fundamental principles that underlie our understanding of probability. We learn the addition and multiplication rules of probability, how the normal curve can be used to make predictions, and how these tools can be used to make decisions. Specifically, we learn to calculate the probabilities of particular events occurring and, maybe more importantly, we learn how to take the lessons of probability and apply them to social research. A few symbols and formulas that are used in this chapter are shown in Table 5.1.

TABLE 5.1	*Symbols and Formulas*	
TERM/SYMBOL	**MEANING OF SYMBOL**	**FORMULA**
Probability (*P*)	The likelihood of a particular event occurring	$\dfrac{Number\ of\ outcomes\ in\ the\ event}{Number\ of\ all\ possible\ outcomes\ that\ can\ occur}$
Z-score (standard score)	The value of a particular case (*x*) relative to the mean (μ), measured in units of standard deviation (σ)	$z = \dfrac{x - \mu}{\sigma}$
Percentile	The value of a case below which a percentage of other cases fall	Calculated using Table A

Intelligence, Life Chances, and Inequality

Not many social phenomena are truly random occurrences. In fact, the goal for many if not most social scientists is to uncover the structures and processes that channel behavior into, at least somewhat, predictable patterns. While many of these patterns are easily identifiable (working during the day, eating three meals a day, graduating from school at a particular age), others are more subtle (the type of work we do, the type of food we eat, the number of years of education we receive, and overall intelligence).

Measuring human intelligence has long been a goal for researchers from a variety of academic disciplines, including biology/genetics, psychology, education, and sociology. Each discipline has its own set of explanations of why some people exhibit greater levels of intelligence than others, yet debates exist within each discipline. Is intelligence a genetic trait passed down from parents to children? Are some people predisposed to enjoy academic study more than others? Is our narrow definition of what constitutes intelligence measuring only certain types of intelligence to the exclusion of others? Is intelligence a function of opportunity structures and life chances that are afforded only to some people and not others? Each of these is an important question and each contributes to a more complete understanding of human intelligence. In this way, each field makes important and unique contributions.

German sociologist Max Weber (1864–1920) coined the term "life chances" to describe class position and how it influences opportunities that people have to pursue lifestyles of their choice (Marshall, 1998). Weber theorized that life chances are probabilistic and that being wealthy does not guarantee pathways to upward mobility, it only increases the likelihood that those pathways will present themselves. For example, if you were born into a politically powerful family, such as the Clinton, Bush, or Kennedy family, it is likely that you would have more opportunities to

Life chances Opportunities to achieve personal goals that originate in class standing. Higher class standing affords people greater life chances.

Social capital Networks of relations between individuals.

develop the social capital necessary to go into public office than would people from more typical families. In this case, social capital refers to the number and range of connections one has with other people who are part of the political structure or have access to it. On the other hand, if you were born into a typical working-class family, it is not as likely that you would be able to achieve political prominence; not impossible, but less likely.

Similarly, people raised in wealthier families are more likely to be afforded educational opportunities (educational life chances) than are people raised in lower income families. This is not to say that people from wealthy families are smarter, but they probably do have more opportunities to attend schools of their choice, engage in extracurricular activities, partake in travel opportunities, receive specialized tutoring, and purchase learning resources (computers, software, books, etc.). Figure 5.1 is based on data from the 2006 General Social Survey (National Opinion Research Center, 2006) and offer some support for this hypothesis. People with higher levels of education don't have smarter children, but they do have more resources to provide those children with more educational opportunities. This education can then be parlayed into higher paying jobs, greater levels of social capital, and even more life chances. Is it any wonder then that wealth begets more wealth? This raises questions about how unevenly education is distributed in our society.

Sadly, the process by which social capital generates more social capital is not a common story in the mass media outlets of our time. Instead, we tend to hear more about the opposite—of people with little or no social capital finding ways to "make it to the top." The Horatio Algers of our time tend to consist of lottery winners, professional athletes, and entertainers from poor backgrounds with few life chances who have "pulled themselves up by the bootstraps," symbolizing the American Dream of hard work and success. The marketing of these stories over the internet, radio, television, and magazines smothers the fact that most working-class people have relatively few life chances (compared to the life chances of the wealthy) and lays the blame for failure to achieve these lofty ideals at the feet of those who don't make it to the top. In other words, we are taught to blame individuals for their failures rather than to blame social structures for failing to provide life chances to all people equally. Interestingly, the tendency to "blame the victim" camouflages the very structures that create victims in the first place.

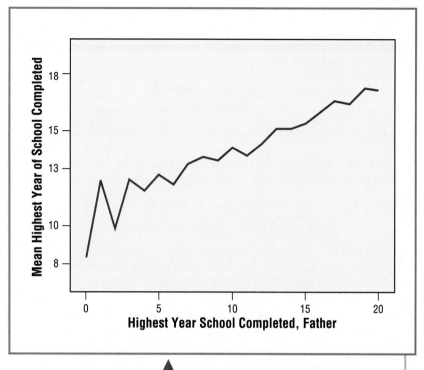

Figure 5.1 **Mean Years of School Completed by Father's Education**

The Fundamentals of Probability

Probability is a useful tool because it allows us to predict the likelihood of events taking place. Probability is used to forecast weather, earthquakes, election results, the impact of social policies, and many other events that impact our lives. You can use it to calculate the probability of winning the lottery, the probability of rolling double sixes with a pair of dice, the probability of getting into a car accident, or the probability of living past a particular age. Statistically, probability is represented as P.

Interestingly, probability is based entirely on theory. If you continue to flip a coin, eventually you will get five heads in a row. You might even get 10 in a row if you flip it enough times; however, if you keep flipping long enough, you will eventually get about 50% heads and 50% tails. Heads and tails will eventually balance out. For example, if you flip a coin 1,000 times, you might get 525 heads and 475 tails. Do it again and those outcomes might be reversed, 525 tails and 475 heads. If we flip the coin an infinite number of times, recording each result, *the theoretical relative frequency* of each is .5. Because we have two possible outcomes, each with a relative frequency of .5, the sum of the two relative frequencies is equal to 1.0. This requires a little more explanation as it will constitute the basis of our calculations for much of the chapter.

Relative frequency The proportion of times that we can expect an event to occur.

Probability can be thought of as the likelihood of a particular event occurring. More specifically, it is the number of outcomes in the event relative to the number of outcomes than can occur. For example, we know that the chance of flipping a coin and having it come up heads is 50/50 because 50% of the time it comes up heads and 50% of the time it comes up tails. Expressed as a proportion, the probability of heads is .5 ($P = .5$). Think of it this way: when we flip a coin, there are two possible outcomes—heads or tails. Therefore, the total number of possible outcomes is two. Out of the two possible outcomes, only one is heads.

$$P = \frac{Number\ of\ outcomes\ in\ the\ event}{Number\ of\ all\ possible\ outcomes\ that\ can\ occur}$$

Using the formula for probability shown above, if we are predicting the likelihood of flipping heads, there is only one head on the coin. And there are only two sides to a coin. Therefore, the number of outcomes in the event ('heads') can occur is one and the number of all possible outcomes that can occur (heads or tails) is two.

$$P = \frac{Number\ of\ outcomes\ in\ the\ event}{Number\ of\ all\ possible\ outcomes\ that\ can\ occur} = \frac{1}{2} = .5$$

If we calculate the probability of getting tails, we get the same probability of .5. The sum of the two probabilities is 1.0. This means that the probability of getting either heads or tails on a flip of the coin is equal to 1.0, a logical conclusion since the coin must come up one or the other. This is shown in Table 5.2.

The same logic can be applied to rolling dice. For example, suppose that we want to know the probability of rolling a die and having it come up "5." Because a die has only one '5' on it, the number of outcomes in the event 'rolling a 5' is equal to one. And because a die has six sides, the number of all possible outcomes that can occur is equal to six. Therefore:

$$P = \frac{Number\ of\ outcomes\ in\ the\ event}{Number\ of\ all\ possible\ outcomes\ that\ can\ occur} = \frac{1}{6} = .167$$

Ultimately, each value on the die (1, 2, 3, 4, 5, and 6) has the same probability of occurring. If we sum these probabilities we get 1.0, just as we did in the coin-flipping example.

When you stop and think about it, this is all pretty amazing! Although we cannot predict the outcome of each toss of a coin or roll of a die, we can predict the long-term trend of tosses of a coin and rolls of a die. Probabilities are expressed as numbers that range between 0 and 1.0, the same way that proportions are expressed. A probability of 0 indicates that an event has no chance of occurring and a probability of 1.0 means that an event will occur no matter what. Generally, when we calculate a probability, we take it to at least three decimal places, as in the example above. The probability of rolling a "5" is equal to .167. This is the same as saying that a "5" will be rolled 16.7% of the

TABLE 5.2

EVENT	PROBABILITY
Heads	.5
Tails	.5
Sum	1.0

TABLE 5.3

EVENT	PROBABILITY
1	.167
2	.167
3	.167
4	.167
5	.167
6	.167
Sum	1.0

time. Of course, rounding is a subjective process that is a function of how specific we need to be. For example, we may only need to round to one decimal place when describing the percent of a population that lives in poverty; however, we may need to round to many more decimal places when determining appropriate dosages for patients receiving chemotherapy.

The Addition Rule of Probability

There are a couple of rules of probability, one of which we have already begun to discuss. It is called the addition rule. The addition rule allows us to determine the probability of a range of outcomes by summing the probability of each individual outcome. Using the example of coin-flipping, we know that the probability of a head is .5 and we know that the probability of a tail is .5. By adding the two probabilities together, we see that the probability of flipping *either* a head *or* a tail is .5 + .5, or 1.0.

The addition rule applies to what are called *disjoint events*. Disjoint events are events in which the occurrence of one event precludes the occurrence of other events. For example, when flipping a coin, if a head comes up, it means that a tail did not/cannot come up.

We can also apply the addition rule to the example of rolling a die. We saw in a previous example that the probability of rolling a "5" is equal to $\frac{1}{6}$, or .167. Suppose we want to know the probability of rolling either a "5" or a "6." We now have two events that can take place out of a total of six possible events. The probability of either event taking place is .167. Therefore, we can sum the two probabilities to determine the probability of either one occurring.

$$P = .167 + 1.67 = .334$$

The probability of rolling either a "5" or a "6" is .334.

Another way, and a better way to avoid rounding errors, of thinking of this is to sum the fractions:

$$\frac{1}{6} + \frac{1}{6} = \frac{2}{6} = .333$$

The probability of rolling either a "5" or a "6" is .333. As you can see, we arrived at two slightly different answers. The reason is because of rounding error. To help avoid rounding error, it is necessary to sum the frequencies rather than summing the individual probabilities. Remember, any time that we sum final answers, we are apt to encounter some rounding error, so try to work with frequencies to avoid this fact.

The Multiplication Rule of Probability

We have seen how to calculate the probability of a range of possible events. Now it is useful to look at the probability of independent events. *Independent events* are events in which the occurrence of one event has no impact on the occurrence of other events.

Disjoint events Events in which the occurrence of one event precludes the occurrence of other events.

Addition rule of probability The probability of a range of possible disjoint events is equal to the sum of their individual probabilities.

Independent events Events in which the occurrence of one event has no impact on the occurrence of other events.

Multiplication rule of probability The probability of independent events occurring simultaneously is equal to the product of their individual probabilities.

For example, we may want to know the probability "of rolling" two 6s in a row with our die. The two rolls are independent because the outcome of the first roll has no influence on the outcome of the second role. In other words, if our first roll is a 6, it neither increases nor diminishes the likelihood of the second roll being a 6.

We can therefore calculate the probability of rolling two 6s in a row as follows.

1. First roll: $P = \dfrac{1}{6} = .167$

2. Second roll: $P = \dfrac{1}{6} = .167$

3. *P of First Roll* $\times$ *P of Second Roll* $= .167 \times .167 = .028$

4. $P = .028$

We could also calculate it as follows:

$$\frac{1}{6} \times \frac{1}{6} = \frac{1}{36} = .028$$

The addition and the multiplication rules are very useful tools in the field of probability. Students often get confused trying to remember which one to use. Here is a helpful hint: If you see a question that contains an *either/or* phrase in it (e.g., What is the probability of buying either a Toyota or a Honda?), use the addition rule. In this case the question is asking for a range of possible outcomes, Toyota or Honda; therefore, the addition rule applies. If, on the other hand, you see a question that contains a *first x, then y* phrase in it (e.g., What is the probability of correctly picking the winner of two consecutive baseball games?), use the multiplication rule. In this case the outcome of one game does not influence the outcome of the second, so the games are considered independent events and thus the multiplication rule applies.

If you have a lot of time on your hands, try rolling a pair of dice 100 times and count how many times you roll double 6s. Theoretically, you should roll double 6s once out of every 36 rolls. Because the outcomes of the two dice are independent, we must use the multiplication rule to calculate the probability of both being a 6. Therefore, our equation is as follows:

$$P = \frac{1}{6} \times \frac{1}{6} = \frac{1}{36} = .028$$

While probability states that we should roll double 6s 2.8% of the time, we might have to roll the dice a hundred times or more before we get double 6s. Remember, probability theory is based on an infinite number of trials or attempts. It is possible, though not probable, to roll double 6s on each of our first two rolls, but then not roll them again for the next 100 attempts. Interestingly, probability cannot predict the outcome of any particular roll of the dice, yet it can predict long-term patterns of outcomes.

Replacement The act of returning a case to the population after it has been selected. Replacement maintains N at its original value. Failure to replace a case means that subsequent calculations must use $N - 1$.

Probability with and without Replacement.   One final consideration in the basic rules of probability is the difference between calculating probabilities with replacement and without replacement. Replacement refers to selecting a case and then putting it back into the list of all possible cases, whereas without replacement refers to selecting a case and then removing it from the list of possible cases. Imagine that we have the whole alphabet of refrigerator magnets, letters A to Z. We put all the letters into a bag so that $N = 26$. Suppose that we want to calculate the probability of selecting the letter A. Because there is only one A out of 26 letters, the probability is equal to $\frac{1}{26} = .038$. Now suppose that we want to calculate the probability of selecting the letter B. Our formula is the same as it was for selecting the letter A only if we put the letter A back into the bag. If we do not put the letter A back in the bag, then the formula for the probability of selecting the letter B is $\frac{1}{25} = .04$. This is the difference between probability with replacement and probability without replacement.

Now You Try It 1

See if you can calculate probabilities for the following events. Be sure to ask yourself if the events are disjoint or independent, so that you use the appropriate rule (if necessary).

Imagine a box with 10 ping pong balls in it. The balls are numbered 1–10.

1. What is the probability of selecting the ball with a number 7 on it?
2. What is the probability of selecting either the ball with a number 7 or a number 8 on it?
3. What is the probability of selecting on consecutive picks (without replacement) the ball with a number 3, followed by the ball with a number 2, followed by the ball with a number 1?

Probability Using Frequency Tables

Although it may not be immediately obvious, it is a small step to move from flipping coins and rolling dice to working with social data. For example, Table 5.4 shows data taken from the 2006 General Social Survey. The number of years of education is operationalized as "Less than 12 Years," "12 Years," and "More than 12 Years."

TABLE 5.4 *Education*

		FREQUENCY	PERCENT	VALID PERCENT	CUMULATIVE PERCENT
Valid	Less than 12 Years	781	17.3	17.3	17.3
	12 Years	1,204	26.7	26.7	44.0
	More than 12 Years	2,525	56.0	56.0	100.0
	Total	4,510	100.0	100.0	

Assuming that our sample is random, 17.3% of the population has less than 12 years of education, 26.7% has 12 years of education, and 56.0% has more than 12 years of education. Therefore, out of our 4,510 respondents, the probability of randomly selecting a respondent with less than 12 years of education is $P = .173$. Similarly, the probability of randomly selecting a respondent with 12 years of education is .267. To get this, we divide the percentage by 100 to obtain the proportion, which is equal to the probability.

The addition and multiplication rules hold true when working with frequency tables the same way they do when working with dice-rolling or coin-flipping. Suppose we want to know the probability of selecting either a respondent with less than 12 years of education or a respondent with more than 12 years of education. Because we have

781 respondents with less than 12 years and 2,525 respondents with more than 12 years, using the addition rule, our equation looks as follows:

$$P = \frac{781 + 2,525}{4,510} = .733$$

Now suppose we want to know the probability of selecting first a respondent with less than 12 years of education followed by a respondent with more than 12 years of education. To do this we must (1) calculate separate probabilities for the two events and then (2) multiply those probabilities together to find our answer. The equations look as follows:

$$P\ for\ Less\ than\ 12\ Years = \frac{781}{4,510} = .173$$

$$P\ for\ More\ than\ 12\ Years = \frac{2,525}{4,509} = .560$$

Multiplying the two probabilities, we get: $.173 \times .560 = .097$

Therefore, the probability of selecting first a respondent with less than 12 years of education followed by a respondent with more than 12 years of education is .097. It is also possible to solve the equation as follows:

$$P = \frac{781}{4,510} \times \frac{2,525}{4,509} = \frac{1,972,025}{20,340,100} = .097$$

Either technique is acceptable and choice usually depends on which makes more logical sense to the person doing the calculation.

Getting back to our discussion of Weber's concept of "life chances" from Chapter 1, Table 5.5 shows the distribution of education by race. As you can see, among White respondents, 59.0% have more than 12 years of education ($P = .590$) compared to 52.4% of Black respondents ($P = .542$) and only 42.9% of Other ($P = .429$). It is important to realize that these probabilities are calculated using the number of respondents within each subgroup of race. In other words, it is important to specify which populations our probabilities are based on when doing calculations.

TABLE 5.5 *Education*

RACE OF RESPONDENT			FREQUENCY	PERCENT	VALID PERCENT	CUMULATIVE PERCENT
WHITE	Valid	Less than 12 Years	428	13.0	13.0	13.0
		12 Years	917	27.9	27.9	41.0
		More than 12 Years	1,939	59.0	59.0	100.0
		Total	3,284	100.0	100.0	
BLACK	Valid	Less than 12 Years	137	21.6	21.6	21.6
		12 Years	165	26.0	26.0	47.6
		More than 12 Years	332	52.4	52.4	100.0
		Total	634	100.0	100.0	
OTHER	Valid	Less than 12 Years	216	36.5	36.5	36.5
		12 Years	122	20.6	20.6	57.1
		More than 12 Years	254	42.9	42.9	100.0
		Total	592	100.0	100.0	

EXAMPLE 1

Education, Race, and Life Chances

Consider the following statements:

1. Among Whites, what is the probability of randomly selecting a respondent with less than 12 years of education?
2. What is the probability of selecting a respondent who is White and has less than 12 years of education?

The first statement specifies that the population upon which the probability should be determined is "Whites." Therefore, our equation is as follows:

$$P = \frac{428}{3,284} = .130$$

The second statement specifies a population consisting of Whites, Blacks, and Others, thereby increasing the value of the denominator. Therefore our equation is as follows:

$$P = \frac{428}{3,284 + 634 + 592} = .095$$

Now You Try It 2

Use the frequency table below to answer the following questions.

Marital Status

		FREQUENCY	PERCENT	VALID PERCENT	CUMULATIVE PERCENT
Valid	MARRIED	2,170	48.1	48.2	48.2
	WIDOWED	366	8.1	8.1	56.3
	DIVORCED	732	16.2	16.3	72.6
	SEPARATED	156	3.5	3.5	76.0
	NEVER MARRIED	1,080	23.9	24.0	100.0
	Total	4,504	99.9	100.0	
Missing	NA	6	.1		
Total		4,510	100.0		

1. What is the probability of randomly selecting a divorced respondent?
2. What is the probability of randomly selecting either a married or a widowed respondent?
3. What is the probability of selecting first a separated respondent, then a never married respondent on consecutive turns?
4. What is the probability of selecting, on consecutive picks, first either a widowed or a divorced respondent and second a separated respondent?

Eye on the Applied

The Gamblers Fallacy and a Trip to the Casino

In the movie *Ocean's Eleven*, Danny Ocean, played by actor George Clooney, states, "Cause the house always wins. Play long enough, you never change the stakes. The house takes you. Unless, when that perfect hand comes along, you bet big, then you take the house." It seems logical that the house always wins because if they lost money, casinos would not be able to remain in business. Therefore, they must take in more money than they pay out. How do they do it?

Many gamblers don't understand probability or the odds they face and continue to gamble on the rationale of "feeling lucky." The probability of winning money in modern casinos is electronically controlled. Slot machines are run by computers that are programmed to generate winners a given number of times per 100 coins deposited. Let's suppose that for every 100 coins deposited, a slot machine will generate 10 winners who receive eight coins each. That means the probability of winning is 10/100 or .10. If you played this machine an infinite number of times, you would eventually win back 80 coins for every 100 you deposited. You never know if you are going to win three times in a row or only once in 30 tries or once in 300 tries; but over the long haul, you win only 80 coins for each 100 spent. This is how the house always wins—they are guaranteed 20 coins for each 100 deposited, a 20% return. For the house, this is a statistically calculated business transaction. For many gamblers, it is a "lucky feeling." Would you rather be the house or the gambler?

Another way of analyzing life chances is to see if levels of education reproduce themselves across generations. For example, how likely are people who receive less than a high school degree to have parents who also received less than a high school degree? And how likely are people who receive a college degree to have parents who also received a college degree? To test this, we can split our database by "Mother's Highest Degree" and then run a frequency table for Respondent's Highest Degree. The results are shown in Table 5.6.

The data support the claim that Mother's Highest Degree has an effect on Respondent's Highest Degree. For example, of those whose mother received less than a high school degree, 29.9% received less than a high school degree. This means that children whose mother received less than a high school degree have only a .701 probability of receiving at least a high school degree. By contrast, children whose mother received a high school degree have a .943 probability of receiving at least a high school degree. And

TABLE 5.6 *Respondent's Highest Degree*

MOTHER'S HIGHEST DEGREE			FREQUENCY	PERCENT	VALID PERCENT	CUMULATIVE PERCENT
LT HIGH SCHOOL	Valid	LT HIGH SCHOOL	276	29.9	29.9	29.9
		HIGH SCHOOL	452	48.9	48.9	78.8
		JUNIOR COLLEGE	58	6.3	6.3	85.1
		BACHELOR	88	9.5	9.5	94.6
		GRADUATE	50	5.4	5.4	100.0
		Total	924	100.0	100.0	
HIGH SCHOOL	Valid	LT HIGH SCHOOL	72	5.7	5.7	5.7
		HIGH SCHOOL	713	56.3	56.3	62.0
		JUNIOR COLLEGE	137	10.8	10.8	72.8
		BACHELOR	237	18.7	18.7	91.5
		GRADUATE	108	8.5	8.5	100.0
		Total	1,267	100.0	100.0	
JUNIOR COLLEGE	Valid	LT HIGH SCHOOL	5	3.6	3.6	3.6
		HIGH SCHOOL	49	35.3	35.3	38.8
		JUNIOR COLLEGE	25	18.0	18.0	56.8
		BACHELOR	45	32.4	32.4	89.2
		GRADUATE	15	10.8	10.8	100.0
		Total	139	100.0	100.0	
BACHELOR	Valid	LT HIGH SCHOOL	5	1.9	1.9	1.9
		HIGH SCHOOL	85	32.3	32.3	34.2
		JUNIOR COLLEGE	25	9.5	9.5	43.7
		BACHELOR	101	38.4	38.4	82.1
		GRADUATE	47	17.9	17.9	100.0
		Total	263	100.0	100.0	
GRADUATE	Valid	LT HIGH SCHOOL	4	3.3	3.3	3.3
		HIGH SCHOOL	39	32.0	32.0	35.2
		JUNIOR COLLEGE	9	7.4	7.4	42.6
		BACHELOR	29	23.8	23.8	66.4
		GRADUATE	41	33.6	33.6	100.0
		Total	122	100.0	100.0	
NAP	Valid	LT HIGH SCHOOL	296	17.5	17.6	17.6
		HIGH SCHOOL	881	52.2	52.3	69.9
		JUNIOR COLLEGE	115	6.8	6.8	76.7
		BACHELOR	254	15.1	15.1	91.8
		GRADUATE	138	8.2	8.2	100.0
		Total	1,684	99.8	100.0	
	Missing	NA	3	.2		
	Total		1,687	100.0		

(Continued)

TABLE 5.6 *Continued*

	MOTHER'S HIGHEST DEGREE		FREQUENCY	PERCENT	VALID PERCENT	CUMULATIVE PERCENT
DK	Valid	LT HIGH SCHOOL	23	29.5	29.5	29.5
		HIGH SCHOOL	47	60.3	60.3	89.7
		JUNIOR COLLEGE	2	2.6	2.6	92.3
		BACHELOR	5	6.4	6.4	98.7
		GRADUATE	1	1.3	1.3	100.0
		Total	78	100.0	100.0	
NA	Valid	LT HIGH SCHOOL	10	33.3	33.3	33.3
		HIGH SCHOOL	7	23.3	23.3	56.7
		JUNIOR COLLEGE	6	20.0	20.0	76.7
		BACHELOR	4	13.3	13.3	90.0
		GRADUATE	3	10.0	10.0	100.0
		Total	30	100.0	100.0	

children whose mother received a bachelor's degree have a .981 probability of receiving at least a high school degree.

As these data indicate, institutional forces do have the potential to reproduce existing class structure. While the data in this table do not tell us why this is the case, it is likely that a lack of resources and opportunity rather than academic ability holds some students back. Clearly, life chances are a function of the social strata in which we live.

Probability and the Normal Curve

Before getting too far into this discussion, it's worth repeating that the normal curve is only a theoretical construct. In other words, while many distributions may approximate the shape of a normal curve, we assume that the normal curve only exists as an ideal, not as a reality. It is important, however, to learn the theory before we move on to adjusting for the difference between theory and reality (the subject of Chapter 6).

You may recall from Chapter 4 that the normal curve has special properties related to the mean and standard deviation. Specifically, for any normal curve, about 34% of all cases fall between the mean and +1 standard deviations from the mean. Similarly, about 34% of all cases fall between the mean and −1 standard deviations from the mean. Therefore, we can say that about 68% of all cases in a distribution fall within one standard deviation of the mean. This is represented by the shaded area under the curve in Figure 5.2.

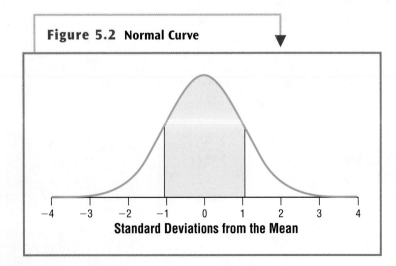

Figure 5.2 Normal Curve

Standard Deviations from the Mean

Based on this logic, we can conclude that as we move away from the mean (in either direction), a certain percentage of cases are located between the mean and the distance we have moved away from the mean. When we get to a full standard deviation from the mean, we can expect that about 34% of all the cases will fall between the mean and 1 standard deviation. Therefore, as we go from .1 standard deviations above or below the mean to .2 standard deviations all the way up to 4.0 standard deviations from the mean, we are steadily increasing our percentage of cases that fall between the mean and our number of standard deviations above or below the mean. This is a very useful property of the normal curve, as we shall now see.

EXAMPLE 2

Student Test Scores

Suppose that we give an exam to a group of students and find that the scores are normally distributed with a mean of 75 and a standard deviation of 6, as shown in Figure 5.3. Now suppose that we have a student who received a grade of 81 on the exam. We can express this student's score in either of two ways. The first is as a raw score of 81. The second is as a standardized score. Standardized scores are the number of standard deviations a case falls from the mean; they are also referred to as z-scores.

Integrating Technology

A number of online statistics "applets" can be found with a simple Internet search. One of these applets that is particularly useful in demonstrating the concept of randomness in the normal curve can be found at http://www.ms.uky.edu/~mai/java/stat/GaltonMachine.html. In it, ping pong balls are dropped into the top center point of a matrix of "bumpers." Under the matrix is an outline of a normal curve. As the balls make their way through the matrix, bouncing randomly, they tend to take the shape of a normal curve with very few making it out to the tails of the distribution and most falling into the center of the distribution. Applets such as this help us to visualize statistics and to better understand the random nature of distribution curves.

Z-Scores

In this example, Student A received an 81, which is 6 points above the mean. The standard deviation happens to be equal to 6 points. Therefore, our student who received an 81 is +1 standard deviation above the mean. This student's z-score is equal to +1. For Student B who receives a grade that is 6 points below the mean, 69, or one standard deviation below the mean, the z-score is equal to −1.

The formula to calculate z-scores is:

$$z = \frac{x - \mu}{\sigma}$$

In this formula

- x is equal to the raw score that is to be standardized
- μ is equal to the population mean
- σ is equal to the standard deviation of the population

z-scores Also known as standardized scores, z-scores tell us how many standard deviations a particular case falls from the mean. Cases above the mean have positive z-scores and cases below the mean have negative z-scores.

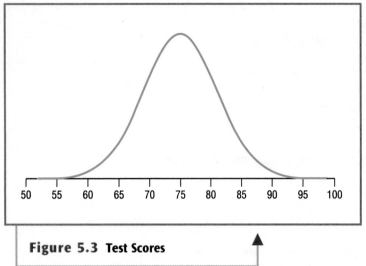

Figure 5.3 Test Scores

It is important to remember that we are dealing with theoretical concepts, therefore we use the population parameters (μ and σ) rather than $\overline{X}$ and s. In Chapter 6, we look at how to make corrections for the differences between samples and populations; but for now we focus on the theoretical concepts. The z-score calculations for Student A and Student B are shown below.

$$\text{Student A: } z = \frac{x - \mu}{\sigma} = \frac{81 - 75}{6} = \frac{6}{6} = 1$$

$$\text{Student B: } z = \frac{x - \mu}{\sigma} = \frac{69 - 75}{6} = \frac{-6}{6} = -1$$

As you can see, z-scores allow us to express each student's performance in relation to the mean in standardized units. It is a new way of expressing individuals' scores. While this may not have obvious uses when dealing with only one population, such as a group of students in a class, it has very useful applications when comparing students' performance across different populations. For example, suppose you and a friend each take the SAT test. You happen to live in New York City and your friend happens to live in Los Angeles. Let's say that you get a combined SAT score of 1250 and your friend in LA gets a combined SAT score of 1280. At first glance it may appear that your friend scored higher than you; however, we need to ask a couple of questions to confirm this.

The first question we should ask is, "What was the mean score for each test?" and the second question is "What is the standard deviation for each test?" With this information, we can standardize the scores and compare them across populations (NYC and LA). Table 5.7 provides us with the necessary information to standardize each test score.

The z-scores are calculated as follows:

$$\text{Your z-score: } z = \frac{x - \mu}{\sigma} = \frac{1250 - 1180}{35} = \frac{70}{35} = 2$$

$$\text{Friend's z-score: } z = \frac{x - \mu}{\sigma} = \frac{1280 - 1230}{50} = \frac{50}{50} = 1$$

Relative to the average score for each city's test, you actually scored higher than your friend. Whereas you scored two standard deviations above the mean for your

TABLE 5.7

YOU (NEW YORK CITY)	FRIEND (LOS ANGELES)
Score (x) = 1250	Score (x) = 1280
Mean (μ) = 1180	Mean (μ) = 1230
Standard deviation (σ) = 35	Standard deviation (σ) = 50

group, your friend scored only one standard deviation above the mean for her group. Assuming that not all SAT exams are of equal difficulty (in other words, some are harder than others), we conclude that the New York City test was more difficult because it has a lower average score (μ). In contrast to raw scores, which do not take the mean and standard deviation into account, z-scores allow us to compare scores across different populations.

Now You Try It 3

Calculating z-Scores (Standardized Scores)

Imagine that we survey a group of employees at a local company and find that the average hourly wage is $14.25 with a standard deviation of $1.80.

1. What is the z-score for an employee who makes $15.00 per hour?
2. What is the z-score for an employee who makes $13.50 per hour?
3. What is the z-score for an employee who makes $17.50 per hour?

Imagine that we survey a group of communities and find that the average annual family income is $47,525. We also find that the standard deviation for these communities is $6,330.

4. What is the z-score for a community with an average family income of $36,000?
5. What is the z-score for a community with an average family income of $55,987?

Statistical Uses and Misuses

Expressing the value of a particular case as a standard score (z-score) helps not only to compare cases across populations but also helps put variables of different scales into a common scale. For example, suppose we want to operationalize a variable that reflects a community's capacity to control the quality of its local environment. Research shows that working-class communities and communities of color tend to bear a disproportionate burden from ecological hazards relative to middle-class communities and white communities. Therefore, we might decide to combine income and the percentage of a community's population that is nonwhite into a single variable called "Control Capacity."

One challenge in developing such a variable is to find a way to combine income (which may consist of values like $36,245) with the percentage of a community's population that is nonwhite (which may consist of values like 6.2%). Z-scores can simplify this problem.

SPSS for Windows has the ability to read all of the cases for a variable, determine the average, and express the z-score for each case as a second variable. For example, suppose that data in the table below represent the median family income, percent of population that is white, and number of hazardous waste sites for 15 towns.

TOWN	SITES	MEDIAN HOUSEHOLD INCOME ($)	% WHITE	Z INCOME	Z % WHITE	Z INCOME + Z % WHITE (CONTROL CAPACITY)
1	10	55,690	89	−.19	−.18	−.37
2	12	59,400	92	.08	.25	.33
3	14	55,524	91	−.21	.11	−.10

(Continued)

TOWN	SITES	MEDIAN HOUSEHOLD INCOME ($)	% WHITE	Z INCOME	Z % WHITE	Z INCOME + Z % WHITE (CONTROL CAPACITY)
4	6	72,318	94	1.05	.53	1.58
5	20	34,965	73	−1.74	−2.44	−4.18
6	13	60,900	92	.20	.25	.45
7	18	48,601	82	−.72	−1.17	−1.89
8	5	68,905	93	.80	.39	1.19
9	0	88,990	96	2.30	.82	3.12
10	23	31,520	75	−2.00	−2.16	−4.16
11	16	48,450	83	−.74	−1.03	−1.77
12	12	58,332	86	.00	−.60	−.60
13	10	58,900	94	.05	.53	.58
14	9	57,350	96	−.07	.82	.75
15	14	39,860	92	−1.38	.25	−1.13
16	7	66,972	98	.65	1.10	1.75
17	3	71,100	98	.96	1.10	2.06
18	8	66,900	96	.65	.82	1.47
19	12	59,500	92	.09	.25	.34
20	10	61,200	93	.22	.39	.51

The mean number of waste sites is 11.1 with a standard deviation of 5.6.
The mean White is 90.3 with a standard deviation of 7.1.
The mean income is $58,269 with a standard deviation of $13,358.

We could hypothesize on the basis of previous findings in the field that higher median income and a greater percentage of the population that is white act as a "barrier" to protect communities from contamination from toxic hazards. By adding the z-scores for each town's income and % White, we effectively create a new ratio variable that can be used to measure the degree of "insulating factors" in communities. For example, in community 1, if we add the z-score for income (−.19) to the z-score for % White (−.18),

we get a combined score of −.37. This tells us that the community's lower income and lower percentage of white population combine to put it at greater risk of toxic contamination.

Whether our new variable actually predicts the number of sites in each community remains unknown, however, this demonstrates the usefulness of z-scores in creating standard units out of variables originally operationalized in completely different scales.

Calculating Probabilities with the Normal Curve

We can think of the total area under a normal curve as equal to 1.0. Therefore, 50% of the area under the curve falls to the left of the mean and 50% falls to the right of the mean. Figures 5.4 and 5.5 show that as we move away from the mean, the area between the mean and our z-score changes; however, the total area between the mean and the tail of the distribution always remains 50%. Therefore, it is possible to determine how this area under the normal curve is divided for any z-score value.

As you can see from Figures 5.4 and 5.5, the total area under the curve is always equal to 100%, with 50% on either side of the mean. Moving away from the mean

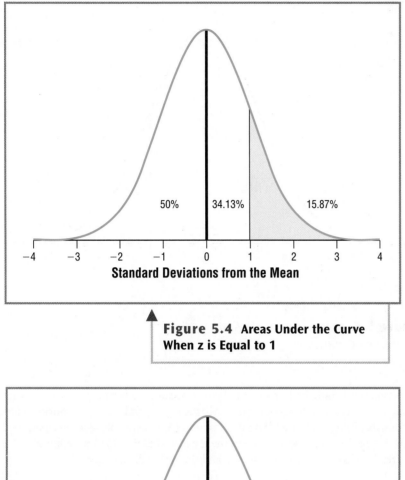

Figure 5.4 Areas Under the Curve When z is Equal to 1

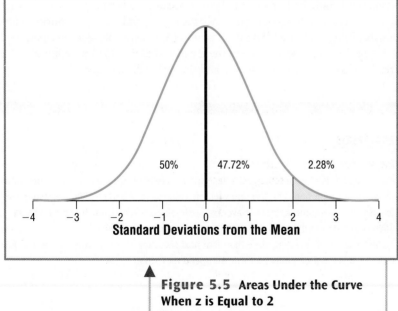

Figure 5.5 Areas Under the Curve When z is Equal to 2

increases the area under the curve between the mean and z and decreases the area between the z and the tail of the curve; but the sum of the two regions (between the mean and z and beyond z) is always 50%.

Fortunately for us, statisticians have already calculated all of the possible areas under the normal curve for different z values. These values are shown in Table A in Appendix A.

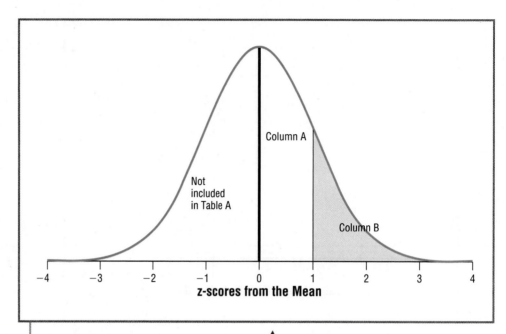

Figure 5.6 **Referencing Table A in the Normal Curve.**

Table A represents only half of a normal curve because each half is a mirror image of the other. So imagine that Table A describes only the right-hand side of the normal curve. The table consists of three columns. The first column (A) consists of z-score values; the second column (B) consists of the area between the mean and z; and the third column (C) consists of the area beyond z (the area between z and the tail of distribution).

EXAMPLE 3

Paying for College Textbooks

At the beginning of each semester, college students nationwide shell out incredible sums of money for their books for the semester, oftentimes far exceeding $500. Let's suppose, for the sake of argument, that the average textbook expenditure for students is in fact $500 with a standard deviation of $40. Because the mean is $500, we know that we have a 50/50 chance of spending more than that next semester *(P = .5)*. Now let's pose a question: What is the probability that you will spend more than $550?

To answer this question, we must first calculate a z-score for $550 using the z-score formula:

$$z = \frac{x - \mu}{\sigma}$$

In this example,

- *x* is equal to $550
- μ is equal to $500
- σ is equal to $40

Therefore,

$$z = \frac{550 - 500}{40} = \frac{50}{40} = 1.25$$

We now know that a semester in which we spend $550 on textbooks is 1.25 standard deviations above the mean. This can be thought of in either of two ways: Figure 5.7 shows the distribution in units of standard deviation and Figure 5.8 shows the distribution in units of dollars. The two figures show the same data.

Because our original question was "What is the probability of spending more than $550?" we must focus our attention on the tail of the distribution, the shaded area that indicates amounts of $550 or more (or the shaded area that indicates z-scores of 1.25 and greater). In Table A, this means that we are concerned with the area "Beyond Z."

When we locate $z = 1.25$ and read Column B (area beyond z), we find a value of .1056. This is the probability of having a semester in which we spend more than $550 on textbooks ($P = .1056$). Conversely, we have a .8944 probability of having a semester in

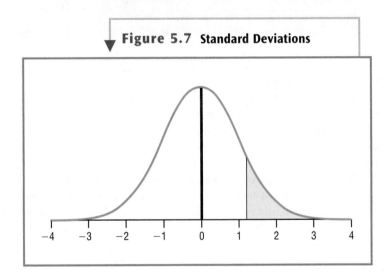

Figure 5.7 **Standard Deviations**

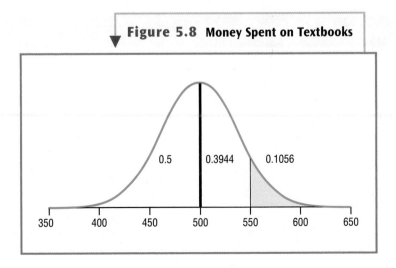

Figure 5.8 **Money Spent on Textbooks**

which we spend less than $550 because .3944 + .5 = .8944. We also know that we have a .3944 probability of spending between $500 and $550.

These probabilities can be used just like the probabilities we found earlier with coin-flipping and dice-rolling. For example, let's suppose we want to know the probability of spending more than $550 two semesters in a row. In this case, because the two events are independent from one another, we use the multiplication rule and multiply the probability of spending more than $550 by itself (.1056 × .1056 = .011). We now know that we have a probability of only .011 (a 1.1% chance) of having to spend more than $550 two semesters in a row.

We may also ask ourselves "What is the probability of spending either more than $550 or less than $500?" In this case because the two events are disjointed, we would use the addition rule to sum the two probabilities (.1056 + .5 = .6056). We now know that we have a probability of .6056 of spending either less than $500 or more than $550 in any given semester.

Integrating Technology

SPSS for Windows has a unique feature that transforms raw scores into z-scores for any interval/ratio variable. This can be useful for a variety of statistical calculations; but it also benefits researchers by providing a unique visualization of data when it is sorted. For example, suppose we have data representing the socioeconomic index of 19 respondents. If we list the cases in the order they appear in our database, we get Table A on the next page. If you first transform the raw scores into z-scores and sort the data, we can generate Table B on the next page.

TABLE A

	CASE SUMMARIES[a]
	RESPONDENT SOCIOECONOMIC INDEX
1	35.7
2	36.5
3	38.4
4	62.0
5	44.7
6	49.6
7	68.1
8	91.2
9	76.4
10	43.4
11	38.4
12	22.9
13	64.1
14	37.7
15	84.7
16	32.7
17	63.5
18	33.6
19	50.7
Total N	19

a. Limited to first 100 cases.

TABLE B

	CASE SUMMARIES[a]	
	RESPONDENT SOCIOECONOMIC INDEX	Z-SCORE: RESPONDENT SOCIOECONOMIC INDEX
1	22.9	−1.48180
2	32.7	−.97009
3	33.6	−.92310
4	35.7	−.81345
5	36.5	−.77168
6	37.7	−.70902
7	38.4	−.67247
8	38.4	−.67247
9	43.4	−.41140
10	44.7	−.34352
11	49.6	−.08767
12	50.7	−.03023
13	62.0	.55980
14	63.5	.63812
15	64.1	.66945
16	68.1	.87831
17	76.4	1.31169
18	84.7	1.74507
19	91.2	2.08446
Total N	19	19

a. Limited to first 100 cases.

As you can see, by virtue of sorting the cases and expressing them as both raw scores and z-scores, we are better able to visualize the overall dispersion of the data and the position of cases in relation to the mean.

EXAMPLE 4

Years of Education

According to the 2006 General Social Survey, Americans average 13 years of education ($\mu = 13.29$) with a standard deviation of 3 ($\sigma = 3.23$). For Whites the mean is higher ($\mu = 13.66$, $\sigma = 2.93$) and for Blacks the mean is lower ($\mu = 12.87$, $\sigma = 2.95$). At first glance, the two groups don't seem radically different from one another; however, we must look more closely to be sure.

Suppose we want to compare Blacks and Whites by determining the probabilities of randomly selecting a person with 15 or more years of education. The equations to determine the z-score in each group is shown below:

For Whites: $z = \dfrac{x - \mu}{\sigma} = \dfrac{15 - 13.66}{2.93} = \dfrac{1.34}{2.93} = .46$

For Blacks: $z = \dfrac{x - \mu}{\sigma} = \dfrac{15 - 12.87}{2.95} = \dfrac{2.13}{2.95} = .72$

Z-scores allow us to use Table A to determine the probabilities of selecting respondents with 15 or more years of education. As Figures 5.9 and 5.10 show, we are concerned with area beyond the z-scores. For Whites, when we go to a z-score of .46 in Table A and read the value in column B, we find that the probability is equal to $P = .3228$. Therefore, Whites have a .3228 probability of having 15 or more years of education. Another way

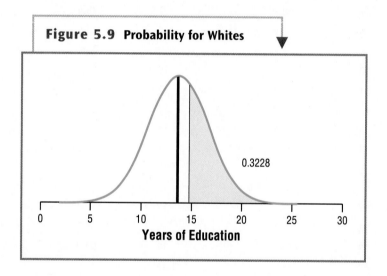

Figure 5.9 Probability for Whites

0.3228

Years of Education

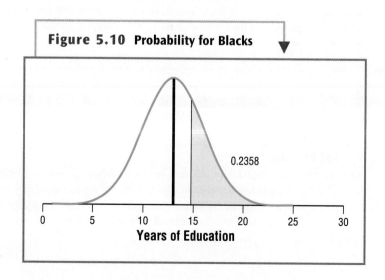

Figure 5.10 Probability for Blacks

0.2358

Years of Education

of thinking about this is that we can now predict that 32.28% of Whites have 15 or more years of education.

For Blacks, when we go to a z-score of .72 in Table A and read the value in column B, we find that the probability is equal to $P = .2358$. Therefore, Blacks have a .2358 probability of having 15 or more years of education. Another way of thinking about this is that we can now predict that 23.58% of Blacks have 15 or more years of education. Overall, Whites are about 9% more likely to receive 15 or more years of education than are Blacks. This difference represents significant differences in the life chances available in the two populations.

Now You Try It 4

Suppose we find that the average height among a group of college males is 5'10" (70 inches) with a standard deviation of 2.5 inches. Use this information to calculate the probability of randomly selecting:

1. A male who is more than 72 inches tall.
2. A male who is less than 73 inches tall.
3. A male more than 65 inches tall.
4. A male between 66 and 71 inches tall.

Now suppose you want to calculate the probabilities for different seasonal snowfall amounts in Lake Placid, New York. You find that the average seasonal snowfall is 200 inches with a standard deviation of 15 inches. Use this information to calculate the probabilities of the following events.

5. A season in which they get more than 210 inches of snow.
6. A season in which they get less than 165 inches of snow.
7. A season in which they get more than 175 inches of snow.
8. A season in which they get between 175 and 210 inches of snow.

Hint: It is very useful to draw a normal curve and shade in the area that represents the answer. This will make it easier to visualize the problem and use Table A.

Using Z-Scores to Find Percentiles

Now that we have seen how to calculate the area under the normal curve, it is a small step to learn how to use the normal curve to calculate percentiles. You have probably heard of percentiles before, particularly in reference to test scores or class rank. Percentiles are a way of standardizing scores to better understand their relative position in a distribution. For example, a student who takes the SAT exam and scores in the 88th percentile is ranked higher than a student who is ranked in the 80th percentile. Unlike z-scores, which can have negative values, percentiles are always positive and range from 0 to 100.

On a normal curve, the lowest possible score is represented by 0 and the highest possible score is represented by the 100th percentile. To determine the percentile for a particular case, it is necessary to (1) calculate the z-score for that case and

Percentile The value of a particular case below which a certain percent of all cases fall.

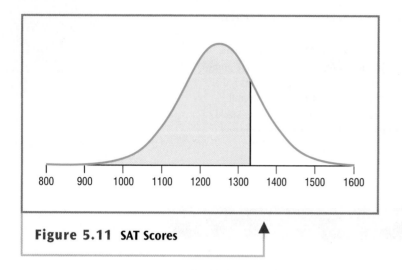

Figure 5.11 **SAT Scores**

(2) locate the probability for that case using Table A. For example, suppose that a student scores 1330 on his SAT exam. The mean score is 1250 with a standard deviation of 40 ($\mu = 1250, \sigma = 40$). Using the formula for z, we find that:

$$z = \frac{x - \mu}{\sigma} = \frac{1330 - 1250}{40} = \frac{80}{40} = 2.00$$

Using Table A, we find that the area between the mean and z is equal to .4772 and the area beyond z is equal to .0228. The distribution is shown in Figure 5.11.

The percentile for an SAT score of 1330 can be calculated in one of two ways. The first method is to take all of the area under the curve (1.0) and subtract from it the area beyond z (.0228). This leaves only the shaded area under the curve in Figure 5.11. Therefore:

$$\text{Percentile} = 1 - .0228 = .9772$$

After rounding, this means that an SAT score of 1330 falls in the 98th percentile because 98% of the area under the curve falls in the shaded area. A second way to calculate the percentile is to find the area under the curve that falls between the mean and z (.4772) and add to it the other side of the curve (.5). Therefore:

$$\text{Percentile} = .4772 + .5 = .9772$$

It is important to note that it almost always helps to draw a rough sketch of a normal curve and shade in the area we are trying to find. For example, suppose a student scores 1180 on their SAT exam. In this case, the percentile we wish to find is below 50 because the shaded area under the curve does not reach all the way to the mean (as shown in Figure 5.12).

Therefore, when we use Table A, we need only to look for the area beyond z. In this case, the area beyond z is equal to .0401, placing this score in the 4th percentile.

Figure 5.12 **SAT Scores**

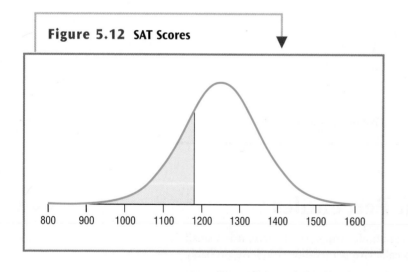

Now You Try It 5

Suppose that you do a study of people who commute to your campus and find that the average commuting time is 17.4 minutes with a standard deviation of 4.1 minutes ($\mu = 17.4, \sigma = 4.1$).

1. What is the percentile ranking for a person who commutes 20.2 minutes?
2. What is the percentile ranking for a person who commutes 14.7 minutes?

Chapter Summary

This chapter has introduced the basic concepts that make up the theory of probability. Using a wide range of examples, emphasis is placed on (1) the two basic rules of probability (the addition rule and the multiplication rule), (2) how probability can be applied to frequency tables, (3) how probability can be applied to the concept of the normal curve, (4) the concept of z-scores, and (5) how z-scores can be applied to the normal curve to determine probabilities and percentile rankings. It is important to stress that the lessons in this chapter constitute the building blocks for future concepts. Specifically, Chapter 6 looks at the process of moving from how probability works in theory to how we apply probability to sample data.

Exercises

Remember, probability is always expressed as ($P = .xx$). Example: What is the probability of getting "heads" when you flip a coin? $P = .50$. Do not answer in percentage form if the question asks for probability. Put your answers on the answer sheet and turn in only the answer sheet.

1. What is the probability of rolling a 5 with a die that has nine sides?

2. What is the probability of rolling either a 5 or a 4 with a die that has nine sides?

3. What is the probability of rolling a 5 with a nine-sided die, then rolling another 5 with the same die?

4. Four people are sitting on a couch. Two are wearing red shirts, one is wearing a blue shirt, and one is wearing a green shirt. What is the probability of a person with a red shirt being the next one to get up and walk out the door?

5. Seventeen people are sitting in a room. Fifteen of them are female and two are male. If we randomly select a person, what is the probability that the person will be male?

6. Using the same scenario as in question #5, if we randomly select two people (without replacement), what is the probability that they will both be female?

Use the frequency table below to answer questions 7 through 12. $N = 819$.

Think of Self as Liberal or Conservative

		FREQUENCY	PERCENT	VALID PERCENT	CUMULATIVE PERCENT
Valid	Extremely liberal	16	1.9	2.0	2.0
	Liberal	94	10.9	11.5	13.4
	Slightly liberal	119	13.9	14.5	28.0
	Moderate	312	36.3	38.1	66.1
	Slightly conservative	129	15.0	15.8	81.8
	Conservative	127	14.8	15.5	97.3
	Extremely conservative	22	2.6	2.7	100.0
	Total	819	95.3	100.0	
Missing	DK	34	4.0		
	NA	6	.7		
	Total	40	4.7		
Total		859	100.0		

7. What is the probability of randomly selecting a respondent who claims to be "moderate"?

8. What is the probability of randomly selecting a respondent who claims to be "extremely conservative"?

9. What is the probability of randomly selecting a respondent who is more liberal than "moderate"?

10. What is the probability of randomly selecting a respondent who is more conservative than "moderate"?

11. What is the probability of randomly selecting a respondent who is either "slightly liberal" or "slightly conservative"?

12. What is the probability of randomly selecting two respondents, the first one being "moderate" and the second being "extremely conservative"?

Suppose the city of Knoxville, Tennessee, has an average July temperature of 87 degrees (F) with a standard deviation of 4 degrees. This information was gathered over the past 100 years. Calculate the z-scores for the next five July temperatures if those temperatures are equal to the following (the mean and standard deviation do not change):

13. 82

14. 84

15. 86

16. 92

17. 94

A normal distribution of the number of parking tickets BSC students receive in a typical semester shows a mean of 2.5 with a standard deviation of .6. Calculate z-scores for each of the following numbers of parking tickets.

18. 1 ticket

19. 4 tickets

20. 2 tickets

21. 3 tickets

22. 0 tickets

Two people, one in Los Angeles and one in New York, take the Graduate Record Entrance exam. These were different exams, but we would like to compare their scores. The person in Los Angeles received a 647 while the average was 640 with a standard deviation of 20. The person in New York received a 570 while the average was 560 with a standard deviation of 25. First, calculate the z-score for each person, then indicate who scored higher after standardizing the scores.

23. Person 1 (Los Angeles)

24. Person 2 (New York)

25. Which person scored higher, NY or LA?

Suppose the college is trying to decide whether to build more parking lots on campus. They decide to count the number of cars in BSC parking lots at 2:00 in the afternoon. They count the number for 15 straight days and find the number of cars takes the shape of a normal distribution with a mean of 670 and a standard deviation of 49. By calculating z-scores and using Table A, determine the following probabilities.

26. A day with less than 624 cars

27. A day with more than 624 cars

28. A day with less than 780 cars

29. A day with more than 677 cars

30. A day with somewhere between 650 and 750 cars

Computer Exercises

Use the GSS2006 database to answer the remaining questions. You will need to run frequency tables, sometimes using the "split file" command first.

31. What is the probability of randomly selecting a female?

32. What is the probability of randomly selecting a person with a graduate degree?

33. What is the probability of randomly selecting a female with a graduate degree?

34. Are you more likely to randomly select a male with a graduate degree or a female with a graduate degree?

35. Of males, what is the probability of being working class?

36. Of females what is the probability of being working class?

37. Of Whites, what is the probability of being working class?

38. Of Blacks, what is the probability of being working class?

39. Among Whites, what is the probability of having either a bachelor's degree or a graduate degree?

40. Among females, what is the probability of randomly selecting first a respondent with a high school degree and then a respondent with a bachelor's degree?

41. What is the z-score for a respondent with four siblings?

42. What is the z-score for a respondent with no siblings?

43. What is the z-score for a male respondent who was married at age 30?

44. What is the z-score for a female respondent who was married at age 30?

45. What is the z-score for a respondent whose first child was born when they were 35?

46. What is the probability of a respondent having their first child born when they were 35 or older?

47. What is the probability of a respondent having less than 13 years of education?

48. What is the probability of a respondent having an SEI score of less than 60?

49. What is the probability of a respondent having an SEI score of more than 65?

50. What is the probability of randomly selecting first a respondent with an SEI score of 60 or less and then a respondent with an SEI score of 65 or higher?

Now You Try It Answers

1: 1. .1 2. .2 3. .001
2: 1. .163 2. .563 3. .008 4. .008
3: 1. .42 2. −.42 3. 1.81 4. −1.82 5. 1.34

4: 1. .2119 2. .8849 3. .9772 4. .6006 5. .2514
6. .0099 7. .9525 8. .7011
5: 1. .7517 = 75th percentile 2. .2456 = 25th percentile

Key Terms

Addition rule of probability, 141
Disjoint events, 141
Independent events, 141
Life chances, 137

Multiplication rule
 of probability, 142
Percentile, 159
Probability, 136

Relative frequency, 139
Replacement, 142
Social capital, 137
z-score, 149

Works Cited

Marshall, G. (1998). *Dictionary of Sociology*. Oxford, UK: Oxford University Press.

National Opinion Research Center. (2006). *General Social Survey*. Chicago: Author.

Soderbergh, S. (Director). (2001). *Oceans Eleven* [Film]. Warner Brothers. Las Vegas.

Zhou, M. (n.d.). *An Illustration of Basic Probability: The Normal Distribution*. Retrieved May 24, 2010, from http://www.ms.uky.edu/~mai/java/stat/Galton Machine.html

Probability—From Samples to Statistics

Introduction

We have learned the basic concepts that underlie the theory of probability and how to apply the addition rule, the multiplication rule, and the normal curve to our analysis. As stated in the last chapter, dealing with probability in theory and reality are two different processes. We now turn our attention to addressing probability when we are working with data that come from samples; in other words, data that vary from theoretical ideal types discussed in Chapter 5.

165

Population All of the possible units that could be studied (individuals, objects, countries, etc.).

Parameters Measures used to describe the characteristics of a population.

Sample A subset of a population, the characteristics of which are often used to generalize to a population.

Statistics Measures used to describe characteristics of a sample.

Do female students tend to have higher GPAs than male students? How do we know that freshmen are the most likely students to drop out of college? How do we know that students prefer one professor over another? These questions, and others like them, can be answered by sampling females and males to compare their mean GPAs; or by sampling people who dropped out of college and asking them how far along in their studies they were; or by asking students to rank their professors. In each case, answers are provided not by asking everyone, but by taking a sample of a population.

A sample is a subset of a population. All statistics are based on samples. Numeric descriptions of a census (when everyone in a population provides data) are called parameters; however, it is almost never feasible to gather data from entire populations (too costly, too time-consuming). It must therefore be assumed that any time we generate statistics, our results will vary from the population parameters, sometimes by a little and sometimes by a lot, depending on the quality of the sample. Statisticians have developed ways to incorporate this uncertainty into statistical calculations based on the theory of probability.

In this chapter we learn a variety of techniques that researchers use to overcome the uncertainty of statistics. Specifically, we learn the standard error of the mean, the standard error of the proportion, confidence intervals, and the *t*-test (Table 6.1). These are what are called *inferential statistics*, as opposed to the *descriptive statistics* that we have learned in previous chapters. Ultimately, inferential statistics allow us to answer the question: How sure of our results can we be? Or, how much confidence can we place in our statistics?

TABLE 6.1 *Symbols and Formulas*

TERM/SYMBOL	MEANING OF SYMBOL	FORMULA
Standard error of the mean For populations: $(\sigma_{\bar{x}})$ For samples: $(s_{\bar{x}})$	A measure of variability in the sampling distribution of the mean	For population data: $\sigma_{\bar{x}} = \dfrac{\sigma}{\sqrt{N}}$ For sample data: $s_{\bar{x}} = \dfrac{s}{\sqrt{N}}$
Dispersion in a percentage	A measure of uniformity of responses	$p(1-p)$
Standard error of the proportion (s_p)	A measure of variability in a sampling distribution	$s_p = \sqrt{\dfrac{p(1-p)}{N}}$

(Continued)

TABLE 6.1 *Continued*

TERM/SYMBOL	MEANING OF SYMBOL	FORMULA
Confidence interval (CI)	A range of values in which the true population parameter is expected to fall	$95\% \; CI \; for \; Proportion = P \pm (1.96)s_p$ $95\% \; CI \; for \; Mean = \bar{X} \pm (1.96)s_{\bar{x}}$
t Ratio	A distribution that is used to determine probabilities when population parameters are unknown and estimated	$t = \dfrac{\bar{X} - \mu}{s_{\bar{x}}}$
Standard error of the difference between means	A statistic that uses the standard deviations of two samples to estimate the difference between means	$S_{\bar{X}_1 - \bar{X}_2} = \sqrt{\left(\dfrac{N_1 S_1^2 + N_2 S_2^2}{N_1 + N_2 - 2}\right)\left(\dfrac{N_1 + N_2}{N_1 N_2}\right)}$
t test	A statistic used to determine the level of confidence at which the null hypothesis can be rejected when comparing two means	$t = \dfrac{\bar{X}_1 - \bar{X}_2}{S_{\bar{X}_1 - \bar{X}_2}}$

The Politics of Sampling: Global Warming and Political Party

The burning of fossil fuels appears to be contributing enough additional carbon dioxide to Earth's atmosphere to cause overall temperatures to rise, a process known as global warming. The effects of global warming are unpredictable, with regional changes in both temperature and precipitation. In fact, global warming may even cause some regions to have lower temperatures. According to Al Gore's documentary *An Inconvenient Truth* (2006), there is no scientific literature that contests claims of global warming. While there may be some debate over why the warming is taking place, the warming trend itself is considered a basic truth. As the NASA (2006) data in Figure 6.1 show, the world has experienced a relatively steady increase in warming since the 1920s.

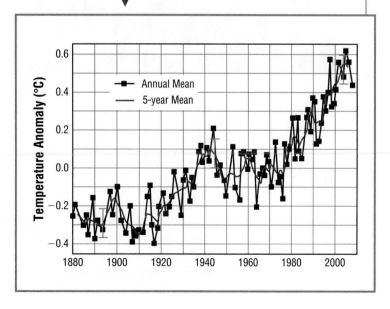

Figure 6.1 Global Land–Ocean Temperature Index

If no scientific literature contests the claim that temperatures are rising, where does the debate over global warming originate? The answer may surprise you. The arguments appear to focus on why global warming occurs, not if it occurs at all. One claim is the possibility that natural fluctuations in global temperatures are at work and that the problem does not originate in human activities. Another debate centers on claims that even if the earth does warm up, it will not result in serious outcomes. You probably have your own position on these debates, but they are debates nonetheless.

An explanation for the lack of consensus on the sources and dangers of global warming is that people's understandings of it are, at least partially, ideologically informed rather than scientifically informed. In other words, people tend to believe what they want to believe. This raises the question of what influences their understandings. Related to this difference of opinion is political party membership. According to sociologists Riley Dunlap and Aaron McCright (2008), significant differences between Republicans and Democrats can be found in their attitudes and opinions toward global warming. For example, while 76% of Democrats feel that the effects of global warming have already begun, only 42% of Republicans feel the same way. They also find that Republicans are more likely to feel that the seriousness of global warming is exaggerated in the news, less likely to say that scientists believe global warming is occurring, less likely to say that global warming is caused by human activities, and less likely to say that global warming will pose a serious threat to their way of life in their lifetimes. It is interesting to note that different people with the same data come to different conclusions. You decide for yourself.

Before we can accept Dunlap and McCright's findings as statistically sound, we must take a closer look at how they calculated their statistics. It is possible that they could be wrong. How big was their sample? Can the results of their sample be generalized to the larger population of the United States? Just how sure can we be when we say 76% of Democrats and 42% of Republicans? These are essentially questions of probability, the kind of issue that social scientists must address when working with sample data.

We need to learn how to incorporate a certain degree of error (think of it as "wiggle room") into these percentages. In other words, if we were to conduct two samples of Democrats asking them if the effects of global warming have already begun, it is unlikely that each sample would yield 76%. One might be 74% and another 77%. This indicates that any sample contains a certain amount of error. Ultimately, we need to express our findings in the language of probability so that we might say, "We are 95% confident that between 74% and 78% of Democrats say the effects of global warming have already begun." This is an example of what is called the *standard error of the proportion*. We begin our discussion, however, by considering sampling and then moving on to the *standard error of the mean*.

To better demonstrate the logic of these statistics, we begin with the assumption that we have certain knowledge about the population parameters; however, we almost never do (that's why we sample in the first place). We then move on to more realistic situations in which we must estimate the standard error of the mean because we do not have certain knowledge about the population parameters.

> **Standard error of the mean** An estimate of the standard deviation of a distribution of means from a series of samples. It is based on a single sample.

Sampling and Statistics

If you've taken a research methods course, there is a good chance that you've been introduced to the logic of sampling. If not, you will get a brief overview here. First, let's define what we mean by a *sample*. A sample is a subset of a population that we use to infer characteristics of the entire population. Samples can be done well or they can be done poorly. The characteristics of a good sample closely reflect the characteristics of the population from which it was drawn. When this occurs, we say that the sample has generalizability. Ultimately, the goal in developing a sample is to maximize its generalizability.

> **Generalizability** The degree to which the results of a sample can be generalized to the population.

Random and Nonrandom Samples

Samples can be divided into two broadly defined groups: random and nonrandom. In random sampling, each member of a population has an equal probability of being included. Randomness, one of the underlying principles of probability, is difficult to achieve because each and every member of the population must be known before they can be given an equal chance of being included in the sample. You can think of random samples as being based on a list. The members of this list are referred to as elements and the list must contain everyone in the population. Such a list is difficult, if not impossible, to create; however, once it has been created, a variety of techniques can be used to select which elements are included in the sample. Common types of random samples include *simple random samples, systematic random samples, cluster samples, multistage cluster samples,* and *stratified random samples*.

Nonrandom samples are used when a list of all of the elements in a population cannot be obtained. Although nonrandom samples cannot be expected to reflect the characteristics of the population from which they were drawn, at least compared to random samples, they can still be extremely useful. For example, suppose you want to study gang members' attitudes toward increased police patrols in a community. It is unlikely that you would be able to compile a list of all the members of a particular gang (let alone deal with the problem of what constitutes membership) and it is unlikely that you would be able to contact these members at random. You might, however, have a good working relationship with one or two members of the gang. In this case, you could start by interviewing the gang members you know and then asking them to refer you to other members of the gang who might be willing to participate. This type of sample is called a *snowball sample*. Other common types of nonrandom samples include *availability or convenience samples, quota samples,* and *purposive samples*. Because the focus for this text is on random samples and their statistical implications, you should look in a research methods text for more detailed descriptions of different sampling techniques.

> **Random sample** A sample in which each member of the population has a known and equal probability of being selected.
>
> **Nonrandom sample** A sample in which members of the population have unknown or different probabilities of being selected.
>
> **Elements** All of the members of a population who are eligible to be included in the sample.

> **68% Confidence interval** A range of values between which 68% of all sample means (or proportions) will fall. It indicates the probability that the population mean will fall between the two values.

When social researchers are concerned with making generalizations to a larger population, it is necessary to work with random samples. For example, you might want to know more about students who attend your college, residents of your hometown, or other students in your department's major. Finding sufficient time, money, and other resources to include everyone in these populations is usually impossible; consequently, sampling is a far more efficient alternative. The size of a sample is usually a function of resources, sampling method, and what is deemed statistically necessary for the study. In other words, why sample 2,000 students when a sample of 1,000 is nearly as good? Although a large sample, done in an identical manner as a small sample, will lead to more reliable data, researchers get diminishing returns on their efforts as sample size increases. Is it worth increasing our reliability by one tenth of one percent if it requires substantial resources? This is an important question when planning a research project.

No matter how large our sample is, probability tells us that the characteristics of the sample will differ from the characteristics of the population. In other words, all samples contain a certain amount of error known as *sampling error*. This refers to the likelihood that no matter how hard we try, the characteristics of our samples tend to differ from the characteristics of our populations. Often, the amount of sampling error is a function of the research strategies that are used to gather the data in the first place; however, this text does not focus on those kinds of methodological issues. Instead, our focus is on dealing with sampling error that exists even when the most rigorous of methodologies are applied.

Sampling error The difference between the characteristics of a random sample and the characteristics of the population from which the sample was drawn.

For example, the very best efforts may reveal that the average number of years of education for a typical female resident of the United States is 13 years while in fact, the actual average might be 13.3 years. The question then becomes, how much faith can we put in statistics that are based on our sample? How do we handle sample data and report results that contain sampling error in them? This chapter begins to answer these kinds of questions and starts by addressing a statistic called the *standard error of the mean*.

The Standard Error of the Mean

Any time we calculate a statistic, we must assume that our results do not match the parameters of the population. For example, your school may have 10,000 students. If you wanted to know the average amount they take out in student loans each semester, you could take a sample of 10, 100, or 500 students (or any number of students). One sample might yield an average of $1,300 and another might yield an average of $5,000. How do you know which one is closer to the average for the population? Every sample yields a slightly different average and unless you gather data from all 10,000, you must assume that none of the results of your samples will perfectly reflect the population parameters. You can also assume that if your sample is truly random, the more people you sample, the more your statistics will approximate the population parameters.

It is important that we have tools with which to handle these kinds of issues. One such tool is the standard error of the mean. It is a commonly used statistic that allows us to estimate (on the basis of probability) the likelihood that an average falls between a higher and a lower value. For example, referring back to the average number of years of education for females in the United States, our sample data might indicate a mean of 13 years. Using the rules of probability, the standard error of the mean allows us to state our results as 13 years plus or minus half a year. This means that it is likely the actual mean falls somewhere between 12.5 and 13.5 years of education. How likely? That is a question to be addressed later in the chapter in a section on *confidence intervals*. In sum, the standard error of the mean helps us to express how much error we can expect to find in a mean based on a sample.

If we had complete population data, we could calculate the standard error using the following formula:

$$\sigma_{\bar{x}} = \frac{\sigma}{\sqrt{N}}$$

However, because population data is rarely available, we must adjust the formula to make it applicable to sample data. We make our adjustment by substituting the standard deviation of the sample for the standard deviation of the population.

$$\sigma_{\bar{x}} = \frac{\sigma}{\sqrt{N}} \text{ is replaced with } s_{\bar{x}} = \frac{s}{\sqrt{N}}$$

Although the two formulas may look quite similar, the differences are important. Remember that σ refers to populations while s refers to samples. It is important to realize that this is a simplification of a more sophisticated theoretical problem. In practice, it makes little difference whether we divide the standard deviation by N or by $N - 1$, particularly when working with large samples of say 1,000 or 1,500. However, by dividing by $N - 1$ we end up with a slightly larger standard error that helps to overcome the differences between samples and populations. For our purposes, we will use N in the denominator. We now turn to an example of carbon dioxide emissions.

EXAMPLE 1

Per Capita Carbon Dioxide Emissions

Every year, each American contributes roughly 21 tons of carbon dioxide to the atmosphere. Some comes from heating our homes, using electricity, and driving automobiles. Suppose we want to know how many tons of carbon dioxide each of us puts into the atmosphere every year through our use of privately owned automobiles. To gather our data, we find some way of measuring the total CO_2 from everyone in the United States. At the end of the year, we find that each person emitted an average of 11 tons of carbon dioxide ($\mu = 11$) with a standard deviation of 4 tons ($\sigma = 4$).

Now let's change the situation. Because measuring everyone in the country is impossible, we decide to measure the emissions of 25 people in a rural community who have very long commutes to work. We find that they have an average annual emission of 25 tons with a standard deviation of 4 tons (substantially higher than the population mean). Remember, had we sampled 25 other people, the results might be quite different, so our goal is to determine just how much error is in our mean of 25 tons per person per year. This error is called the standard error of the mean. The formula is shown below:

$$s_{\bar{x}} = \frac{s}{\sqrt{N}}$$

Therefore, to calculate the standard error of the mean, we need only to divide the standard deviation of the population (s) by the square root of our sample size, (N).

$$s_{\bar{x}} = \frac{s}{\sqrt{N}} = \frac{4}{\sqrt{25}} = \frac{4}{5} = .8$$

We now know that the standard error of the mean is equal to .8 tons of carbon dioxide. Remember our goal in calculating the standard error of the mean is to determine the average amount of error in our average. The standard error of the mean ($s_{\bar{x}} = .8$) tells us that we can expect typical variations of .8 tons of carbon dioxide should we take additional samples of 25 people. How typical? It is important to understand exactly what *typical* means.

If you recall, 68% of all cases fall within 1 standard deviation of the mean. The same property holds true for standard errors: 68% of all means fall within 1 standard error of the mean. Therefore, if we conducted 100 samples of people in rural areas with long commutes, each sample consisting of $N = 25$, we can expect 68 of those samples to have means that fall within 1 standard error of 11 tons of carbon dioxide. In other words, 68 of those 100 means would be between 10.2 and 11.8 tons of carbon dioxide.

In fact, if we were to plot those 100 means in the form of a histogram, we would find that they take the shape of a normal curve. While this may not sound too impressive at first, it allows us to apply the logic of probability to means in the same way we applied the logic to cases in a distribution, allowing us to calculate the probability of getting a mean above or below any given value.

As you can see from the formula for the standard error of the mean, it is influenced by (1) the amount of dispersion in the data (i.e., the standard deviation) and (2) the number of cases in the sample. Logically, this makes sense for the following reasons. First, data amount of dispersion require greater amounts of space for errors. Second, samples that consist of small numbers of cases are more likely to contain errors than samples with larger numbers of cases. Let's go back to our example.

Suppose that in our study of carbon dioxide emissions, we decide to sample only 9 people instead of 25. Our calculation for the standard error of the mean now looks like this:

$$s_{\bar{x}} = \frac{s}{\sqrt{N}} = \frac{4}{\sqrt{9}} = \frac{4}{3} = 1.33$$

As you can see, the standard error of the mean increased from .8 tons to 1.33 tons. Rather than 68% of all means falling within 10.2 and 11.8 tons of carbon dioxide, 68% of means now fall between 9.67 and 12.33 tons. Now consider the effect of increasing our sample size to $N = 100$.

$$s_{\bar{x}} = \frac{s}{\sqrt{N}} = \frac{4}{\sqrt{100}} = \frac{4}{10} = .4$$

The standard error has now fallen to .4 tons of carbon dioxide, meaning that 68% of all samples of $N = 100$ will have means between 10.6 and 11.4 tons. As sample size increases, the range of possible values in which we can expect to find the mean narrows. This trend is shown in Figures 6.2, 6.3, and 6.4.

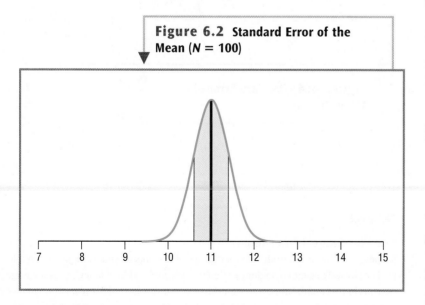

Figure 6.2 Standard Error of the Mean ($N = 100$)

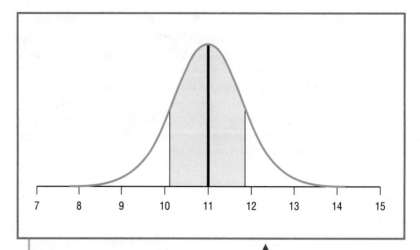

Figure 6.3 Standard Error of the Mean ($N = 25$)

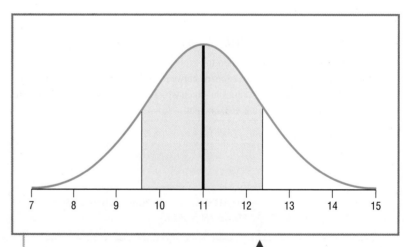

Figure 6.4 Standard Error of the Mean ($N = 9$)

EXAMPLE 2

Sampling Students on Campus

Suppose we want to determine the average age of students on your campus. We sample students by walking into a randomly selected classroom and calculating the average age of students in that room. Suppose we come up with a mean age of 20.4 years. If we randomly select another classroom we might find that the average age is 20.9 years. It is likely that very few of the hundreds of classrooms on your campus would yield identical averages. It is also possible that evening courses would have higher means because they are more likely to be filled with graduate students who have already completed their undergraduate work several years ago. This, however, is more of a methodological issue than a statistical issue and we address only the statistical issues here.

Ultimately, we have little ability to predict exactly what the average age in any particular classroom will be. We can, however, be relatively sure that the average age in any classroom will fall between certain ages. For example, we could be 100% certain that the average age would fall between 0 and 100 years old. We could probably also be certain that the average age would fall between 18 and 32, but not as sure as we could be with 0 and 100. As our upper and lower age boundaries get closer together, we cannot be as sure that our average will fall between them as when they were farther apart. For example, we might only be 80% certain that the average age will fall between 20 and 23. We need a way to express the degree of uncertainty in a mean that helps us to determine the amount of "flexibility" we wish to incorporate into it. This degree of uncertainty is a function of dispersion and sample size, the two parts of the equation for the standard error of the mean.

Remember that means are ways of describing where cases tend to cluster. Standard deviations, on the other hand, are ways of describing how dispersed cases are around the mean. The standard error of the mean is a way of describing the degree of possible variation in a group of means. Ultimately, we can be more certain of means based on tightly clustered cases (small standard deviations). Similarly, as shown in the previous example, some means are based on large samples and others on small samples. Assuming that a sampling method generates reliable data, we can say that larger samples provide greater certainty than smaller samples. For example, if I conduct two samples to determine the average age of Buffalo State College (BSC) students, one based on 250 students and the other based on 500 students, we could put more faith in the one based on 500 students. In this way, the amount of error in a mean is a function of two factors: dispersion and sample size.

As stated earlier, these two factors (dispersion and sample size) are included in the calculation of the standard error of the mean.

$$s_{\bar{x}} = \frac{s}{\sqrt{N}}$$

In calculating the standard error of the mean we are essentially taking the amount of dispersion and controlling for the number of cases upon which the dispersion is based. This provides us with a way to express the amount of certainty we can place in the mean.

For example, let's use the two samples mentioned, one based on 250 cases and one based on 500 cases. In this example, it doesn't matter what the actual mean is, but let us suppose that the mean is 20.7 (average age of a BSC student is 20.7 years) and for each sample the standard deviation is 3.4 years. As Table 6.2 shows, the standard error based on 500 cases is much smaller than the standard error based on 250 cases. This is because we can be more confident in statistics based on larger samples and less confident in statistics based on smaller samples.

TABLE 6.2

Examples shown below are based on a mean of 20.7 ($\bar{X}$ = 20.7), with a standard deviation of 3.4 (s = 3.4).

Sample Size ($N = 250$)

$$s_{\bar{x}} = \frac{s}{\sqrt{N}} = \frac{3.4}{\sqrt{250}} = \frac{3.4}{15.8} = .22$$

This indicates that the standard error of the mean is equal to .22 years. Therefore, 68% of all students fall within .22 years of the mean (20.7 years). We can therefore expect 68% of all students to fall between the ages of 20.48 and 20.92. The 20.48 is called the lower bound and the 20.92 is called the upper bound of the 68% confidence interval. It is expressed as:

$$68\% \text{ CI} = 20.48 \text{ to } 20.92$$

Sample Size ($N = 500$)

$$s_{\bar{x}} = \frac{s}{\sqrt{N}} = \frac{3.4}{\sqrt{500}} = \frac{3.4}{22.3} = .15$$

This indicates that the standard error of the mean is equal to .15 years. Therefore, 68% of all students fall within .15 years of the mean (20.7 years). We can therefore expect 68% of all students to fall between the ages of 20.55 and 20.85. The 20.55 is the lower bound and the 20.85 is the upper bound of the 68% confidence interval. It is expressed as:

$$68\% \text{ CI} = 20.55 \text{ to } 20.85$$

As you can see, the difference between the two standard errors is fairly minimal. This raises the question of whether it is worth putting the resources into sampling 500 students as opposed to 250 students. Ultimately this decision should be guided by how we plan to use the data. If we deem it necessary to measure age down to the 10th of a year, we should then use our resources to sample 500 students rather than 250.

Now You Try It 1

Scenario 1: In a study of 100 students who live off-campus, you find that each respondent pays an average $675 a month for rent and utilities combined. The standard deviation for these monthly expenses is $100. Use this information to calculate (A) the standard error of the mean and (B) the 68% confidence interval.

Scenario 2: In a study of 200 college graduates who graduated in 2008, you find that average amount owed on student loans is $22,673 with a standard deviation of $2,500. Use this information to calculate (A) the standard error of the mean and (B) the 68% confidence interval.

The Standard Error of the Proportion

According to a recent Gallup poll (Saad, 2009), 41% ($p = .41$) of Americans say that the seriousness of global warming is exaggerated. This percent is a significant increase since 1998 when 31% ($p = .31$) felt it was exaggerated—interesting given that 10 of the hottest years on record have occurred in the past 12 years. The Gallup poll is based on responses from 1,012 U.S. adults age 18 and older.

Standard error of the proportion An estimate of the standard deviation of a distribution of proportions from a series of samples. It is based on a single sample.

Often we are unable to compute a mean given the type of data with which we are working. For example, we cannot calculate an average (or a standard deviation) when working with data based on percents. A critical statistician might then ask how sure we are of our claim. As is the case with all statistics, which are based on samples, our answer would be a function of (1) our sample size and (2) the amount of dispersion in our data.

In the case of sample size, we cannot place much confidence if our claim that 41% of Americans say the seriousness of global warming is exaggerated if the sample consists of only 100 respondents. However, as sample size increases, to 410 out of 1,000 respondents or 4,110 out of 10,000 respondents, we can be more confident in our results. The larger our sample size (N), the greater our confidence, and the smaller our standard error. In the case of dispersion, we do not have a standard deviation when working with percents, but we do have a measure of uniformity.

■ % Exaggerated   ■ % Correct/Underestimated

Gallup Poll: *Thinking about what is said in the news, in your view is the seriousness of global warming — [generally exaggerated, generally correct, or is it generally underestimated]?*

Think about it this way. It is possible to take any percentage and measure how far it falls from 100%. For example, 50% falls 50% from 100—this is as far from uniform as possible. If our percentages were 60% and 40%, our data is more uniform. Therefore, a 0/100 split is as uniform as possible and as we move away from this (10/90—20/80—30/70—40/60—50/50), our data become more dispersed. It is possible to express this variation using the following formula *dispersion* $= p(1 - p)$. Consider the following equations:

$$0\% \quad 0(1 - 0) = 0$$

$$10\% \quad .1(1 - .1) = .09$$

$$20\% \quad .2(1 - .2) = .16$$

$$30\% \quad .3(1 - .3) = .21$$

$$40\% \quad .4(1 - .4) = .24$$

$$50\% \quad .5(1 - .5) = .25$$

$$60\% \quad .6(1 - .6) = .24$$

$$70\% \quad .7(1 - .7) = .21$$

$$80\% \quad .8(1 - .8) = .16$$

$$90\% \quad .9(1 - .9) = .09$$

$$100\% \quad 1(1 - 1) = 0$$

As you can see, maximum dispersion (a value of .25) is achieved with a percent value of 50%. We can use our measure of dispersion and sample size in the same way we used them to calculate the standard error of the mean, only this time we are calculating the standard error of the proportion. In each case, we divide the level of dispersion by sample size. Formulas are shown below to highlight their similarities.

$$\textit{Standard Error of the Mean for a Population } \sigma_{\bar{x}} = \frac{\sigma}{\sqrt{N}}$$

$$\textit{Standard Error of the Mean for a Sample } s_{\bar{x}} = \frac{s}{\sqrt{N}}$$

$$\textit{Standard Error of the Proportion } s_p = \sqrt{\frac{p(1 - p)}{N}}$$

EXAMPLE 3

Attitudes Toward Global Warming

We can now use this formula to determine the amount of error in the Gallup poll that claimed 41% of Americans say the seriousness of global warming is exaggerated.

$$s_p = \sqrt{\frac{p(1 - p)}{N}} = \sqrt{\frac{.41(1 - .41)}{1012}} = \sqrt{\frac{.242}{1012}} = \sqrt{.0002} = .015 \textit{ or } 1.5\%$$

We now know that the standard error of the proportion is equal to .015. Therefore, if Gallup conducted multiple polls, 68% of those polls would conclude that 41% $\pm$ 1.5% of Americans would say that the effects of global warming are exaggerated. Another way of looking at this is to say that we can be 68% confident that somewhere between 39.5% and 42.5% of Americans feel this way. This is determined as follows:

$$41\% \pm 1.5\% = 39.5\% \text{ to } 42.5\%$$

The 39.5% is called the lower bound and the 42.5% is called the upper bound of the 68% confidence interval. It is expressed as:

$$68\% \text{ CI} = 39.5\% \text{ to } 42.5\%$$

We can put a greater amount of faith in our proportion as sample size increases and as dispersion in the responses decreases.

EXAMPLE 4

Perceptions of Health

Daily reports of obesity, cancer, heart disease, failure to exercise, unhealthy diets, and sedentary lifestyles are constant reminders of just how unhealthy we are as a society. While millions of people around the world go hungry from too few calories and a lack of nutrition, Americans tend to get sick from too many calories and a lack of nutrition. Despite the overwhelming amount of bad news we receive, seldom do we hear how people rate their own health. How do people feel about their own health?

The General Social Survey includes an item that asks respondents to indicate whether they feel their overall health is excellent, good, fair, or poor. The results are shown in Table 6.3.

TABLE 6.3 *Condition of Health*

		FREQUENCY	PERCENT	VALID PERCENT	CUMULATIVE PERCENT
Valid	EXCELLENT	976	21.6	27.8	27.8
	GOOD	1641	36.4	46.7	74.4
	FAIR	704	15.6	20.0	94.5
	POOR	195	4.3	5.5	100.0
	Total	3516	78.0	100.0	
Missing	NAP	989	21.9		
	DK	1	.0		
	NA	4	.1		
	Total	994	22.0		
Total		4510	100.0		

This tells us that 27.8% of respondents feel that their health is excellent and another 46.7% feel their health is good. This means that only 25.6% of respondents feel their health is either fair or poor. Compared to what we tend to hear on a daily basis, these statistics seem to offer hope that maybe Americans are a little healthier than we are led to believe!

To determine the amount of error in these percentages, we need to select one. Let's take the first group, those who feel that their health is excellent (27.8%). The proportion (p) of the sample to answer "excellent" is therefore .278. We also know from the table that $N = 3,516$. Our formula for the standard error of the proportion is therefore:

$$s_p = \sqrt{\frac{p(1-p)}{N}} = \sqrt{\frac{.278(1-.278)}{3516}} = \sqrt{\frac{.201}{3516}} = \sqrt{.00006} = .008$$

When expressed as a percent, this becomes .8%. We can now say that we are 68% confident that 27.8% of respondents ($\pm$ .8%) rate their health as excellent.

$$68\% \text{ CI} = 27.8\% \pm .8\% \text{ or } 68\% \text{ CI} = 27.72\% \text{ to } 27.88\%$$

Now You Try It 2

Scenario 1: In a sample of 1,000 students you find that 72% feel that public transportation is lacking in their community. Use this information to calculate (A) the standard error of the proportion and (B) the 68% confidence interval.

Scenario 2: A survey finds that 244 out of 767 students live off-campus. Use this information to calculate (A) the standard error of the proportion and (B) the 68% confidence interval.

Other Confidence Intervals

95% Confidence interval A range of values, between which we can be 95% confident that a population mean or proportion will fall.

99% Confidence interval A range of values, between which we can be 99% confident that a population mean or proportion will fall.

This is all very useful, but one problem is fairly obvious: Why would anyone want to be only 68% confident in the results of their work? If someone told you that you had a 68% chance of getting to work safely in your car today, you might decide to walk or ride your bike instead. In fact, you might choose not to take your car even if you had a 99% chance of getting there safely. After all, if you drive to work 300 times a year, you could count on having three accidents a year just going to work! Clearly this is unacceptable.

While most science does not require that we achieve 99.9999999% confidence, it is necessary to achieve levels higher than 68%. So where did this 68% come from in the first place? If you recall from an earlier discussion, just as 68% of all cases fall within 1 standard deviation of the mean, so too do 68% of all sample means fall within 1 standard error of the population mean. A distribution of sample means takes the shape of the normal curve just as randomly selected cases tend to do so. Ultimately, the 68% comes from the z-score table in the back of your book.

Consider the following normal curves (Figures 6.5 and 6.6). The first normal curve is shaded from −1 to +1 standard deviations and the second is shaded from −1.96 to +1.96 standard deviations.

If you recall, when the standard deviation is equal to 1.0, Table A indicates that 34.13% of the area under the curve is shaded to the left of the mean and another 34.13% of the area under the curve is shaded to the right of the mean. Notice that if we add the two shaded areas together, we get 68.26%, or roughly 68%. Only when $z = 1.00$ do we find 68.26% of the area under the curve shaded and 31.74% not shaded (15.87% in each of the two tails of the distribution).

This is the source of the 68% confidence interval. When we calculate a standard error (mean or proportion), we always take the result and multiply it by a z-score to get the margin of error for the confidence interval.

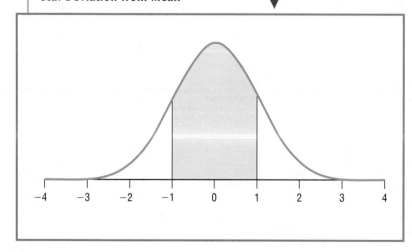

Figure 6.5 Normal Curve: −1 to +1 Std. Deviation from Mean

By default, we always calculate the 68% confidence interval because the z-score for 68% confidence happens to be 1.00.

Now let's contrast this to another confidence interval, the 95% confidence interval (95% CI). Using Figure 6.6 you can see that 95% of the area under the curve is shaded. This leaves 5% not shaded, 2.5% in the left-hand tail and 2.5% in the right-hand tail. Using Table A in the back of your book, find the z-score when the area beyond z is equal to 2.5%. The z is equal to 1.96. This means that if you want to be 95% confident in your results, you need to take the standard error and multiply by 1.96 to get the margin of error for the confidence interval.

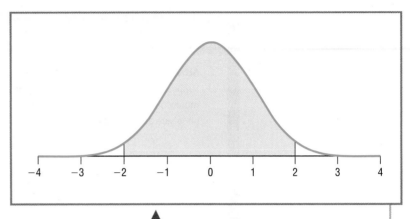

Figure 6.6 **Normal Curve: –1.96 to +1.96 Std. Deviation from Mean**

We can calculate any confidence interval we want using Table A by (1) determining how confident we want to be, (2) multiplying the standard error by the corresponding z-score, and (3) adding/subtracting our result from the mean (or proportion).

The formulas for determining confidence intervals are as follows:

$$CI \text{ for a Mean} = \overline{X} \pm Z(\sigma_{\bar{x}}) \text{ OR } CI \text{ for a Proportion} = p \pm Z(S_{\bar{p}})$$

$$95\% \text{ } CI \text{ for Mean} = \overline{X} \pm (1.96)s_x$$

$$95\% \text{ } CI \text{ for Proportion} = p \pm (1.96)s_p$$

$$99\% \text{ } CI \text{ for Mean} = \overline{X} \pm (2.58)s_x$$

$$99\% \text{ } CI \text{ for Proportion} = p \pm (2.58)s_p$$

Now You Try It 3

Suppose you are conducting research and analyzing the concentration of carbon dioxide in air samples from various locations around the world. If your goal is to achieve certain confidence levels in your results, what Z value should you multiply your standard error by to achieve:

1. a 95% confidence level?
2. a 99% confidence level?
3. a 70% confidence level?
4. an 80% confidence level?
5. an 88% confidence level?

EXAMPLE 5

68%, 95%, and 99% Confidence Intervals for the Standard Error of the Mean

Suppose we conduct a study on your campus to learn more about how students spend their money. We sample 25 students and find that, on average, students spend $50 each weekend on leisure activities (dinners, movies, etc.) with a standard deviation of $8. Therefore:

$$N = 25$$
$$\bar{X} = \$50$$
$$s = \$8$$

Using the formula for the standard error of the mean, we find:

$$s_{\bar{x}} = \frac{s}{\sqrt{N}} = \frac{8}{\sqrt{25}} = \frac{8}{5} = \$1.60$$

The 68% CI. Because we know that the corresponding z-score for the 68% confidence interval is equal to 1.00, there is no need to multiply the standard error ($1.60) by anything. Therefore:

$$68\% \text{ CI} = \$50 \pm \$1.60 \text{ } or \text{ } \$48.40 \text{ to } \$51.60$$

This tells us that if we conduct another sample of 25 students, we have a 68% probability that the mean for that sample would fall between $48.40 and $51.60. If you were doing this for a market research firm and your boss asked you how sure you are that the mean will fall between these two values, you could say that you are 68% sure. In other words, you cannot be very confident; so let's be 95% confident instead.

The 95% CI. Because we already know that the standard error of the mean is equal to $1.60, we only need to put our data into the equation for the 95% confidence interval for a mean.

$$95\% \text{ CI for Mean} = \bar{X} \pm (1.96)s_{\bar{x}}$$

Therefore:

$$95\% \text{ CI} = 50 \pm 1.96(1.60) = 50 \pm 3.14$$
$$95\% \text{ CI} = \$46.86 \text{ to } \$53.14$$

You can now tell your boss that you are 95% confident that the average amount spent by a typical college student on a weekend is between $46.86 and $53.14. What if your boss wants to be 99% confident?

The 99% CI. Again, because we already know that the standard error of the mean is equal to $1.60, we need only to put our data in the equation for the 99% confidence interval for a mean.

$$99\% \text{ CI for Mean} = \bar{X} \pm (2.58)s_{\bar{x}}$$

Therefore:

$$99\% \text{ CI} = 50 \pm 2.58(1.60) = 50 \pm 4.13$$
$$99\% \text{ CI} = \$45.87 \text{ to } \$54.13$$

You can now tell your boss that you are 99% confident that the average amount spent by a typical college student on a weekend is between $45.87 and $54.13.

Now You Try It 4

Suppose you are studying Facebook users and want to find the average number of "friends" each user has. You sample 60 students and find that, on average, each user has 92 "friends" with a standard deviation of 11.

1. What is the 95% confidence interval for this data?
2. What is the 99% confidence interval?
3. What is the 90% confidence interval?
4. What is the 80% confidence interval?

EXAMPLE 6

68%, 95%, and 99% Confidence Intervals for the Standard Error of the Proportion

A recent Gallup poll found that between November 2004 and May 2009, the percentage of weekly churchgoers who favor allowing openly gay men and women to serve in the military rose from 49% to 60% (Morales, 2009). Suppose we want to learn more about students' attitudes toward being openly gay on campus. We conduct a survey of 62 students and find that 87% support being openly gay. Based on these data, we will now calculate the 68%, 95%, and 99% confidence intervals.

The 68% CI. To calculate any confidence interval, we must begin by determining the standard error. For the standard error of the proportion, the formula is:

$$s_p = \sqrt{\frac{p(1-p)}{N}}$$

We know that $N = 62$ and that $p = .87$. Therefore:

$$s_p = \sqrt{\frac{p(1-p)}{N}} = \sqrt{\frac{.87(1-.87)}{62}} = \sqrt{\frac{.1131}{62}} = \sqrt{.0018} = .0427 \text{ or } 4.3\%$$

Because the corresponding z-score for the 68% confidence interval is equal to 1.00, we do not need to multiply our standard error by it. Consequently, the 68% confidence interval is:

$$87\% \pm 4.3\% \text{ or } 82.7\% \text{ to } 91.3\%$$

We can be 68% confident that the percent of students who support being openly gay is between 82.7% and 91.3%.

The 95% CI. Because we already know that the standard error of the proportion is 4.3%, we only need to put our data into the equation for the 95% confidence interval.

$$95\% \text{ CI for Proportion} = p \pm (1.96)s_p$$

Therefore:

$$95\% \text{ CI} = 87\% \pm 1.96(4.3\%) = 87\% \pm 8.4\%$$

$$95\% \text{ CI} = 78.6\% \text{ to } 95.4\%$$

We can now say that we are 95% confident that between 78.6% and 95.4% of students on campus support being openly gay. Now suppose we need to be more confident.

The 99% CI. Again, because we already know that the standard error of the proportion is 4.3%, we need only to put our data into the equation for the 99% confidence interval.

$$99\% \text{ CI for Proportion} = p \pm (2.58)s_p$$

Therefore:

$$99\% \text{ CI} = 87\% \pm 2.58(4.3\%) = 87\% \pm 11.1\%$$

$$99\% \text{ CI} = 75.9\% \text{ to } 98.1\%$$

We can now say that we are 99% confident that between 75.9% and 98.1% of students on campus support being openly gay. Notice how we sacrifice precision for confidence. If we want to be more confident, we must widen the range of the upper and lower bound of the confidence interval. Think of it as a target. The bigger (wider) the target, the more confident you can be that you will hit the target.

Eye on the Applied

Once every 10 years the government attempts to count all Americans by conducting a census of the population. The cost for Census 2010 is estimated to be over $10 billion. Is it worth it? The U.S. Census provides a great deal of information to policy-makers, researchers, and citizens by providing easily accessed data (via the Internet) to just about anyone who wants it. In fact, the American Sociological Association advocates that sociology departments search for ways to incorporate working with census data into undergraduate curriculums.

The census provides an incredible amount of data for social scientists. Census variables range from the predictable (age, race, ethnicity, sex, income, education, etc.) to the unexpected (commuting distance to work, whether your house has functional plumbing, how long you have lived at your current residence, etc.).

The data are useful because it allows us to "paint a portrait" of whatever geographic location we choose. For example, census data can be organized into a variety of levels: states, counties, minor civil divisions, census tracts, block groups, blocks, or congressional districts. The two maps of New York shown below demonstrate how census data can be illustrated using geographic information systems software. The first shows the distribution of median household income by minor civil division and the other shows it by county.

Map A: New York State Median Household Income by Minor Civil Division, 2000

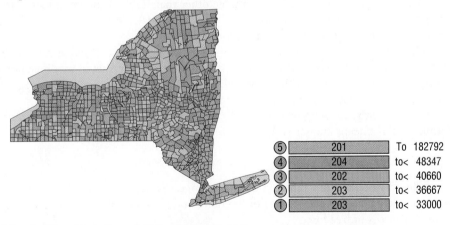

Map B: New York State Median Household Income by County, 2000

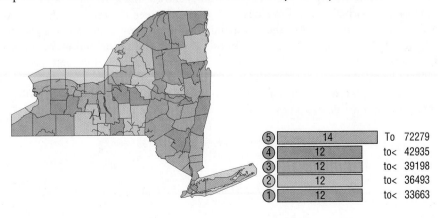

Useful as these maps may be, it is important to remember the old rule that statistics (and parameters) are only as good as the data with which they were generated. In other words, would the two maps shown above look different if not everyone was counted in the last census?

Critics of the census say that not everyone gets counted. For example, the homeless are less likely to be counted. This can have the effect of misrepresenting the actual population of a community and making it less likely to be politically represented and less eligible for federal funds such as community development grants. To overcome these problems, many scientists advocate the adoption of a series of nationwide and regional samples to supplement the census data.

The *t* Distribution

t Distribution A family of curves, each differing slightly more from the normal curve depending on the number of degrees of freedom. As degrees of freedom increase, the curves are more similar to the normal curve.

If you recall, we have a problem with the way that we have been calculating the standard error of the mean and confidence intervals for the mean. We are using Table A, which is based entirely on theory. In theory, a normal curve can only be achieved with an infinite number of samples. In other words, we need to incorporate a way to account for error in our distribution (because it can never be based on an infinite number of samples).

Our adjustment consists of using a table other than Table A, one that incorporates greater variation. We must add some flexibility to our statistical methods to overcome the fact that we do not know the population parameters.

Degrees of freedom A concept used to account for the difference in shape between a sampling distribution and a normal curve.

The second adjustment that we make is abandoning the use of Table A in favor of something called the *t distribution*. The *t* distribution is actually a set of modified normal curves that vary from one another depending on the size of the sample. The bigger the sample, the more likely the *t* distribution matches the normal curve.

Consequently, knowing which *t* distribution to use is a function of sample size. The formula for a concept known as *degrees of freedom* (*df*) is equal to $N - 1$.

$$df = N - 1$$

The *t* distribution is a function of how many cases are in the sample. If we sample 10 respondents, we have 9 degrees of freedom; and if we sample 100 respondents, we have 99 degrees of freedom.

The variable nature of the *t* distribution is shown in Figure 6.7. Notice how the shape of the normal curve for *t* changes as the degrees of freedom change. As the degrees of freedom increase, the *t* distribution increasingly approximates the normal curve (the tallest curve in Figure 6.7). In other words, the *t* distribution for our sample of nine students would be shorter and wider than would our *t* distribution for our sample of 99 students.

Ultimately, we will be using values from Table B (critical values of *t*) rather than values of Z in our calculation of confidence intervals. We replace the formula:

$$CI\ for\ a\ Mean = \overline{X} \pm Z(\sigma_{\overline{X}})$$

with

$$CI\ for\ a\ Mean = \overline{X} \pm t(s_{\overline{X}})$$

Although the two formulas are nearly identical, the second one will generate slightly wider confidence intervals to compensate for the error involved in working with samples. The following is an example of how to use the *t* distribution to calculate confidence intervals for a sample mean.

Finding Confidence Intervals Using *t*. Suppose we sample 10 students and find that average time spent in the library each week is 11 hours ($\overline{X} = 11$) with a standard deviation of 1.5 ($S = 1.5$). We then decide that we want to be 95% confident of our results. First, we must find the standard error of the mean using the equation:

$$s_{\bar{x}} = \frac{s}{\sqrt{N}} = \frac{1.5}{\sqrt{10}} = \frac{1.5}{3.2} = .5$$

Second, we use the formula for degrees of freedom (*df*) to determine how many degrees of freedom are in our data.

$$df = N - 1 = 10 - 1 = 9$$

Third, we use Table B from Appendix A to find our *t* value. Doing so requires that we know (1) which level of significance to use and (2) our degrees of freedom. As stated

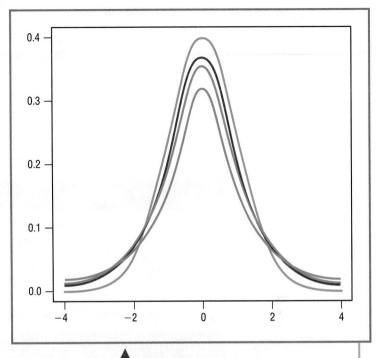

Figure 6.7 *t* Distribution for 1, 2, and 3 Degrees of Freedom and the Normal Curve

earlier, we want to be 95% confident in our results, meaning the chance of error is 5% or .05. This value (.05) is called the *level of significance* and is represented with the symbol α. The level of significance can be thought of as the probability of our making an error. In this sense, the 95% confidence interval is referred to as "being significant to the .05 level."

We now know that our data have 9 degrees of freedom and our desired level of significance is .05. Locating the point at which these two values intersect in Table B, we find a *t* value of 2.262. Inserting this *t* value in the formula for a confidence interval, we find the following:

$$95\% \text{ Confidence Interval for Mean} = \overline{X} \pm ts_{\bar{x}} = 11 \pm 2.262(.5)$$

$$95\% \text{ CI} = 11 \pm 1.1 \text{ or } 9.9 \text{ to } 12.1 \text{ hours}$$

We can be 95% confident that students spend between 11.1 and 12.1 hours in the library each week.

Finding Confidence Intervals Using *t*: Another Example. Now suppose that we want to be more confident of our results. Two options are available. We could either increase our sample size or we could widen our confidence intervals to the 99% level. If we choose to be 99% confident using the data we have already collected, it is necessary to recalculate the confidence interval using a different value of *t*. It is not necessary, however, to recalculate the standard error of the mean because we have not made any changes to the data. Therefore, $S_{\bar{x}}$ remains .5.

Using Table B, we find that for data with 9 degrees of freedom, the t value at the .01 level of significance is 3.250. Therefore,

$$99\% \; \textit{Confidence Interval for Mean} = \overline{X} \pm ts_{\bar{x}} = 11 \pm 3.250(.5)$$

$$99\% \; \text{CI} = 11 \pm 1.6 \; or \; 9.4 \text{ to } 12.6 \text{ hours}$$

We can be 99% confident that students spend between 9.4 and 12.6 hours in the library each week. Notice how the range of our confidence interval has increased from *9.9 to 11.1* to *9.4 to 12.6*. By widening the confidence interval, we can be more confident that the mean will actually fall between the upper and lower bound.

Now You Try It 5

Suppose that we want to study the overall health of students on your campus. We decide to sample students to determine how many times they missed a day of class due to illness in the past year. Our sample consists of 100 students with a mean of 4 and a standard deviation of 2. Use this information to determine (A) the standard error of the mean and (B) the 95% confidence interval.

Integrating Technology

As you may suspect, SPSS is capable of calculating standard errors and confidence intervals with a few simple clicks of the mouse. A function called "Explore" allows users to select an interval/ratio variable for which confidence intervals will be calculated. It also allows users to select a categorical variable (nominal or ordinal) for which confidence intervals will be calculated for each attribute. For example, if we were to select "Age when first Married" as our interval/ratio variable, we could then select "Sex of Respondent" as our categorical variable. SPSS will then organize the output into two groups, males and females as shown in the table below.

Descriptives

	RESPONDENT'S SEX			STATISTIC	STD. ERROR
AGE WHEN FIRST MARRIED	MALE $N = 525$	Mean		24.85	.261
		95% Confidence Interval for Mean	Lower Bound	24.34	
			Upper Bound	25.36	
		5% Trimmed Mean		24.28	
		Median		23.00	
		Variance		35.697	
		Std. Deviation		5.975	
		Minimum		16	
		Maximum		65	
		Range		49	
		Interquartile Range		6	
		Skewness		1.829	.107
		Kurtosis		5.774	.213

RESPONDENT'S SEX			STATISTIC	STD. ERROR
FEMALE N = 636	Mean		22.08	.237
	95% Confidence Interval for Mean	Lower Bound	21.61	
		Upper Bound	22.54	
	5% Trimmed Mean		21.47	
	Median		21.00	
	Variance		35.619	
	Std. Deviation		5.968	
	Minimum		13	
	Maximum		90	
	Range		77	
	Interquartile Range		5	
	Skewness		4.272	.097
	Kurtosis		35.102	.194

You can see from the table above that the first four statistics for each group are mean, standard error, lower bound of the 95% confidence interval, and upper bound of the 95% confidence interval. The results here tell us that males marry for the first time at an average age of 24.85 while females marry for the first time at an average age of 22.08. This may seem young to you, but remember that these statistics are based on a sample of the entire U.S. population, not just people closer to college age.

The 95% confidence interval for males tells us that if we were to conduct this sample over and over, 95% of our means would fall between the ages of 24.34 and 25.36 years old. The 95% confidence interval for females tells us that if we were to conduct this sample over and over, 95% of our means would fall between the ages of 21.61 and 22.54 years old. Notice that there is no overlap between the confidence interval for males and the confidence interval for females. This indicates that there really is a difference between male and females, which is ultimately what we are testing. This is discussed in greater detail in the following section.

Hypotheses and Testing Differences between Means

When we compare the means from two or more populations, say males to females, how do we know if the difference between them is real or a function of sampling error? For example, Table 6.4 shows that the mean Socioeconomic Index score for males is 49.541 and for females is 49.303. The two means barely differ from one another (by only .238). Can we really be sure that this difference is real? Can we really say that, on average, females have lower SEI scores than males? Before answering these questions, it is important to discuss the difference between research hypotheses and null hypotheses.

TABLE 6.4 *Descriptives*

RESPONDENT'S SEX				STATISTIC	STD. ERROR
RESPONDENT SOCIOECONOMIC INDEX	MALE N = 1,906	Mean		49.541	.4570
		95% Confidence Interval for Mean	Lower Bound	48.644	
			Upper Bound	50.437	
		5% Trimmed Mean		48.592	
		Median		44.200	
		Variance		398.095	
		Std. Deviation		19.9523	
		Minimum		17.1	
		Maximum		97.2	
		Range		80.1	
		Interquartile Range		31.2	
		Skewness		.635	.056
		Kurtosis		−.823	.112
	FEMALE N = 2,336	Mean		49.303	.3995
		95% Confidence Interval for Mean	Lower Bound	48.519	
			Upper Bound	50.086	
		5% Trimmed Mean		48.846	
		Median		39.600	
		Variance		372.893	
		Std. Deviation		19.3104	
		Minimum		17.1	
		Maximum		97.2	
		Range		80.1	
		Interquartile Range		32.7	
		Skewness		.385	.051
		Kurtosis		−1.180	.101

Research Hypotheses and Null Hypotheses

Null hypothesis A prediction that patterns do not exist in data.

A great deal of social research is based on hypothesis testing. Often, but not always, this involves comparing means across different groups or populations. Do whites have higher income than blacks? Do men have higher status than women? Do women have higher grade point averages than men? This could be a very long list of questions, but you get the point: Comparing averages is an important part of conducting research.

Research hypothesis A prediction that patterns exist in data.

Throughout the research process scientists tend to engage in "evidence gathering," a process that collects the data necessary to test hypotheses. Our predictions about the world, for example that males have higher status than females, are known as research hypotheses. Research hypotheses do not emerge out of thin air. They are often (but not always) supported by a body of literature that contains both empirical and theoretical justifications for them.

While the research hypothesis predicts that we will find patterns in our data, such as a difference between the status of males and females, the null hypothesis predicts that no such pattern exists. In other words, the null hypothesis predicts that males and females will have the same social status with no difference between them.

This is an important concept in the world of statistics and hypothesis testing because it provides us with a standard against which to assess the likelihood that any patterns in our data are random occurrences, as opposed to reflections of reality. As scientists and statisticians our goal is not to look for reasons to accept our research hypothesis. Instead, the goal is to look for reasons to reject the null hypothesis. In fact, think of confidence intervals (95%, 99%) as expressing the degree of confidence we have in rejecting the null hypothesis.

Getting back to our discussion of the differences between male and female SEI, we know from Table 6.4 that males tend to have higher socioeconomic status than females. What we do not know is whether this difference is real or a result of sampling error. We do not yet know whether to reject or retain the null hypothesis. The two means are different, but are they different enough to warrant rejecting the null and claiming that the difference is real?

The key to answering this question lies in a statistic called the *standard error of the difference between means*. The equation is symbolized as:

$$S_{\bar{X}_1 - \bar{X}_2} = \sqrt{\left(\frac{N_1 S_1^2 + N_2 S_2^2}{N_1 + N_2 - 2}\right)\left(\frac{N_1 + N_2}{N_1 N_2}\right)}$$

Standard error of the difference between means A technique used to estimate the variability in the differences between means from two random samples using standard deviations.

While this may look like one of those equations that justifies never taking a statistics course, bear in mind that the entire equation consists of just four different numbers (*N* for the first group, *N* for the second group, the variance for the first group, and the variance for the second group). Looking at it this way, it really isn't so bad! The following example should help.

Let's suppose that we are comparing the hourly wages of two groups, males and females. The data for males will be indicated by the use of a subscript 1 and the data for females indicated by a subscript 2. Our sample yields the results in Table 6.5.

TABLE 6.5

MALES	FEMALES
$N_1 = 20$	$N_2 = 25$
$\bar{X}_1 = 13$	$\bar{X}_2 = 12$
$S_1^2 = 1$	$S_2^2 = 1$

Beginning with our equation for the standard error of the difference between means, we find:

$$S_{\overline{X}_1 - \overline{X}_2} = \sqrt{\left(\frac{N_1 S_1^2 + N_2 S_2^2}{N_1 + N_2 - 2}\right)\left(\frac{N_1 + N_2}{N_1 N_2}\right)}$$

$$= \sqrt{\left(\frac{(20)(1) + (25)(1)}{20 + 25 - 2}\right)\left(\frac{20 + 25}{(20)(25)}\right)}$$

$$= \sqrt{\left(\frac{45}{43}\right)\left(\frac{45}{500}\right)}$$

$$= \sqrt{(1.0465)(.09)}$$

$$= \sqrt{.0942}$$

$$= .31$$

Thus the standard error of the difference between means is .31. With this we can calculate a t value and use it in Table B to determine our level of significance. The formula for t is:

$$t = \frac{\overline{X}_1 - \overline{X}_2}{S_{\overline{X}_1 - \overline{X}_2}}$$

Therefore,

$$t = \frac{13 - 12}{.31}$$

$$t = \frac{1}{.31}$$

$$= 3.225$$

t A measure of how far two sample means differ from 0, expressed in units of standard error.

Now we use the t distribution (Table B in the back of your book) to determine our level of significance (α). Our data include a total of 45 respondents (20 males and 25 females); therefore, we have 43 degrees of freedom. As you can see from Table B, there is no point at which $df = 43$. Instead, we must use the closest value that is less than N. Using a higher df assumes that our data conform more closely to the shape of the normal distribution than they actually do. For this example, our degrees of freedom is equal to 40 ($df = 40$). So we must use the row in the table associated with 40 df.

At the .20 level of significance, the t value is 1.303. Because or t value of 3.225 exceeds the t at the .20 level of significance, we can say that our results are significant to the .20 level. This means that our data, which show that males average higher hourly wages than females, will be in error 20% of the time. In looking more closely at Table B, our t value exceeds the t value in the table at the .10 level, the .05 level, the .02 level, and the .01 level. It does not, however, surpass the value of t at the .001 level. Therefore, we can say that our data are significant to the .01 level ($\alpha = .01$), meaning that only one out of every 100 samples of 20 males and 25 females would result in error. In other words, we can be 99% confident in our results.

Now You Try It 6

Suppose you want to know who is more likely to attend guest speaker events on campus, lower classmen or upper classmen. To find out, you wait until the end of the semester and then ask students how many guest speaker events they attended over the past semester. Your data are as follows:

LOWER CLASSMEN	UPPER CLASSMEN
$N_1 = 15$	$N_2 = 18$
$\bar{X}_1 = 3.4$	$\bar{X}_2 = 5.2$
$S_1^2 = .8$	$S_2^2 = 1.4$

Find the level of significance (α) using the formula for the standard error of the difference between means

$$S_{\bar{X}_1 - \bar{X}_2} = \sqrt{\left(\frac{N_1 S_1^2 + N_2 S_2^2}{N_1 + N_2 - 2}\right)\left(\frac{N_1 + N_2}{N_1 N_2}\right)}$$

and the formula for t.

$$t = \frac{\bar{X}_1 - \bar{X}_2}{S_{\bar{X}_1 - \bar{X}_2}}$$

Potential Errors: Type I and Type II

It is important to remember that any time we work with sample data, the potential for error is always present. Errors can be broadly classified into two types: Type I errors and Type II errors. Think of them in the following ways:

- **Type I Errors**—Errors in our reasoning that occur when we claim that something is significant when it really is not significant.
- **Type II Errors**—Errors in our reasoning that occur when we fail to claim that something is significant when it really is significant.

Statistics and the theory of probability upon which inferential statistics is built are not surefire ways to avoid all errors. After all, if something is significant to the .05 level ($\alpha = .05$), we should expect errors to occur 5% of the time. This means that despite our best efforts, we will be wrong one out of every 20 times.

Often students will ask me how confident we need to be in our results. This is a very difficult question to answer, and will be dependent on what we are analyzing. For example, if we want to know what percent of students on campus smoke, an alpha level of .05 ($\alpha = .05$) may be sufficient. If, however, we are discussing whether a new drug will result in a severe allergic reaction, we would want to be far more confident. As a general rule, social scientists often use the 95% confidence level. This is both traditional and convenient, but not necessarily applicable in all situations. Sometimes, as in studies with very small sample sizes, a lower confidence level may be acceptable. Other times, particularly when outcomes are severe, a much higher confidence level is needed.

Type I error An error that occurs when we reject the null hypothesis when in fact the null hypothesis is true.

Type II error An error that occurs when we fail to reject the null hypothesis when in fact the null hypothesis is false.

You may have noticed that we have been dealing exclusively with Type I errors, which are symbolized by α (alpha). For example, if we are 95% confident in rejecting the null, we will incorrectly reject the null 5% of the time ($\alpha = .05$). Therefore, alpha represents Type I errors. On the other hand, Type II errors are symbolized by β (beta). Remember, Type II errors occur when we fail to reject the null hypothesis when we should have rejected it. The reason we use α rather than β is because we can never know when we have made a mistake by failing to reject the null. Therefore, in hypothesis testing, we deal exclusively with alpha and the probability of error when we do reject the null (α).

Statistical Uses and Misuses

The uses of probability are far-reaching and cross nearly all disciplines. Engineers use it to determine safety levels when they test-drive and test-crash cars; drug manufacturers use it to determine the risk of side effects; meteorologists use it to predict the weather; and social scientists apply it to all kinds of different problems.

One such application is the theory of risk and the concept of "risk society" put forth by Ulrich Beck. Essentially, risk is something that we often feel the government should effectively manage. We all take risks everyday by living and working in polluted areas, injecting vaccines, and crossing streets; but we tend to trust that the government will effectively regulate chemicals known to make us ill, ban vaccines and drugs that are unsafe, and provide safe ways to cross streets. In fact, all of our actions come with a certain set of risks, but who is responsible for them is debatable. Is risk something that the state should manage for us? Or are risks borne and dealt with at the individual level? The problem that modern societies face is that citizens are simultaneously losing their faith in the ability of governments, businesses, and other social institutions to effectively assess and guard against risk at the same time that management of risk is increasingly displaced to the level of the individual. At least one example supports this claim.

When Hurricane Katrina hit New Orleans on August 29, 2005, the storm surge and rainfall brought enough water to breach the levees and flood roughly 80% of the city, killing over 1,800 people. For some reason engineers, politicians, and real estate companies like to apply a concept called the *100-year flood line*. The 100-year flood line represents the highest point at which water has risen in the past 100 years. The problem in New Orleans is that the entire city is below sea level and relies on levees for protection. Therefore the levees must be capable of withstanding *at least* a 100-year flood. But is a 100-year flood levee really enough? If it has been 60 years since the last 100-year flood, what is the probability of a failure in the next 50 years?

Should anyone build under this line? Discussions of the Hurricane Katrina disaster raise questions of who is at fault. Are the citizens living below the 100-year flood line responsible for themselves and the damage they suffered? Or is the state responsible for safeguarding the citizenry?

These are difficult questions, but it may be time for the Army Corps of Engineers to begin thinking in terms of 1,000-year flood lines, with additional adjustments for error. Many feel that the decision to use 100-year flood lines upon which to base levee construction is woefully inadequate and is costing people their lives. Looked at this way, it is easy to find support for Beck's predictions of the "risk society."

Chapter Summary

Seldom do samples yield a perfect picture of an entire population. Consequently, we need to find ways to incorporate probabilities into the statistics generated by our sample data. By taking into account the size of the sample and the amount of dispersion in the data, standard errors are ways of expressing the amount of error that we can expect in our statistics. In the case of averages, our confidence level is a function of sample size and dispersion. When samples are large we have greater confidence in the data and this confidence is reflected in smaller standard errors. In the case of proportions, our confidence level is a function of sample size and magnitude of the proportion relative to the size of the sample. Standard errors are an important part of inferential statistics and a good understanding of them is necessary for understanding confidence intervals.

Confidence intervals are based on standard errors. They allow us to express our certainty in a mean or a proportion as falling within a given range of values. These ranges of values all have a high and a low value. For example, we might claim that the average age of a college student is 20 years. Are we 100% sure it is 20 years? No. We might not even be 50% sure of this claim. Therefore, we need to find a way to say we are 95% sure that the average age falls between two values or 99% sure the average age falls between two values. It is logical to claim that the further apart we make the two ages between which we predict the mean will fall that the more confident we can be in our claim that the actual average falls between them. For example, we can be almost 100% confident that the average age will fall between 13 and 27. We can be less confident that the average age will fall between 17 and 23. And we can even be less confident that it will fall between 19 and 21. This trend can be expressed in the following way: *The greater the range between the low and high values of our confidence interval, the greater the confidence we can place in our claim.* Therefore, in determining confidence intervals, we sacrifice confidence to be more specific.

Exercises

We sample 20 new cars (sedans) and find the average miles per gallon (mpg) to be 26 with a standard deviation of 1.7.

1. What is the standard error of the mean?

2. If we increase our sample size to 40, what is the standard error of the mean?

3. If we increase our sample size to 200, what is the standard error of the mean?

In a sample of 100 BSC students, we find that on average students eat at a fast-food restaurant four times a week with a standard deviation of .5.

4. What is the standard error of the mean?

5. If our sample size is only 10, what is the standard error?

6. If our sample size is 1000, what is the standard error?

In a sample of 212 BSC students, we find that 82% are binge drinkers.

7. What is the standard error of the proportion?

8. If we increase the sample size to 500, what is the standard error of the proportion?

Thirty out of 167 students have been involved in a violent conflict in the past year.

9. What is the standard error of the proportion?

10. If 90 students reported a violent conflict, what is the standard error of the proportion?

We sample 20 new cars (sedans) and find the average mpg to be 26 with a standard deviation of 1.7.

11. What is the 68% confidence interval (CI)?

12. What is the 95% CI?

13. What is the 99% CI?

14. What is the 75% CI?

In a sample of 100 BSC students, we find that on average students eat at a fast-food restaurant four times a week with a standard deviation of .5.

15. What is the 68% CI?

16. What is the 95% CI?

17. What is the 99% CI?

18. What is the 80% CI?

In a sample of 212 BSC students, we find that 82% are binge-drinkers.

19. What is the 95% CI?

20. What is the 99% CI?

21. What is the 90% CI?

Thirty out of 167 students have been involved in a violent conflict in the past year.

22. What is the 95% CI?

23. What is the 99% CI?

24. What is the 82% CI?

25. What is the 86% CI?

26. What is the 48% CI?

Computer Exercises

Use the GSS2006 database to answer the following questions.

For the variable YEARSJOB, indicate the following values:

27. Mean: _____

28. Standard error of the mean: _____

29. 95% confidence interval: _____ to _____

Repeat question 7, except this time split the database by SEX and compare males to females.

30. Mean for males: _____

31. Standard error of the mean for males: _____

32. 95% confidence interval for males: _____

33. Mean for females: _____

34. Standard error of the mean for females: _____

35. 95% confidence interval for females: _____

For the variable AGE, indicate the following values (do not split the file):

36. Mean: _____

37. Standard error of the mean: _____

38. 95% confidence interval: _____

39. 99% confidence interval: _____

For the variable EDUC, indicate the following values:

40. Mean: _____

41. Standard error of the mean: _____

42. 99% confidence interval: _____

43. 95% confidence interval: _____

44. 80% confidence interval: _____

45. 68% confidence interval: _____

46. 50% confidence interval: _____

47. Explain why we can put more faith in wider confidence intervals.

Use the table below to answer questions 48–52.

Marital Status

		FREQUENCY	PERCENT	VALID PERCENT	CUMULATIVE PERCENT
Valid	married	795	53.0	53.0	53.0
	widowed	165	11.0	11.0	64.0
	divorced	213	14.2	14.2	78.3
	separated	40	2.7	2.7	80.9
	never married	286	19.1	19.1	100.0
	Total	1499	99.9	100.0	
Missing	NA	1	.1		
Total		1500	100.0		

48. What is the standard error of the proportion for "married"?

49. What is the standard error of the proportion for "separated"?

50. What is the 95% confidence interval for "divorced"?

51. What is the 99% confidence interval for "divorced"?

52. What is the 80% confidence interval for "divorced"?

Now You Try It Answers

1: Scenario 1 — A. $10.05 B. $664.95 to $685.05
Scenario 2 — A. $177.22 B. $22,495.75 to $22,850.22
2: Scenario 1 — A. .014 B. 70.6 to 73.4%
Scenario 2 — A. .017 B. 30.3 to 33.7%
3: 1. 1.96 2. 2.58 3. 1.03 4. 1.28 5. 1.55
4: 1. 89.22 to 94.78 2. 88.34 to 95.66 3. 89.67 to 94.33
4. 90.21 to 93.19

5: A. .20 B. 3.6 to 4.4
6: Standard error of the difference between
means = .383 t = 4.70
Significance level = .001

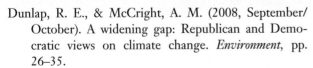

Key Terms

68% Confidence interval, 169
95% Confidence interval, 180
99% Confidence interval, 180
Degrees of freedom, 186
Elements, 169
Generalizability, 169
Nonrandom sample, 169
Null hypothesis, 190

Parameters, 166
Population, 166
Random sample, 169
Research hypothesis, 190
Sample, 166
Sampling error, 170
Standard error of the difference
between means, 191

Standard error of the mean, 169
Standard error of the
proportion, 177
Statistics, 166
t Distribution, 186
t-Ratio, 192
Type I error, 193
Type II error, 193

Works Cited

Dunlap, R. E., & McCright, A. M. (2008, September/October). A widening gap: Republican and Democratic views on climate change. *Environment*, pp. 26–35.

Guggenheim, D. (Director). (2006). *An Inconvenient Truth* [Motion Picture]. Lawrence Bender Productions. Hollywood, CA.

Morales, L. (2009, June 5). *Conservatives Shift in Favor of Openly Gay Service Members*. Retrieved June 16, 2009, from http://www.gallup.com/poll/120764/Conservatives-Shift-in-Favor-of-Openly-Gay-Service-Members.aspx

NASA. (2006, June 11). *Data Sets and Images*. Retrieved June 11, 2009, from http://data.giss.nasa.gov/gistemp/graphs/

Saad, L. (2009, March 11). *Increased Number Think Global Warming is Exaggerated*. Retrieved June 12, 2009, from http://www.gallup.com/poll/116590

Cross-tabulation Tables and Chi-Square

Introduction

Our discussions of statistical significance have thus far focused exclusively on particular statistics, specifically means and percentages. But data are often presented in tables that contain lots of frequencies and percents (such as frequency tables). Suppose we are trying to assess the statistical significance of a table. How do we go about determining whether trends in a table are statistically significant? In this chapter we extend our understanding of how data can be presented in tabular form to include *cross-tabulation tables*.

199

Cross-tabulation table (also known as a contingency table) Two variables organized into a table with the attributes of one in rows and the attributes of the other in columns. Cross-tabulation tables reveal the relationship between the two variables.

We also learn the most common measure of statistical significance used for frequency and cross-tabulation tables, a statistic known as the *chi-square measure of statistical significance*, or simply *chi-square* (χ^2).

Chi-square can be used to assess statistical significance in two kinds of tables: frequency and cross-tabulation. You are already familiar with frequency tables from Chapter 2; however, we have yet to discuss cross-tabulation tables. This chapter therefore begins with a discussion of cross-tabulation tables, specifically how to read them and how to construct them. The chapter then demonstrates the manners in which chi-square can be used to assess the statistical significance of frequency tables (one-way chi-square) and cross-tabulation tables (two-way chi-square). A number of important symbols and formulas, many of which you are already familiar, are shown in Table 7.1.

TABLE 7.1

SYMBOL	MEANING OF SYMBOL	FORMULA
N	The number of cases in a table	
f	The frequency of cases for a particular attribute	
cf	The cumulative frequency of cases for a group of attributes	Σf
P	The sample proportion	$P = \dfrac{f}{N}$
π	The population proportion	$\pi = \dfrac{f}{N}$
$\%$	Percent	$\% = \dfrac{f}{N}(100)$
$c\%$	Cumulative percent	$c\% = \dfrac{cf}{N}(100)$
$column\,\%$	Column percent	$column\,\% = \dfrac{f}{N_{column}}(100)$
$row\,\%$	Row percent	$row\,\% = \dfrac{f}{N_{row}}(100)$
χ^2	Chi-square	$\chi^2 = \sum \dfrac{(f_o - f_e)^2}{f_e}$
df	Degrees of freedom for a frequency table	$df = \#\,rows - 1$
df	Degrees of freedom for a cross-tabulation table	$df = (\#\,rows - 1)(\#\,columns - 1)$
α	Level of statistical significance	

The "Environmental Decade" and Environmentalism

In a recent publication, sociologist Robert Brulle argues that the U.S. environmental movement is the single largest social movement in the country's history, "with over 6,500 national and 20,000 local environmental organizations, along with an estimated 20-30 million members" (Brulle, 2009, p. 211). Many environmental scholars feel the modern environmental movement began in the 1960s with the publication of Rachel Carson's *Silent Spring* (1962) and peaked in the 1970s, a time often referred to as "the environmental decade" by many. The 1970s were a time when the federal government passed a significant amount of environmental legislation, including the Clean Air Act, the Clean Water Act, the National Environmental Policy Act, and the Endangered Species Act, to name a few. It was also a time when a number of federal bureaucracies designed to address environmental problems were formed, including the Environmental Protection Agency (EPA), which began operating in December 1970.

It is interesting to note that most of these actions on behalf of the government took place in the early part of the decade, during the Nixon administration and prior to the Carter administration. This is somewhat surprising, especially in light of the partisan politics of global warming discussed in the last chapter. Rising and falling levels of environmentalism among the population and among groups (Republicans, Democrats, etc.) suggests that people's attitudes toward environmental issues vary over time and are influenced by a multitude of factors. Consider the following findings from the National Opinion Research Center's 2000 General Social Survey:

- 97% of Americans feel that air pollution caused by industry is at least somewhat dangerous to the environment.
- 92% feel that pesticides and chemicals used in farming are at least somewhat dangerous to the environment.
- 95% feel that water pollution is at least somewhat dangerous to the environment.
- 87% feel that the greenhouse effect is at least somewhat dangerous to the environment.
- 68% feel that genetically modified crops are at least somewhat dangerous to the environment.

In the following section we analyze a variety of different data, including data to assess whether overall levels of environmental concern are rising. Specifically, we assess differences in public opinion toward government spending on the environment by comparing males to females, Democrats to Republicans, and older Republicans to younger Republicans. Our analyses are conducted using cross-tabulation tables.

Data Presented in Cross-tabulation Tables

Referring back to our discussion of environmental protection from Chapter 2, we know that 68.6% of Americans feel that we are spending too little on protecting the environment (National Opinion Research Center, 2006). We do not know, however, if this opinion is consistent across different demographic groups. For example, we do not know if males and females tend to feel the same about spending on the environment. Similarly, we do not know if Republicans and Democrats feel the same. To check, we could run two separate frequency tables, one for males and one for females, or we could run a single cross-tabulation table.

Reading Cross-tabulation Tables

EXAMPLE 1

Assessing Attitudes toward Environmental Spending with a Cross-tabulation Table

Unlike frequency tables, cross-tabulation tables allow us to compare groups (e.g., males and females) using any variable that we choose (education levels, income levels, various behaviors, or attitudes toward spending on the environment). You can think of cross-tabulation tables as based on hypotheses that predict the relationship between two variables. Hypotheses are educated guesses, predictions about the patterns we think we will find in data. Hypotheses are not limited to relationships between two variables. For example, we may predict that most of the students in a particular college are female or that most Americans feel that we spend too little on protecting the environment.

Cross-tabulation tables allow us to compare males to females by answering the following questions: Of males, what percent feel that we are spending too little on environmental protection? Of females, what percent feel that we are spending too little on environmental protection? Table 7.2 helps us to answer these questions. Generally, the independent variable in a hypothesis is placed in the columns in a cross-tabulation table and the dependent variable is placed in the rows.

TABLE 7.2 *Protecting the Environment by Sex*

| | | | RESPONDENT'S SEX | | |
			MALE	FEMALE	TOTAL
Improving Protecting Environment	TOO LITTLE	Count	418	574	992
	ABOUT RIGHT	Count	164	201	365
	TOO MUCH	Count	52	37	89
	Total	Count	634	812	1,446

Column variable The variable with attributes in the columns of a cross-tabulation table. In this book, the column variable is the independent variable in hypotheses (when applicable).

Column percent The percent of cases within the population of a particular attribute of the column variable in a cross-tabulation table.

Table 7.2 is referred to as a 3 × 2 cross-tabulation table because it contains a row variable with three attributes and a column variable with two attributes. Because it is a 3 × 2 table, it contains six cells. The column to the far right and the bottom row of the table contain what are called marginal values, or totals. We can read this table in one of two ways: either "down and over" or "across and up." Reading "down and over," we can state that *of males, 418 feel we are doing too little*. If we read across and up, we can state that *of those who feel we are doing too little, 418 are male*.

Don't be fooled. While these may sound like the same statement, each is based on a different population of respondents. The first statement is based on 634 males ($N = 634$) and the second is based on 992 ($N = 992$) people who feel we are doing too little about environmental protections. This will be very important when we begin calculating percentages.

If we want to compare male to female attitudes toward environmental protections, it is customary to put the variable sex (the independent variable) in the columns. Unless you are like Dustin Hoffman's character in the movie *Rainman,* it is unlikely that you can reliably determine which group is more likely to feel that we are doing too little to protect the environment. Yes, more females answered "too little," but there are more females in the sample. To overcome this problem, it is useful to calculate the percentage of males who answered "too little" and compare it to the percentage of females who answered "too little." We do so using the following equation for column percents:

$$column \ \% \ = \ \frac{f}{N_{column}}(100)$$

$$\text{For males: } column \ \% \ = \ \frac{418}{634}(100) \ = \ 65.9\%$$

$$\text{For females: } column \ \% \ = \ \frac{574}{812}(100) \ = \ 70.7\%$$

We can now insert these percentages into the appropriate cells in the table and *compare the percent of those who feel we are spending "too little" across categories of the independent variable.* Of males, 65.9% feel we are spending too little. Of females, 70.7% feel we are spending too little. Therefore, females are more likely than males to feel that we are spending too little.

TABLE 7.3   *Protecting the Environment by Sex*

			RESPONDENT'S SEX		
			MALE	FEMALE	TOTAL
Improving Protecting Environment	TOO LITTLE	Count	418	574	992
		% within RESPONDENT'S SEX	65.9%	70.7%	68.6%
	ABOUT RIGHT	Count	164	201	365
		% within RESPONDENT'S SEX	25.9%	24.8%	25.2%
	TOO MUCH	Count	52	37	89
		% within RESPONDENT'S SEX	8.2%	4.6%	6.2%
	Total	Count	634	812	1446
		% within RESPONDENT'S SEX	100.0%	100.0%	100.0%

We can determine that the table contains column percents by checking to see if they add up to 100 in each column. The table also contains percents in the marginal column to the right. The 68% indicates that of all the respondents in the table ($N = 1,446$), 68% feel we are doing too little to protect the environment. In effect, the cross-tabulation table is three frequency tables in one: one for males, one for females, and one for both males and females combined.

EXAMPLE 2

Assessing Levels of Education with a Cross-tabulation Table

Using Table 7.4, we see that most of the respondents from a particular college are female. This does not mean, however, that most of the people with college degrees are female (85 females to only 54 males). It may be that the ratio of females to males in school has increased in recent years and, therefore, we could hypothesize that males are more likely than females to hold a college degree. To test this hypothesis, we must create a cross-tabulation table in which Sex is the independent (column) variable and College Degree is the dependent (row) variable. In this book, independent variables are always placed in the columns of the cross-tabulation table and dependent variables are always placed in the rows. This is simply a matter of preference.

TABLE 7.4 *College Degree by Sex*

		RESPONDENT'S SEX		
		MALE	FEMALE	TOTAL
Does *R* have a college degree?	No	36	66	102
	Yes	18	19	37
	Total	54	85	139

Table 7.4 is a cross-tabulation of College Degree by Sex. College Degree is the dependent variable and Sex is the independent variable. The table is based on data that consists of 54 males (36 without a college degree and 18 with a college degree) and 85 females (66 without a college degree and 19 with a college degree), for a total of 139 respondents ($N = 139$).

Remember that our hypothesis is that males are more likely than females to have a college degree. Another way of stating this is to say:

If a respondent is male, then they are more likely to have a college degree.

Stated this way, the variable that is referenced after the word "If" is the independent variable and the variable that is referenced after the word "then" is the dependent variable. Sex is our independent variable and College Degree is our dependent variable. In other words, we are predicting that the probability of holding a college degree is dependent on whether one is male or female.

To test our hypothesis, that males are more likely than females to hold a college degree, we need to compare percentages across populations males and females. Therefore, we need to calculate percentages within each column. These are called column percent. For males, 18 out of 54 have a college degree. Using the formula for column percents (shown below), we see that:

$$column \% = \frac{f}{N_{column}}(100)$$

Males without a college degree:

$$column \% = \frac{36}{54}(100) = 66.7\%$$

Males with a college degree:

$$column \ \% \ = \frac{18}{54}(100) = 33.3\%$$

Females without a college degree:

$$column \ \% \ = \frac{66}{85}(100) = 77.6\%$$

Females with a college degree:

$$column \ \% \ = \frac{19}{85}(100) = 22.4\%$$

Table 7.5 shows the column percents. As you can see, these are called column percentages because the values of the cells in each column add up to 100%. For example, 66.7% males do not have a college degree and 33.3% do. Together these add up to 100%. Similarly for females, 77.6% do not have a college degree and 22.4% do. On some occasions, the two column percents do not add up to 100%, but this is only due to rounding error.

TABLE 7.5 *College Degree by Sex*

		RESPONDENT'S SEX		
		MALE	FEMALE	TOTAL
Does *R* have a college degree?	No	36 66.7%	66 77.6%	102 73.4%
	Yes	18 33.3%	19 22.4%	37 26.6%
	Total	54 100.0%	85 100.0%	139 100.0%

We can now compare the percentage of males to the percentage of females (across categories of the independent variable). Of males, 33.3% have a college degree. Of females, 22.4% have a college degree. Therefore males are more likely than females to have a college degree. The data offer support for our hypothesis.

The third column in Table 7.5 is labeled "Total." As you can see the top cell in this table contains a value of 102. This refers to the total number of respondents that do not have a college degree (36 males and 66 females). The 73.4% value is calculated by dividing the total number of respondents without a college degree ($f = 102$) by the total number of respondents ($N = 139$).

$$\% = \frac{36 + 66}{139}(100) = 73.4\%$$

The same process is used to calculate the frequency and percent of respondents with a college degree.

$$\% = \frac{18 + 19}{139}(100) = 26.6\%$$

Integrating Technology

Creating a Cross-tabulation Table Using SPSS for Windows

SPSS for Windows offers a quick and easy way to generate cross-tabulation tables from raw data. With just a few clicks of the mouse, users can create tables that contain any combination of row, column, and total percents. It also allows users to pick which variables will be in the columns and rows, allowing for individual preferences of users.

SPSS for Windows also provides users with the ability to enter a third variable into the cross-tabulation. At first this may seem a bit odd; however, it is a relatively common practice. Suppose, for example, that you were interested in the relationship between political party affiliation and attitudes toward abortion, but you suspect there may be differences between males and females. SPSS has the ability for users to generate a cross-tabulation table and then add what is called a *control variable*. The control variable has the effect of splitting the data file into attributes of the control variable and running separate analyses for each population. Consider the following table.

Abortion if Woman Wants for Any Reason *Political Party Affiliation *Respondent's Sex Cross-tabulation

	RESPONDENT'S SEX			POLITICAL PARTY AFFILIATION		
				DEMOCRAT	REPUBLICAN	TOTAL
MALE	ABORTION IF WOMAN WANTS FOR ANY REASON	YES	Count	103	81	184
			% within Political Party Affiliation	46.6%	33.5%	39.7%
		NO	Count	118	161	279
			% within Political Party Affiliation	53.4%	66.5%	60.3%
		Total	Count	221	242	463
			% within Political Party Affiliation	100.0%	100.0%	100.0%
FEMALE	ABORTION IF WOMAN WANTS FOR ANY REASON	YES	Count	204	75	279
			% within Political Party Affiliation	51.6%	27.1%	41.5%
		NO	Count	191	202	393
			% within Political Party Affiliation	48.4%	72.9%	58.5%
		Total	Count	395	277	672
			% within Political Party Affiliation	100.0%	100.0%	100.0%

As you can see, we have two cross-tabulation tables of Abortion by Political Party, one for males and one for females. The tables show that Democrats have more permissive attitudes toward abortion *and* that this trend is more pronounced among females than among males.

Now You Try It 1

Use the cross-tabulation table to (A) fill in the two missing column percents and (B) read the two column percents that are in bold.

| | | | RESPONDENT'S SEX | | |
			MALE	FEMALE	TOTAL
Favor or Oppose Death Penalty for Murder	FAVOR	Count	875	1010	1885
		% within RESPONDENT'S SEX	____%	**63.8%**	67.0%
	OPPOSE	Count	357	573	930
		% within RESPONDENT'S SEX	____%	**36.2%**	33.0%
	Total	Count	1232	1583	2815
		% within RESPONDENT'S SEX	100.0%	100.0%	100.0%

Generating Cross-tabulation Tables Using Raw Data

EXAMPLE 3

Assessing Attitudes toward Abortion Rights

The keys to creating a cross-tabulation table are (1) determining the column and row variables and (2) determining the frequency of cases for each cell. Attributes of the dependent variable are usually displayed in the rows and attributes of the independent variable are displayed in the columns; again, this is a just a matter of preference.

The cases listed in Table 7.6 are color-coded so that all similar cases have identical variable attributes. For example, to be coded in blue, a respondent must meet two criteria: they must be female and they must support abortion rights. As Table 7.6 shows, four respondents meet these criteria.

TABLE 7.6   *Position on Abortion Rights by Sex*

CASE NUMBER	SEX	POSITION ON ABORTION RIGHTS
1	Female	Support
2	Female	Support
3	Male	Support
4	Female	Oppose
5	Male	Oppose

(Continued)

TABLE 7.6 *Continued*

CASE NUMBER	SEX	POSITION ON ABORTION RIGHTS
6	Female	Support
7	Male	Oppose
8	Female	Support
9	Male	Oppose
10	Male	Support

All of the females who support abortion rights are then summed and placed in the appropriate cell in the cross-tabulation table. The same is done for each of the other three types of respondents in Table 7.7.

TABLE 7.7 *Position on Abortion Rights by Sex*

		RESPONDENT'S SEX		
		MALE	FEMALE	TOTAL
Position on Abortion Rights	Support	2	4	6
	Oppose	3	1	4
	Total	5	5	10

The sums of the rows and columns are found in the margins. The intersection of the margins in the lower right-hand corner of the table shows the total number of cases in the table, or N. Once a cross-tabulation table has been created, then the row, column, and total percentages can be calculated.

We can now add column percentages to the table to better compare differences in attitude toward abortion rights between males and females in Table 7.8.

TABLE 7.8 *Position on Abortion Rights by Sex*

			RESPONDENT'S SEX		
			MALE	FEMALE	TOTAL
Position on Abortion Rights	Support	Count	2	4	6
		% within Sex of Respondent	40.0%	80.0%	60.0%
	Oppose	Count	3	1	4
		% within Sex of Respondent	60.0%	20.0%	40.0%
	Total	Count	5	5	10
		% within Sex of Respondent	100.0%	100.0%	100.0%

These data can be shown in the form of a bar chart in Figure 7.1.

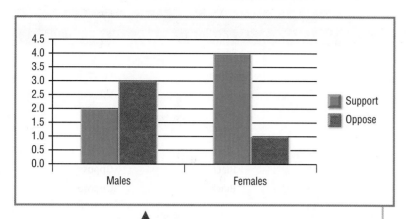

Figure 7.1 **Position on Abortion Rights by Sex**

EXAMPLE 4

Assessing Attitudes Toward the Death Penalty for Murder

About two-thirds (67%) of Americans support the death penalty for murder; however, it is unclear as to why they support it. Many people argue that the death penalty reduces the murder rate by deterring such acts. Others argue that it saves money by reducing prison costs for those convicted of murder. Both claims are rather dubious since evidence supports neither; yet support for the death penalty remains high. Sociologist Jack Levin (1999) maintains that the death penalty for murder is widely supported because it provides a vehicle for revenge. Class discussions with my own students support this claim as many indicate that they feel it is "the right thing to do." Apparently, Americans find some satisfaction in seeing a convicted murderer put to death. Is this true for all Americans?

A significant portion of inmates on death row are people of color. Similarly, a vast majority of those who are put to death each year are non-White. Do people of all racial backgrounds support the death penalty for murder equally? A cross-tabulation table of "Attitude toward the Death Penalty for Murder by Race" can help us to answer this question.

Imagine that we conduct a sample of 44 Americans and obtain the following data in Table 7.9.

TABLE 7.9 *Favor or Oppose Death Penalty for Murder by Race*

CASE NUMBER	RACE	FAVOR OR OPPOSE DEATH PENALTY FOR MURDER
1	White	Favor
2	Black	Oppose
3	Black	Favor
4	White	Oppose

(Continued)

TABLE 7.9 *Continued*

CASE NUMBER	RACE	FAVOR OR OPPOSE DEATH PENALTY FOR MURDER
5	Other	Oppose
6	White	Favor
7	Black	Oppose
8	White	Oppose
9	White	Favor
10	Black	Favor
11	Black	Oppose
12	Black	Oppose
13	White	Oppose
14	Black	Oppose
15	White	Favor
16	White	Favor
17	Black	Favor
18	Black	Oppose
19	Other	Oppose
20	White	Favor
21	White	Favor
22	White	Favor
23	Black	Oppose
24	White	Oppose
25	Black	Oppose
26	White	Oppose
27	White	Oppose
28	White	Favor
29	Black	Oppose
30	Black	Oppose
31	White	Favor
32	White	Favor
33	Black	Favor
34	Black	Oppose
35	White	Oppose
36	Black	Oppose
37	White	Favor
38	Other	Favor
39	White	Favor
40	Other	Oppose
41	Black	Favor
42	Black	Favor
43	White	Favor
44	Other	Oppose

Summing the frequency of each cell, we find 14 Whites who favor, 7 Whites who oppose, 6 Blacks who favor, 12 Blacks who oppose, 1 Other who favors, and 4 Others who oppose. When we fill in the cells of our table, it looks like Table 7.10.

TABLE 7.10 *Favor or Oppose Death Penalty for Murder by Race*

		RACE OF RESPONDENT			
		WHITE	BLACK	OTHER	TOTAL
Favor or Oppose Death Penalty for Murder	FAVOR	14	6	1	21
	OPPOSE	7	12	4	23
	Total	21	18	5	44

To better compare differences between Whites, Blacks, and Others, we include column percents in Table 7.11.

TABLE 7.11 *Favor or Oppose Death Penalty for Murder by Race*

		RACE OF RESPONDENT			
		WHITE	BLACK	OTHER	TOTAL
Favor or Oppose Death Penalty for Murder	FAVOR	14	6	1	21
		66.7%	33.3%	20.0%	47.7%
	OPPOSE	7	12	4	23
		33.3%	66.7%	80.0%	52.3%
	Total	21	18	5	44
		100.0%	100.0%	100.0%	100.0%

As you can see by comparing the column percents, Whites are twice as likely as Blacks, and more than three times as likely as Others, to favor the death penalty for murder. This indicates that while Americans as a whole tend to view the death penalty as a vehicle for revenge, the dominant opinions among populations can be overlooked far too easily.

Finally, we can graph the data in a bar chart, as in Figure 7.2.

According to data from the 2006 General Social Survey (National Opinion Research Center, 2006), 73.2% of Whites, 42.3% of Blacks, and 56.5% of Others support the death penalty for murder. Although these data differ from the hypothetical data used in our example, whites overwhelmingly favor the death penalty for murder.

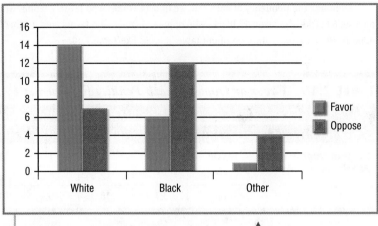

Figure 7.2 **Favor or Oppose Death Penalty for Murder by Race**

Now You Try It 2

Use the data below to construct a cross-tabulation table. Be sure to include all appropriate labels, frequencies, column percents, and marginal values.

CASE NUMBER	SEX	EMPLOYED
1	Male	Yes
2	Female	No
3	Female	Yes
4	Female	No
5	Male	No
6	Female	Yes
7	Male	Yes
8	Male	Yes
9	Female	Yes
10	Female	No
11	Male	No
12	Male	Yes
13	Male	No
14	Female	Yes
15	Female	No
16	Female	Yes

(Continued)

CASE NUMBER	SEX	EMPLOYED
17	Female	Yes
18	Female	No
19	Male	Yes
20	Female	Yes
21	Male	Yes
22	Male	No
23	Female	No
24	Male	Yes
25	Female	Yes
26	Male	Yes
27	Female	Yes
28	Female	No
29	Female	Yes
30	Female	Yes

Other (Less Common) Statistics in a Cross-tabulation Table

Row Percents. Another kind of percentage can be calculated with cross-tabulation tables. It is called a *row percent*. Row percentages are similar to column percentages except they are calculated using the row total instead of the column total. For example, using Table 7.12 we may ask, "Of those who favor the death penalty for murder, what percent are White?" This is very different from our earlier question, "Of Whites, what percent favor the death penalty for murder?" because the questions are based on different

Row variable The variable with attributes in the rows of a cross-tabulation table. In this book, the row variable is the dependent variable in hypotheses (when applicable).

Row percent The percent of cases within the population of a particular attribute of the row variable in a cross-tabulation table.

TABLE 7.12 *Favor or Oppose Death Penalty for Murder by Race*

		RACE OF RESPONDENT			
		WHITE	BLACK	OTHER	TOTAL
Favor or Oppose Death Penalty for Murder	FAVOR	14	6	1	21
		66.7%	28.6%	4.8%	100.0%
	OPPOSE	7	12	4	23
		30.4%	52.2%	17.4%	100.0%
	Total	21	18	5	44
		47.7%	40.9%	11.4%	100.0%

populations. The first is concerned only with those who favor the death penalty for murder and the second is concerned only with whites. While these populations overlap in many cases, they are not entirely the same individuals.

As the table shows, the two questions refer to different populations. One is concerned with the percentage of Whites. The other is concerned with the percentage of those who favor the death penalty for murder. The row percents are shown in Table 7.12. To calculate the row percents, we take the total number of White respondents who favor the death penalty for murder (14), divide that number by the total number of respondents who favor the death penalty for murder (21), and multiply the result by 100.

$$row \% = \frac{f}{N_{row}}(100)$$

$row \% = \dfrac{14}{21}(100) = 66.7\%$ Therefore, of those who favor the death penalty for murder, 66.7% are White.

$row \% = \dfrac{6}{21}(100) = 28.6\%$ Therefore, of those who favor the death penalty for murder, 28.6% are Black.

$row \% = \dfrac{1}{21}(100) = 4.8\%$ Therefore, of those who favor the death penalty for murder, 4.8% are Other.

Total Percents.   A final type of percent that can be found in cross-tabulation tables is the total percent. Total percents tell us what percent of respondents satisfy two criteria. For example, we might want to know what percent of respondents are both Black and oppose the death penalty for murder. To calculate this we must first determine the frequency of respondents who satisfy both of these two criteria (being Black and opposing the death penalty for murder). The table indicates that there are 12 such respondents. Therefore, we divide this frequency (12) by the total number of respondents in the table ($N = 44$) to determine the total frequency for that cell in the table. To do this we use the same formula that we use to calculate percents:

> **Total percent** The percent of all cases located in a single cell of a cross-tabulation table.

$$\% = \frac{f}{N}(100)$$

$\% = \dfrac{12}{44}(100) = 27.3\%$ Therefore, 27.3% of our sample ($N = 44$) consists of Blacks who oppose the death penalty for murder.

Similarly,

$\% = \dfrac{7}{44}(100) = 15.9\%$ Therefore, 15.9% of our sample ($N = 44$) consists of Whites who oppose the death penalty for murder.

$$\% = \frac{4}{44}(100) = 9.1\%$$ Therefore, 9.1% of our sample ($N = 44$) consists of Others who oppose the death penalty for murder.

It should be mentioned that cross-tabulation tables offer us insight regarding the *association* between two variables. For example, if we identify changes when comparing percentages across categories of the independent variable, we can then say that the two variables are associated with one another. In Table 7.12, we see that changes in the attribute of the independent variable are accompanied by percentage changes in the dependent variables. Consequently, the variables Race and Death Penalty are associated with one another. The differences in percentages across columns of the independent variables are a relatively simplistic method for determining that an association exists; however, it does offer some "quick and easy" insight on the data. Later chapters address the concept of statistical association in much greater detail and discuss a variety of measures that are appropriate for different types of variables.

Eye on the Applied

International Analysis of Women's Literacy and Population

It has long been argued that incentive-based methods of population control are unjust and illogical. For example, it is often argued that the best way to control poverty is to control population growth. Consequently, women in third world countries who engage in voluntary, and sometimes involuntary, sterilization have been rewarded with economic incentives and household necessities. Similarly, women who agree to use birth control devices (some of which are outlawed in the United States, such as the intra-uterine device) "earn" economic rewards.

Fertility Rate Female Literacy Rate Cross-tabulation

| | | | FEMALE LITERACY RATE | | |
			LOW	HIGH	TOTAL
Fertility Rate	Low	Count	3	30	33
		% within Female Literacy Rate	7.3%	68.2%	38.8%
	High	Count	38	14	52
		% within Female Literacy Rate	92.7%	31.8%	61.2%
Total		Count	41	44	85
		% within Female Literacy Rate	100.0%	100.0%	100.0%

It is likely that the opposite is true, that the best way to control population growth is to control poverty. Literacy rates are considered a valid indicator of poverty for

cross-cultural analyses. In the case of population growth and women's rights, female literacy rate is chosen for this example. The table on the previous page represents 85 countries. In each, female literacy rate and fertility rate are coded "high" and "low." Of countries with a high female literacy rate, 68.2% have low fertility rates. Even more dramatic is the trend in countries with low female literacy rates, where 92.7% of countries have high fertility rates.

The cross-tabulation table offers an easily understandable way to analyze the connection between literacy and population growth.

A Final Thought on Environmental Spending

Before concluding our discussion of cross-tabulation tables, a final table needs to be run. It may shed some light on a question posed at the beginning of this chapter. It was noted that the "environmental decade" of the 1970s was characterized by a number of federal bureaucracies built during the Nixon administration. It was also noted that Republicans are more likely to feel that current spending on the environment is sufficient. Could this mean that the Republican Party has undergone an ideological shift away from environmental concerns?

Hypothesis: Older Republicans are more likely to support environmental spending than younger Republicans.

To test this hypothesis, we must select only Republicans for our analysis. We then divide them into groups (in this case we will divide them into "younger than 50" and "50 and older"). Finally, we need to run a cross-tabulation table, "Environmental Spending" dependent by "Age." If the older group is more likely to feel that environmental spending is too little, it would offer support for claims of an ideological shift in party thinking. In short, it would help us to understand why Republicans pushed for environmental legislation in the past, but are more likely to oppose environmental spending today. The results are shown in Table 7.13.

TABLE 7.13 *Improving Protecting Environment Age of Respondent Cross-tabulation*

			AGE OF RESPONDENT		
			YOUNGER THAN 50	50 AND OLDER	TOTAL
Improving Protecting Environment	TOO LITTLE	Count	124	88	212
		% within Age of Respondent	59.6%	52.4%	56.4%
	ABOUT RIGHT	Count	73	57	130
		% within Age of Respondent	35.1%	33.9%	34.6%
	TOO MUCH	Count	11	23	34
		% within Age of Respondent	5.3%	13.7%	9.0%
	Total	Count	208	168	376
		% within Age of Respondent	100.0%	100.0%	100.0%

The data do not support our hypothesis. In fact, younger Republicans are more likely to feel that we are spending too little on environmental protection. This example just goes to show that despite making logical sense, data should support our hypotheses before we put much faith in our ideas.

The Next Step: From Descriptive to Inferential Statistics

Now that we have learned how to use a cross-tabulation table to describe the distribution of cases, it is time to consider the amount of confidence we can put in those results. In other words, how sure can you be that younger Republicans are more likely to feel we are spending too little on environmental protections? Are you 100% sure of these findings? These are questions of *statistical significance*. Statistical significance is denoted by the symbol α (alpha).

When working with frequency and cross-tabulation tables, social scientists often employ a commonly used technique called the chi-square (χ^2) test of statistical significance. We now turn our attention to applying the chi-square test of statistical significance to both frequency tables and cross-tabulation tables.

> **Statistical significance** The amount of faith we can put in our statistics.

Cross-tabulation and the Chi-Square Test of Statistical Significance

When working with tables that contain nominal or ordinal variables, we need to find new ways to express the amount of confidence in our statistics. Confidence intervals are applicable to percentages and means, but don't work when it comes to assessing the overall trends found in a table. Therefore, we need to find a way to express confidence in our results when working with frequency tables and cross-tabulation tables. The chi-square test of statistical significance is a common and useful tool for this.

Chi-square is based on a relatively simple comparative logic. It compares the strength of the pattern in our table to a similar table with no pattern in the data. The bigger the difference between them, the less likely it is that the pattern in our table is the result of random error. Social scientists call these the *observed frequencies* and the *expected frequencies*. Together, they make up the formula for chi-square.

As you can see from the formula below, chi-square is based solely on frequencies. In fact, the entire equation is based on two values: f_o represents *observed* frequencies and f_e represents *expected* frequencies. Observed frequency refers to the frequencies in our table. Expected frequency refers to the frequencies we would expect to see in our table if there were no trend.

> **Observed frequencies** The actual distribution of cases in a frequency table or a cross-tabulation table.
>
> **Expected frequencies** A distribution of cases in either a frequency table or a cross-tabulation table that we would expect to see if no trends exist in the data.

$$\chi^2 = \sum \frac{(f_o - f_e)^2}{f_e}$$

Essentially, chi-square is based on a comparison of our data to a "gold standard" of data with no trends. If you have had a research methods course, this may sound familiar. It is based on the concepts of the null hypothesis and research hypothesis. A brief review of the null and research hypotheses will assist in your understanding of chi-square.

We can define *research hypothesis* as a prediction of a trend or pattern in the data. We can define *null hypothesis* as a prediction of the lack of a trend or pattern in the data.

> **Research hypothesis** A prediction that a trend or pattern exists in data.
>
> **Null hypothesis** A prediction that no trend or pattern exists in the data.

Thus, while research hypotheses predict trends, null hypotheses predict no trends. This raises an interesting question: Why should we have a hypothesis that predicts no trend? The answer is a logical one: scientific research is not based on proving research hypotheses; it is based on rejecting null hypotheses. The question then becomes, How sure can we be of our rejection?

It's not easy, but we need to stop looking at data as being either "correct" or "incorrect." Instead, we need to ask ourselves the question, How far from no trend at all is the trend in my data? The usefulness of this approach is that it allows us to express confidence in our results by comparing our results to data with no trend in it. In other words, scientists do not look for evidence to support research hypotheses. They look for evidence to reject null hypotheses. This way, scientists can express the amount of confidence they have in their rejection of the null hypothesis.

Two questions must be addressed when analyzing data: (1) What are the trends in the data? and (2) how much faith can we put in these trends? The chi-square test of statistical significance is a way to express the amount of faith we can put in our rejection of the null hypothesis. As noted in the introduction to this chapter, we can use chi-square for frequency tables and for cross-tabulation tables. When chi-square is used for frequency tables, it is called a one-way chi-square. When it is used for cross-tabulation tables, it is called a two-way chi-square. We begin with one-way chi-squares; but first one important note: A minimum expected frequency of 5 is necessary for chi-square to be considered accurate. In other words, if any attribute in a frequency table or any cell in a cross-tabulation table has an expected frequency of less than 5, chi-square should not be used.

One-Way Chi-Square

EXAMPLE 5

Calculating a One-Way Chi-Square for a Frequency Table

The purpose of calculating chi-square is to determine the amount of confidence we can put in the results shown in our frequency table. To successfully complete this task, we must accomplish the following: (1) calculate chi-square and (2) use the chi-square value to look up our confidence level in the *Distribution of Critical Values of Chi-Square* table in your textbook. Let's say you do a sample of students in an on-campus coffee shop and want to see if males or females are more likely to go to the coffee shop. Table 7.14 shows your results.

TABLE 7.14	*Coffee Shop Customers*
Males	9
Females	21
Total	30

We see in this table that more females (21) than males (9) use the coffee shop. This is what we call our observed frequency—the frequency of males and females that we actually observed in our sample. We now calculate chi-square to compare this uneven

One-way chi-square A chi-square test for a frequency table.

distribution to an even distribution. If the 30 patrons were evenly divided by gender, we would expect to find 15 males and 15 females. This is what we call the expected frequency—the frequency of males and females with no trend in the data. In calculating chi-square we want to find the difference between observed and expected frequencies. See Table 7.15.

TABLE 7.15 *Coffee Shop Customers (Expected Frequencies are in Bold Parentheses)*

Males	9 **(15)**
Females	21 **(15)**
Total	30

The formula for chi-square is shown below.

$$\chi^2 = \sum \frac{(f_o - f_e)^2}{f_e}$$

To summarize, for each row of data in the table, we find the difference between observed and expected frequencies, then square this difference (hence the name chi-*square*). We then divide this value by the expected frequency. After we complete this process for each row of data in the table (once for each attribute), we sum the results. The sum of the results is equal to chi-square. In our example the calculation is as follows:

$$\text{Males: } \frac{(f_o - f_e)^2}{f_e} = \frac{(9-15)^2}{15} = \frac{(-6)^2}{15} = \frac{36}{15} = 2.4$$

$$\text{Females: } \frac{(f_{1o} - f_{1e})^2}{f_{1e}} = \frac{(21-15)^2}{15} = \frac{(6)^2}{15} = \frac{36}{15} = 2.4$$

$$\text{Sum: } 4.8 = \chi^2$$

Finally, 2.4 for males added to 2.4 for females yields a chi-square value of 4.8. ($\chi^2 = 4.8$).

The next and final step is to plug this chi-square value of 4.8 into the *Distribution of Critical Values of Chi-Square* table (Table C) in the back of this book. As you can see, this table can be a little tricky to figure out. The top row of data (.05 and .01) refers to what are called alpha (α) values. These values indicate the degree of risk in rejecting the null hypothesis. The higher the alpha value, the higher the amount of risk you are taking. For example, an alpha value of .01 means that we have a 1% chance of incorrectly rejecting the null hypothesis whereas an alpha value of .05 means that we have a 5% chance of incorrectly rejecting the null hypothesis. As in the case of confidence intervals, it is up to the researcher to determine an acceptable level of risk.

You may have also noticed that the first column of data in Table C is labeled *df*, which refers to *degrees of freedom*. In this case, degrees of freedom are a function of the size of the table, not the number of cases. The degrees of freedom column in Table C allows you to control for the size of your frequency table. Why? Well, if you have a very small frequency table as is the case with our example, we only have two equations to calculate chi-square. This does not leave much opportunity for a large χ^2. On the other hand, if we have a variable with 25 attributes, we would have 25 equations and we would expect our chi-square value to come out much larger after summing the results of all 25.

Degrees of freedom are calculated in the following way: Imagine that we already know we have 30 respondents in our sample, but we have none of the data for the rows (male and female) entered. Beginning at the top of the table, the frequency for males could vary anywhere from 0 to 30, but as soon as we enter a value, the remainder of the table is determined. For example, if we enter 10 for males, the frequency of females must be 20 because we know there are only 30 respondents total. Therefore, the table has one degree of freedom because only one row of data is free to vary before the rest of the table is determined.

Now that we know our frequency table has only one degree of freedom, we look only at the first row of values in the *Distribution of Critical Values of Chi-Square* table. The rest of the table is unimportant to us. As we look at the values in the table, we want to move from left to right until we get as close as we can to our chi-square value without exceeding it. Our chi-square value is 4.8, so we can move to the right until we get to 3.841. We cannot go to the 5.412 because we have exceeded our chi-square value. At the top of the column, the alpha value is equal to .05. This means that the probability of committing an error when rejecting the null hypothesis is .05, or a 5% chance of error. In other words, we can be 95% confident that the data in our table are not the result of a random sampling error—females are more common patrons than males.

Integrating Technology

One-Way Chi-Square Using SPSS for Windows

SPSS for Windows allows users to generate one-way chi-square values for using a function called *nonparametric tests*. Chi-square is one such test. In this case, parametric refers to interval/ratio variables (variables with which we can calculate a mean) and non-parametric refers to nominal and ordinal variables. For example, a frequency table for the variable Labor Force Status is shown below.

Labor Force Status

		FREQUENCY	PERCENT	VALID PERCENT	CUMULATIVE PERCENT
Valid	WORKING FULL TIME	2321	51.5	51.5	51.5
	WORKING PART TIME	440	9.8	9.8	61.3
	TEMP NOT WORKING	84	1.9	1.9	63.1
	UNEMPL, LAID OFF	143	3.2	3.2	66.3
	RETIRED	712	15.8	15.8	82.1
	SCHOOL	139	3.1	3.1	85.2
	KEEPING HOUSE	490	10.9	10.9	96.1
	OTHER	177	3.9	3.9	100.0
	Total	4506	99.9	100.0	
Missing	NA	4	.1		
Total		4510	100.0		

When we run a chi-square test for the variable Labor Force Status, we get the following output:

Labor Force Status

	OBSERVED *N*	EXPECTED *N*	RESIDUAL
WORKING FULL TIME	2321	563.2	1757.8
WORKING PART TIME	440	563.2	−123.2
TEMP NOT WORKING	84	563.2	−479.2
UNEMPL, LAID OFF	143	563.2	−420.2
RETIRED	712	563.2	148.8
SCHOOL	139	563.2	−424.2
KEEPING HOUSE	490	563.2	−73.2
OTHER	177	563.2	−386.2
Total	4506		

Test Statistics

	LABOR FORCE STATUS
Chi-square	6866.996[a]
df	7
Asymp. sig.	.000

[a]0 cells (.0%) have expected frequencies less than 5. The minimum expected cell frequency is 563.3.

As you can see, the first table in the output shows both the observed and expected frequencies for each attribute for the variable. It also shows the *residual* value, the difference between the observed and expected. The second table shows the chi-square value, the number of degrees of freedom, and something labeled *Asymp. sig.*, which is the alpha (α) value.

EXAMPLE 6

Calculating a One-Way Chi-Square for an SPSS Table

Now let's take an example from the 2006 General Social Survey. As Table 7.16 shows, 3,516 respondents provided data on their overall health. When working with chi-square, the question we ask is, How likely is it that these results reflect reality? In other words, we are again asking, what is the probability of making an error if we choose to reject the null hypothesis? To answer this question, we must calculate a chi-square and use it to obtain an alpha value in Table C.

TABLE 7.16 *Condition of Health*

		FREQUENCY	PERCENT	VALID PERCENT	CUMULATIVE PERCENT
Valid	EXCELLENT	976	21.6	27.8	27.8
	GOOD	1641	36.4	46.7	74.4
	FAIR	704	15.6	20.0	94.5
	POOR	195	4.3	5.5	100.0
	Total	3516	78.0	100.0	
Missing	NAP	989	21.9		
	DK	1	.0		
	NA	4	.1		
	Total	994	22.0		
Total		4510	100.0		

Table 7.16 contains observed frequencies, so we must determine the expected frequencies using $N(N = 3,516)$ and the number of attributes (four) for the variable. Therefore,

$$Expected\ frequencies = \frac{3516}{4} = 879$$

We can now use the expected frequency in the chi-square formula:

Excellent: $\dfrac{(f_o - f_e)^2}{f_e} = \dfrac{(976 - 879)^2}{879} = \dfrac{(97)^2}{879} = \dfrac{9409}{879} = 10.7$

Good: $\dfrac{(f_o - f_e)^2}{f_e} = \dfrac{(1641 - 879)^2}{879} = \dfrac{(762)^2}{879} = \dfrac{580644}{879} = 660.6$

Fair: $\dfrac{(f_o - f_e)^2}{f_e} = \dfrac{(704 - 879)^2}{879} = \dfrac{(-175)^2}{879} = \dfrac{30625}{879} = 34.8$

Poor: $\dfrac{(f_o - f_e)^2}{f_e} = \dfrac{(195 - 879)^2}{879} = \dfrac{(-684)^2}{879} = \dfrac{467856}{879} = 532.3$

Sum: $1238.4 = \chi^2$

This is an exceptionally large value for a chi-square. Our next step is to use Table C, which first necessitates that we determine the number of degrees of freedom in the table. The formula for degrees of freedom is:

$$df = 4 - 1 = 3$$

As you can see, for a table with three degrees of freedom, the largest value for a chi-square in Table C is 11.345. If our chi-square value exceeds the table value, then our results are significant to the .01 level. This means that we can be 99% confident in our findings (a 1% chance of error).

Now You Try It 3

Use the frequency table below to (A) calculate chi-square, (B) determine the number of degrees of freedom, and (C) determine the alpha value using Table C. Space is provided in the table for you to put the expected values in parentheses.

CLASS STATUS	FREQUENCY
Sophomore	6 ( )
Junior	13 ( )
Senior	10 ( )
Total	29

Two-Way Chi-Square

EXAMPLE 7

Calculating a Two-Way Chi-Square for a Cross-tabulation Table

Now that you understand one-way chi-squares, two-way chi-squares will be easy. The only difference between the two is in the manner in which expected frequencies are calculated and the manner in which degrees of freedom are calculated. The *Distribution of Critical Values of Chi-Square* table and the interpretation of alpha values are all the same. Remember that two-way chi-squares refer to cross-tabulation tables, so let's add another variable to our example of coffee shop patrons.

TABLE 7.17 *Coffee Shop Patrons by Sex and Residence*

	ON-CAMPUS	OFF-CAMPUS	TOTALS
Males	30	10	*40*
Females	25	35	*60*
Totals	*55*	*45*	*100*

Calculating expected frequencies in a cross-tabulation table is different from that of a frequency table. For example, in this table we need to determine expected frequencies for each cell in the table. We then need to complete four separate calculations (one for each cell) and sum them to determine the chi-square value.

To determine the expected frequency for a cell in the table, we begin by identifying the column and row totals for that particular cell. For example, for On-Campus Males, the row total is equal to 40 and the column total is equal to 55. We then multiply these two values together and divide by the total number of respondents in the table (*N*). The formula for an expected frequency in a cell is shown below.

Two-way chi-square A chi-square test for a cross-tabulation table.

$$Expected\ frequency\ for\ a\ cell\ in\ a\ cross\text{-}tabulation\ table = \frac{(Row\ Total)(Column\ Total)}{N}$$

For off-campus males, we have an observed frequency of 30; however, if there were no trend in the table, we might not expect to find a value of 30 in this cell. To determine the expected value, we multiply the row total (40) by the column total (55) and divide by *N* (100), as shown below.

$$On\text{-}campus\ males: \frac{(Row\ Total)(Column\ Total)}{N} = \frac{40 \times 55}{100} = \frac{2200}{100} = 22$$

Doing this equation for the other three cells in the table, we get the following:

$$Off\text{-}campus\ males: \frac{(Row\ Total)(Column\ Total)}{N} = \frac{40 \times 45}{100} = \frac{1800}{100} = 18$$

$$On\text{-}campus\ females: \frac{(Row\ Total)(Column\ Total)}{N} = \frac{60 \times 55}{100} = \frac{3300}{100} = 33$$

$$\text{Off-campus females: } \frac{(Row\ Total)(Column\ Total)}{N} = \frac{60 \times 45}{100} = \frac{2700}{100} = 27$$

Inserting these values into our cross-tabulation table, we get Table 7.18.

TABLE 7.18 *Sex of Coffee Shop Patrons by Residence*

	ON-CAMPUS	OFF-CAMPUS	TOTALS
Males	30	10	*40*
	(22)	**(18)**	
Females	25	35	*60*
	(33)	**(27)**	
Totals	*55*	*45*	*100*

We now use these values to complete the formula for chi-square. Once we have completed the formula for each cell, we sum the results to obtain chi-square. Our chi-square calculation is as follows:

Cell 1 (On-campus males): $\dfrac{(f_o - f_e)^2}{f_e} = \dfrac{(30 - 22)^2}{22} = \dfrac{(8)^2}{22} = \dfrac{64}{22} = 2.9$

Cell 2 (Off-campus males): $\dfrac{(f_o - f_e)^2}{f_e} = \dfrac{(10 - 18)^2}{18} = \dfrac{(-8)^2}{18} = \dfrac{64}{18} = 3.5$

Cell 3 (On-campus females): $\dfrac{(f_o - f_e)^2}{f_e} = \dfrac{(25 - 33)^2}{33} = \dfrac{(-8)^2}{33} = \dfrac{64}{33} = 1.9$

Cell 4 (Off-campus females): $\dfrac{(f_o - f_e)^2}{f_e} = \dfrac{(35 - 27)^2}{27} = \dfrac{(8)^2}{27} = \dfrac{64}{27} = 2.3$

$$\text{Sum: } = 10.6 = \chi^2$$

You may have noticed that some of the values calculated could have been rounded up. For example, the answer to the equation for Cell 4 was actually 2.370. Often, this is rounded to 2.4; however, in the case of probability, it is better not to round up. This prevents mistakes by artificially inflating the chi-square value, resulting in a lower alpha value. Essentially, it prevents us from overestimating our level of confidence in rejecting the null hypothesis.

Degrees of freedom are also calculated differently. Here, degrees of freedom are equal to the *number of rows – 1* multiplied by the *number of columns – 1*. The equation is shown below.

$$df = (\#\ rows\ -\ 1)(\#\ columns\ -\ 1)$$

Because we are working with a 2 $\times$ 2 table, our equation for degrees of freedom looks like this:

$$df = (2 - 1)(2 - 1) = (1)(1) = 1$$

Using Table C in the back of the book, we see that when degrees of freedom is equal to 1, a chi-square value of 3.841 is significant to the .05 level ($\alpha = .05$). Because our chi-square value is 10.6, we can move to the right where we see a chi-square value of 6.635 is significant to the .01 level ($\alpha = .01$). Therefore, we know that the trends in our data are significant to at least the .01 level. This means that we can be 99% confident in rejecting the null hypothesis. In other words, we can be 99% confident in the results of our survey of coffee shop patrons.

Integrating Technology

Two-Way Chi-Square Test Using SPSS for Windows

Obtaining chi-square values when using SPSS for Windows is quite simple. After selecting the column variable, row variable, and column percents, users can pick from a wide range of statistics. One of these statistics is chi-square. Using the table shown earlier (Abortion by Political Party Affiliation), the output looks as follows.

Abortion if Woman Wants for Any Reason Political Party Affiliation Cross-tabulation

| | | | POLITICAL PARTY AFFILIATION | | |
			DEMOCRAT	REPUBLICAN	TOTAL
Abortion If Woman Wants for Any Reason	YES	Count	307	156	463
		% within Political Party Affiliation	49.8%	30.1%	40.8%
	NO	Count	309	363	672
		% within Political Party Affiliation	50.2%	69.9%	59.2%
	Total	Count	616	519	1135
		% within Political Party Affiliation	100.0%	100.0%	100.0%

Chi-Square Tests

	VALUE	DF	ASYMP. SIG. (TWO-SIDED)	EXACT SIG. (TWO-SIDED)	EXACT SIG. (ONE-SIDED)
Pearson Chi-Square	45.629[a]	1	.000		
Continuity Correction[b]	44.814	1	.000		
Likelihood Ratio	46.203	1	.000		
Fisher's Exact Test				.000	.000
Linear-by-Linear Association	45.589	1	.000		
N of Valid Cases	1135				

[a] 0 cells (.0%) have expected count less than 5. The minimum expected count is 211.72.
[b] Computed only for a 2 × 2 table

As you can see, the first output table is the cross-tabulation table. The second provides a number of statistics related to the chi-square test. The first of these is Pearson Chi-Square with a value of 45.629 with 1 degree of freedom and an alpha value of .000. This tells us that should we reject the null hypothesis, we would be in error less than 1 in 1,000 times. In other words, these results are statistically significant.

Statistical Uses and Misuses

Significant Opinions versus Statistically Significant Arguments

Often in our everyday lives, we take anecdotal evidence and use it as the foundation upon which we base our beliefs and, sometimes, argue for what we believe to be certain "truths." For example, using the story of a 92-year-old relative who has smoked two packs a day for the past 80 years, someone may argue that cigarette smoking does not cause cancer. Now, there is some significance in this story in that it tells us that not *everyone* will necessarily get cancer from smoking cigarettes. In this sense, we can say that this is a significant piece of information. Significant as it may be, in and of itself it is not *statistically significant*. As you well know by now, sample size plays a very important role in determining statistical significance and a sample of $N = 1$ is not good science. In the nonscientific world, significant does not usually mean statistically significant.

In the world of social science, these ideas are often turned around. For example, thousands upon thousands of statistically significant findings are passed over almost every day as being not newsworthy or not of great enough importance to be acted upon. And often for good reasons. Does it really matter that birthrates increased one tenth of one percent during the month of October? This offers somewhat of a window into the political nature of science. What is not news today may end up being news tomorrow, not because of any change in the reality of newsworthy problems (statistically significant findings on global warming, crime rates, incarceration rates, suicide rates, etc., are relatively steady over the course of a few years); but because what gets labeled as significant often has less to do with statistics and more to do with substantive significance.

Consider our example of the difference between mean socioeconomic status for males and females. We know from Chapter 6 that on average, males have higher SEI scores than females (males = 49.5, females = 49.3). This is a statistically significant finding, but is it substantively significant? That is a difficult question to answer. The means are almost identical. In a perfect world, they should be equal (and probably much higher), but this is a pretty minimal difference. A more important question might address how the difference between males and females has changed over the past 5, 10, or 25 years. If the past 25 years show the gap closing, then maybe this is not so significant.

Next time you are watching the news, ask yourself how much of what gets reported is rooted in statistically significant findings and how much is substantively significant findings. Is there any news that is both?

EXAMPLE 8

Calculating a Two-Way Chi-Square for an SPSS Cross-tabulation Table

Now let's take a look at another example of two-way chi-square, the relationship between race and attitudes toward crime. As Table 7.19 shows, nonwhites are more likely to feel that too little is being done to address rising crime rates.

TABLE 7.19 *Halting Rising Crime Rate Race of Respondent Cross-tabulation*

| | | | RACE OF RESPONDENT | | |
			WHITE	NONWHITE	TOTAL
Halting Rising Crime Rate	TOO LITTLE	Count	636	261	897
		% within Race of Respondent	60.3%	66.4%	61.9%
	ABOUT RIGHT	Count	357	99	456
		% within Race of Respondent	33.8%	25.2%	31.5%
	TOO MUCH	Count	62	33	95
		% within Race of Respondent	5.9%	8.4%	6.6%
	Total	Count	1055	393	1448
		% within Race of Respondent	100.0%	100.0%	100.0%

We now calculate chi-square for this table and use it to determine an alpha value. We begin by finding the expected frequency for each cell. Remember, the formula for expected frequencies in a cross-tabulation table is:

$$Expected\ Frequency\ for\ a\ cell\ in\ a\ Cross\text{-}tabulation\ Table = \frac{(Row\ Total)(Column\ Total)}{N}$$

Therefore,

$$\text{Whites/Too Little: } \frac{897 \times 1055}{1448} = 653.5$$

$$\text{Nonwhites/too little: } \frac{897 \times 393}{1448} = 243.5$$

$$\text{Whites/about right: } \frac{456 \times 1055}{1448} = 332.2$$

$$\text{Nonwhites/about right: } \frac{456 \times 393}{1448} = 123.8$$

$$\text{Whites/too much:} \quad \frac{95 \times 1055}{1448} = 69.2$$

$$\text{Non-whites/too much:} \quad \frac{95 \times 393}{1448} = 25.8$$

Now that the expected frequencies are determined, we can put them into Table 7.20.

TABLE 7.20 *Halting Rising Crime Rate*
Race of Respondent Cross-tabulation

			RACE OF RESPONDENT		
			WHITE	NONWHITE	TOTAL
Halting Rising Crime Rate	TOO LITTLE	Count	636	261	897
		Expected Count	**653.5**	**243.5**	897.0
		% within Race of Respondent	60.3%	66.4%	61.9%
	ABOUT RIGHT	Count	357	99	456
		Expected Count	**332.2**	**123.8**	456.0
		% within Race of Respondent	33.8%	25.2%	31.5%
	TOO MUCH	Count	62	33	95
		Expected Count	**69.2**	**25.8**	95.0
		% within Race of Respondent	5.9%	8.4%	6.6%
	Total	Count	1055	393	1448
		Expected Count	1055.0	393.0	1448.0
		% within Race of Respondent	100.0%	100.0%	100.0%

The next step is to calculate the chi-square value using the formula,

$$\chi^2 = \sum \frac{(f_o - f_e)^2}{f_e}$$

Remember, this means that we calculate $\frac{(f_o - f_e)^2}{f_e}$ for each cell in the table and sum the results.

$$\text{Whites/too little: } \frac{(636 - 653.5)^2}{653.5} = .48$$

$$\text{Nonwhites/too little: } \frac{(261 - 243.5)^2}{243.5} = 1.25$$

$$\text{Whites/about right: } \frac{(357 - 332.2)^2}{332.2} = 1.85$$

$$\text{Nonwhites/about right: } \frac{(99 - 123.8)^2}{123.8} = 4.96$$

$$\text{Whites/too much: } \frac{(62 - 69.2)^2}{69.2} = .74$$

$$\text{Nonwhites/too much: } \frac{(33 - 25.8)^2}{25.8} = 2.00$$

Sum: $11.26 = \chi^2$

The next step in our process is to determine the number of degrees of freedom in our table using the formula:

$$df = (\# \; rows - 1)(\# \; columns - 1)$$

Therefore,

$$df = (3 - 1)(2 - 1) = 2 \times 1 = 2$$

Now that we have calculated chi-square and the degrees of freedom, we can use them to determine the alpha value for our table. Remember, the reason for calculating chi-square is to find out how much statistical significance is in our results.

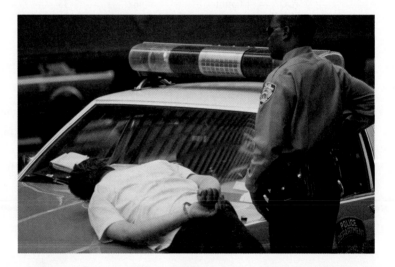

Using Table C, we identify the appropriate number of degrees of freedom and find that, in order to be significant at the .05 level, chi-square must exceed a value of 5.991.

And to be significant at the .01 level, chi-square must exceed a value of 9.210. Because our chi-square value is larger than 9.210, we know that alpha (α) is equal to .01. This tells us that the distribution of cases in our table is such that it would be the result of random sampling error only 1% of the time. Therefore, we can have 99% confidence in our results.

Now You Try It 4

Use the cross-tabulation table below to calculate chi-square, degrees of freedom, and the alpha value.

Political Party Affiliation Race of Respondent Cross-Tabulation

			RACE OF RESPONDENT			
			WHITE	BLACK	OTHER	TOTAL
Political Party Affiliation	Democrat	Count	859	394	183	1436
		% within RACE OF RESPONDENT	45.3%	92.9%	73.8%	55.9%
	Republican	Count	1037	30	65	1132
		% within RACE OF RESPONDENT	54.7%	7.1%	26.2%	44.1%
	Total	Count	1896	424	248	2568
		% within RACE OF RESPONDENT	100.0%	100.0%	100.0%	100.0%

Chapter Summary

The concept of statistical significance applies not only to means and percentages, but also to frequency and cross-tabulation tables. By showing how cross-tabulation tables are constructed and read, this chapter demonstrated their usefulness in effectively organizing data and revealing relationships between two variables. It then introduced the chi-square measure of statistical significance and how to calculate both one-way and two-way chi-square. As in the use of other inferential statistics from previous chapters, chi-square is ultimately used to help us determine the probability of making an error when we choose to reject the null hypothesis. This probability is reflected in alpha values (α) in Table C.

Exercises

Use the cross-tabulation table below to answer the following questions.

Homeowner or Renter Race of Respondent Cross-tabulation

| | | RACE OF RESPONDENT | | | |
		WHITE	BLACK	OTHER	TOTAL
Homeowner or Renter	owns home	590	45	27	662
	pays rent	241	57	24	322
	other	21	4	3	28
Total		852	106	54	1012

1. How many respondents provided data for the table?
2. How many respondents own a home?
3. How many respondents are black?

4. Of Whites, what percent own a home?
5. Of Blacks, what percent own a home?
6. Which of the three groups is most likely to pay rent?

Use the table below to answer the remaining questions.

Rap Music (3) Respondent's Sex Cross-tabulation

| | | | RESPONDENT'S SEX | | |
			MALE	FEMALE	TOTAL
Rap Music (3)	Like It	Count	56	55	111
		% within Respondent's Sex	15.3%	11.1%	12.9%
	Mixed Feelings	Count	60	109	169
		% within Respondent's Sex	16.4%	22.0%	19.6%
	Dislike It	Count	250	332	582
		% within Respondent's Sex	68.3%	66.9%	67.5%
Total		Count	366	496	862
		% within Respondent's Sex	100.0%	100.0%	100.0%

7. Of all respondents, what percent like rap music?
8. Of females, what percent like rap music?
9. Of males, what percent like rap music?
10. Are males or females more likely to like rap music?

Suppose that we want to know if males are more likely than females to live off-campus. Use the data on the next page to construct a cross-tabulation table. Be sure to include frequencies, column percents, and marginal values.

SEX	RESIDENCE	SEX	RESIDENCE
Male	On-Campus	Female	On-Campus
Female	On-Campus	Female	On-Campus
Female	On-Campus	Female	On-Campus
Female	Off-Campus	Female	Off-Campus
Male	On-Campus	Male	On-Campus
Female	On-Campus	Female	On-Campus
Female	On-Campus	Female	Off-Campus
Male	On-Campus	Female	Off-Campus
Female	On-Campus	Male	Off-Campus
Female	Off-Campus	Female	On-Campus
Female	On-Campus	Female	On-Campus
Male	On-Campus		

11. How many respondents are female?

12. What percent of respondents are male?

13. Of males, what percent live on-campus?

14. Of females, what percent live off-campus?

15. What percent of respondents are males who live on-campus?

16. Of those who live off-campus, what percent are female?

17. Use the table below to calculate chi-square: _____

Blues and R&B Music

		FREQUENCY	PERCENT	VALID PERCENT	CUMULATIVE PERCENT
Valid	Like It	505	56.1	58.6	58.6
	Mixed Feelings	220	24.4	25.5	84.1
	Dislike It	137	15.2	15.9	100.0
	Total	862	95.8	100.0	
Missing	System	38	4.2		
Total		900	100.0		

18. Use the table below to calculate chi-square: _____

Voting in 1992 Election

		FREQUENCY	PERCENT	VALID PERCENT	CUMULATIVE PERCENT
Valid	Voted	659	73.2	73.6	73.6
	Did not vote	211	23.4	23.6	97.2
	Not eligible	20	2.2	2.2	99.4
	Refused	5	.6	.6	100.0

(Continued)

Continued

		FREQUENCY	PERCENT	VALID PERCENT	CUMULATIVE PERCENT
	Total	895	99.4	100.0	
Missing	DK	3	.3		
	NA	2	.2		
	Total	5	.6		
Total		900	100.0		

19. Use the table below to calculate chi-square (expected frequencies are given in the table): _____

Rap Music (3) Respondent's Sex Cross-tabulation

			RESPONDENT'S SEX		
			MALE	FEMALE	TOTAL
Rap Music (3)	Like It	Count	56	55	111
		Expected Count	47.1	63.9	111.0
	Mixed Feelings	Count	60	109	169
		Expected Count	71.8	97.2	169.0
	Dislike It	Count	250	332	582
		Expected Count	247.1	334.9	582.0
Total		Count	366	496	862
		Expected Count	366.0	496.0	862.0

20. Use the table below to calculate chi-square: _____

Classical Music (3) Education Cross-tabulation

			EDUCATION		
			LESS THAN HIGH SCHOOL	HIGH SCHOOL OR HIGHER	TOTAL
Classical Music (3)	Like It	Count	35	403	438
		% within Education	30.4%	54.2%	51.0%
	Mixed Feelings	Count	23	196	219
		% within Education	20.0%	26.3%	25.5%
	Dislike It	Count	57	145	202
		% within Education	49.6%	19.5%	23.5%
Total		Count	115	744	859
		% within Education	100.0%	100.0%	100.0%

Computer Exercises

Use the information in the table below to create a database.
Use the database to answer the questions that follow.

SEX (IS R MALE OR FEMALE?) MALE FEMALE	CLASS (R'S PROGRESS IN ACADEMIC CAREER) FRESHMAN SOPHOMORE JUNIOR SENIOR OTHER	CAMPUS (DOES R LIVE ON CAMPUS?) YES NO	CAR (DOES R OWN A CAR?) YES NO	AGE (R'S AGE IN YEARS)
SEX	CLASS	CAMPUS	CAR	AGE
1	3	2	1	18
1	2	2	1	20
1	3	2	1	19
1	4	1	1	18
2	2	2	1	20
2	1	1	2	32
1	3	2	1	24
2	2	1	1	21
1	4	1	1	22
2	5	1	2	21
1	5	2	2	21
1	5	1	1	20
2	4	2	1	20
1	3	1	2	21
2	2	1	1	21
1	4	2	2	21
2	1	2	1	21
1	3	1	2	21
2	1	1	1	20
1	4	1	1	20

21. How many respondents are male?

22. How many respondents are seniors?

23. How many respondents own a car?

24. How many respondents live on campus?

25. How many respondents are 21 years old?

26. What percent of respondents are female?

27. What percent of respondents are freshmen?

28. What percent of respondents are sophomores?

29. What percent of respondents are either juniors or seniors?

30. What percent of respondents are not seniors?

31. What percent of respondents do not own a car?

32. What percent of respondents are 18 years old?

33. What percent of respondents are more than 18 years old?

34. What percent of respondents are between the ages of 20 and 22 (inclusive)?

35. What percent of respondents live on campus?

36. What is chi-square equal to for the variable Sex?

37. What is the alpha value for the chi-square for the variable Sex?

38. What is chi-square equal to for the table Campus by Sex?

39. What is alpha equal to for the table Campus by Sex?

40. In your own words, describe what alpha is telling us about the table Campus by Sex.

Now You Try It Answers

1: A) 71.0% 29.0% B) Of females, 63.8% favor the death penalty for murder.

Of females, 36.2% oppose the death penalty for murder.

2:

Is Respondent Employed Sex of Respondent Cross-tabulation

| | | | RESPONDENT'S SEX | | |
			MALE	FEMALE	TOTAL
Is Respondent Employed	No	Count	4	7	11
		% within Sex of Respondent	33.3%	38.9%	36.7%
	Yes	Count	8	11	19
		% within Sex of Respondent	66.7%	61.1%	63.3%
	Total	Count	12	18	30
		% within Sex of Respondent	100.0%	100.0%	100.0%

3: Degrees of freedom = 2 Chi-square = 2.570
Alpha = Not significant to .05 level

4: Degrees of freedom = 2 Chi-square = 354.3
Alpha = .01

Key Terms

Column percent, 202
Column variable, 202
Cross-tabulation table, 200
Expected frequencies, 217
Null hypothesis, 217

Observed frequencies, 217
One-way chi-square, 218
Research hypothesis, 217
Row percent, 213
Row variable, 213

Statistical significance, 217
Total percent, 214
Two-way chi-square, 224

Works Cited

Brulle, R. J. (2009). U.S. environmental movements. In K. A. Gould & T. L. Lewis (Eds.), *Twenty lessons in environmental sociology* (pp. 211–227). New York: Oxford University Press.

Carson, R. (1962). *Silent spring*. Boston: Houghton Mifflin.

Levin, J. (1999). *Sociological snapshops: Seeing social structure in everyday life* (3rd ed.). Thousand Oaks, CA: Pine Forge.

National Opinion Research Center. (2006). General Social Survey. Chicago: Author.

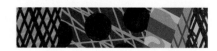

Measures of
Association for
Categorical Variables

Introduction

Measures of association are commonly used statistics that allow
us to express the degree to which changes in one variable co-vary
with changes in another variable. They enable us to express this co-
variation with a single number that ranges between 0 and 1. The
closer a measure is to 1.0, the stronger the association. For example,
income and race are associated. Whites tend to have higher income
than blacks. Also, income and education are associated with one

Statistical Association A condition that exists when changes in one variable are accompanied by changes in another variable.

Causality A condition in which changes in one variable are caused by changes in another variable.

Strength of Association All statistical associations range between 0 and 1.0; 0 indicates no association and 1.0 indicates a perfect association.

Direction of Association Refers to whether an increase in one variable is accompanied by an increase (positive association) or decrease (negative association) in another variable.

another. People with more education tend to have more income. Therefore, increases in education tend to be associated with increases in income.

All measures of association indicate the strength of association, but not all indicate the *direction of association*. In cases involving a nominal variable, such as the association between income and race (e.g., Black/White/Other), the association cannot have direction because race is a nominal variable. In cases involving no nominal variables, the concept of direction does apply. For example, if increases in education are associated with increases in income, the association is positive. On the other hand, if increases in education are associated with decreases in income, the association is negative.

Statistical association refers only to a condition involving co-variation in two or more variables. It does not imply that one variable causes a change in another variable. A common saying among social scientists is "association does not imply causation."

In this chapter, we discuss measures of association that can be used when working with categorical (nominal and ordinal) variables in a cross-tabulation table. The nominal measures of association addressed include phi, the contingency coefficient (C), Cramer's V (V), and lambda (λ) The ordinal measures of association addressed are gamma and Somer's *d*. See Table 8.1.

TABLE 8.1 *Symbols and Formulas*

TERM/SYMBOL	MEANING OF TERM/SYMBOL	FORMULA
Measures of association	A group of descriptive statistics that indicate the strength of a relationship between two variables. Some, but not all, measures of association indicate the direction of the association.	
Proportionate reduction of error	The degree to which our ability to predict outcomes in the dependent variable are influenced by the independent variable.	*PRE*
Phi (ϕ)	A chi-square-based measure of association used with 2 × 2 cross-tabulation tables that contain at least one nominal variable	$\phi = \sqrt{\dfrac{X^2}{N}}$
Contingency coefficient (C)	A chi-square-based measure of association used with cross-tabulation tables that are square in shape and contain at least one nominal variable	$C = \sqrt{\dfrac{X^2}{N + X^2}}$

(Continued)

TABLE 8.1 *Continued*

TERM/SYMBOL	MEANING OF TERM/SYMBOL	FORMULA
Cramer's V (V)	A chi-square-based measure of association used with cross-tabulation tables that are rectangular in shape and contain at least one nominal variable	$V = \sqrt{\dfrac{X^2}{N(k-1)}}$
Lambda	A PRE measure of association used when at least one of the two variables in a cross-tabulation table is nominal	$\lambda = \dfrac{E_1 - E_2}{E_1}$
Gamma	A PRE measure of association based on the concept of concordant (same-order) and discordant (opposite-order) pairs that is used when both variables in a cross-tabulation table are ordinal	$G = \dfrac{S - O}{S + O}$
Somer's d	A PRE measure of association based on the concept of concordant (same-order), discordant (opposite-order), and tied pairs that is used when working with two ordinal variables	$d = \dfrac{S - O}{S + O + T_y}$

Social Institutions and Social Control

In October 1972, a Uruguayan rugby team, along with numerous family and friends, was flying across the Andes Mountains to Santiago, Chile, for a match when their plane crashed deep in the heart of the mountains. Many of the passengers were killed in the crash and others died shortly after from injury. The survivors were stranded for nearly 3 months before being rescued and were able to survive by eating the bodies of those who were killed in the crash. Upon hearing this, most of my students immediately reject the possibility that they themselves would partake in this seemingly unthinkable act. Before jumping to any conclusions about what each of us would or would not do in a similar situation, let us consider the power of social institutions.

Sociologist Richard Schaefer defines social institutions as "organized patterns of beliefs and behavior centered on basic social needs, such as replacing personnel (the family) and preserving social order (the government)" (2009, p. 113). Social institutions also have the effect of channeling human behavior into identifiable patterns. Religion can be considered a social institution in that it consists of organized patterns of beliefs and behavior that serve a variety of functions at the individual and social levels. A great deal of debate takes place between sociologists who argue that religion is becoming secularized and moving increasingly in the direction of formal organizations and those who challenge such claims. In either case, it seems safe to consider religion a social institution.

You may recall our discussion of Emile Durkheim's study of suicide from Chapter 1. Durkheim (1897/1951) argued that in times of uncertainty, suicide rates tend to rise. However, he considered suicide to be only one type of deviance that could result from a societal state of anomie. Rises in the rates of other types of deviant behavior might also emerge. He concluded that increases in suicide rates would not be consistent across all groups. Certain groups in society, those who are most integrated into communities that can effectively act as a barrier to anomie by providing social structure, would be less likely to see increases in suicide rates. Another way of thinking about this is in the context of social control. Was Durkheim writing about the functions of social institutions or was he writing about the manners in which social institutions can exert control over individuals (for better or worse)? I suppose it depends on how you choose to read his work.

In this way, Durkheim viewed social control (or we may think of it as socialization) as taking place along two axes: regulation and integration. Normal amounts of regulation and integration are represented by the green shaded area in Figure 8.1 while pathological amounts are shown in red. It is in these red zones that Durkheim predicted rising levels of deviant behavior. Too little regulation can lead to anomie and too much regulation can lead to fatalism. Likewise, too little integration can lead to egoism and

Figure 8.1 A Durkheimian Model of Socialization/Social Control

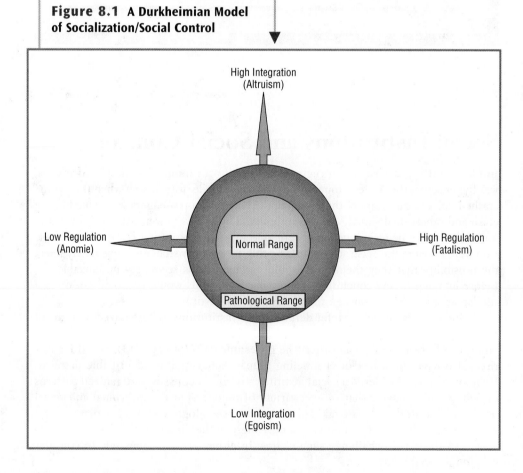

too much can lead to altruism. This raises interesting questions about what kinds of institutions are socializing (controlling?) people in our society.

As it turned out, the survivors of the plane crash in the Andes resolved their dilemma over eating human flesh in two ways, one moralistically and the other religiously. First, they concluded that should they themselves die, they would want the other survivors to eat them in order to live. Second, the crash survivors likened the act of eating human flesh to partaking in communion in the Catholic Church (most, if not all, the passengers were Catholic). In his book *Alive* (2005), author Piers Paul Read notes that upon the survivors' return to civilization, the Church went so far as to state that they did not need to be forgiven, for they had committed no sin. In this case, the social control of the Church may have saved the survivors.

We now turn our attention to measures of association using examples of social institutions and the degree to which people are integrated into these institutions. We begin with nominal measures of association and then discuss ordinal measures of association.

Nominal Measures of Association

Nominal measures of association are used when at least one of the two variables in a cross-tabulation table is operationalized at the nominal level. Because nominal values do not have increasing or decreasing relative values, nominal measures of association can only be positive; the concept of the direction of association does not apply.

We discuss four nominal measures of association: phi (ϕ), the contingency coefficient (C), Cramer's V (V), and lambda (λ). Phi, the contingency coefficient, and Cramer's V are very similar to one another in that all three are based on chi-square. They are referred to as chi-square-based measures of association and are so similar to one another that only one, phi, will be given full attention; C and V are given brief discussions. Lambda is based on a logic that differs significantly from chi-square.

> **Nominal Measures of Association** Measures of association that are used when working with a cross-tabulation table that contains at least one nominal variable. They include phi, the contingency coefficient, Cramer's *V*, and lambda.

Chi-Square-Based Measures of Association

You may recall from our discussion of chi-square in Chapter 7 that the number of cases in a table has a direct effect on the size of the chi-square statistic. This in turn has a direct effect on the alpha value obtained from the *Critical Values of Chi-Square* table. Therefore, assuming that some difference exists between the observed frequency and the expected frequency, the degree of statistical significance is a function of the number of cases. Add enough cases to any table and eventually it will become statistically significant. This means that any measure of association based on chi-square must find some way to control for the number of cases (N).

One other consideration for measures of association based on chi-square is that the actual value of chi-square is a squared value (as the name implies). Therefore, it is necessary to take the square out of chi-square by taking its square root. As you can see from the formula below, phi controls for the number of cases by putting in the denominator and it controls for the squared nature of chi-square by taking the square root of the entire equation. All chi-square-based measures of association do essentially the same thing, but with slight variations. Consider the equations for phi, C, and V in Table 8.2.

TABLE 8.2   *Equations for Phi, C, and V*

$\phi = \sqrt{\dfrac{\chi^2}{N}}$	χ^2 = Chi-square N = Number of cases Only used when working with 2 × 2 cross-tabulation tables.
$C = \sqrt{\dfrac{\chi^2}{N + \chi^2}}$	χ^2 = Chi-square N = Number of cases Used with larger tables that are square in shape (3 × 3, 4 × 4, etc.)
$V = \sqrt{\dfrac{\chi^2}{N(k - 1)}}$	χ^2 = Chi-square N = Number of cases k = Number of rows in the table or the number of columns in the table (whichever is smaller) Used when working with tables that are rectangular in shape (3 × 5, 2 × 6, etc.)

Chi-square-based measures of association are based, as you might expect, on the magnitude of difference between the frequencies that we observe in our data and the frequencies that we would expect if there were no trends at all. In other words, as the difference between observed and expected increases, the more likely that there is an association. It is essentially the same logic used in the calculation of chi-square to assess statistical significance, except that we control for the number of cases. For example, suppose we sample 20 respondents, 10 males and 10 females, and ask them if they attend religious services on a weekly basis and get the results shown in Table 8.3 (expected frequencies are in parentheses).

As you can see, there is no difference between the observed and expected frequencies, therefore the value of chi-square and chi-square-based measures of association will be .00, no association. On the other hand, if our results are like those shown in Table 8.4, we would have perfect association of 1.0. In this case, the difference between observed and expected frequencies is maximized. And as you can see, all males in the sample do not attend weekly services while all females do attend weekly services.

By itself, chi-square cannot function as a measure of association because it is strongly influenced by sample size (N). By keeping the proportion of each respondent in each cell the same while increasing the overall frequencies (and therefore N), chi-square increases from a small value to a larger value. It is therefore necessary to control for sample size when using chi-square-based measures of association. We now turn our

TABLE 8.3   *Weekly Service Attendance*

	MALES	FEMALES	TOTAL
Attends Weekly Services	5 (5)	5 (5)	10
Does Not Attend Weekly Services	5 (5)	5 (5)	10
Total	10	10	20

TABLE 8.4 *Weekly Service Attendance*

	MALES	FEMALES	TOTAL
Attends Weekly Services	0 (5)	10 (5)	10
Does Not Attend Weekly Services	10 (5)	0 (5)	10
Total	10	10	20

attention to demonstrating how to calculate phi, *C*, and *V* using data from the 2006 General Social Survey. The examples below draw on variables related to the social institution of religion and the degree to which integration into this social institution influences beliefs and behaviors.

Phi A chi-square-based measure of association used with 2 × 2 cross-tabulation tables that contain at least one nominal variable.

EXAMPLE 1

Calculating Phi (ϕ) to Assess toward Abortion

In a 1973 ruling known as *Roe v. Wade,* the Supreme Court legalized abortion. It would be an understatement to say that this remains a disputed ruling. Suppose we are interested in learning more about how religion influences attitudes toward abortion. The General Social Survey (GSS) operationalizes a number of variables related to religiosity, including how fundamental respondents are in their religious beliefs, how often respondents attend religious services, and whether respondents feel the bible is the word of God. Likewise, the GSS contains a number of items that measure respondents' attitudes toward abortion. For this example, religion is operationalized as whether respondents consider themselves fundamentalist or liberal in their beliefs and abortion is operationalized as whether respondents feel that a woman should be able to have an abortion for any reason. Table 8.5 is

TABLE 8.5 *Abortion if Woman Wants for Any Reason by Religious Beliefs*

			IS R FUNDAMENTALIST OR LIBERAL IN RELIGIOUS BELIEFS		
			FUNDAMENTALIST	LIBERAL	TOTAL
ABORTION IF WOMAN WANTS FOR ANY REASON	YES	Count	143	337	480
		Expected Count	229.7	250.3	480.0
	NO	Count	403	258	661
		Expected Count	316.3	344.7	661.0
	Total	Count	546	595	1141
		Expected Count	546.0	595.0	1141.0

generated using these variables and it includes both observed and expected frequencies. Suppose we hypothesize that attitudes toward abortion are a function of religious beliefs.

To calculate phi, we must first calculate chi-square using the formula:

$$\chi^2 = \sum \frac{(f_o - f_e)^2}{f_e}$$

Fundamentalist/Yes: $\dfrac{(f_o - f_e)^2}{f_e} = \dfrac{(143 - 229.7)^2}{229.7} = \dfrac{(-86.7)^2}{229.7} = \dfrac{7516.89}{229.7} = 32.7$

Fundamentalist/No: $\dfrac{(f_o - f_e)^2}{f_e} = \dfrac{(403 - 316.3)^2}{316.3} = \dfrac{(86.7)^2}{316.3} = \dfrac{7516.89}{316.3} = 23.8$

Liberal/Yes: $\dfrac{(f_o - f_e)^2}{f_e} = \dfrac{(337 - 250.3)^2}{250.3} = \dfrac{(86.7)^2}{250.3} = \dfrac{7516.89}{250.3} = 30.0$

Liberal/No: $\dfrac{(f_o - f_e)^2}{f_e} = \dfrac{(258 - 344.7)^2}{344.7} = \dfrac{(-86.7)^2}{344.7} = \dfrac{7516.89}{344.7} = 21.8$

Chi-square = 108.3

Once we have calculated chi-square (108.3) and N (1,141), we can use them in the formula for phi.

$$\phi = \sqrt{\frac{\chi^2}{N}} = \sqrt{\frac{108.3}{1141}} = \sqrt{.0949} = .308$$

χ^2 = Chi-square

N = Number of cases

This tells us that a moderately strong association characterizes the relationship between respondents' religiosity and attitudes toward abortion and offers some support for our hypothesis. Based on the value of phi, we cannot say which group tends to be more liberal or fundamentalist in their religious beliefs because the concept of direction of association does not apply to phi, or to any nominal measures of association. To determine which group tends to be more liberal we must compare column percents in the table, as was shown in Chapter 7.

Before we leave this example, one more consideration must be taken into account: the significance of this association. In other words, we now know the strength of the association between religiosity and attitude toward abortion, but we do not know how statistically significant this association is. To determine the significance level, we can use Table C (Critical Values of Chi-Square) in Appendix A using the same technique we used in Chapter 7. Our chi-square value of 108.3 far exceeds the table value of 6.635 and therefore our results are significant to the .01 level ($\alpha = .01$).

Now You Try It 1

A. Use the table below to calculate phi. Expected frequencies are in parentheses.

	MALES	FEMALES	TOTAL
Attends Weekly Services	3 (5)	7 (5)	10
Does Not Attend Weekly Services	7 (5)	3 (5)	10
Total	10	10	20

   1. Phi =
   2. Are the results significant to the .05 level? the .01 level?

B. Use the table below to calculate phi.

Is the Bible the Word of God How Often R Attends Religious Services Cross-tabulation

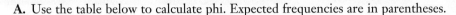

			HOW OFTEN R ATTENDS RELIGIOUS SERVICES		
			LESS THAN ONCE A WEEK	ONCE A WEEK OR MORE	TOTAL
IS THE BIBLE THE WORD OF GOD	YES	Count	591	416	1007
		Expected Count	740.7	266.3	1007.0
	NO	Count	1570	361	1931
		Expected Count	1420.3	510.7	1931.0
	Total	Count	2161	777	2938
		Expected Count	2161.0	777.0	2938.0

   1. Phi =
   2. Are the results significant to the .05 level? the .01 level?

Contingency Coefficient A chi-square-based measure of association used with cross-tabulation tables that are square in shape and contain at least one nominal variable.

EXAMPLE 2

Calculating the Contingency Coefficient to Assess Feelings about the Bible

Let us now suppose that we are interested in learning about how race is associated with feelings about the Bible. Like phi, the logic behind the contingency coefficient is based on chi-square (the difference between observed and expected frequencies). The more our observed frequencies differ from our expected frequencies, the larger chi-square will be. As you can see in Table 8.6, our two variables each have three attributes, resulting in a 3×3 table, which makes it appropriate for using the contingency coefficient (C). Suppose that we hypothesize that feelings about the Bible are a function of race.

TABLE 8.6 *Feelings About the Bible by Race of Respondent*

| | | | RACE OF RESPONDENT | | | |
			WHITE	BLACK	OTHER	TOTAL
FEELINGS ABOUT THE BIBLE	WORD OF GOD	Count	609	256	145	1010
		Expected Count	738.7	143.2	128.1	1010.0
	INSPIRED WORD	Count	1079	127	157	1363
		Expected Count	996.8	193.3	172.9	1363.0
	BOOK OF FABLES	Count	411	24	62	497
		Expected Count	363.5	70.5	63.0	497.0
	Total	Count	2099	407	364	2870
		Expected Count	2099.0	407.0	364.0	2870.0

Because we have spent ample time calculating chi-square, let us assume that we now know that the chi-square value for Table 8.6 is equal to 181.73. Now that we have determined chi-square (181.73) and N (2,870), we can use them in the formula for the contingency coefficient:

$$C = \sqrt{\frac{\chi^2}{N + \chi^2}} = \sqrt{\frac{181.73}{2870 + 181.73}} = \sqrt{\frac{181.73}{3051.73}} = \sqrt{.0595} = .244$$

χ^2 = Chi-square

N = Number of cases

This indicates that an association does exist between the variables Race and Feelings about the Bible and offers support for our hypothesis, although not a lot of support. It does not, however, tell us anything about which group or groups tend to feel a particular way. The final step is to determine whether our results are statistically significant. To do this, we use our chi-square value of 181.73. To determine the significance level, we use Table C (Critical Values of Chi-Square) in the back of the book using the same technique we used in Chapter 7. With four degrees of freedom, our chi-square value of 181.73 far exceeds the table value of 13.277 and therefore our results are significant to the .01 level ($\alpha = .01$).

Now You Try It 2

A. Use the table below to calculate the contingency coefficient. Expected frequencies are in parentheses.

	WHITE	BLACK	OTHER	TOTAL
Attends Weekly Services	30 (32)	25 (21)	20 (21)	75
Attends Services Less than Weekly	10 (13)	10 (9)	10 (9)	30
Never Attends Services	20 (15)	5 (10)	10 (10)	35
Total	60	40	40	140

1. C =
2. Are the results significant to the .05 level? the .01 level?

B. Use the table below to calculate the contingency coefficient.

Is Life Exciting or Dull by RS Religious Preference

			RS RELIGIOUS PREFERENCE			
			PROTESTANT	CATHOLIC	JEWISH	TOTAL
IS LIFE EXCITING OR DULL	EXCITING	Count	493	244	18	755
		Expected Count	507.7	234.5	12.7	755.0
	ROUTINE	Count	502	207	8	717
		Expected Count	482.2	222.7	12.1	717.0
	DULL	Count	42	28	0	70
		Expected Count	47.1	21.7	1.2	70.0
	Total	Count	1037	479	26	1542
		Expected Count	1037.0	479.0	26.0	1542.0

1. C =
2. Are the results significant to the .05 level? the .01 level?

Cramer's V A chi-square based measure of association used with cross-tabulation tables that are rectangular in shape and contain at least one nominal variable.

EXAMPLE 3

Calculating Cramer's V to Assess Interpretations of the Bible

Cramer's V is the third and final chi-square-based measure of association that we will learn. It is used when working with cross-tabulation tables that contain at least one nominal variable when the table is not square. Cramer's V is interpreted the same way that phi and the contingency coefficient are interpreted. Suppose we want to know more about the relationship between respondents' level of education and their interpretation of the bible and obtain the data shown in Table 8.7. We hypothesize that interpretations of the bible are a function of education.

TABLE 8.7 *Is the Bible the Word of God by Education*

			EDUCATION			
			LESS THAN 12 YEARS	12 YEARS	MORE THAN 12 YEARS	TOTAL
IS THE BIBLE THE WORD OF GOD	YES	Count	262	298	450	1010
		Expected Count	167.8	254.6	587.5	1010.0
	NO	Count	227	444	1262	1933
		Expected Count	321.2	487.4	1124.5	1933.0
	Total	Count	489	742	1712	2943
		Expected Count	489.0	742.0	1712.0	2943.0

To calculate the Cramer's V we must first calculate chi-square. Again, because we have spent ample time working on the calculations for chi-square, we move ahead knowing that chi-square is equal to 140.76. Now that we have determined chi-square (140.76) and N (2,943), we can use them in the formula for Cramer's V.

$$V = \sqrt{\frac{\chi^2}{N(k-1)}} = \sqrt{\frac{140.76}{2943(2-1)}} = \sqrt{\frac{140.76}{2943}} = \sqrt{.0478} = .219$$

χ^2 = Chi-square

N = Number of cases

k = Number of rows in the table or the number of columns in the table (whichever is smaller)

This indicates that there is a fairly weak association between the variables Education and Interpretation of the Bible and offers support for our hypothesis, although not a lot of support. Again, it does not tell us anything about which group or groups tend to feel a particular way, only that there are patterns in the data. The final step is to determine whether our results are statistically significant. To do this, we use our chi-square value of 140.76. To determine the significance level, we use Table C (Critical Values of Chi-Square) in the back of the book using the same technique we used in Chapter 7. With two degrees of freedom, our chi-square value of 140.76 far exceeds the table value of 9.210 and therefore our results are significant to the .01 level ($\alpha = .01$).

Now You Try It 3

A. Use the table below to calculate Cramer's V. Expected frequencies are in parentheses.

	WHITE	BLACK	OTHER	TOTAL
Attends Weekly Services	30 (28)	20 (21)	20 (21)	70
Attends Services Less than Weekly	10 (12)	10 (9)	10 (9)	30
Total	40	30	30	100

1. Cramer's V =
2. Are the results significant to the .05 level? the .01 level?

B. Use the table below to calculate Cramer's V.

Political Party Affiliation by RS Religious Preference

			RS RELIGIOUS PREFERENCE			
			PROTESTANT	CATHOLIC	JEWISH	TOTAL
POLITICAL PARTY AFFILIATION	DEMOCRAT	Count	748	335	46	1129
		Expected Count	785.8	312.6	30.6	1129.0
	REPUBLICAN	Count	740	257	12	1009
		Expected Count	702.2	279.4	27.4	1009.0
	Total	Count	1488	592	58	2138
		Expected Count	1488.0	592.0	58.0	2138.0

1. Cramer's V =
2. Are the results significant to the .05 level? the .01 level?

Lambda (λ)

Lambda is the final nominal measure of association that we will learn. It is not a chi-square-based measure of association; instead, it is based on the logic of proportionate reduction of error. Proportionate reduction of error (PRE) refers to the extent to which knowledge of the categories of an independent variable reduce errors in predicting categories of the dependent variable. Like all measures of association, lambda can range from 0 to 1.0 in strength. The more errors are reduced, the stronger the association between the variables. Again, because it is a nominal measure of association, the direction of association does not apply.

Lambda A PRE measure of association used when at least one of the two variables in a cross-tabulation table is nominal.

Proportionate Reduction of Error (PRE) The proportion of errors that are eliminated in predicting values on the dependent variable by knowing values on the independent variable.

The formula for lambda is fairly simple in that it contains only two values, E_1 and E_2.

$$\lambda = \frac{E_1 - E_2}{E_1}$$

E_1 is the number of errors without knowledge of the independent variable.

E_2 is the number of errors with knowledge of the independent variable.

EXAMPLE 4

Applying the Concept of Proportionate Reduction of Error (PRE)

Suppose we are trying to predict the outcome of some event (it doesn't matter what the event is) and over the course of 154 guesses we make 100 errors. Now suppose that someone gives us some information that we can use to help predict the outcome of the event. Over the course of the next 154 guesses, we only make 50 errors. Clearly, we have been given some very important information because we used it to cut the number of our errors in half. In this example, E_1 is our original number of errors (100) and E_2 is our new number of errors with the new information. The 154 prediction is not important; it could just as easily have been 254 predictions. What is important are the numbers of errors.

The formula for lambda now looks like this:

$$\lambda = \frac{E_1 - E_2}{E_1} = \frac{100 - 50}{100} = \frac{50}{100} = .5$$

It makes sense that lambda is equal to .5 because the information we received reduced the number of errors that we made by 50% (i.e., .5). If that information had reduced our errors by one-third, then lambda would be equal to .33. This is the nature of PRE measures of association: knowledge of values on the independent variable reduces the number of errors that we make in predicting values on the dependent variable. The value of lambda is equal to the ratio by which the original number of errors is reduced. This logic can be applied to cross-tabulation tables to assess the strength of the association between two variables.

EXAMPLE 5

Calculating Lambda to Predict Library Use

Suppose we want to know more about the relationship between living on campus and using the library.

TABLE 8.8 *Library Use by Residency*

	ON-CAMPUS	OFF-CAMPUS	TOTALS
Uses Library Often	25	65	90
Uses Library Seldom	75	35	110
Totals	100	100	200

To determine the value of E_1, we only use data from the Totals column where $N = 200$. From this column, we know that 90 students use the library often and 110 use the library seldom. If we were to randomly select one of the 200 respondents and had to predict whether they used the library often or seldom, we would predict that this randomly selected respondent uses the library seldom. We would make this selection on the basis of there being more respondents who use the library seldom than there are respondents who use the library often. If we applied this same method to all 200 respondents, we would make 110 correct predictions and 90 errors. These 90 errors are the value for E_1. Another way of thinking about E_1 is to select the mode in the Totals column, and everything else is an error.

$E_1 = 90$

To determine E_2, we use the same method that we used to determine E_1, except we apply it first to the column for On-Campus students and then to the column for Off-Campus students. The sum of the two is equal to the value of E_2. For example, we know that 100 students live On-Campus *and* we know that 75 of them seldom use the library. Therefore, when randomly selecting On-Campus students, we would predict that each one seldom uses the library. This technique results in 75 correct predictions and 25 errors. Similarly, for the 100 Off-Campus students, we would predict that each one uses the library often. This results in 65 correct predictions and 35 errors. The sum of errors for On-Campus and Off-Campus students is the value for E_2. In this case $E_2 = 25$ On-Campus Errors $+ 35$ Off-Campus Errors $= 60$ Total Errors.

$E_2 = 60$

As you can see, knowing whether students live on-campus or off-campus reduces our number of errors that we make in our predictions from 90 to 60. We can then plug these values into the formula for lambda.

$$\lambda = \frac{E_1 - E_2}{E_1} = \frac{90 - 60}{90} = \frac{30}{90} = .33$$

Reducing our errors from 90 to 60 translates into a 33% reduction in the number of errors. Therefore, lambda is equal to .33 and is translated as follows: Knowing whether a student lives On-Campus or Off-Campus reduces our errors in predicting library use by 33%. You can begin to see why lambda is considered a PRE measure of association. In this example, our proportionate reduction of error is .33.

EXAMPLE 6

Calculating Lambda to Describe the Association of Religion with Race

Now let's consider an example of lambda using the relationship between race and religion. As you can see from Table 8.9 (Race is the independent variable and Religious Preference is the dependent variable), 69.8% of Whites are Protestant compared to 92.3% of Blacks, and only 26.3% of Others. This wide discrepancy in percentages indicates that some type of association exists between race and religious affiliation. We can assess the strength of this association using lambda, but first we must determine the values of E_1 and E_2.

TABLE 8.9 *Is R Catholic or Protestant by Race of Respondent*

| | | | RACE OF RESPONDENT | | | |
			WHITE	BLACK	OTHER	TOTAL
IS R CATHOLIC OR PROTESTANT	PROTESTANT	Count	1721	490	117	2328
		% within Race of Respondent	69.8%	92.3%	26.3%	67.6%
	CATHOLIC	Count	745	41	328	1114
		% within Race of Respondent	30.2%	7.7%	73.7%	32.4%
	Total	Count	2466	531	445	3442
		% within Race of Respondent	100.0%	100.0%	100.0%	100.0%

To determine E_1 we need only to select the mode in the Total column and consider everything else an error. This means that the mode is Protestant and the frequency of Catholics ($f = 1114$) is equal to E_1.

To determine E_2 we must apply the same methods as we did for E_1, except this time we must do it for Whites, Blacks, and Others and sum the results. For Whites the mode is Protestant, so $E_{2 \text{ for Whites}} = 745$. For Blacks the mode is Protestant, so $E_{2 \text{ for Blacks}} = 41$. And for Others the mode is Catholic, so $E_{2 \text{ for Others}} = 117$. The sum of these values is

$$E_2 = 745 + 41 + 117 = 903$$

We now know that $E_1 = 1114$ and $E_2 = 903$. Our formula for lambda is:

$$\lambda = \frac{E_1 - E_2}{E_1} = \frac{1114 - 903}{1114} = \frac{211}{1114} = .189$$

It is important to note that if lambda is calculated with Race dependent, rather than Religious Preference, the result will not be the same. It is also possible to calculate a symmetric lambda, a technique that does not differentiate between independent and dependent variables in the table. For the purposes of this book, however, only one version is discussed (that which places the independent variable in the columns of the cross-tabulation table). It should also be noted that the significance test for lambda is based on a highly complex formula based on standard errors and is not discussed in this text.

We now turn our attention to ordinal measures of association and the concept of ordered pairs.

Now You Try It 4

These problems use the same tables that you used to calculate phi in *Now You Try It 1*. Notice how the results differ. Remember, you do not need to use the expected frequencies to calculate lambda.

A. Use the table below to calculate lambda. Expected frequencies are in parentheses.

Religious Service Attendance by Sex

	MALES	FEMALES	TOTAL
Attends Weekly Services	3	7	10
Does Not Attend Weekly Services	7	3	10
Total	10	10	20

Lambda =

B. Use the table below to calculate lambda.

Is the Bible the Word of God by How Often R Attends Religious Services

			HOW OFTEN R ATTENDS RELIGIOUS SERVICES		
			LESS THAN ONCE A WEEK	ONCE A WEEK OR MORE	TOTAL
IS THE BIBLE THE WORD OF GOD	YES	Count	591	416	1007
		Expected Count	740.7	266.3	1007.0
	NO	Count	1570	361	1931
		Expected Count	1420.3	510.7	1931.0
	Total	Count	2161	777	2938
		Expected Count	2161.0	777.0	2938.0

Lambda =

Integrating Technology

Often, it is useful to be able to specify whether results hold true across an entire population or only across certain demographic groups. For example, suppose we are interested in the relationship between race and attitudes toward the death penalty and find the following:

Favor or Oppose Death Penalty for Murder by Race of Respondent

			RACE OF RESPONDENT			
			WHITE	BLACK	OTHER	TOTAL
FAVOR OR OPPOSE DEATH PENALTY FOR MURDER	FAVOR	Count	1522	159	204	1885
		% within Race of Respondent	73.2%	42.3%	56.5%	67.0%
	OPPOSE	Count	556	217	157	930
		% within Race of Respondent	26.8%	57.7%	43.5%	33.0%
	Total	Count	2078	376	361	2815
		% within Race of Respondent	100.0%	100.0%	100.0%	100.0%

As you can see, Whites are far more likely to favor the death penalty for murder compared to Blacks or Others. This finding is supported by a Cramer's V value of .239 (.000). We may be interested in knowing if this finding holds true across categories of sex. In other words, is the feeling among Whites common between males and females?

To answer this question, we can add a third variable to our analysis. SPSS for Windows calls this a "Layer" variable; most researchers call it a "control" variable. Adding the control variable Sex will produce two cross-tabulation tables (because the variable Sex is made up of two attributes). The results are shown below.

Favor or Oppose Death Penalty for Murder by Race of Respondent by Respondent's Sex

				RACE OF RESPONDENT			
RESPONDENT'S SEX				WHITE	BLACK	OTHER	TOTAL
MALE	FAVOR OR OPPOSE DEATH PENALTY FOR MURDER	FAVOR	Count	716	64	95	875
			% within Race of Respondent	76.9%	47.1%	57.6%	71.0%
		OPPOSE	Count	215	72	70	357
			% within Race of Respondent	23.1%	52.9%	42.4%	29.0%
	Total		Count	931	136	165	1232
			% within Race of Respondent	100.0%	100.0%	100.0%	100.0%
FEMALE	FAVOR OR OPPOSE DEATH PENALTY FOR MURDER	FAVOR	Count	806	95	109	1010
			% within Race of Respondent	70.3%	39.6%	55.6%	63.8%
		OPPOSE	Count	341	145	87	573
			% within Race of Respondent	29.7%	60.4%	44.4%	36.2%
	Total		Count	1147	240	196	1583
			% within Race of Respondent	100.0%	100.0%	100.0%	100.0%

By comparing the column percentages we see that in all three categories of race, males are more likely to approve of the death penalty for murder than are females. This difference, however, is not reflected in Cramer's V (.235 (sig. $= .000$)). It is always a good idea to compare column percents when analyzing associations because they often provide insight to the data that is not possible when using measures of association.

Ordinal Measures of Association

So far we have focused on measures of association that are used when at least one of the variables in a cross-tabulation table is nominal. When both variables in the table are ordinal, another group of statistics can be applied—ordinal measures of association. We have seen how the logic of observed and expected frequencies is used to calculate chi-square-based measures of association and we have seen how the logic of errors (E_1 and E_2) is used to calculate lambda. A third kind of logic, based on the concept of ordered pairs, is now presented. It is necessary to understand the concept of ordered pairs for the calculation of gamma G and Somer's d (d).

> **Ordinal Measures of Association** A group of statistics based on the concept of ordered pairs that are used when both variables in a cross-tabulation table are operationalized at the ordinal level.

The Concept of Ordered Pairs

When working with ordinal variables, researchers can apply the concept of direction to the data, whereas with nominal variables they cannot. For example, suppose we are interested in studying education and operationalize the variable *Highest Degree*, as shown in Table 8.10 below.

As you can see, the cases tend to cluster around High School, which is relatively low in the ordered list of possible degrees. If they clustered around Graduate, we could then say that they cluster higher. When applied to cross-tabulation tables, the properties of ordinal variables allow us to make predictions (hypotheses) about the relationship between two variables. For example, suppose we are studying the relationship between education and income. We might hypothesize that respondents with lower levels of education will be likely to have lower income and respondents with higher levels of

TABLE 8.10 *RS Highest Degree*

		FREQUENCY	PERCENT	VALID PERCENT	CUMULATIVE PERCENT
Valid	LT High School	691	15.3	15.3	15.3
	High School	2273	50.4	50.4	65.8
	Junior College	377	8.4	8.4	74.1
	Bachelor	763	16.9	16.9	91.1
	Graduate	403	8.9	8.9	100.0
	Total	4507	99.9	100.0	
Missing	NA	3	.1		
Total		4510	100.0		

TABLE 8.11 *Income*

	LOW EDUCATION	HIGH EDUCATION
High Income	*	**
Low Income	***	*

education would be likely to have higher income. Therefore, we would expect the cases in Table 8.11 to cluster in the lower left-hand cell and the upper right-hand cell.

The concept of ordered pairs provides a way to assess the degree to which cases align according to our predictions (higher scores on one variable tend to cluster with higher scores on the second variable). We can think of such clustering as support for our hypothesis.

In Table 8.11, we see that respondents with low education tend to have low income and cases with high education tend to have high income. Suppose that instead of having our cases represented by stars (*), we give them actual names. See Table 8.12.

The next step is to pair up all of the respondents with low education and low income with those who have high education and high income. The total number of pairs will act as an indicator of the tendency for our data to support the hypothesis because the more that cases cluster in these cells the more our data support our prediction. We can create the following pairs:

Betty/Wilma

Betty/Hillary

Betty/Barney

Jane/Wilma

Jane/Hillary

Jane/Barney

Fred/Wilma

Fred/Hillary

Fred/Barney

This gives a total of nine pairs. These are known as *concordant pairs* or *same-direction pairs*. Concordant pairs are pairs that support the hypothesis. The table also

TABLE 8.12 *Income Levels by Education*

	LOW EDUCATION	HIGH EDUCATION
High Income	Sam	Wilma Hillary Barney
Low Income	Betty Jane Fred	Bill

TABLE 8.13 *Income Levels by Education*

	LOW EDUCATION	HIGH EDUCATION
High Income	1	3
Low Income	3	1

contains a *discordant pair* or *opposite-direction pair* that does not support the hypothesis. This pair is:

Sam/Bill

Sam has low education and high income, something that our hypothesis does not predict. And Bill has high education and low income, which is also something that we did not predict. Calculating the number of same- and opposite-direction pairs is actually quite simple. Rather than using names in our table, let us put frequencies in each cell, as in Table 8.13.

To calculate the number of same-direction pairs, we multiply the frequency of the Low Education/Low Income cell ($f = 3$) by the frequency of the High Education/High Income cell ($f = 3$). This results in $3 \times 3 = 9$. Therefore, the number of same-direction pairs is 9. We do the same for opposite-direction pairs, multiplying the frequency of the Low Education/High Income cell ($f = 1$) by the frequency of the High Education/Low Income cell ($f = 1$). This results in $1 \times 1 = 1$. Therefore, the number of opposite-direction pairs is 1.

Integrating Technology

Understanding the relationship between two variables requires a thorough understanding of both the database one uses and the hypothesis one wishes to test. SPSS for Windows simplifies the process of understanding relationships by incorporating the measures of association into the same function as cross-tabulation tables. This way, any time you wish to run a cross-tabulation table, you have the choice of asking for any one (or several) measures of association. SPSS breaks these measures down into categories of Nominal Measures, Ordinal Measures, and Nominal by Interval/Ratio (the subject of Chapter 9). SPSS also offers users the option of a clustered bar chart that shows the frequencies of the cross-tabulation table.

For example, suppose that we want to learn more about the relationship between education and socioeconomic standing. We hypothesize that lower levels of education are associated with lower socioeconomic standing. To test this hypothesis, we run a cross-tabulation table with Education independent and Socioeconomic Status dependent. The independent and dependent variables are not all that clear in this analysis because we could claim that education leads to higher socioeconomic status or that socioeconomic status leads to higher levels of education. Therefore we will use the asymmetric measure gamma to assess the strength and direction of this association. The results (the cross-tabulation table, gamma statistic, and clustered bar chart) are shown on the next page.

Socioeconomic Standing by Education

		EDUCATION			
		LESS THAN 12 YEARS	12 YEARS	MORE THAN 12 YEARS	TOTAL
Socioeconomic Status	Low	520	493	465	1478
	Middle	243	640	1224	2107
	High	18	71	836	925
	Total	781	1204	2525	4510

Symmetric Measures

		VALUE	ASYMP. STD. ERROR[a]	APPROX. T[b]	APPROX. SIG.
Ordinal by Ordinal	Gamma	.642	.015	34.889	.000
	N of Valid Cases	4510			

[a]Not assuming the null hypothesis.

[b]Using the asymptotic standard error assuming the null hypothesis.

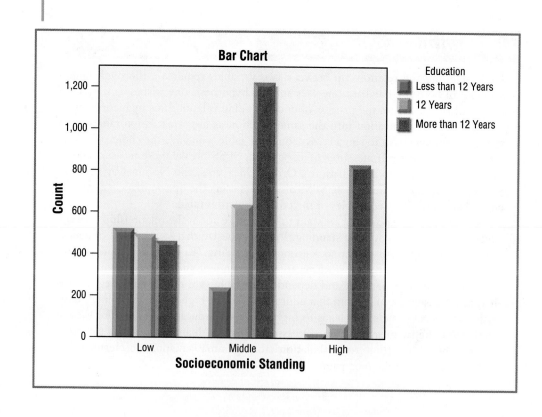

As you can see, the association between these variables is positive and quite strong, with a gamma of .642 that is significant to the .000 level. This means that knowing values on Education helps us to reduce errors in predicting values on Socioeconomic Status by 64.2%. The bar chart gives us a kind of window into the strength of the association. As you can see, respondents with more than 12 years of education tend to cluster strongly around middle and high socioeconomic status. It is no surprise then that by knowing values on one variable, we can better predict outcomes on the other variable.

Bar charts, a wide variety of statistical techniques, and easy to use software are just some of the benefits of a good statistical analysis program like SPSS for Windows.

Gamma

Gamma is the common name for Goodman's and Kruskal's Gamma. It is a PRE measure of association that is based on the concept of same- and opposite-direction pairs. It is a proportion based on the difference between same-direction pairs and opposite-direction pairs to the total number of pairs in the table. Gamma is an asymmetric measure and can be either positive or negative, depending on whether same-direction pairs outnumber opposite-direction pairs or not.

Gamma A PRE measure of association based on ordered pairs that is used with cross-tabulation tables containing two ordinal variables. Gamma is symmetric, meaning that it does not distinguish between independent and dependent variables.

$$G = \frac{S - O}{S + O}$$

To calculate gamma, we insert the number of same- and opposite-direction pairs into the equation as follows:

$$\text{Same-direction pairs} = 9$$

$$\text{Opposite-direction pairs} = 1$$

$$G = \frac{S - O}{S + O} = \frac{9 - 1}{9 + 1} = .80$$

A gamma of .80 tells us that the association of Education with Income is positive and quite strong. In fact, a gamma value of .80 indicates that we can predict values on the dependent variable with 80% greater accuracy by knowing values of the independent variable.

Explaining the PRE Logic of Gamma. Suppose that with a total of 10 ordered pairs (S + O), we have a 50/50 chance of predicting whether they happen to be same-order pairs or opposite-order pairs. Probability tells us that should we assume that all pairs are same-direction pairs, we would be correct half the time and make a total of five errors. Now suppose that we know the rank order of education for all of our pairs. This means that we now know that Higher Education is more likely to be paired with Higher Income. Because there is only one opposite-order pair in our table, probability tells us that should we assume that each pair is a same-direction pair, we will be making only one error. Reducing our errors from five to one is an 80% reduction of error; consequently, gamma is equal to .80.

In other words, if we know the relative order of pairs, we can predict with 80% more accuracy whether a randomly selected respondent is going to be High Income or Low Income.

EXAMPLE 7

Calculating Gamma to Describe the Association of Fundamentalism with Education

Suppose that we want to learn more about the relationship between religious fundamentalism and education. We hypothesize that liberal religious beliefs tend to be positively associated with higher levels of education. Our research results in Table 8.14.

TABLE 8.14   *Degree of Fundamentalism by Education*

	LT 12 YEARS	12 YEARS	MT 12 YEARS	TOTAL
Liberal	171	317	839	1327
Moderate	311	452	947	1710
Fundamentalist	282	387	628	1297
Total	764	1156	2414	4334

The first step in calculating gamma is to determine the number of same-direction (concordant) and opposite-direction (discordant) pairs in the table. To find the number of same-direction pairs, it is best to begin by asking, Where do we expect cases to cluster? Based on our hypothesis that respondents with the highest level of education will tend to be liberal and respondents with the lowest level of education will tend to be fundamentalist, we predict that most cases will fall in the lower left-hand cells and the upper right-hand cells. We now begin calculating same-direction ordered pairs.

TABLE 8.14A   *Degree of Fundamentalism by Education*

	LT 12 YEARS	12 YEARS	MT 12 YEARS	TOTAL
Liberal	171	317	839	1327
Moderate	311	452	947	1710
Fundamentalist	282	387	628	1297
Total	764	1156	2414	4334

TABLE 8.14B   *Degree of Fundamentalism by Education*

	LT 12 YEARS	12 YEARS	MT 12 YEARS	TOTAL
Liberal	171	317	839	1327
Moderate	311	452	947	1710
Fundamentalist	282	387	628	1297
Total	764	1156	2414	4334

TABLE 8.14C *Degree of Fundamentalism by Education*

	LT 12 YEARS	12 YEARS	MT 12 YEARS	TOTAL
Liberal	171	317	839	1327
Moderate	311	452	947	1710
Fundamentalist	282	387	628	1297
Total	764	1156	2414	4334

TABLE 8.14D *Degree of Fundamentalism by Education*

	LT 12 YEARS	12 YEARS	MT 12 YEARS	TOTAL
Liberal	171	317	839	1327
Moderate	311	452	947	1710
Fundamentalist	282	387	628	1297
Total	764	1156	2414	4334

Referring to the shaded areas in the tables above, our calculation of same-direction pairs is:

$$282(317 + 452 + 839 + 947) + 311(317 + 839) + 387(839 + 947) + 452(839) = 2{,}150{,}436$$

The opposite-direction pairs are calculated as follows:

TABLE 8.14E *Degree of Fundamentalism by Education*

	LT 12 YEARS	12 YEARS	MT 12 YEARS	TOTAL
Liberal	171	317	839	1327
Moderate	311	452	947	1710
Fundamentalist	282	387	628	1297
Total	764	1156	2414	4334

TABLE 8.14F *Degree of Fundamentalism by Education*

	LT 12 YEARS	12 YEARS	MT 12 YEARS	TOTAL
Liberal	171	317	839	1327
Moderate	311	452	947	1710
Fundamentalist	282	387	628	1297
Total	764	1156	2414	4334

TABLE 8.14G *Degree of Fundamentalism by Education*

	LT 12 YEARS	12 YEARS	MT 12 YEARS	TOTAL
Liberal	171	317	839	1327
Moderate	311	452	947	1710
Fundamentalist	282	387	628	1297
Total	764	1156	2414	4334

TABLE 8.14H *Degree of Fundamentalism by Education*

	LT 12 YEARS	12 YEARS	MT 12 YEARS	TOTAL
Liberal	171	317	839	1327
Moderate	311	452	947	1710
Fundamentalist	282	387	628	1297
Total	764	1156	2414	4334

Referring to the shaded areas in the tables above, our calculation of opposite-direction pairs is:

$$171(452 + 387 + 947 + 628) + 311(387 + 628) + 317(947 + 628) + 452(628) = 1{,}511{,}590$$

As you can see, calculating gamma often entails very large numbers of ordered pairs. We now know that $S = 2{,}150{,}436$ and $O = 1{,}511{,}590$. Using these values in our equation for gamma, we find:

$$G = \frac{S - O}{S + O} = \frac{2{,}150{,}436 - 1{,}511{,}590}{2{,}150{,}436 + 1{,}511{,}590} = \frac{638{,}846}{3{,}662{,}026} = .174$$

This indicates a relatively weak association between Education and Degree of Fundamentalism. Specifically, it tells us that when we know the relative order of pairs, we can predict outcomes on the other variable with 17.4% greater accuracy. Remember that gamma is a symmetric measure of association and does not distinguish between an independent and dependent variable. We now continue our investigation of the relationship between Education and Religious Fundamentalism using a statistic that does distinguish between the independent and dependent variable, Somer's *d*.

Now You Try It 5

Suppose we want to learn more about the relationship between socioeconomic status and happiness, specifically whether people find life exciting, routine, or dull. We hypothesize that happiness is a function of higher socioeconomic status. Our data are shown below. Use the table below to calculate Gamma.

Is Life Exciting or Dull by Socioeconomic Status

COUNT		SOCIOECONOMIC STATUS			TOTAL
		LOW	MIDDLE	HIGH	
IS LIFE EXCITING OR DULL	EXCITING	286	451	247	984
	ROUTINE	311	422	155	888
	DULL	48	46	8	102
	Total	645	919	410	1974

Gamma =

What does this tell us about the relationship between socioeconomic status and happiness?

Statistical Uses and Misuses

When working with ordinal measures of association, it is important to understand the structure of your data and the nature of your research hypothesis. For example, suppose we want to learn about the relationship between socioeconomic status and marital satisfaction. We operationalize socioeconomic status as Low, Medium, and High and we operationalize marital satisfaction as Very Happy, Pretty Happy, and Not Too Happy. We hypothesize that respondents of higher socioeconomic status will be more happily married than those of lower socioeconomic status and obtain the following results.

Happiness of Marriage by Socioeconomic Status

COUNT		SOCIOECONOMIC STATUS			TOTAL
		LOW	MIDDLE	HIGH	
HAPPINESS OF MARRIAGE	VERY HAPPY	216	421	224	861
	PRETTY HAPPY	179	212	121	512
	NOT TOO HAPPY	17	13	7	37
	Total	412	646	352	1410

Symmetric Measures

		VALUE	ASYMP. STD. ERROR[a]	APPROX. T[b]	APPROX. SIG.
Ordinal by Ordinal	Gamma	−.153	.044	−3.454	.001
	N of Valid Cases	1410			

[a]Not assuming the null hypothesis.
[b]Using the asymptotic standard error assuming the null hypothesis.

You can see from the results (gamma $= -.153$) that the direction of effect is negative, indicating a weak negative association between socioeconomic status and marital happiness. Does this mean that marital happiness increases with socioeconomic status? Or does it mean the opposite? To know for sure, we must know how the variables are coded in our data. If it turns out that "Not Too Happy" is coded 1 and "Low Socioeconomic Status" is also coded 1, then we can believe the SPSS for Windows output results. If, however, "Not Too Happy" is coded 3 and Low Socioeconomic Status is coded 1, then we must reverse the direction of association provided in the SPSS output.

As it turns out, the two variables are coded as follows:

> Socioeconomic Status: 1, Low;
>   2, Middle; 3, High
> Marital Happiness: 1, Very Happy;
>   2, Pretty Happy; 3, Not Too
>   Happy

This means that one of the variables is coded in reverse order. It doesn't matter which; all that matters is that they are coded in opposite directions. This means that we need to change the direction of effect in our results. Consequently, our original gamma value of $-.153$ should be $+.153$. This means that the data do offer support for our hypothesis. We do not know *why* people of higher socioeconomic status tend to be more happily married, we just know that they are.

Somer's d (d)

Somer's d A PRE measure of association based on ordered pairs that is used when working with cross-tabulation tables that contain two ordinal variables. Somer's d is one variable identified as dependent and the other independent.

Somer's d is much like gamma in that it is based on the concept of ordered pairs. The difference between the two is whereas gamma is an asymmetric measure, Somer's d is not. Somer's d is based on one variable being independent and the other dependent. Researchers using Somer's d must therefore indicate which variable is dependent in their hypothesis. Like all measures of association, Somer's d ranges between 0 and 1.0. The direction of effect also applies, meaning that it can be positive or negative.

Because Somer's d is an extension of the logic of gamma, we use examples similar to those that we used for gamma to demonstrate how Somer's d is calculated. As you can see, the formula for Somer's d is identical to that of gamma with one exception: the denominator includes one more set of pairs, pairs that are tied on the axis of the dependent variable. In this book, we have always put our independent variable on the x-axis (column variable) and our dependent variable on the y-axis (row variable); therefore, we use the following formula for Somer's d.

$$d = \frac{S - O}{S + O + T_y}$$

d = Somer's d

S = Same-direction pairs

O = Opposite-direction pairs

T_y = Tied pairs on the y-axis

Drawing on our earlier example of Education and Income, we use Table 8.15:

TABLE 8.15 *Income*

	LOW EDUCATION	HIGH EDUCATION
High Income	1	3
Low Income	3	1

Therefore,

$$S = 3 \times 3 = 9$$

$$O = 1 \times 1 = 1$$

To determine the number of pairs tied on the y-axis (Income), we must take each row in the table and calculate the total number of pairs that have the same value on the dependent variable. For example, among Low Income respondents, we can create pairs using the three respondents with Low Education and the one respondent with High Education.

$$3 \times 1 = 3$$

And among High Income respondents, we can create pairs using the one respondent with Low Education and the three respondents with High Education.

$$1 \times 3 = 3$$

Together these result in six tied pairs on the y-axis.

$$T_y = 6$$

We now have all three values necessary to calculate Somer's d (S, O, and T_y). Therefore, our equation is,

$$d = \frac{S - O}{S + O + T_y} = \frac{9 - 1}{9 + 1 + 6} = \frac{8}{16} = .5$$

Somer's d is equal to .5. Somer's d will always be smaller, assuming that there are tied pairs on the y-axis, because the denominator is larger than it is for gamma.

EXAMPLE 8

Calculating Somer's *d* to Describe the Association of Fundamentalism with Education

Using our earlier example of Degree of Fundamentalism by Education, we already have the following values:

$$S = 2,150,436$$

$$O = 1,511,590$$

Therefore, to calculate Somer's *d*, we must first determine the total number of tied pairs on the *y*-axis. Using Tables 18.6A and B, we begin with respondents who consider themselves Liberal. We can pair the 171 Liberals with Less Than 12 Years of Education with those 317 with 12 Years of Education and those 839 with More Than 12 Years of Education. Additionally, we can pair the 317 with 12 Years of Education with the 839 with More than 12 Years of Education. Our equation then looks like this:

$$\text{Tied Pairs for Liberal} = 171(317 + 839) + (317)839 = 463,639$$

Moving on the Moderates, and using Tables 8.16C and D, we can pair the 311 Moderates with Less than 12 Years of Education with the 452 with 12 Years of Education and the 947 with More than 12 Years of Education. Additionally, we can pair the 452 with 12 Years of Education with the 947 with More than 12 Years of Education. Our equation then looks like this:

$$\text{Tied Pairs for Moderate} = 311(452 + 947) + (452)947 = 863,133$$

Moving on to Fundamentalists, using Tables 8.16E and F we can pair the 282 with Less than 12 Years of Education with the 387 with 12 Years of Education and the 628 with More than 12 Years of Education. Additionally, we can pair the 387 with 12 Years of Education with the 628 with More than 12 Years of Education. Our equation then looks like this:

$$\text{Tied Pairs for Fundamentalist} = 282(387 + 628) + (387)628 = 529,266$$

TABLE 8.16A *Degree of Fundamentalism by Education*

	LT 12 YEARS	12 YEARS	MT 12 YEARS	TOTAL
Liberal	171	317	839	1327
Moderate	311	452	947	1710
Fundamentalist	282	387	628	1297
Total	764	1156	2414	4334

TABLE 8.16B *Degree of Fundamentalism by Education*

	LT 12 YEARS	12 YEARS	MT 12 YEARS	TOTAL
Liberal	171	317	839	1327
Moderate	311	452	947	1710
Fundamentalist	282	387	628	1297
Total	764	1156	2414	4334

TABLE 8.16C *Degree of Fundamentalism by Education*

	LT 12 YEARS	12 YEARS	MT 12 YEARS	TOTAL
Liberal	171	317	839	1327
Moderate	311	452	947	1710
Fundamentalist	282	387	628	1297
Total	764	1156	2414	4334

TABLE 8.16D *Degree of Fundamentalism by Education*

	LT 12 YEARS	12 YEARS	MT 12 YEARS	TOTAL
Liberal	171	317	839	1327
Moderate	311	452	947	1710
Fundamentalist	282	387	628	1297
Total	764	1156	2414	4334

TABLE 8.16E *Degree of Fundamentalism by Education*

	LT 12 YEARS	12 YEARS	MT 12 YEARS	TOTAL
Liberal	171	317	839	1327
Moderate	311	452	947	1710
Fundamentalist	282	387	628	1297
Total	764	1156	2414	4334

TABLE 8.16F *Degree of Fundamentalism by Education*

	LT 12 YEARS	12 YEARS	MT 12 YEARS	TOTAL
Liberal	171	317	839	1327
Moderate	311	452	947	1710
Fundamentalist	282	387	628	1297
Total	764	1156	2414	4334

The total number of tied pairs on the y-axis is then:

$$\text{Liberal} = 463,639$$

$$\text{Moderate} = 863,133$$

$$\underline{\text{Fundamentalist} = 529,266}$$

$$T_y = 1,856,038$$

We now have all three values necessary to complete the equation for Somer's d.

$$S = 2{,}150{,}436$$

$$O = 1{,}511{,}590$$

$$T_y = 1{,}856{,}038$$

$$d = \frac{S - O}{S + O + T_y} = \frac{2{,}150{,}436 - 1{,}511{,}590}{2{,}150{,}436 + 1{,}511{,}590 + 1{,}856{,}038} = \frac{638{,}846}{5{,}518{,}064} = .116$$

As you can see, the value of Somer's d is smaller than that of gamma. Somer's d is a more rigorous measure of association because the denominator is almost always larger due to the addition of tied pairs. As a PRE measure of association, Somer's d is interpreted similarly to gamma; however, whereas gamma ignores cases that are tied on the y-axis, Somer's d recognizes them and assumes that they do not affect the relationship between two variables. By including them in the denominator of the equation, Somer's d eliminates the effect that these tied pairs have on the relationship of X (independent) and Y (dependent). Therefore, Somer's d is almost always a smaller value than gamma and is considered a more rigorous measure of association. Remember that Somer's d is used when clearly defined independent and dependent variables are identified in the research hypothesis.

Now You Try It 6

Suppose we want to know more about the relationship between education and religious fundamentalism. We hypothesize that greater levels of education will be associated with a more liberal religious outlook. We collect data and generate the table below.

How Fundamentalist is R Currently by Education Cross-tabulation

| | | EDUCATION | | |
		LESS THAN BACHELOR'S DEGREE	BACHELOR'S DEGREE OR HIGHER	TOTAL
HOW FUNDAMENTALIST IS R CURRENTLY	FUNDAMEN-TALIST	1098	199	1297
	MODERATE	1258	452	1710
	LIBERAL	877	450	1327
	Total	3233	1101	4334

Use the table to calculate Somer's d.

What does this tell us about the relationship between education and religious fundamentalism?

Eye on the Applied

The Toxic Waste Trade in Your Community

Social scientists (Krieg, 2003) argue that polluting industries pay towns property taxes in exchange for the "right" to pollute. This fee takes the form of local taxes. Consequently, we could predict that the towns most dependent on polluting industries are the towns with the greatest number of hazardous sites. A study of communities in Vermont shows that those towns with the greatest number of hazardous sites are also those towns that make the greatest gains from commercial and industrial taxes.

The cross-tabulation table below categorizes towns by whether they receive above median or below-median taxes from commercial and industrial sources and whether they have above or below-median numbers of hazardous sites. Values for gamma and Somer's *d* are calculated and shown below.

Frequency of Hazardous Sites by % of Taxes from Commercial/Industrial

COUNT		% OF TAXES FROM COMMERCIAL/INDUSTRIAL		
		LOW	HIGH	TOTAL
Frequency of Hazardous	Low	86	33	119
Sites	High	38	91	129
Total		124	124	248

Gamma = .724 Somer's *d* = .427

As you can see, both measures of association indicate that a strong association exists between tax structures and hazardous sites. Those towns dependent on commercial and industrial taxes tend to be the same towns with the most hazardous sites. This raises questions regarding whether towns willfully engage in such an exchange and whether local residents are aware of these trends. Where do taxes come from in your community?

Chapter Summary

To determine whether variables in a cross-tabulation table are associated requires a number of considerations: the levels at which the variables are operationalized, the presence of independent and dependent variables, the shape of the table, and the wording of the research hypothesis. This chapter has divided nonparametric measures of association into two types, nominal and ordinal. Nominal measures of association (phi, *C*, *V*, and lambda) apply to cross-tabulation tables that contain at least one nominal variable. The direction of association does not apply to these measures. Ordinal measures of association (gamma, Somer's *d*) apply to cross-tabulation tables that contain two ordinal variables. Direction of effect applies to ordinal measures of association; however, when using SPSS for Windows or other statistical software packages, the direction of effect is a function of variable coding and not the research hypothesis and should therefore be interpreted carefully.

Exercises

Use the table below to answer questions 1–3. The table shows *percentages*, not frequencies.

HOW MUCH R LIKES JAZZ BY AGE CATEGORY

	18–35	36–60	61+
Very Little	60%	33%	10%
Somewhat	30	34	30
A Lot	10	33	60
Total	100%	100%	100%

1. By looking at the percentages, would you say that Jazz and Age are associated with one another, yes or no?
2. How did you come to your conclusion in question #1?
3. If there is an association, is it positive or negative?

For each of the tables below, calculate lambda and phi.

Use the table below to answer questions 4–6. The table shows frequencies.

SHOE PREFERENCE BY SEX

	MALE	FEMALE	
Nike	72	45	117
Reebok	40	86	126
Total	112	131	243

4. Who is most likely to prefer Nike shoes, males or females (offer evidence for your answer that is based on percentages)?
5. Calculate lambda.
6. By knowing if a respondent is male or female, what is the percentage by which we reduce our errors in predicting their footwear preference?

Have You Ever Considered Transferring Out of BSC? by Sex

			RESPONDENTS SEX		
			MALE	FEMALE	TOTAL
Have you ever considered transferring out of BSC?	No	Count	75	160	235
		% within Respondent's sex	42.6%	50.6%	47.8%
	Yes	Count	101	156	257
		% within Respondent's sex	57.4%	49.4%	52.2%
Total		Count	176	316	492
		% within Respondent's sex	100.0%	100.0%	100.0%

7. Lambda = _____
8. Phi = _____

Membership in BSC by Sex

			RESPONDENTS SEX		
			MALE	FEMALE	TOTAL
Are you a member of a BSC sports team or club?	No	Count	106	228	334
		% within Respondent's sex	60.6%	74.8%	69.6%
	Yes	Count	69	77	146
		% within Respondent's sex	39.4%	25.2%	30.4%
Total		Count	175	305	480
		% within Respondent's sex	100.0%	100.0%	100.0%

9. Lambda = _____
10. Phi = _____

Have You Ever Considered Transferring Out of BSC? Year/Class Standing

			YEAR/CLASS STANDING					
			FRESHMAN	SOPHOMORE	JUNIOR	SENIOR	OTHER	TOTAL
Have you ever considered transferring out of BSC?	No	Count	21	26	79	89	14	229
		% within Year/Class standing	45.7%	32.1%	46.2%	53.9%	73.7%	47.5%
	Yes	Count	25	55	92	76	5	253
		% within Year/Class standing	54.3%	67.9%	53.8%	46.1%	26.3%	52.5%
Total		Count	46	81	171	165	19	482
		% within Year/Class standing	100.0%	100.0%	100.0%	100.0%	100.0%	100.0%

11. Lambda = _____
12. List the three criteria for demonstrating causality.

13. Gamma: _____
14. Somer's *d:* _____

Use the tables below to calculate gamma and Somer's *d.* Remember that same-direction pairs can be thought of as pairs that offer support for the hypothesis we are testing.

	R IS POOR	R IS WEALTHY
R owns an expensive car	4	23
R owns an inexpensive car	15	12

	R IS POOR	R IS MIDDLE CLASS	R IS WEALTHY
R owns an expensive car	4	20	23
R owns an inexpensive car	15	15	12

15. Gamma: _____

16. Somer's *d:* _____

17. Gamma: _____

18. Somer's *d:* _____

	R IS POOR	R IS MIDDLE CLASS	R IS WEALTHY
R owns an expensive car	4	20	23
R owns a medium-priced car	7	15	10
R owns an inexpensive car	15	15	12

Computer Exercises

Use the GSS2006 database to answer the remaining questions. It is important that you set up each of your tables (row × column); another way of thinking about this is (dependent × independent). Otherwise, it will be difficult to know which values to use for your answer (in some cases).

Indicate the strength of the association for the following tables. If a measure does not apply, indicate so by writing "NA" for your answer. Remember to consider the size and shape of the table when deciding which measures apply.

Attitude toward abortion (abany) by sex:

19. Phi _____

20. *C* _____

21. *V* _____

22. Lambda _____

Degree by sex:

23. Phi _____

24. *C* _____

25. *V* _____

26. Lambda _____

Degree by race:

27. Phi _____

28. *C* _____

29. *V* _____

30. Lambda _____

Grass by degree:

31. Phi _____

32. *C* _____

33. *V* _____

34. Lambda _____

Cappun by degree:

35. Phi _____

36. *C* _____

37. *V* _____

38. Lambda _____

Health by Age2:

39. Gamma _____

40. Somer's *d* _____

Polviews by Educ3:

41. Gamma _____

42. Somer's *d* _____

Polviews by race:

43. Phi _____

44. *C* _____

45. *V* _____

46. Lambda _____

Postlife by attend:

47. Phi _____

48. *C* _____

49. *V* _____

50. Lambda _____

Wrkstat by race:

51. Phi _____

52. *C* _____

53. *V* _____

54. Lambda _____

Now You Try It Answers

1: A. 1. .40   2. No, No
    B. 1. phi = .243   2. Yes, Yes
2: A. 1. .20   2. No, No
    B. 1. .08   2. Yes, No
3: A. .088   2. No, No
    B. 1. .105   2. Yes, Yes

4: A. .4   B. .054
5: .188
6: .21

Key Terms

Causality, 238
Contingency coefficient, 246
Cramer's *V*, 248
Direction of association, 238
Gamma, 259

Lambda, 249
Nominal measures of
    association, 241
Ordinal measures of association, 255
Phi, 243

Proportionate reduction of error
    (PRE), 249
Somer's *d*, 264
Statistical association, 238
Strength of association, 238

Works Cited

Durkheim, E. (1897/1951). *Suicide: A study in sociology* (J. A. Spaulding & G. Simpson, Trans.; G. Dimpson, Ed.). New York: Free Press.

Krieg, E. J. (2003). Hazardous site and local taxes: An application of social cost theory. *Journal of Applied Sociology Sociological Practice*, Volume 20, Issue 1: 115–129.

Read, P. P. (2005). *Alive*. New York: HarperPerennial.

Schaefer, R. T. (2009). *Sociology: A brief introduction*. Boston: McGraw-Hill.

CHAPTER

9

Analysis of Variance

Introduction

You may recall from Chapter 6 that variance is an important part of analyzing whether two means are truly different from one another. Specifically we looked at the difference in socio-economic status between male and females by calculating the standard error of the difference between means and used it to conduct a *t*-test. The *t*-test informed us to the degree of certainty we could place in the difference between males and females. It was a useful test and is used very often; unfortunately, it can only be used to compare two groups (two means).

Often we are in a position of having to compare more than two means. For example, we may be asked to compare income differences between the six New England states (Maine, New Hampshire, Vermont, Massachusetts, Connecticut, and Rhode Island), average socioeconomic status across neighborhoods in a city, or the average number of stored phone numbers on cell phones for different groups of college students. Whatever the measure, the point is that we might have to compare more than two groups.

Suppose we had to compare four groups: freshmen, sophomores, juniors, and seniors. While it is possible to run separate *t*-tests for each possible pair (freshmen/sophomores, freshmen/juniors, freshmen/seniors, sophomores/juniors, sophomores/seniors, juniors/seniors) it tends to be cumbersome, prone to cumulative errors, and inconclusive. Therefore, a new statistical method is introduced here to make such analyses possible. It is called analysis of variance, or ANOVA for short.

ANOVA is an inferential statistic used when working with interval ratio variables (dependent) and categorical variables (nominal or ordinal as the independent). It allows us to compare across groups of the categorical variable to determine whether the difference between the means (any one of them) is statistically significant or not. One-way ANOVA refers to working with one independent and one dependent variable, while two-way ANOVA refers to working with two independent variables. Our discussion in this book is limited to one-way ANOVA. Table 9.1 presents relevant terms and symbols that are used in our discussion of analysis of variance.

Analysis of variance (ANOVA) An inferential statistic to assess the statistical significance of the relationship between two variables across multiple populations.

TABLE 9.1 *Symbols and Formulas*

TERM/SYMBOL	MEANING OF SYMBOL	FORMULA
ANOVA	Analysis of variance	
SS	Sum of squares is equal to the sum of squared deviations from the mean	
SS_{within}	Within-group sum of squares	$SS_{within} = \sum (X - \bar{X}_K)^2$
$SS_{between}$	Between-group sum of squares	$SS_{between} = \sum N_k (\bar{X}_k - \bar{X}_{total})^2$
SS_{total}	Total sum of squares	$SS_{total} = \sum (X - \bar{X}_{total})^2$

(Continued)

TABLE 9.1 *Continued*

TERM/SYMBOL	MEANING OF SYMBOL	FORMULA
$df_{between}$	The number of degrees of freedom between groups	$df_{between} = k - 1$
df_{within}	The number of degrees of freedom among the subgroups	$df_{within} = N_{total} - Nk$
MS	Mean square is a way to control for variance in the analysis by dividing appropriate sums of squares by appropriate degrees of freedom	
$MS_{between}$	Mean square between populations	$MS_{between} = \dfrac{SS_{between}}{df_{between}}$
MS_{within}	Mean square within populations	$MS_{within} = \dfrac{SS_{within}}{df_{within}}$
F-Ratio	A statistic used with ANOVA equal the ratio of $MS_{between}$ to MS_{within}	$F = \dfrac{MS_{between}}{MS_{within}}$
Eta^2	The ratio of the SSB to the SST	$Eta^2 = \dfrac{SSB}{SST}$

k = the different subgroups being compared
N_k = the number of subgroups in the analysis
$\bar{X}_k$ = the mean for a subgroup

Smoking on Campus

On March 26, 2003, New York Governor George Pataki signed into law a bill to ban smoking in places where employees would be exposed to secondhand smoke, a demonstrated health risk. One day restaurant and bar patrons could freely smoke while they dined and drank, the next day they could not. Initially a large number of news stories featured bar and restaurant owners claiming that business would decline and that they risked losing the very jobs they provided. Not much has been made of it since.

In recent years, a large number of college campuses have banned smoking while others have banned all tobacco use. The call for smoking bans led to student protests, letter-writing campaigns to lawmakers, and claims that such action would lower student enrollments on smoke-free campuses. Critics of the ban argue that people have the right to choose when and where they smoke and that smoking is a personal choice that each citizen should have the right to make. Supporters of the ban argue that nonsmokers should not be forced to breath secondhand smoke, that smoking leads to littering (particularly when ashtrays are not readily available), and that smoking leads to higher health care costs for everyone by increasing the incidence of a variety of long-term and terminal illnesses. In New York, a supporter of a proposed ban at the University at

Buffalo responded by stating, "Owning a gun is legal, but you're not allowed to have a gun on campus either" (Przepasniak, 2009).

Research has found that about 30% of college students have smoked cigarettes in the past 30 days and that tobacco use is highest at the beginning and end of the academic year and on weekends (Dierker et al., 2008). Students taking my research methods course surveyed student smokers and found some surprising results. First, nearly one-third of all students consider themselves to be smokers. Second, about half the smokers on campus did not smoke until they moved to the campus. This may indicate that college campuses produce smokers. Third, about 80% of all smokers wanted to quit *and* tried to quit *and* failed to quit. This seems to indicate that choosing to smoke is a decision individuals make, but choosing to quit is a decision mediated by addiction. In other words, it is easy to start smoking and nearly impossible to quit (think of wanting to quit and having only .20 probability of kicking the habit!).

Analysis of Variance

The Sum of Squares: The Basis for ANOVA

Sum of squares The sum of squared deviations from a mean.

As we saw in Chapter 4, the sum of squares is a necessary concept in understanding variance (it is also a necessary step in the calculation of the variance). If you recall, the process for determining the sum of squares is to use the following formula to sum the squared deviations from the mean:

$$\sum (X - \overline{X})^2$$

We then divided this by N to get the variance and took the square root of the variance to get the standard deviation. Although we are not using either the variance or the standard deviation per se, the discussions ahead of us will sometimes use the term *variance* to refer to the size of the sum of squares.

TABLE 9.2 *A Brief Summary of ANOVA*

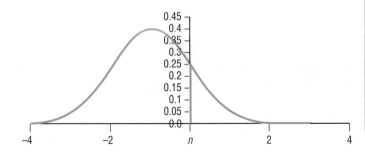

Group A: Mean = −1 $S = 1$

Consider the three figures to the left. Suppose they represent the responses from three different groups (A, B, and C) to an item on a questionnaire on a proposed smoking ban on campus. A value of −4 represents total opposition to the ban and a +4 represents total support. You can see from the distributions that A has the least support, B somewhat more support, and C the most support. You can also see that a certain degree of overlap exists among the three groups. The question we must ask ourselves is this: Is the degree of overlap (variance) such that the groups are really not so different from one another?

(Continued)

TABLE 9.2 *Continued*

Group B: Mean = 0 S = 1 N = 20

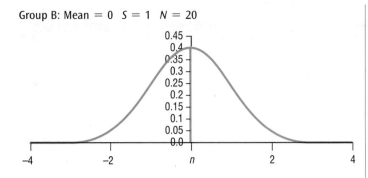

ANOVA helps us to answer this question by breaking down the total amount of variance in the sample of 60 into two types: (1) the amount of variance within each group and (2) the amount of variance between the groups. If ratio of between-group variance to within-group variance is large enough, we can claim that the difference between the groups is significant.

Group C: Mean = 1 S = 1 N = 20

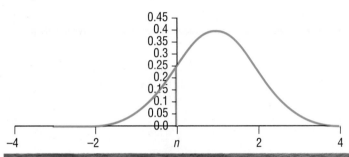

You can see that the amount of variance within each group is the same ($S = 1$); however, there is also variance between each of the groups. Evidently, whatever variable divides the respondents into Groups A, B, and C influences their opinion toward a campus smoking ban.

EXAMPLE 1

Using ANOVA for a Survey of Students

Suppose we wanted to find out how students feel about a proposal to ban smoking on campus. We decide that we would like to compare students who currently smoke, students who formerly smoked, and students who never smoked. We decide to conduct a preliminary sample of 15 ($N = 15$) to test our questionnaire (and because calculating ANOVA by hand is a cumbersome process, it will simplify our example). Therefore, each of our subgroups (Current Smokers – Group 1, Former Smokers – Group 2, and Never Smoked – Group 3) will each have five respondents. Therefore,

$$N = 15$$

$$N_1 = 5$$

$$N_2 = 5$$

$$N_3 = 5$$

These different groups of smokers represent the categorical, or independent, variable in our analysis. Our dependent variable is how students feel about a smoking ban. We operationalize this by asking students to indicate on a scale of 0 to 10 how much support they have for the ban (0 is equal to no support and 10 is equal to full support). The results of our survey are shown in Table 9.3.

TABLE 9.3 *Attitudes Towards a Smoking Ban*

CURRENT SMOKERS	FORMER SMOKERS	NEVER SMOKED
2	4	6
3	5	7
4	6	8
5	7	9
6	8	10
$N_1 = 5$	$N_2 = 5$	$N_3 = 5$
$\bar{X}_1 = 4$	$\bar{X}_2 = 6$	$\bar{X}_3 = 8$
	$N_{total} = 15$	
	$\bar{X}_{total} = 6$	

Total Mean. The first step in our analysis is to determine the total mean ($\bar{X}_{total}$) and total sum of squares (SST) for all 15 cases. To calculate the mean we use the following equation:

$$\bar{X}_{total} = \frac{\sum X}{N} = \frac{2 + 3 + 4 + 5 + 6 + 4 + 5 + 6 + 7 + 8 + 6 + 7 + 8 + 9 + 10}{15} = \frac{90}{15} = 6$$

To calculate the total sum of squares (SST) (shown in Table 9.4), we use the same method as if we were calculating the standard deviation:

Total sum of squares The amount of variance that exists for all cases in a sample relative to the mean for the entire sample. It is equal to the sum of within-group and between-group variance.

TABLE 9.4 *Sum of Squares for All Respondents*

X	$(X - \bar{X})$	$(X - \bar{X})^2$
2	$2 - 6 = -4$	16
3	$3 - 6 = -3$	9
4	$4 - 6 = -2$	4
5	$5 - 6 = -1$	1
6	$6 - 6 = 0$	0
4	$4 - 6 = -2$	4
5	$5 - 6 = -1$	1
6	$6 - 6 = 0$	0
7	$7 - 6 = 1$	1
8	$8 - 6 = 2$	4
6	$6 - 6 = 0$	0
7	$7 - 6 = 1$	1
8	$8 - 6 = 2$	2
9	$9 - 6 = 3$	9
10	$10 - 6 = 4$	16
		SST = 70

$$SST = \sum(X - \bar{X}_{total})^2 = 70$$

SST = 70

Group Means. The second step in our analysis is to determine the amount of variation within each group. To do so we follow the same procedure as we just completed, except this time we do it for each of the groups (populations) in our analysis: Current Smokers, Former Smokers, and Never Smoked. To do this we use the formula for the within-group sum of squares (SSW).

$$SS_{within} = \sum(X - \bar{X}_k)^2$$

Remember that the subscript k in this equation means that we conduct the equation independently for all three groups before we sum the results. This means we need to calculate the sum of squares for each group while using the mean specific to each group. The equations for the means and sum of squares for each group are shown below and in Tables 9.5–9.7.

Mean for Current Smokers:

$$\bar{X}_1 = \frac{\sum X}{N} = \frac{2 + 3 + 4 + 5 + 6}{5} = \frac{20}{5} = 4$$

> **Within-group sum of squares** The amount of variance that exists for all cases in a sample relative to their subgroup means.

TABLE 9.5 *Sum of Squares for Current Smokers*

X	$(X - \bar{X})$	$(X - \bar{X})^2$
2	$2 - 4 = -2$	4
3	$3 - 4 = -1$	1
4	$4 - 4 = 0$	0
5	$5 - 4 = 1$	1
6	$6 - 4 = 2$	4
	Sum of Squares = 10	

Mean for Former Smokers:

$$\bar{X}_2 = \frac{\sum X}{N} = \frac{4 + 5 + 6 + 7 + 8}{5} = \frac{30}{5} = 6$$

TABLE 9.6 *Sum of Squares for Former Smokers*

X	$(X - \bar{X})$	$(X - \bar{X})^2$
4	$4 - 6 = -2$	4
5	$5 - 6 = -1$	1
6	$6 - 6 = 0$	0
7	$7 - 6 = 1$	1
8	$8 - 6 = 2$	4
	Sum of Squares = 10	

Mean for Never Smoked:

$$\bar{X}_3 = \frac{\sum X}{N} = \frac{6 + 7 + 8 + 9 + 10}{5} = \frac{40}{5} = 8$$

TABLE 9.7 *Sum of Squares for Never Smoked*

X	$(X - \bar{X})$	$(X - \bar{X})^2$
6	$6 - 8 = -2$	4
7	$7 - 8 = -1$	1
8	$8 - 8 = 0$	0
9	$9 - 8 = 1$	1
10	$10 - 8 = 2$	4

Sum of Squares $= 10$

We can now add the results of our sum of squares for each group to get the SSW.

$$SSW = 10_1 = 10_2 = 10_3 = 30$$

SSW = 30

Between-group sum of squares The amount of variance that exists for all cases in a sample when comparing subgroup means to the overall mean.

Between-Group Sum of Squares. The third step in our analysis is to determine the between-group sum of squares (SSB). To do this we use the following formula:

$$SS_{between} = \sum N_k(\bar{X}_k - \bar{X}_{total})^2$$

The formula tells us that for each group, we must multiply the number of cases in that group by the squared difference between the group mean and the total mean, then add them together. The result is the sum of the squared deviations of the group means from the total mean. Again, remember that subscript k refers to a specific group. The calculations are shown below.

For Current Smokers:

$$N_k(\bar{X}_k - \bar{X}_{total})^2 = 5(4 - 6)^2 = 5(4) = 20$$

For Former Smokers:

$$N_k(\bar{X}_k - \bar{X}_{total})^2 = 5(6 - 6)^2 = 5(0) = 0$$

For Never Smoked:

$$N_k(\bar{X}_k - \bar{X}_{total})^2 = 5(8 - 6)^2 = 5(4) = 20$$

Therefore, the sum of these equations is $20 + 0 + 20 = 40$. The sum of squares between equals 40.

SSB = 40

As you can see, the sum of the SSB and the SSW are equal to the SST. This will always be the case. You can think of it this way. In any data set, there is a certain amount of total variance (SST). This variance is distributed both across groups (SSB) and within groups (SSW). Whatever variance does not occur across groups must occur within groups. The ANOVA statistics break down this distribution and turn it into a ratio of between-group variance to within-group variance to help us decide if the difference between groups is statistically significant or not. Specifically, it tells us if any one of the groups under consideration differs from the others. It does not, however, identify which group.

Calculating Mean Squares. The next step in our process is to make a couple of corrections to the sums of squares, specifically to the SSB and the SSW.

This is necessary because the variances that we have calculated (the sums of squares) are based on samples that could contain a large or small number of cases. By controlling for the number of degrees of freedom in our data, we can calculate both a *between-group mean square* and a *within-group mean square* that we can then use for our ratio of between- to within-group variance. The formulas for between-group mean square and within-group mean square are shown below.

$$MS_{between} = \frac{SS_{between}}{df_{between}}$$

$$MS_{within} = \frac{SS_{within}}{df_{within}}$$

In this case, $df_{between}$ is equal to $k - 1$, where k is equal to the number of groups. Therefore,

$$MS_{between} = \frac{SS_{between}}{df_{between}} = \frac{40}{3 - 1} = \frac{40}{2} = 20$$

Also, df_{within} is equal to $N_{total} - k$, where N_{total} is the total number of cases in all groups and k is the number of groups. Therefore,

$$MS_{within} = \frac{SS_{within}}{df_{within}} = \frac{30}{15 - 3} = \frac{30}{12} = 2.5$$

Calculate the *F*-Ratio. At this point, we are ready to calculate the *F*-ratio or *F*-statistic using $MS_{between}$ and MS_{within}. The formula for *F* is shown below.

$$F = \frac{MS_{between}}{MS_{within}} = \frac{20}{2.5} = 8$$

Use *F* in Table D or Table E. We are not at the final stage of our ANOVA. We need only to plug our value for *F* into either Table D or Table E in Appendix A to determine whether our findings are statistically significant. Table D tells us if our findings are significant to the .05 level and Table E tells us if our findings are significant to the .01 level. Let's say we want to see if our findings are significant to the .01 level using Table E.

As you can see for Table E, it is necessary to know the degrees of freedom for both the numerator and the denominator in our equation for F. Since we just calculated the two mean squares, this is quite simple. The *df* for the numerator is 2 (the number of groups − 1) and the *df* for the denominator is 12 (the total number of cases − the number of groups). These two degrees of freedom intersect at a value of 6.93. Because our *F*-ratio of 8 exceeds the table value of 6.93, we know that the findings from our 15-student survey are statistically significant to the .01 level. This means that we would be wrong only 1% of the time should we choose to reject the null hypothesis (that no differences exist between the three groups).

Mean square between populations A technique used to control for sampling error in which the between-group sum of squares is divided by its corresponding degrees of freedom.

Mean square within populations A technique used to control for sampling error in which the within-group sum of squares is divided by its corresponding degrees of freedom.

F-Ratio (F-Statistic) The outcome of an ANOVA calculation equal to the ratio of the mean square between groups to the mean square within groups. It is then used in either Table D or Table E to determine the significance level of our analysis.

Now You Try It 1

Suppose that we are interested in learning about whether video gaming is associated with grade point average. We gather data in which 100 respondents are grouped by the number of hours of video games they play each day. The groups are:

0 hours of gaming $N = 30$
Less than 1 hour of gaming $N = 22$
1 to less than 3 hours of gaming $N = 18$
3 to less than 5 hours of gaming $N = 21$
5 or more hours of gaming $N = 9$

Our data yield the following sums of squares:

$$SS_{between} = 76.3$$

$$SS_{within} = 18.6$$

$$SS_{total} = 94.9$$

Use this information to determine the following:

1. $df_{between}$?
2. df_{within}?
3. $MS_{between}$?
4. MS_{within}?
5. F-ratio?
6. Are the results of our survey significant to the .05 level?
7. Are the results of our survey significant to the .01 level?

Eta² A measure of association used when the independent variable is categorical (nominal or ordinal) and the dependent variable is interval/ratio.

The *Eta²* Statistic

It is important to note that neither the F-ratio nor anything else we have calculated so far in our discussion of ANOVA can function on its own as a measure of association. We can, however, use the ratio of the SSB to the SST as a measure of association. It is called eta^2, a correlation ratio (Chapter 10) that is always a positive value, and can be interpreted in the same way that gamma is interpreted (Chapter 8).

$$Eta^2 = \frac{SSB}{SST}$$

Essentially, eta^2 tells us the proportion of variance in the dependent variable that is explained by the independent variable. Remember that SST is equal to SSB + SSW, therefore SSB appears in both the numerator and denominator in the equation. Whereas gamma is used with two ordinal variables and Pearson's r (as we will see in Chapter 10) is used with two interval/ratio variables, Eta^2 is used with an interval/ratio dependent variable and a categorical independent variable.

Let's apply it to our example of smoking on campus. We know that the SSB is 40 and that our SST is 70. Using these values, our equation is shown below.

$$Eta^2 = \frac{SSB}{SST} = \frac{40}{70} = .57$$

A value of .57 tells us that we have a strong association between smoking status and attitude toward a smoking ban. Because the independent variable is nominal, the concept of direction does not apply. We can, however, go back to the original means for the three groups and identify how attitude toward a smoking ban varies by smoking status. In this case, the group most opposed is Current Smokers and the group most in favor is Never Smoked. Former Smokers falls between them.

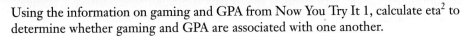

Now You Try It 2

Using the information on gaming and GPA from Now You Try It 1, calculate eta^2 to determine whether gaming and GPA are associated with one another.

1. What is the value of eta^2?
2. What does this tell us about the association of gaming with GPA?
3. What does this not tell us about the association of gaming with GPA?

Summary of Steps to Calculate ANOVA. Calculating ANOVA is a relatively complicated process requiring a lot of steps. A couple of suggestions will make this a much easier process. First, think about when and why ANOVA is used. It is used when working with a categorical independent variable and an interval/ratio dependent variable. It is used to assess whether the differences between groups are significant after accounting for the degree of "overlap" in their variance. Second, try calculating a couple of these on your own. Use a small number of cases in each group to simplify the process. If you have access to SPSS for Windows, you can enter your data and run an ANOVA to check your work. Table 9.8 shows a quick list of the steps to take when calculating an ANOVA by hand.

TABLE 9.8 *Steps for Calculating ANOVA*

1. Determine the mean for the entire sample.
2. Determine the mean for the subgroups.
3. Determine the total sum of squares (SST).
4. Determine the within-groups sum of squares (SSW).
5. Determine the between-group sum of squares (SSB).
6. Determine the mean square between.
7. Determine the mean square within.
8. Determine the *F*-ratio.
9. Use the *F*-ratio for either Table D or Table E.

Integrating Technology

Calculating ANOVA by hand is a long and tedious process when working with a limited number of cases. You can imagine what it might be like when working with large databases with hundreds or thousands of cases. SPSS for Windows allows researchers to conduct ANOVA analyses with thousands or tens of thousands of cases in the blink of an eye while greatly reducing the chances of committing mathematical errors. It can also provide graphs of how cases tend to be distributed. For example, suppose we wanted to find out if there is a statistically significant difference in the average age of different labor force statuses. In our database, labor force status is a nominal variable and age is an interval/ratio variable. Using SPSS for Windows, we find that labor force status is distributed as follows:

Labor Force Status

		FREQUENCY	PERCENT	VALID PERCENT	CUMULATIVE PERCENT
Valid	Working Full Time	2321	51.5	51.5	51.5
	Working Part Time	440	9.8	9.8	61.3
	Temp Not Working	84	1.9	1.9	63.1
	Unempl, Laid Off	143	3.2	3.2	66.3
	Retired	712	15.8	15.8	82.1
	School	139	3.1	3.1	85.2
	Keeping House	490	10.9	10.9	96.1
	Other	177	3.9	3.9	100.0
	Total	4506	99.9	100.0	
Missing	NA	4	.1		
Total		4510	100.0		

When running an ANOVA using SPSS for Windows, we have the option of viewing several descriptive statistics for each of the populations being analyzed. These statistics include the number of cases, mean, standard deviation, standard error of the mean, confidence intervals, and high and low values. The descriptive statistics for our example are shown below.

Descriptives
Age of Respondent

	N	MEAN	STD. DEVIATION	STD. ERROR	95% CONFIDENCE INTERVAL FOR MEAN		MINIMUM	MAXIMUM
					LOWER BOUND	UPPER BOUND		
Working Full Time	2309	41.83	11.818	.246	41.35	42.31	18	87
Working Part Time	439	44.11	16.376	.782	42.57	45.65	18	88
Temp not Working	84	43.49	11.664	1.273	40.96	46.02	20	74
Unempl, Laid Off	141	41.35	13.010	1.096	39.18	43.51	19	70
Retired	711	71.57	9.511	.357	70.87	72.27	20	89
School	139	27.94	11.576	.982	26.00	29.88	18	86
Keeping House	490	46.01	17.030	.769	44.50	47.52	19	89
Other	177	50.37	12.661	.952	48.49	52.25	18	89
Total	4490	47.14	16.891	.252	46.65	47.64	18	89

SPSS for Windows also generates a table that summarizes the sums of squares, degrees of freedom, mean squares, F-ratio, and alpha value. These statistics for our example are shown in the table below.

ANOVA

Age of Respondent

	SUM OF SQUARES	df	MEAN SQUARE	F	Sig.
Between Groups	553170.077	7	79024.297	486.836	.000
Within Groups	727528.551	4482	162.322		
Total	1280698.628	4489			

SPSS for Windows also provides users with the option of plotting the mean age by group as shown in the chart below.

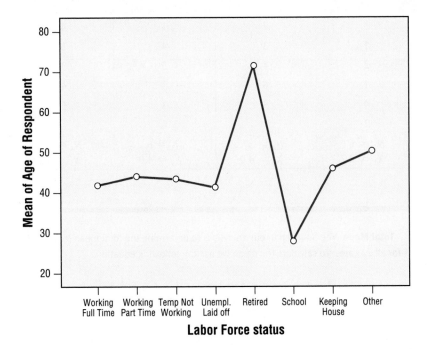

As the chart shows, among the eight populations in our analysis, respondents who are in school have the lowest mean age and respondents who are retired have the highest mean age. Little difference exists between other groups and there is little reason to predict that differences would exist. It is this difference between those who are retired and those who are in school that generates a significant portion of the between-group sum of squares ($SS_{Between} = 79,024.3$) and, consequently, a large F-ratio ($F = 486.8$).

Viewing all of the output in neatly organized formats often helps researchers to visualize and better understand the nature of the data they are analyzing.

EXAMPLE 2

Using ANOVA to Analyze Social Networking and Smoking

Let's take one more example of an ANOVA that we calculate by hand before moving on to an example using SPSS for Windows. Again, in the interest of keeping our calculations to a minimum, this example is hypothetical and uses a limited number of cases. Evidence suggests that smoking has a social component to it. A recent study in the *Journal of American College Health* (Ott, Cashin, & Altekruse, 2005) argues that students who smoke are more likely to have student friends who also smoke.

Based on this and the fact that the probability of quitting is so low, suppose we hypothesize that the farther along a student is in their college career, the more friends they will have who smoke. We then sample freshmen, sophomores, juniors, and seniors and collect the data in Table 9.9. (*Note:* All calculations are rounded to one decimal place for this ANOVA.)

TABLE 9.9

FRESHMEN	SOPHOMORES	JUNIORS	SENIORS
3	2	3	4
1	3	4	5
2	4	5	3
1	6	3	4
4	5	3	5
2		6	
$N_1 = 6$	$N_2 = 5$	$N_3 = 6$	$N_4 = 5$
$\bar{X}_1 = 2.2$	$\bar{X}_2 = 4.0$	$\bar{X}_3 = 4.0$	$\bar{X}_4 = 4.2$

$$N = 22$$
$$\bar{X}_{total} = 3.5$$

Total Mean. The first step in our analysis is to determine the total mean $(\bar{X}_{total})$ and SST for all 22 cases. To calculate the mean we use the following equation:

$$\bar{X}_{total} = \frac{\sum X}{N} = \frac{\begin{array}{c} 3 + 1 + 2 + 1 + 4 + 2 + 2 + 3 + 4 + 6 + 5 \\ + 3 + 4 + 5 + 3 + 3 + 6 + 4 + 5 + 3 + 4 + 5 \end{array}}{22} = \frac{78}{22} = 3.5$$

$$\bar{X}_{total} = 3.5$$

To calculate the SST, we use the same method as if we were calculating the standard deviation. See Table 9.10.

TABLE 9.10

X	$(X - \bar{X})$	$(X - \bar{X})^2$
3	$3 - 3.5 = -.5$	.25
1	$1 - 3.5 = -2.5$	6.25
2	$2 - 3.5 = -1.5$	2.25
1	$1 - 3.5 = -2.5$	6.25
4	$4 - 3.5 = .5$	.25
2	$2 - 3.5 = -1.5$	2.25
2	$2 - 3.5 = -1.5$	2.25
3	$3 - 3.5 = -.5$	.25
4	$4 - 3.5 = .5$	.25
6	$6 - 3.5 = 2.5$	6.25
5	$5 - 3.5 = 1.5$	2.25
3	$3 - 3.5 = -.5$	.25
4	$4 - 3.5 = .5$	.25
5	$5 - 3.5 = 1.5$	2.25
3	$3 - 3.5 = -.5$	.25
3	$3 - 3.5 = -.5$	.25
6	$6 - 3.5 = 2.5$	6.25
4	$4 - 3.5 = .5$	.25
5	$5 - 3.5 = 1.5$	2.25
3	$3 - 3.5 = -.5$	.25
4	$4 - 3.5 = .5$	.25
5	$5 - 3.5 = 1.5$	2.25
		SST = 43.5

$$SST = \sum (X - \bar{X}_{total})^2 = 43.5$$

SST = 43.5

Group Means. The second step in our analysis is to determine the amount of variation within each group. To do so we follow the same procedure as we just completed, except this time we do it for each of the groups (populations) in our analysis: freshmen, sophomores, juniors, and seniors. To do this we use the formula for the SSW.

$$SS_{within} = \sum (X - \bar{X}_K)^2$$

Remember that the subscript k in this equation means that we conduct the equation independently for all four groups before we sum the results. This means we need to calculate the sum of squares for each group while using the mean specific to each group. The equations for the means and sums of squares for each group are shown below and in Tables 9.11–9.14.

Mean for Freshmen:

$$\bar{X}_1 = \frac{\sum X}{N} = \frac{3 + 1 + 2 + 1 + 4 + 2}{6} = \frac{13}{6} = 2.2$$

TABLE 9.11 *Sum of Squares for Freshmen*

X	$(X - \bar{X})$	$(X - \bar{X})^2$
3	$3 - 2.2 = .8$	.6
1	$1 - 2.2 = -1.2$	1.4
2	$2 - 2.2 = -.2$	.04
1	$1 - 2.2 = -1.2$	1.4
4	$4 - 2.2 = 1.8$	3.2
2	$2 - 2.2 = -.2$	.04
		Sum of Squares $= 6.7$

Mean for Former Sophomores:

$$\bar{X}_2 = \frac{\sum X}{N} = \frac{2 + 3 + 4 + 6 + 5}{5} = \frac{20}{5} = 4$$

TABLE 9.12 *Sum of Squares for Sophomores*

X	$(X - \bar{X})$	$(X - \bar{X})^2$
2	$2 - 4 = -2$	4
3	$3 - 4 = -1$	1
4	$4 - 4 = 0$	0
6	$6 - 4 = 2$	4
5	$5 - 4 = 1$	1
		Sum of Squares $= 10$

Mean for Juniors:

$$\bar{X}_3 = \frac{\sum X}{N} = \frac{3 + 4 + 5 + 3 + 3 + 6}{6} = \frac{24}{6} = 4$$

TABLE 9.13 *Sum of Squares for Juniors*

X	$(X - \bar{X})$	$(X - \bar{X})^2$
3	$3 - 4 = -1$	1
4	$4 - 4 = 0$	0
5	$5 - 4 = 1$	1
3	$3 - 4 = -1$	1
3	$3 - 4 = -1$	1
6	$6 - 4 = 2$	4
		Sum of Squares $= 8$

Mean for Seniors:

$$\bar{X}_4 = \frac{\sum X}{N} = \frac{4 + 5 + 3 + 4 + 5}{5} = \frac{21}{5} = 4.2$$

TABLE 9.14 *Sum of Squares for Seniors*

X	$(X - \bar{X})$	$(X - \bar{X})^2$
4	$4 - 4.2 = -.2$	.04
5	$5 - 4.2 = .8$	.6
3	$3 - 4.2 = -1.2$	1.4
4	$4 - 4.2 = -.2$	.04
5	$5 - 4.2 = .8$	.6
		Sum of Squares = 2.7

We can now add the results of our sum of squares for each group to get the SSW.

$$SS_{within} = \sum (X - \bar{X}_k)^2 = 6.7 + 10 + 8 + 4.7 = 27.4$$

SSW = 29.4

Between-Group Sum of Squares. The third step in our analysis is to determine the SSB. To do this we use the following formula:

$$SS_{between} = \sum N_k (\bar{X}_k - \bar{X}_{total})^2$$

The formula tells us that for each group, we must multiply the number of cases in that group by the squared difference between the group mean and the total mean, then add them together. The result is the sum of the squared deviations of the group means from the total mean. Again, remember that subscript k refers to a specific group. The calculations are shown below.

For Freshmen:

$$N_k = [(\bar{X}_k - \bar{X}_{total})^2 = 6(2.2 - 3.5)^2 = 5(1.7) = 10.2$$

For Sophomores:

$$N_k (\bar{X}_k - \bar{X}_{total})^2 = 5(4 - 3.5)^2 = 5(.25) = 1.25$$

For Juniors:

$$N_k (\bar{X}_k - \bar{X}_{total})^2 = 6(4 - 3.5)^2 = 6(.25) = 1.5$$

For Seniors:

$$N_k (\bar{X}_k - \bar{X}_{total})^2 = 5(4.2 - 3.5)^2 = 5(.7) = 3.5$$

Using the formula for the between-group sum of squares, we find that SSB is equal to 16.5.

$$SS_{between} = \sum N_k(\bar{X}_k - \bar{X}_{total})^2 = 10.2 + 1.25 + 1.5 + 3.5 = 16.5$$

SSB = 16.5

Having all of our sums of squares calculated, we can now move on the process of calculating the mean squares.

Calculating Mean Squares. The next step in our process is to make a couple of corrections to the sums of squares, specifically to the SSB and the SSW.

The formulas for between-group mean square and within-group mean square are shown below.

$$MS_{between} = \frac{SS_{between}}{df_{between}}$$

$$MS_{within} = \frac{SS_{within}}{df_{within}}$$

Remember that $df_{between}$ is equal to $k - 1$, where k is equal to the number of groups. Therefore,

$$MS_{between} = \frac{SS_{between}}{df_{between}} = \frac{16.5}{4 - 1} = \frac{16.5}{3} = 5.5$$

Also recall that df_{within} is equal to $N_{total} - k$, where N_{total} is the total number of cases in all groups and k is the number of groups. Therefore,

$$MS_{within} = \frac{SS_{within}}{df_{within}} = \frac{29.4}{22 - 4} = \frac{29.4}{18} = 1.6$$

MSB = 5.5

MSW = 1.6

We can now use the values of the mean square between and the mean square within to calculate the f-ratio.

Calculating the F-Ratio. At this point, we are ready to calculate the f-ratio or f-statistic using $MS_{between}$ and MS_{within}. The formula for F is shown below.

$$F = \frac{MS_{between}}{MS_{within}} = \frac{5.5}{1.6} = 3.438$$

Use F in Table D or Table E. To determine whether our findings are significant to the .05 level, we use Table D in the back of the book. Remember that the formula for degrees of freedom for the numerator is

$$df_{between} = K - 1 = 4 - 1 = 3$$

and the degrees of freedom for the denominator is

$$df_{within} = N_{total} - K = 22 - 4 = 18$$

Using Table D, we find an *F*-ratio of 3.16. Because our *F*-ratio of 3.438 is larger than the value in the table, we can know that our results are significant to the .05 level.

Using Table E, we find that our *F*-ratio must exceed a value of 5.09. In this case, our *F*-ratio does not exceed this value and therefore we cannot state that our findings are significant to the .01 level.

The *Eta²* Statistic. To calculate the *eta²* statistics we use the following formula.

$$Eta^2 = \frac{SSB}{SST}$$

Again, *eta²* indicates the proportion of variance in the dependent variable that is explained by the independent variable. Using the appropriate values from our calculations, our equation is shown below.

$$Eta^2 = \frac{SSB}{SST} = \frac{16.5}{43.5} = .379$$

A value of .38 tells us that 37.9% of the total variation in the dependent variable (the number of friends who smoke) is explained by the independent variable (year of college). This tells us that we have a moderately strong association between year of college and the number of friends who smoke.

Now You Try It 3

Suppose we add one more group to our study of the social components of smoking from example #2 above. We add five graduate students who provide the following data:

2
5
3
6
5

Use this new data to go back to Example #2 and recalculate the following:

1. $SS_{between}$?
2. SS_{within}?
3. SS_{total}?
4. $df_{between}$?
5. df_{within}?
6. $MS_{between}$?
7. MS_{within}?
8. *f*-ratio?
9. Are the results of our survey significant to the .05 level?
10. Are the results of our survey significant to the .01 level?
11. Eta^2?

Statistical Uses and Misuses

ANOVA is a powerful and commonly used method of data analysis. It can be particularly useful when working with experimental data when researchers are interested in how a treatment (such as a drug or teaching method) impacts different populations. For example, in his book *Better: A Surgeon's Notes on Performance* (2007), Atul Gawande includes a chapter titled "The Bell Curve." In it he discusses the average number of years that children diagnosed with cystic fibrosis are likely to survive. Cystic fibrosis is a genetic disease that affects about 1,000 children in the United States each year. According to Gawande, the effect of this disease is that it

> thickens secretions throughout the body, turning them dry and gluey. In the ducts of the pancreas, the flow of digestive enzymes becomes blocked, making a child less and less able to absorb food.... The effects on the lungs, however, are what make the disease lethal. Thickened mucus slowly fills the small airways and hardens, shrinking lunch capacity. (p. 203)

Over time, the average survival rates for these children increased over time, but not evenly from one hospital to the next. Gawande found that some hospitals had much longer average survival times for these children than others. Why were their patients surviving longer than most? Were they just lucky and had somewhat healthier patients? What did these hospitals know and do that other hospitals did not?

Surprisingly, he found that the hospitals with the most success were energetic, tight-knit groups who took the time to know their patients and motivate the patients to adhere to the regimen of treatments. In other words, they didn't know more about the disease, they knew more about how to treat the disease.

Suppose we wanted to test these ideas using a natural experiment. We set up our experiment using 6 hospitals, all of which have low survival rates for patients with cystic fibrosis. In two of them we make no changes. In another two, we begin to model how more successful hospitals run their program. And in the last two, we fully implement how the successful hospitals run their program. Setting our study up this way gives us an independent variable with three attributes. Our dependent variable is the average number of years that their patients survive.

Gathering this kind of data may take years or even decades since people with cystic fibrosis live so much longer than they used to. But over time they will, unfortunately, die. With an ample amount of data, we could use ANOVA to compare the differences between the average years of survival among our three hospital types and determine whether the differences between them are statistically different.

In this case, knowing what kind of data to gather, how to gather it, and how to analyze it are all important steps in improving human health by knowing not more about the disease, but more about how to treat it.

EXAMPLE 3

Using ANOVA to Analyze Racial Disparity and America's Toxics Crisis

The Commonwealth of Massachusetts is home to over 30,000 toxic waste sites. These range in severity from minor spills in sparsely populated areas to Superfund sites in densely populated suburban communities. In 2005, my colleague Daniel Faber and I published a report titled *Unequal Exposure to Ecological Hazards 2005: Environmental Injustices in the Commonwealth of Massachusetts*. In it we identified many types of ecological hazards, including municipal solid waste landfills, sludge landfills, incinerators, waste to energy facilities, facilities reporting the use and disposal of toxic materials, Superfund sites, and many others.

We then devised a point system based on the number and types of ecological hazards in each community. For example, Superfund sites received 25 points, operating landfills received 6 points, and so on. Each community was then assigned a point total such that communities with a high number of points are those facing the greatest risk from toxic hazards.

It is not easy to draw conclusions regarding the actual risks to human health based on the number of sites in each community (in this case towns and cities). For example, not all communities are the same size; therefore, a large town with 100 points may be less contaminated than a small town with 100 points. Similarly, not all sites/points are distributed evenly across a community. While some communities may have sites concentrated near population centers, others may have sites widely dispersed in less populated areas. In addition to these geographic considerations are variations in the types of chemicals found in those sites. Different chemicals have different impacts on human health. Individual responses to exposures vary (the very young and very old are often much more at risk).

To overcome some of these problems, we took the total number of hazard points in each town and divided it by the area (square miles) of the town. This allowed us to take the *extent* of the contamination (total number of hazard points) and convert it to a measure of the *intensity* of contamination (points per square mile).

Not surprisingly, the distribution of hazard points and hazard points per square mile is not even. Some communities contain above the average number of points and others below. For example, the mean number of hazard points for all communities (minor civil divisions, or MCDs) in the Commonwealth of Massachusetts is 133. Yet the city of Boston is home to 3,972 points, while nearby Newton is home to only 467 points. Similarly, for the state as a whole, the number of points per square mile is 5.4 while for Boston it is 84 and for Newton it is 26.

A significant body of literature argues that low-income communities and communities of color are more likely to suffer from toxic contamination than are higher income communities and white communities (Bullard, 1994). The reasons for this are numerous, but let's suppose that we want to test this claim using the data that Daniel Faber and I collected in Massachusetts. Specifically, we want to know if towns with a *greater percentage of nonwhite population* are more likely to have *more ecological hazards per square mile*. To begin, we divide all of the towns and cities in the state into four groups based on the percentage of their populations that are nonwhite. The results of this are shown in Table 9.15.

Obviously there are far too many cases ($N = 351$) in our analysis to compute the ANOVA by hand, so we will use SPSS for Windows instead. Ultimately we are trying to determine whether the amount of variance between the different groups in Table 9.15 is greater than the amount of variance within those same groups.

TABLE 9.15 *Percent of Population that is Nonwhite*

		FREQUENCY	PERCENT	VALID PERCENT	CUMULATIVE PERCENT
Valid	0 to LT 5%	231	65.8	65.8	65.8
	5 to LT 15%	95	27.1	27.1	92.9
	15 to LT 25%	13	3.7	3.7	96.6
	25% or Greater	12	3.4	3.4	100.0
	Total	351	100.0	100.0	

We begin our analysis by generating some descriptive statistics for each of the four groups (Table 9.16).

TABLE 9.16

0 TO LT 5% NONWHITE	5 TO LT 15% NONWHITE	15 TO LT 25% NONWHITE	25% OR GREATER NONWHITE
$N = 231$	$N = 95$	$N = 13$	$N = 12$
$\bar{X} = 3.25$	$\bar{X} = 11.29$	$\bar{X} = 32.95$	$\bar{X} = 50.36$
$s = 3.77$	$s = 12.18$	$s = 33.13$	$s = 40.33$

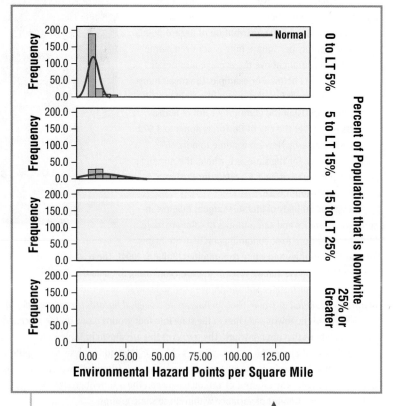

Figure 9.1 **Distribution of Ecological Hazards by Race**

You can see from the statistics in Table 9.16 that as the percent of nonwhite population increases, so do the mean number of hazards and the degree of dispersion. Figure 9.1 shows the normal curve for each of the four groups of communities. As you can see, the very low frequency large standard deviation of the last two groups makes the fit line impossible to see. Nevertheless, the statistics above tell us that normal curve for each group gets flatter, wider, and moves to the right as we go from one figure to the next.

At this point we are ready to run our ANOVA using SPSS. The results are shown in Table 9.17.

TABLE 9.17 *ANOVA*

Environmental Hazard Points per Square Mile

	SUM OF SQUARES	df	MEAN SQUARE	f	Sig.
Between Groups	35,862.329	3	11,954.110	85.920	.000
Within Groups	48,278.432	347	139.131		
Total	84,140.761	350			

If you remember, our number of cases is $N = 351$. Therefore the Total degrees of freedom is 350. Similarly, because we have four groups in our analysis, the between-group degrees of freedom is the number of groups minus 1, so between $df = 3$. Finally, the within-group degrees of freedom is always the difference between the total and between degrees of freedom, so within $df = 347$.

As you can see, the SPSS output table also includes the sums of squares, mean squares, F-ratio, and significance level. Remember that the F-ratio is calculated by dividing the mean square between groups by the mean square within groups.

$$F = \frac{Mean\ Square\ Between}{Mean\ Square\ Within} = \frac{11,954.110}{139.131} = 85.920$$

The significance level of .000 tells us that we are justified in rejecting the null hypothesis and that there is a very high probability that the differences between the means for our four groups of communities indicate real differences, not statistical aberrations.

Eye on the Applied

Nationwide, dairy operators face a serious crisis. Because they are paid by the number of pounds of milk they produce, as milk prices drop dairy operators are forced to search for ways to remain in business. One way is to increase their overall milk production. In Vermont, a number of dairy operators have begun buying up surrounding farms as they go out of business. Consequently, the average number of cows per farm has increased dramatically since 1950 to about 100 cows per farm (with some farms housing thousands of cows). A second way to respond is to transition to organic production where a higher price is received for milk.

In the past few years, I have interviewed a small number of Vermont organic dairy operators to try and learn more about the plans they have for their farms. It appears that the larger organic dairies (60 or more cows) seem to be doing pretty well and the owners feel confident that they will remain in business. This also appears to be true for the very small organic dairies (20 or less cows), which tend to be highly diversified with multiple sources of farm income. The mid-size dairies, however, seem to be facing the greatest crisis.

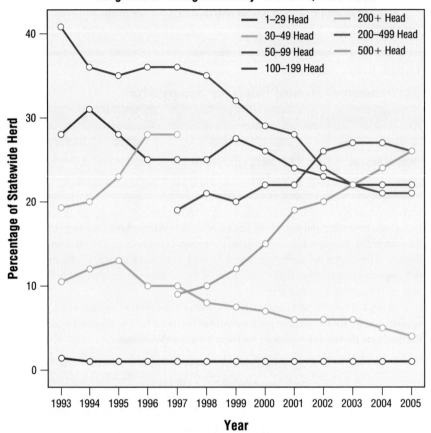

Longitudinal Changes in Dairy Farm Size, 1993-2005

Source: USDA, National Agricultural Statistics Service,
http://www.nass.usda.gov/QuickStats/Pulldata.us.jsp

One of the questions on my questionnaire asks dairy operators to indicate the probability that their farm will be operating 5 years from now (responses can range from 0 to 100%). Given a large enough sample, it would be interesting to run an ANOVA with *size of farm* as the independent variable (small, medium, large) and *probability of being in business 5 years from now* as the dependent variable.

An alternative way to use an ANOVA would also be to operationalize the probability of being in business 5 years from as Likely, Not Sure, Unlikely. This could then be used as the independent variable.

The dependent variable could be operationalized as the number of cows on each farm.

In either case, it is best not to design a study with particular types of statistics in mind. Good statisticians will be able to draw on a wide range of statistical techniques that can be applied to the type of data with which they are working. Ultimately it is more important to focus on gathering quality data because without high-quality data, the old saying "garbage in, garbage out" becomes a reality.

Chapter Summary

When comparing means, we often have to deal with more than two populations at a time. By creating a ratio of the variation between groups to the variation within groups, ANOVA provides researchers with a technique to assess whether the differences between means are statistically significant or not. This assessment is known as the F-ratio and is used in conjunction with a series of tables that help to determine alpha values. As with other measures of statistical significance, ANOVA is a way to guard against the problem of making Type I errors. ANOVA also provides researchers with the data necessary to calculate a measure of association called eta^2. Eta^2 is a measure of association used when comparing independent means from a sample. ANOVA cannot be calculated unless working with interval/ratio data and it should only be used when comparing three or more means.

Exercises

1. Explain when an ANOVA is used.
2. What does ANOVA tell us about our data?
3. Explain why ANOVA is not a measure of association.
4. What does eta^2 tell us that ANOVA does not?
5. If the sum of squares between is equal to 10 and the sum of squares within is equal to 4, what is the value of the total sum of squares?
6. If the sum of squares between is equal to 10 and the sum of squares within is equal to 4, what is the value of eta^2?
7. If the mean square between ($MS_{between}$) is equal to 20 and the mean square within (MS_{within}) is equal to 30, what is eta^2 equal to?

Suppose you want to learn more about which students are most likely to get parking tickets on your campus. You conduct a short survey of 15 students, dividing them into three groups (Driving Commuters, Non-Driving Commuters, Campus-Based Students). The data are shown in the table below. Use the data to calculate the F-ratio and eta^2.

Number of College Parking Tickets Received in the Past Year by Student Type

DRIVING COMMUTERS	NON-DRIVING COMMUTERS	CAMPUS-BASED STUDENTS
2	1	0
5	0	0
3	3	1
4	2	0
2	1	2

8. Is there a statistically significant difference among the means for the three groups?
9. Does eta^2 offer any evidence that getting a parking ticket is associated with students' driving status? Explain.

Suppose you want to learn more about student satisfaction with campus dining services. To investigate, you survey a group of students, asking them which dining hall they usually patron and their overall assessment of the dining experience (on a scale of 1–10). Your survey yields the following data.

DINING HALL #1	DINING HALL #2	DINING HALL #3	DINING HALL #4
5	6	4	6
6	4	5	7
4	5	3	5
5	7	6	8
3	8	4	4
5	4	2	5
6	6	4	7

10. Is there a statistically significant difference among the means for the three groups?
11. Does eta^2 offer any evidence that attitudes toward dining on campus are associated with the dining hall students attend? Explain.

Computer Exercises

Suppose we add two more dining halls to our analysis of dining halls so that our data are as follows. Enter these data into an SPSS for Windows database and use the results to answer the questions that follow.

DINING HALL #1	DINING HALL #2	DINING HALL #3	DINING HALL #4	DINING HALL #5	DINING HALL #6
5	6	4	6	7	5
6	4	5	7	4	6
4	5	3	5	8	4
5	7	6	8	6	7
3	8	4	4	2	3
5	4	2	5	6	5
6	6	4	7	7	6

12. What is the value of the between-group sum of squares?
13. What is the value of the within-group sum of squares?
14. What is the value of the mean square between?
15. What is the value of the mean square within?
16. What is the value of the *F*-ratio?

17. What is the value of eta^2?
18. Are the results statistically significant?
19. Is there an association between the two variables? Explain.

Use the GSS2006 database to answer the following questions.

Suppose you are studying political party affiliation and socioeconomic status.

20. What is the value of the between-group sum of squares?
21. What is the value of the within-group sum of squares?
22. What is the value of the mean square between?
23. What is the value of the mean square within?
24. What is the value of the *F*-Ratio?
25. What is the value of Eta^2?
26. Are the results statistically significant?
27. Is there an association between the two variables? Explain.

Suppose you are studying race and socioeconomic status.

28. What is the value of the between-group sum of squares?
29. What is the value of the within-group sum of squares?

30. What is the value of the mean square between?

31. What is the value of the mean square within?

32. What is the value of the *f*-ratio?

33. What is the value of eta²?

34. Are the results statistically significant?

35. Is there an association between the two variables? Explain.

Now You Try It Answers

1: 1. $df_{between} = 4$ 2: $df_{within} = 96$
   3. $MS_{between} = 19.075$ 4. $MS_{within} = .19375$
   5. $F\text{-}ratio = 98.4$ 6. Yes 7. Yes
2: 1. .804   2. The two are strongly associated and that at least one group is very different from the rest.

3. It does not tell us anything about which group or groups the trend holds true for.
3: 1. 17.6   2. 38.4   3. 56.0   4. 4   5. 2   6. 4.4
   7. 1.7   8. 2.5   9. No   10. No   11. .314

Key Terms

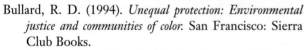

Analysis of variance, 276
Between-group sum of squares, 282
Eta², 284
F-ratio, 283

F-statistic, 283
Mean square between
   populations, 283
Mean square within populations, 283

Sum of squares, 278
Total sum of squares, 280
Within-group sum of squares, 281

Work Cited

Bullard, R. D. (1994). *Unequal protection: Environmental justice and communities of color*. San Francisco: Sierra Club Books.

Dierker, L., Stolar, M., Lloyd-Richardson, E., Tiffany, S., Flay, B., Collins, L., et al. (2008). Tobacco, alcohol, and marijuana use among first-year U.S. college students: A time series analysis. *Substance Use and Misuse*, 680–699.

Faber, D. R., & Krieg, E. J. (2005). *Unequal exposure to ecological hazards 2005: Environmental injustices in the Commonwealth of Massachusetts*. Boston: Philanthropy and Environmental Justice Research Project at Northeastern University.

Gawande, A. (2007). *Better: A surgeon's notes on performance*. New York: Metropolitan Books.

Ott, C. H., Cashin, S. E., Altekruse, M. (2005). Development and validation of the College Tobacco Survey. *Journal of American College Health*, 379–392.

Przepasniak, E. (2009, March 25). *Artvoice*. Retrieved July 29, 2009, from http://artvoice.com/issues/v8n13/news_briefs/ub_smoking_ban

CHAPTER

10

Correlation and Regression

Introduction

On average, how many years of education does it take to reach an income level of $75,000? On average, for each hour of television watched per day, how much is a student's GPA lowered? Do countries with higher median household income tend to have higher literacy rates? These and other questions like them can be answered using statistics known as correlation and regression. In previous chapters we learned how to describe the relationship between two nominal variables (phi, C, V, and lambda),

303

Correlation A symmetrical measure of association used when working with two interval/ratio variables that is based on variance.

Linear Regression A statistical method that assesses the degree to which two variables are correlated and is represented as a straight "best-fitting" line.

a nominal and an ordinal variable (phi, C, V, and lambda), two ordinal variables (gamma and Somer's d) and nominal and interval/ratio variables (ANOVA and eta^2). Correlation and regression are two of the most commonly used methods for assessing the nature of the relationship between interval/ratio variables—variables that can be used to calculate the mean and variance.

Because researchers often gather data at the interval/ratio level, such as census data, these are important statistical tools to have. In many ways they are the crowning achievement of the work that we have done so far because to understand them it is necessary to have a firm grasp on the concepts that have preceded them: central tendency (the mean), dispersion (the sum of squares), and association; therefore, they are the last two concepts that we will address in this text.

In this chapter we learn the underlying concepts behind both correlation and linear regression. Concepts and calculations will be done with small samples using hypothetical data. Then numerous examples will be provided using data from the individual-level data from the General Social Survey, town/city-level data from Census 2000, and country-level data from the United Nations to demonstrate real examples. We begin with correlation, specifically one statistic known as Pearson's r; and then we look at how the concept of correlation can be extended to something called linear regression. Multiple regression, a statistical technique that weighs the relative effects of multiple independent variables on a single dependent variable, is not included in this book. Useful term/symbols and formulas are presented in Table 10.1.

TABLE 10.1 *Symbols and Formulas*

TERM/SYMBOL	MEANING OF SYMBOL	FORMULA
r	Pearson's r	$r = \dfrac{SP}{\sqrt{SS_x SS_y}}$
SS_x	Sum of squares for the independent variable	$SS_x = \sum (x - \bar{x})^2$
SS_y	Sum of squares for the dependent variable	$SS_y = \sum (y - \bar{y})^2$
SP	Sum of products	$\sum (x - \bar{x})(y - \bar{y})$
t	t-ratio	$t = \dfrac{r\sqrt{N - 2}}{\sqrt{1 - r^2}}$
df	Degrees of freedom (based on pairs of cases)	$df = N - 2$

(Continued)

TABLE 10.1 *Continued*

TERM/SYMBOL	MEANING OF SYMBOL	FORMULA
$\hat{Y}$	Predicted value of Y (dependent variable). The predicted value of Y after accounting for changes in X (independent variable)	$\hat{Y} = a + bx$
b	Slope (regression coefficient). The amount of unit(s) change in Y (dependent variable) for each unit change in X (independent variable)	$b = \dfrac{SP}{SS_x}$
Beta	b expressed in units of standard deviation	
a	Y-intercept. It is the expected level of Y (the dependent variable) when X is equal to 0.	$a = \bar{y} - b\bar{x}$

Unequal America

Most of us, at one time or another, have probably heard that America is the "land of opportunity" where everyone has an equal chance of attaining wealth and living a happy life. Looking around, however, we also see that roughly 40 million Americans are without health insurance, nearly 13% of Americans live in poverty, and approximately 18% of children under the age of 18 live in poverty. These are shocking statistics for a country considered to be one of the wealthiest in world history. Assuming that rational people do not voluntarily choose to live in poverty without health insurance, we must conclude that pathways of upward mobility are not available to everyone. You may recall from Chapter 5 that sociologist Max Weber (1864–1920) referred to something called *life chances* to explain inequality and Karl Marx referred to *class conflict* to explain it. Regardless of the explanation you find most plausible, it is hard to believe that pathways to upward mobility are equally available to everyone. History can help us better understand how the United States got to this point.

The immediate post–World War II era brought with it unprecedented growth in the U.S. economy. In the aftermath of the war, America's factories ran at full tilt to supply Europe and Japan with much needed steel and textiles to rebuild their infrastructure. Cities like Buffalo, New York; Pittsburgh, Pennsylvania; and Gary, Indiana, saw their economies flourish as global demands for steel rose to record high levels. This economic growth characterized not only cities and geographic regions, but much of the population as well. Working-class families witnessed consistent gains in their income all the way into the 1970s in an era of economic expansion that came to be known as "Fordism."

The oil crisis of 1973 signaled the end of the Fordist era of economic expansion as the U.S. economy began to slow. "Stagflation" became a popular term to describe a stagnant economy with rising inflation. Stagflation ushered in a new set of challenges for working-class families in the United States. As prices rose, jobs became scarce and the economic gains made in the decades following World War II seemed a distant memory. These changes can be seen in Figures 10.1 and 10.2.

As you can see, between 1947 and 1979, families of all income levels saw their income levels rise. Understand, however, that this does not mean that inequality was on

Fordism A period of unprecedented economic expansion in the U.S. economy in the post–World War II era.

Socioeconomic status A measure of social class that is often based on some combination of income, occupation, and education.

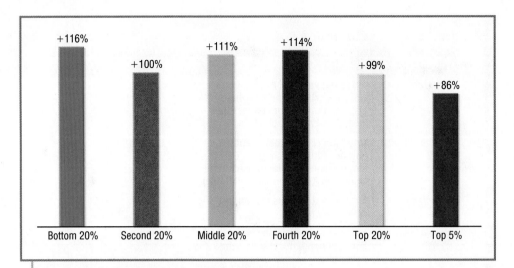

Figure 10.1 **Change in Real Family Income by Quintile and Top 5%, 1947–1979**

Source: U.S. Census Bureau, Historical Income Tables, Table F-3, *http://www.demos.org/inequality/numbers.cfm.*

Figure 10.2 **Change in Real Family Income by Quintile and Top 5%, 1979–2005**

Source: Analysis of U.S. Census Bureau Data in Economic Policy Institute, *The State of Working America, 1994–1995* (Armonk, NY: M. E. Sharpe, 1994) p. 37.

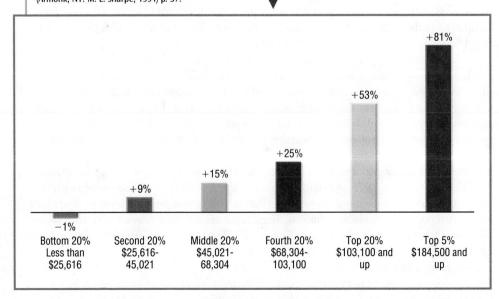

the decline. For example, a family in the bottom 20%, with an income of $10,000, saw their income rise to $21,600, while a family in the top 20%, with an income of $100,000, saw their income rise to $216,000. Therefore, similar percentage increases results in growing disparity in terms of real dollars.

This growing income inequality pales in comparison to what happened between 1979 and 2005. During this period, a family in the bottom 20%, with an income of $10,000 saw their income *decline* to $9,900 while a family in the top 20 percent, an income of $110,000, saw their income rise to $168,300. The 1980s and 1990s represent a historical era in U.S. history characterized by a tremendous widening of the gap between rich and poor. How do you think this may have affected life chances of people from different income levels?

In this chapter, we learn how to use correlation and regression to better understand how variables are related to one another. Pearson's correlation coefficient (*r*) is introduced as a way to summarize both the strength and the direction of an association between two interval/ratio variables. Then linear regression and the coefficient of determination (r^2) are introduced as ways to describe associations, predict individual outcomes, and explain variance (e.g., the percent of total variance in income that is explained by education).

Scatterplots: The Underlying Logic Behind Correlation

Scatterplots are a graphic way of visualizing the relationship between two variables. Each data point on a scatterplot represents two values, an *X* value and a *Y* value. *X* represents the independent variable and *Y* represents the dependent variable. For example, suppose we hypothesize that the more hours students spend studying for an exam, the better they will do on the exam. The number of hours studied is our independent variable and the grades they receive are the dependent variable (grades are dependent on studying). A scatterplot of our results might look like Figure 10.3.

As you can see from Figure 10.3, as the number of hours studied increases, the grades earned on the exam *tend* to increase. In this example, the correlation is positive because the cases that score low on the independent variable (studying) score lower on the dependent variable (grade) and cases that score high on the independent variable score higher on the dependent variable. This trend in the data is not true for each and every case, but it does characterize the pattern found among the 10 respondents in our sample.

It is possible to add what is called a "fit line" to the chart, as shown in Figure 10.4. The degree to which cases cluster along the fit line represents the overall strength of the correlation between studying and grades. Figure 10.5 shows the scatterplot for a perfect correlation between studying and grades.

As you can see in Figure 10.5, each of the cases falls directly on the fit line, indicating a perfect correlation. The slope of the line has no effect on the strength of the correlation, but will be important later in our discussion of linear regression.

Scatterplot A graph that displays the relationship between two interval/ratio variables by plotting the location of each case along two axes (*X* and *Y*).

Positive correlation A relationship between two interval/ratio variables that occurs when cases with lower values on one variable tend to have lower values on the second variable and cases with higher values on one variable tend to have higher values on the second variable.

Negative correlation A relationship between two interval/ratio variables that occurs when cases with lower values on one variable tend to have higher values on the second variable and cases with higher values on one variable tend to have lower values on the second variable.

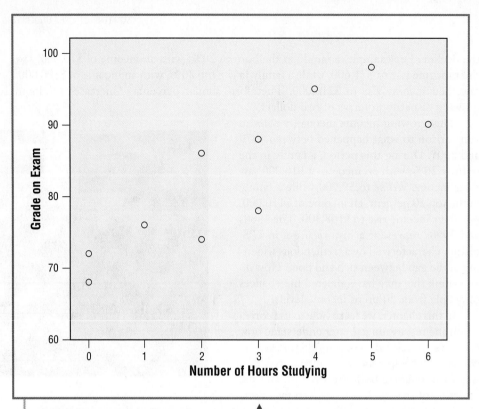

Figure 10.3 Exam Grade by
Number of Hours Studied

Figure 10.4 Exam Grade by Number
of Hours Studied

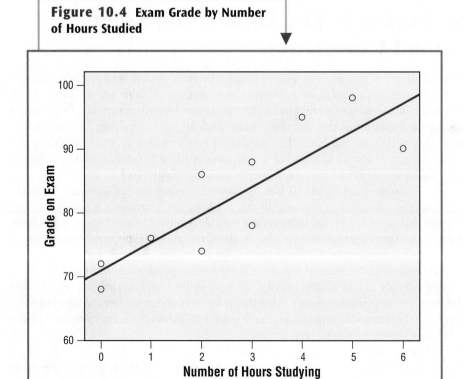

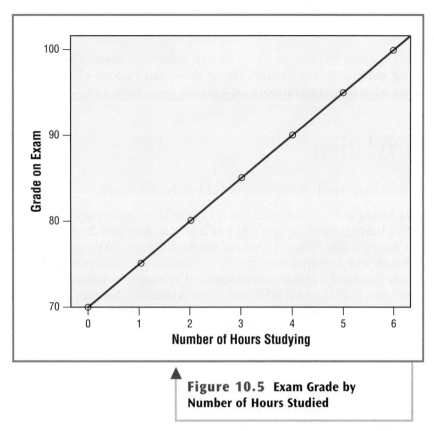

Figure 10.5 Exam Grade by Number of Hours Studied

Suppose a group of students got together to study for a few hours the night before an exam, but instead of studying they ended up having a party. Now we might expect that the number of hours "studying" will be negatively correlated with exam grades, as shown in Figure 10.6.

Figure 10.6 Exam Grade by Number of Hours Studied while Partying

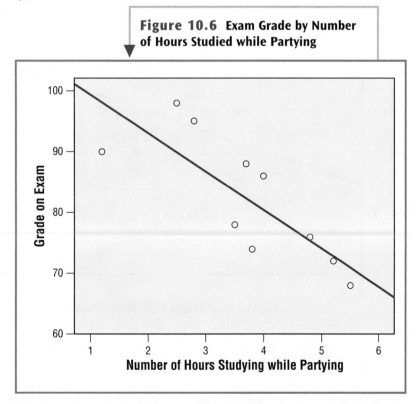

As predicted, the fit line moves downward, indicating a negative correlation between studying and grades. The evidence clearly shows that students who spend more time studying while partying tend to do the worst on their exams.

Correlation

Education and American Class Structure

Having looked at how scatterplots can help us to better understand the nature of relationships between variables, let's now take a look at some data from the 2006 General Social Survey (GSS; National Opinion Research Center, 2006) to better understand life chances and American class structure. Suppose we hypothesize that education is positively associated with mother's education. The scatterplot below uses 100 randomly selected cases from the 2006 GSS to show the relationship between mother's education and respondent's education. As you can see, the two variables are positively associated, yet there is a significant amount of variation in the data (meaning the data do not cluster tightly along the fit line).

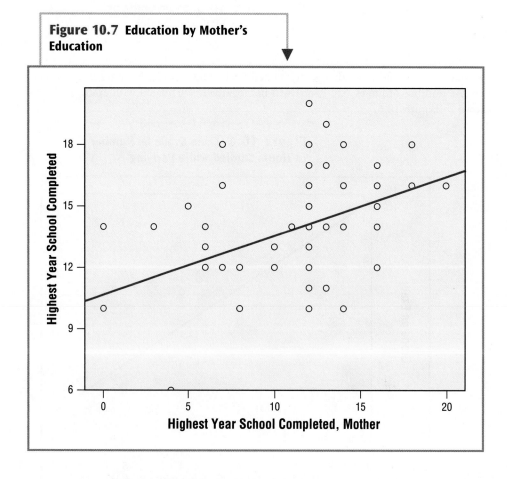

Figure 10.7 Education by Mother's Education

Calculating and Interpreting Pearson's r

EXAMPLE 1

Education and Mother's Education

Figure 10.8 below shows a scatterplot of education by mother's education for 6 hypothetical cases that can be used to demonstrate how to calculate Pearson's r. As in the case of the 2006 GSS data, the association is positive. We need a way, however, to describe the strength of the association. Pearson's r, like other measures of association, ranges between

TABLE 10.2

RESPONDENT	MOTHER'S EDUCATION (X)	RESPONDENT'S EDUCATION (Y)
A	12	12
B	10	13
C	12	14
D	16	16
E	14	16
F	8	13

Figure 10.8 **Education by Mother's Education**

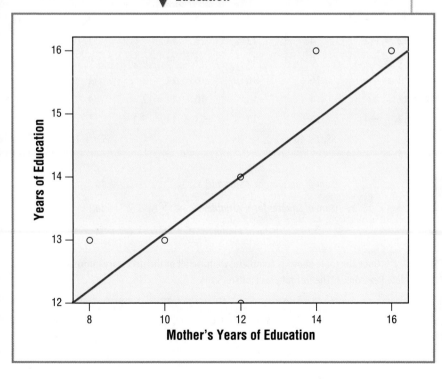

0 and 1.0 with 0 indicating no association and 1.0 indicating a perfect linear association. Pearson's r can also be positive or negative, an indication of the direction of association. Figure 10.8 indicates that the association between our variables is positive. The next step is to calculate the strength of the association.

> **Pearson's r** A symmetrical measure of association that is based on presumed linear relationship between two interval/ratio variables. It can be either positive or negative.

Our hypothesis is: Mother's education (independent variable) is positively associated with respondent's education (dependent variable). Before beginning our calculation of Pearson's r, it is useful to calculate the mean for Education and the mean for Mother's Education. It is also useful to set up a table like Table 10.3. This table may look intimidating, but it consists of material covered in earlier chapters. It is set up to organize the process of finding the sums of squares for the X and Y variables. The only new part of this table is the last column, labeled $(X - \bar{X})(Y - \bar{Y})$. The purpose of this column is to multiply each case's deviation from the mean on one variable with the same case's corresponding deviation from the mean on the other variable. The formulas to calculate the mean for Education $(\bar{X})$ and the mean for Mother's Education $(\bar{Y})$ are shown below.

$$\bar{X} = \frac{12 + 10 + 12 + 16 + 14 + 8}{6} = \frac{72}{6} = 12$$

$$\bar{Y} = \frac{12 + 13 + 14 + 16 + 16 + 13}{6} = \frac{84}{6} = 14$$

To minimize error, it is best to complete the table one row at a time moving from left to right. Then move on to the next row.

TABLE 10.3

X	$X - \bar{X}$	$(X - \bar{X})^2$	Y	$Y - \bar{Y}$	$(Y - \bar{Y})^2$	$(X - \bar{X})(Y - \bar{Y})$
12	$12 - 12 = 0$	0	12	$12 - 14 = -2$	4	0
10	$10 - 12 = -2$	4	13	$13 - 14 = -1$	1	2
12	$12 - 0 = 0$	0	14	$14 - 14 = 0$	0	0
16	$16 - 12 = 4$	16	16	$16 - 14 = 2$	4	8
14	$14 - 12 = 2$	4	16	$16 - 14 = 2$	4	4
8	$8 - 12 = -4$	16	13	$13 - 14 = -1$	1	4
$\Sigma = 72$		$SS_x = 40$	$\Sigma = 84$		$SS_y = 14$	$SP = 18$

$$(\textit{Sum of Squares for X variable}) \; SS_x = \sum (x - \bar{x})^2 = 40$$

$$(\textit{Sum of Squares for Y variable}) \; SS_y = \sum (y - \bar{y})^2 = 14$$

$$(\textit{Sum of Products}) \; SP = \sum (x - \bar{x})(y - \bar{y}) = 18$$

Once the table above is complete, we have all of the necessary information to calculate Pearson's r. The formula for Pearson's r is:

$$r = \frac{SP}{\sqrt{SS_x SS_y}} = \frac{18}{\sqrt{(40)(14)}} = \frac{18}{\sqrt{560}} = \frac{18}{23.7} = .76$$

This tells us that Pearson's *r* is equal to .76. The association between mother's education and respondent's education is positive and very strong.

Only one more question needs to be asked about the relationship between these two variables and that is to what degree are the findings statistically significant? In other words, what is the probability of having made an error in our rejection of the null hypothesis? Remember significance tests are based on the idea of how sure we can be in rejecting the null hypothesis.

To assess the significance of Pearson's *r*, we use the following equation for a *t* ratio shown below.

$$t = \frac{r\sqrt{N-2}}{\sqrt{1-r^2}}$$

In this formula, *r* is equal to Pearson's *r* and *N* is equal to the number of pairs of cases. As you can see in Table 10.3, the table contains 6 pairs of cases. Therefore, our degrees of freedom equal 4. Our *t*-ratio formula then looks as follows:

$$t = \frac{r\sqrt{N-2}}{\sqrt{1-r^2}} = \frac{.76\sqrt{6-2}}{\sqrt{1-.76^2}} = \frac{.76\sqrt{4}}{\sqrt{1-.58}} = \frac{.76(2)}{\sqrt{.42}} = \frac{1.52}{.65} = 2.338$$

Using Table B in the back of the book, we plug our *t*-ratio value of 2.338 into the row with 4 degrees of freedom. At the .10 level of significance, we see that the table value is 2.132. Because our *t*-ratio is larger than the value in the table, we can say that our results are significant to the .10 level ($\alpha = .10$).

Now You Try It 1

Use the information in the table below to complete the table and determine the strength and direction of the association between variable *X* and variable *Y* by calculating Pearson's *r* and the significance level.

X	$X - \bar{X}$	$(X - \bar{X})^2$	Y	$Y - \bar{Y}$	$(Y - \bar{Y})^2$	$(X - \bar{X})(Y - \bar{Y})$
4			10			
4			11			
5			13			
5			14			
6			18			
6			18			
$\Sigma =$		$SS_x =$	$\Sigma =$		$SS_y =$	$SP =$

EXAMPLE 2

Socioeconomic Status and Father's Education

Now let's take a look at the relationship between socioeconomic status and father's education. If class inequalities reproduce themselves across the generations, it stands to reason that people who have fathers with many years of education will be more likely to have higher socioeconomic status than those who have fathers with fewer years of education. Therefore, we can pose the following hypothesis: Respondent's socioeconomic status is positively correlated with father's education. Using a group of randomly selected cases from the 2006 GSS, we see that the nature of the relationship between these variables is positive in Figure 10.9.

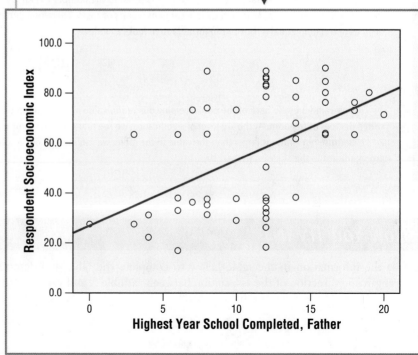

Figure 10.9 Socioeconomic Status by Father's Education

Suppose we sample 10 people in your hometown to determine their socioeconomic status and the father's number of years of education and get the results shown in Figure 10.10 based on the data in Table 10.4.

TABLE 10.4

RESPONDENT	FATHER'S EDUCATION	SEI SCORE
A	16	85
B	12	61
C	14	70
D	12	45
E	11	55
F	13	50
G	18	77
H	16	62
I	16	82
J	12	43

Figure 10.10 **Socioeconomic Status by Father's Education**

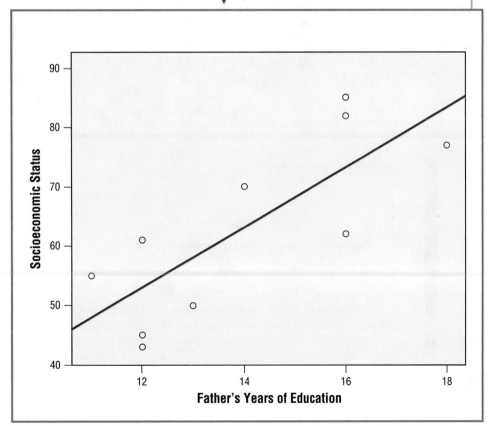

Before we can begin our calculations, it is necessary to determine which variable is independent and which is dependent. To do this we must state our hypothesis: Higher levels of father's education will result in higher levels of socioeconomic status. Therefore, father's education is independent and is considered our X variable and socioeconomic status is dependent and is considered our Y variable.

The first step is to determine the mean for X and the mean for Y. We can then use the values to determine the sum of squares for both X and Y and the sum of products (SP).

$$\bar{X} = \frac{16 + 12 + 14 + 12 + 11 + 13 + 18 + 16 + 16 + 12}{10} = \frac{140}{10} = 14$$

$$\bar{Y} = \frac{85 + 61 + 70 + 45 + 55 + 50 + 77 + 62 + 82 + 43}{10} = \frac{630}{10} = 63$$

The second step is to complete the table (Table 10.5). Remember to complete the table one row at a time, moving from left to right, to minimize error.

TABLE 10.5

X	$(X - \bar{X})$	$(X - \bar{X})^2$	Y	$(Y - \bar{Y})$	$(Y - \bar{Y})^2$	$(X - \bar{X})(Y - \bar{Y})$
16	$16 - 14 = 2$	4	85	$85 - 63 = 22$	484	$(2)(22) = 44$
12	$12 - 14 = -2$	4	61	$61 - 63 = -2$	4	$(-2)(-2) = 4$
14	$14 - 14 = 0$	0	70	$70 - 63 = 7$	49	$(0)(7) = 0$
12	$12 - 14 = -2$	4	45	$45 - 63 = -18$	324	$(-2)(-18) = 36$
11	$11 - 14 = -3$	9	55	$55 - 63 = -8$	64	$(-3)(-8) = 24$
13	$13 - 14 = -1$	1	50	$50 - 63 = -13$	169	$(-1)(-13) = 13$
18	$18 - 14 = 4$	16	77	$77 - 63 = 14$	196	$(4)(14) = 56$
16	$16 - 14 = 2$	4	62	$62 - 63 = -1$	1	$(2)(-1) = -2$
16	$16 - 14 = 2$	4	82	$82 - 63 = 19$	361	$(2)(19) = 38$
12	$12 - 14 = -2$	4	43	$43 - 63 = -20$	400	$(-2)(-20) = 40$
$\Sigma = 140$		$SS_x = 50$	$\Sigma = 630$		$SS_y = 2052$	$SP = 253$

We now have the following values:

$$SS_x = 50$$
$$SS_y = 2{,}052$$
$$SP = 253$$

These values can now be used to compute Pearson's r.

$$r = \frac{SP}{\sqrt{SS_x SS_y}} = \frac{253}{\sqrt{(50)(2{,}052)}} = \frac{253}{\sqrt{102{,}600}} = \frac{253}{320.3} = .79$$

A Pearson's r of .79 indicates a strong positive association between father's education and respondent's socioeconomic status. The only remaining step in our analysis is to determine the significance level. As in Example 1, to assess the significance of Pearson's *r*, we use a *t*-ratio, shown below.

$$t = \frac{r\sqrt{N-2}}{\sqrt{1-r^2}}$$

In this formula, *r* is equal to Pearson's *r* and *N* is equal to the number of pairs of cases. As you can see in Table 10.5, the table contains 10 pairs of cases. Therefore, our degrees of freedom equal 8. Our *t*-ratio formula then looks as follows:

$$t = \frac{r\sqrt{N-2}}{\sqrt{1-r^2}} = \frac{.79\sqrt{10-2}}{\sqrt{1-.79^2}} = \frac{.79\sqrt{8}}{\sqrt{1-.62}} = \frac{.79(2.83)}{\sqrt{.38}} = \frac{2.23}{.62} = 3.597$$

Using Table B in the back of this book, we plug our *t*-ratio value of 3.597 into the row with 8 degrees of freedom. At the .05 level of significance, we see that the table value is 2.306. Because our *t*-ratio is larger than the value in the table, we can say that our results are significant to the .05 level ($\alpha = .05$). Using the table at the .01 level, we see that our *t*-ratio would have to exceed 3.355. Because our *t*-ratio is 3.597, we can say that our results are significant to the .01 level.

Overall, both of the hypothetical examples presented here and both of the examples based on 2006 GSS data indicate that people who have parents with higher levels of education tend to have higher education and higher socioeconomic status. Example 1 is significant to the .10 level and Example 2 is significant to the .01 level. The results raise interesting questions regarding claims that everyone has equal opportunities for success in the United States. The results of our analyses would indicate otherwise—that social class appears to reproduce itself within family units by privileging some and depriving others of opportunities. It would appear that Max Weber was onto something that still applies today when he argued that wealthier people are afforded more life chances and opportunities for upward advancement in capitalist societies.

Integrating Technology

As you might imagine, statistical software programs like SPSS for Windows offer users a great number of options to conduct insightful statistical analyses that can often be presented in visual form. One question that comes to mind in our previous analyses is the issue of bias, specifically sex bias. Do males and females benefit equally from their parents' years of education? In other words, we could predict that parents' education leads to higher socioeconomic status, but the question remains as to whether this is true for both males and females. Or is it as true for females as it is for males?

To test this, the following scatterplot is run using SPSS for Windows. The chart is set up with Father's Years of Education independent and Respondent's Socioeconomic Status dependent. Cases for males and females are marked using different-colored points and each group has its own fit line.

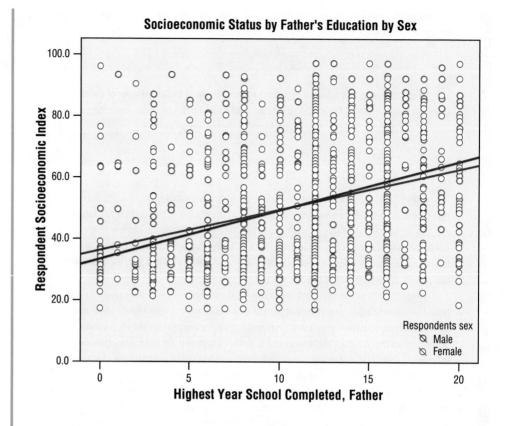

Correlations

	RESPONDENT'S SEX		HIGHEST YEAR SCHOOL COMPLETED, FATHER	RESPONDENT SOCIOECONOMIC INDEX
Male	Highest Year School Completed, Father	Pearson Correlation	1	.358**
		Sig. (two-tailed)		.000
		N	1015	975
	Respondent Socioeconomic Index	Pearson Correlation	.358**	1
		Sig. (two-tailed)	.000	
		N	975	1906
Female	Highest Year School Completed, Father	Pearson Correlation	1	.286**
		Sig. (two-tailed)		.000
		N	1243	1163
	Respondent Socioeconomic Index	Pearson Correlation	.286**	1
		Sig. (two-tailed)	.000	
		N	1163	2336

** Correlation is significant at the 0.01 level (two-tailed).

As the scatterplot indicates, the association between father's education and respondent's socioeconomic status is positive for both males and females. However, you can see that the lines cross somewhere around 10 years of father's education. This indicates that while both males and females benefit from their father's education, males tend to benefit at a greater rate, as indicated by the steeper slope of the fit line. We can also see in the correlation table that, for males, the Pearson's r is equal to .358. On the other hand, for females the Pearson's r is .286. This indicates that the association of father's education with respondent's socioeconomic status is stronger for males than it is for females.

Linear Regression

Regression is an extremely useful statistical technique that builds on the concepts of variance (s^2) and correlation (r). Linear regression is based on the idea that the relationship between two variables is linear, as opposed to curvilinear, and that the line can be drawn on a scatterplot. We have actually been working with regression lines in the section on correlation, but we extend our understanding of them in this section.

Regression analysis offers a more in-depth understanding of the relationship between two variables by providing a technique that allows us to describe the amount of change in the dependent variable that is accounted for by the independent variable. This is referred to as explaining the variance in the dependent variable. Regression analysis also offers the ability to use the formula for a line to make predictions that summarize trends. For example, education (independent) and income (dependent) are positively correlated. A regression line would then allow us to predict that for each additional year of education, an increase of some number of dollars in income can be expected. We begin our analysis of linear regression with a discussion of the formula for lines and the regression model.

> **Linear regression** A tool used to describe the relationship between two interval/ratio variables that relies on the use of scatterplots and a prediction of the "best-fitting" line to describe the trend.
>
> **Y-intercept** The point at which the regression line crosses the y-axis. The expected value of Y when X is equal to 0.
>
> **Slope** The steepness of the regression line (equal to rise divided by run). It indicates the predicted increase in the dependent variable for each unit increase in the independent variable.

Lines and the Regression Model

Lines. The most basic formula for a line is $Y = a + bX$. The symbols in this formula are:

- Y is the value of the dependent variable that we are trying to predict.
- a is the Y-intercept, the value of Y when X is equal to 0.
- b is the slope, also known as "rise divided by run." For each increase in unit on the X-axis is a corresponding increase or decrease on the Y-axis. Statisticians refer to b as the unstandardized regression coefficient.
- Beta is the same as b except that it is expressed in units of standard deviation. Statisticians refer to beta as the standardized regression coefficient. The use of beta is discussed a little later in the chapter.

For example, suppose that we have the following information for workers in a print shop. X is equal to the number of years they have spent on the job and Y is equal to hourly wage.

  $a = 8$ (the base level of pay for anyone on the job)

  $b = 2$ (for each year on the job, wages increase by 2)

  $X = 1, 2, 3, 4$

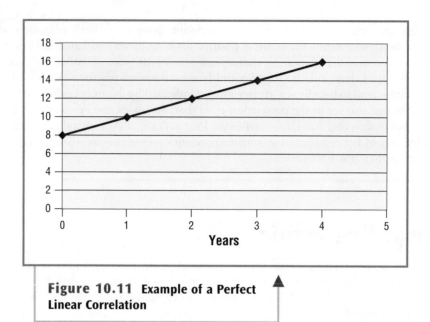

Figure 10.11 **Example of a Perfect Linear Correlation**

We can plot values of Y (wages) if we know the values of X (years) as follows:

- When $X = 0$, $Y = a + bx = 8 + 2(0) = 8$
- When $X = 1$, $Y = a + bx = 8 + 2(1) = 10$
- When $X = 2$, $Y = a + bx = 8 + 2(2) = 12$
- When $X = 3$, $Y = a + bx = 8 + 2(3) = 14$
- When $X = 4$, $Y = a + bx = 8 + 2(4) = 16$

The difference between our example of the formula for a line in Figure 10.11 and that of a line representing real data is that seldom, if ever, do we find a perfect correlation between two variables. In reality, our five employees may be distributed so that few, if any, cases actually fall on the fit line, as in Figure 10.12. This is the difference between a line and a "best-fitting" line. Any best-fitting line is going to have a certain amount of error in it, because it is a predicted line, like that shown in Figure 10.12. Therefore, the formula for a regression line is as follows:

$$\hat{Y} = a + bx + e$$

In this formula

- $\hat{Y}$ represents the *predicted value of Y.*
- a represents the *Y-intercept.*
- b represents the slope, or *regression coefficient.*
- e represents the *error term (it represents the amount of wages that cannot be explained by the number of years on the job).*

Incorporating the error term into our calculations is beyond the scope of this book and we will proceed from this point without using it. Our formula for predicted values of Y will then be:

$$\hat{Y} = a + bx$$

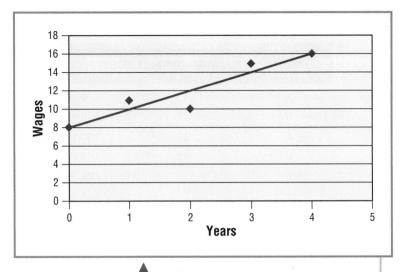

Figure 10.12 **An Example of an Imperfect Correlation**

Now You Try It 2

Plotting a Line

Use the data below to generate the data points for a line. Draw the chart and insert the line along the data points.

$a = 2$
$b = 1$
$X = 3, 5, 7, 9, 11$

The Regression Model. Drawing a regression line is very similar to drawing a line in the previous examples except that we do not know the values of the Y-intercept (a) or the slope (b). The values must be calculated on the basis of means and variances, specifically sums of squares. Therefore, the three formulas we are working with to draw a regression line are as follows:

1. $\hat{Y} = a + bx$ (formula for the predicted value of Y).

2. $b = \dfrac{SP}{SS_x}$ (formula for the regression coefficient, or slope).

3. $a = \bar{y} - b\bar{x}$ (formula for the Y-intercept).

EXAMPLE 3

Grade Point Average and Television Viewing

Suppose we want to learn more about the relationship between students' GPAs and the time they spend watching television. Because watching television takes time away from more academic activities, we hypothesize that the two are negatively associated: As television viewing hours (X) increase, GPA (Y) decreases. To test our hypothesis, we sample 10 students and gather the following data.

TABLE 10.6

RESPONDENT	TELEVISION VIEWING HOURS	GPA
A	3	2.70
B	5	2.10
C	2	3.30
D	0	3.40
E	5	2.00
F	3	3.00
G	1	3.60
H	4	2.80
I	3	3.50
J	4	2.60

Before we can begin to solve for our predicted values of y ($\hat{Y} = a + bx$), we must first determine the regression coefficient (b) and the y-intercept (a). To determine these values, we must first calculate the sum of products (SP), the sum of squares for the independent variable (SS_x), the mean for the dependent variable ($\bar{Y}$), and the mean for the independent variable ($\bar{X}$). To do this, we set up a table similar to the one used to calculate a Pearson's correlation since all of the values in the table will be of use to us at some point.

TABLE 10.7

X	$X - \bar{X}$	$(X - \bar{X})^2$	Y	$Y - \bar{Y}$	$(Y - \bar{Y})^2$	$(X - \bar{X})(Y - \bar{Y})$
3	$3 - 3 = 0$	0	2.70	$2.70 - 2.90 = -.2$	.04	$(0)(-.2) = 0$
5	$5 - 3 = 2$	4	2.10	$2.10 - 2.90 = -.8$	.64	$(2)(-.8) = -1.6$
2	$2 - 3 = -1$	1	3.30	$3.30 - 2.90 = .4$	.16	$(-1)(.4) = -.4$
0	$0 - 3 = -3$	9	3.40	$3.40 - 2.90 = .5$	.25	$(-3)(.5) = -1.5$
5	$5 - 3 = 2$	4	2.00	$2.00 - 2.90 = -.9$	.81	$(2)(-.9) = -1.8$
3	$3 - 3 = 0$	0	3.00	$3.00 - 2.90 = .1$	.01	$(0)(.1) = 0$
1	$1 - 3 = -2$	4	3.60	$3.60 - 2.90 = .7$	.49	$(-2)(.7) = -1.4$
4	$4 - 3 = 1$	1	2.80	$2.80 - 2.90 = -.1$	.01	$(1)(-.1) = -.1$
3	$3 - 3 = 0$	0	3.50	$3.50 - 2.90 = .6$	.36	$(0)(.6) = 0$
4	$4 - 3 = 1$	1	2.60	$2.60 - 2.90 = -.3$	.09	$(1)(-.3) = -.3$
$\Sigma = 30$		$SS_x = 24$	$\Sigma = 29.0$		$SS_y = 2.86$	SP $= -7.1$

We can now calculate the regression coefficient (b) and the y-intercept (a) as follows:

$$b = \frac{SP}{SS_x} = \frac{-7.1}{24} = -.2958$$

$$a = \bar{y} - b\bar{x} = 2.90 - (-.2958)(3) = 2.90 - (-.8874) = 3.79$$

We can now use the values of the regression coefficient and the y-intercept to calculate predicted values of y ($\hat{Y}$) using given values of X to draw two points through which the fit line will pass. It is always a good idea to draw the fit line using the y-intercept as one point and the second point on the basis of using a large value of X in the formula for a line ($\hat{Y} = a + bx$). This will produce two points that are far apart on the scatterplot, making the line easier to draw. First, we draw one point on the y-axis at a GPA of 3.79 (the y-intercept). Second, using an X value of 5, our highest value of X, we calculate the second point using the formula for a line as follows:

$$\hat{Y} = a + bx = 3.79 + (-.2958)(5) = 3.79 - 1.479 = 2.31$$

This tells us that a student with an X value of 5 will have a $\hat{Y}$ value of 2.31. As you can see in Figure 10.13, the fit line passes through these two points. You can also see in Figure 10.13 that a new statistic is given in the lower right-hand corner, R Sq Linear. This is referred to as r^2 and is discussed shortly.

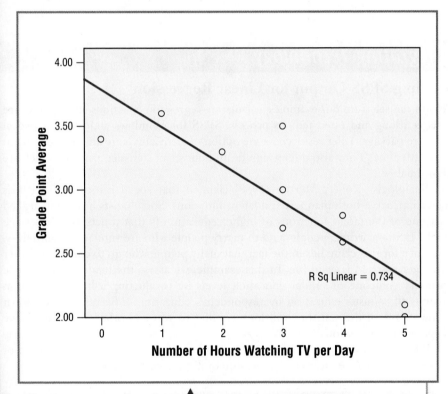

Figure 10.13 **Grade Point Average by Television Viewing**

We first calculate Pearson's r as follows,

$$r = \frac{SP}{\sqrt{SS_x SS_y}} = \frac{-7.1}{\sqrt{(24)(2.86)}} = \frac{-7.1}{\sqrt{68.64}} = \frac{-7.1}{8.28} = -.86$$

Pearson's r indicates a strong negative association between GPA and television viewing. As the number of hours spent watching television each day increases, GPA tends to decrease. Therefore, the data offer support for our hypothesis. The next step is to calculate a *t*-ratio, which we can then use to determine the significance level of R. The formula for the *t*-ratio is:

$$t = \frac{r\sqrt{N-2}}{\sqrt{1-r^2}} = \frac{-.86\sqrt{10-2}}{\sqrt{1-(-.86)^2}} = \frac{-.86\sqrt{8}}{\sqrt{1-.74}} = \frac{-.86(2.83)}{\sqrt{.26}} = \frac{-2.43}{.51} = -4.765$$

The value of *t* can be either positive or negative since all that matters is its size. Because we have 10 pairs of cases, our degrees of freedom (*df*) is equal to 8. Using Table B in the back of the book, we see that our *t*-ratio must exceed a value of 2.306 to be significant to the .05 level and a value of 3.355 to be significant to the .01 level. Since our *t*-ratio exceeds this value, we can say that our results are significant to the .01 level. They are not, however, significant to the .001 level because our *t*-ratio does not exceed the table value of 5.041.

Integrating Technology

Reading SPSS Output for Linear Regression

As you can see from our examples, calculating regression equations and significance tests is a long and often tedious process. SPSS for Windows and other statistical software packages offer researchers the option of analyzing large amounts of data in very little time. They also offer a significant number of statistics, some of which are shown below.

Sociologist Robert Merton (1968) claimed that social institutions, such as education, serve both manifest and latent functions. Sociologists have long argued that one of the latent functions of higher education is that it acts as a "marriage pool." In other words, people tend to marry people who are similar to themselves. Evidence for this claim lies in the fact that many people who go to college together often get married later in life. In this example, we assess the tendency for people to marry someone of similar education levels by conducting a linear regression analysis of spouse's education by respondent's education. The results are shown below. Some of the statistics will look familiar to you and others are beyond the scope of our discussions.

The first group of statistics should be very familiar and consist of a measure of central tendency (the mean) and a measure of dispersion (the standard deviation).

Descriptive Statistics

	MEAN	STD. DEVIATION	N
Highest Year School Completed, Spouse	13.42	3.279	1398
Highest Year of School Completed	13.62	3.222	1398

The second group of statistics is a correlation matrix that describes the strength of the association between the two variables.

Correlations

		HIGHEST YEAR SCHOOL COMPLETED, SPOUSE	HIGHEST YEAR OF SCHOOL COMPLETED
Pearson Correlation	Highest Year School Completed, Spouse	1.000	.632
	Highest Year of School Completed	.632	1.000
Sig. (one-tailed)	Highest Year School Completed, Spouse		.000
	Highest Year of School Completed	.000	
N	Highest Year School Completed, Spouse	1398	1398
	Highest Year of School Completed	1398	1398

A third group of statistics adjusts the value of r^2 after accounting for the magnitude of the standard error.

Model Summary

MODEL	R	R SQUARE	ADJUSTED R SQUARE	STD. ERROR OF THE ESTIMATE
1	.632[a]	.399	.399	2.543

[a]Predictors: (Constant), Highest Year of School Completed

Finally, a fourth group of statistics tells us the value of the Y-intercept (4.66), the corresponding increase in Y for each unit increase in the value of X (.643), and the significance levels (.000).

Coefficients[a]

MODEL		UNSTANDARDIZED COEFFICIENTS		STANDARDIZED COEFFICIENTS		
		B	STD. ERROR	BETA	T	SIG.
1	(Constant)	4.660	.296		15.767	.000
	Highest Year of School Completed	.643	.021	.632	30.448	.000

[a]Dependent Variable: Highest Year School Completed, Spouse

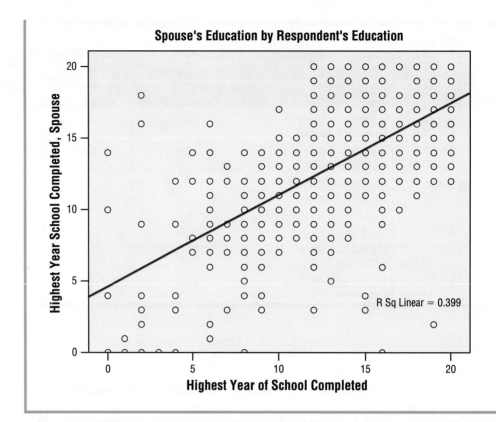

Now You Try It 3

The Regression Line

Use the formulas and values below to draw a regression line. You will need to calculate the Y-intercept (a), the slope (b), the sum of products (SP), and the sum of squares for X (SS_x). Determine the predicted value of Y when $X = 18$. You will need to begin by calculating the mean for X and the mean for Y.

$$\hat{Y} = a + bx$$

$$b = \frac{SP}{SS_x}$$

$$a = \bar{y} - b\bar{x}$$

$$X = 10, 12, 14, 16, 18$$

$$Y = 8, 6, 12, 14, 10$$

$$SP = 24$$

$$SS_x = 45$$

r^2: **Explaining Variance in the Dependent Variable.** As you saw in Figure 10.13, a new statistic called r^2 was introduced. r^2 is nothing more than the square of Pearson's r; but it offers us unique insight on the relationship between the two variables in our analysis. When we square Pearson's r we get:

r square The percent of total variance in the dependent variable that is explained by the independent variable.

$$r^2 = (-.86)(-.86) = .74$$

The difference between the r^2 we just calculated (.74) and the r^2 in Figure 10.13 (.73) is rounding error in our equations. The r^2 value tells us what percent of the total variance in the dependent variable is explained by the independent variable. In other words, 74% of all the variance in GPA can be explained by how many hours of television students watch each day. Obviously these results are based on fabricated data because GPA can be a factor of so many other behaviors and conditions, however, r^2 is a powerful tool that can be used to describe relationships between variables in a concise and easily understood manner.

Now You Try It 4

Use the data in the table below to (1) generate a scatterplot, (2) calculate Pearson's correlation and r^2, (3) draw the fit line for the data, (4) calculate the t-ratio, and (5) determine the significance level.

X	Y
0	88
6	52
4	64
1	60
5	54
3	78
4	40

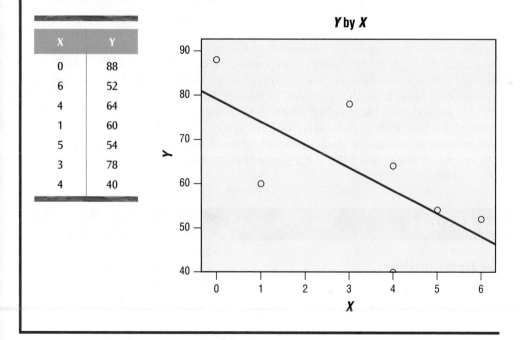

Unstandardized and Standardized Coefficients. Often social scientists study variables that are measured in units that are of different scales. For example, it is one thing to study the relationship between years of education and mothers' years of education (both measured in years) and quite another to study the relationship between income (measured in thousands or millions of dollars) and happiness measured on a scale of 1 to 10. If income is positively associated with happiness, could we really expect to see

TABLE 10.8

HOW MUCH MONEY ARE YOU WORTH?	HOW HAPPY ARE YOU? (1–10)
2,445,500	5
4,635,200	6
6,335,100	7
9,668,700	8
12,578,500	9

an increase in a change in happiness for each $1 increase in income? Theoretically, yes we could; but in reality, probably not. The increase on the happiness scale would be minuscule!

Here is a hypothetical example. Suppose we surveyed a small group of five multi-millionaires and asked them (A) how much money they are worth and (B) how happy they are on a scale of 1 to 10. The results are shown in Table 10.8.

As you can see in Table 10.8, the more money these people have, the happier they are. When this data is analyzed using linear regression, however, we find that the y-intercept is equal to 4.221 and the unstandardized beta coefficient (b), otherwise known as the slope, is equal to .0000003896. In other words, for each additional dollar that these millionaires are worth, we can expect an increase in the happiness scale of .0000003896. Obviously, this is too small of a number to easily comprehend.

Fortunately, social scientists have devised a way to work around this problem using standard deviations to develop an alternative to b. This alternative is called beta. Beta is a measure of change in the dependent variables measured in standard deviations. Beta (standardized regression coefficient) allows us to predict the number of standard deviations of increase in Y for each standard deviation increase in X. In our example, beta is equal to .993 (or just about 1). The standard deviation for X (money) is $s = \$4,029,006$, and the standard deviation for Y (happiness) is $s = 1.58$. So for each $4,029,006 increase in worth, we can expect an increase of about 1 standard deviation, or 1.58 on the happiness scale.

It is worth noting that SPSS output automatically generates both b and Beta values.

Statistical Uses and Misuses

Linear and Curvilinear Relationships

When using regression models to describe the relationship between variables, it is easy to forget that not all relationships are necessarily linear. For example, suppose that we study worker satisfaction at a company that treats their new employees very well and their older employees less well. It may be that newer employees experience rapid advancement, salary increases, and travel opportunities that are offered only for the first few years. We could then hypothe-

size that job satisfaction will rise quickly over the first few years and then decline as the number of years at the job increases. In other words, we might predict a nonlinear relationship. Nonlinear relationships are often referred to as curvilinear relationships.

As the chart below shows, assuming that a relationship is linear can lead to drastic misinterpretations of the data. The r^2 value for the linear regression model shown below is only .018 while the r^2 for the curvilinear relationship is .86. Data do not always take the shapes that we think they might. Probably the two best ways to avoid making such mistakes are: (1) Be familiar with your data and with the literature on the subject you are studying and (2) use scatterplots to get a visual feel for the data to ensure you are not overlooking the obvious. It's often easy to get "lost" in the numbers and miss the big picture right in front of us!

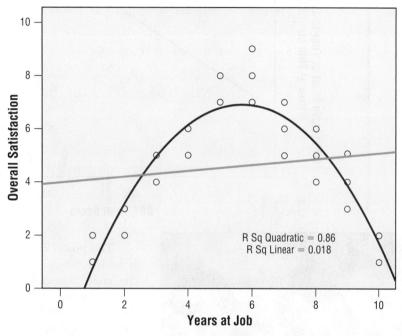

Job Satisfaction by Years at Job

R Sq Quadratic = 0.86
R Sq Linear = 0.018

Eye on the Applied

SAT Scores and Student Success at the College Level

Each year since 2000, the Indiana University Center for Postsecondary Research conducts its National Survey of Student Engagement (NSSE). Over 1,000 colleges have participated and many more use the NSSE data to try and figure out what they are doing well and what could use more work. The data come from students who are asked to respond to questions that deal with class activities, friendship networks, presentations, study habits, and hundreds of other items.

Much to the chagrin of many high school seniors getting ready to take the SAT exams, SAT scores are an excellent predictor of how well students will succeed in college, particularly in their first year of college. The results from one college (the name and year of the data cannot be revealed for purposes of confidentiality) are shown below. The variable Grades was coded C− = 1, C = 2, B− = 3 ... A = 4, so that it could be plotted with a fit line. As you can see from these results, students who score the highest on their SAT tests also tend to have higher grades. In fact, as the chart below indicates, SAT scores explain about 37% of the variance in college grades.

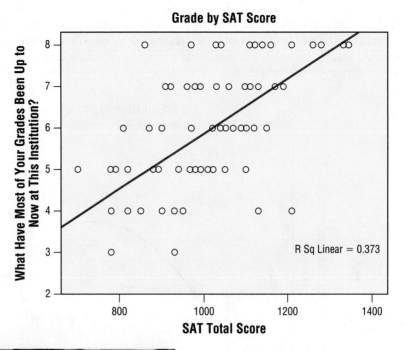

Grade by SAT Score

R Sq Linear = 0.373

The power of these kinds of statistics is evident when we consider the types of challenges that college administrators face in the admissions process. If we assume that colleges prefer to admit the students with the highest scores because they will be the most likely to succeed, then those colleges that can attract such students will gain reputations as being the "most competitive." If those students choose to attend other colleges, then the standard must be lowered so that a greater range of students can gain entry. Ultimately, colleges engage in a game in which they compete against one another to attract those students most likely to succeed.

Can you think of how the stratification of colleges and universities might reflect and contribute to the stratification of society?

Chapter Summary

Assessing the nature of the relationship between two interval/ratio variables can be accomplished in a number of ways. The first of these is to calculate a Pearson's correlation (r). A Pearson's correlation is a symmetric measure that is based on the concepts of means and variances. It indicates both the strength and direction of any association that might exist and, as is the case with other measures of association, its value ranges between 0 and 1.0. A second way to describe the relationship between two interval/ratio variables is to use linear regression. Linear regression is based on the assumption that the nature of the relationship between the variables is linear and can be described using a "best-fitting" line. By using the formula for a line, linear regression allows us to predict the value of a case on the dependent variable by knowing its value on the independent variable. The r^2 value tells us what proportion of the total variance in the dependent variable is explained by the independent variable.

Exercises

For each of the problems below:

A. Draw a scatterplot.

B. Calculate Pearson's r

C. Calculate the y-intercept, slope, and draw a regression line on the scatterplot.

D. Answer the "Prediction" problem.

E. Calculate r^2 and explain what it tells us about the relationship between the variables.

F. Calculate the t-ratio for Pearson's r and determine the level of significance.

1. Sociologists have discovered a phenomenon known as "environmental racism," a condition that exists when people of color bear a disproportionate burden of environmental hazards relative to whites. Suppose we sample 10 communities to determine the number of toxic waste sites in each community and the percent of each community's population that is nonwhite. Use the data in the table below to answer the six questions above.

PERCENT PEOPLE OF COLOR (X)	NUMBER OF TOXIC WASTE SITES (Y)
6	3
20	14
14	10
3	4
9	8
22	17

PERCENT PEOPLE OF COLOR (X)	NUMBER OF TOXIC WASTE SITES (Y)
11	6
8	3
31	15
16	10

Prediction Problem: If a community's population is 37% people of color, what is that community's predicted number of toxic waste sites?

2. A researcher wants to learn more about the relationship between the number of miles traveled to work and earnings. She hypothesizes that wealthier employees live outside the city rather than in the city and decides to sample a group of workers from a bank located downtown. She obtains the following data.

EARNINGS IN $ (X)	MILES TRAVELED TO WORK (Y)
33,250	5
84,500	21
66,350	6
58,425	7
45,600	8
67,240	14
77,900	10

Prediction Problem: How far from the city does an employee earning $50,000 live?

3. A researcher wants to investigate the relationship between social networking and satisfaction with life. She hypothesizes that people who have larger social networks (measured by a social networking index on which scores range from 0 to 10) tend to be happier (measured on a happiness scale on which scores range from 0 to 50). Use the data below to assess her hypothesis.

SOCIAL NETWORK SCORE (X)	HAPPINESS INDEX SCORE (Y)
6	33
4	24
8	25
9	42
7	43
2	21
4	35
6	30
4	20
4	26
10	44
8	32

Prediction Problem: What is the predicted happiness score for a person with a social network score of 3?

4. The same researcher from Question # 3 now wants to learn more about the relationship between social networks and virtual social networks. She predicts that large virtual networks will be associated with large "real" networks. She develops two networking indices to measure networking that each range from 0 to 50. Use the data below to assess her hypothesis.

VIRTUAL SOCIAL NETWORKING SCORE (X)	"REAL" SOCIAL NETWORKING SCORE (Y)
25	20
32	10
16	23
10	19
48	37
22	25
15	41
25	25
34	26
41	18

Prediction Problem: What is the "real" networking score for a respondent with a virtual networking score of 30?

5. Suppose we want to know more about the relationship between family income and time spent on the Internet. We sample a small group of students who recently graduated from high school and obtain the following data.

FAMILY INCOME ($)	HOURS ON THE INTERNET EACH WEEK
55,000	14
35,000	10
65,000	12
40,000	10
125,000	15
85,000	6
95,000	15
70,000	14

Prediction Problem: What is the predicted number of hours spent on the Internet for a respondent with a family income of $150,000 per year?

Computer Exercises

Use the data below to create a database. Then run a regression and scatterplot with a fit line using SPSS for Windows. Use the chart to answer the questions that follow.

X	Y
42	51
30	43
12	15
90	80
34	30
10	65
8	78

6. Are the variables correlated? If so, how?

7. To what level are the results statistically significant?

8. How much of the variance in the dependent variable is explained by the independent variable?

9. For each unit increase in the value of X, how much change can we anticipate in the value of Y?

10. What is the predicted value of Y when X is equal to 50?

Use the data below to create a database. Then run a regression and scatterplot with a fit line using SPSS for Windows. Use the chart to answer the questions that follow.

X	Y
15	25
18	56
23	32
14	48
10	79
9	52
8	10
20	99
14	74
16	63
17	51
18	22

X	Y
12	77
16	64
18	53
20	21
19	84
7	90
15	26
16	46
12	33
10	85
9	72
11	46

11. Are the variables correlated? If so, how?

12. To what level are the results statistically significant?

13. How much of the variance in the dependent variable is explained by the independent variable?

14. For each unit increase in the value of X, how much change can we anticipate in the value of Y?

15. What is the predicted value of Y when X is equal to 22?

Use the table below to create a SPSS database and to answer questions 16–25.

MALES		FEMALES	
X	Y	X	Y
18	4	20	5
22	16	26	6
20	5	24	7
26	13	20	2
24	10	21	6
22	8	25	5
21	15	22	8
25	12	20	3

16. For males, are the variables correlated? If so, how?

17. For females, are the variables correlated? If so, how?

18. To what level are the results statistically significant for males?

19. To what level are the results statistically significant for females?

20. For males, how much of the variance in the dependent variable is explained by the independent variable?

21. For females, how much of the variance in the dependent variable is explained by the independent variable?

22. For males, for each unit increase in the value of X, how much increase can we anticipate in the value of Y?

23. For females, for each unit increase in the value of X, how much increase can we anticipate in the value of Y?

24. For males, what is the predicted value of Y when X is equal to 16?

25. For females, what is the predicted value of Y when X is equal to 17?

Use the GSS2006 database to answer the following questions.

Run a linear regression of education (EDUC independent) by socioeconomic status (SEI dependent) and use the results to answer the following questions.

26. What is Pearson's r equal to?

27. What is the y-intercept equal to?

28. For each additional year of education, what is the expected additional number of socioeconomic status points gained?

29. To what level are the results significant?

Now split the database by race (White, Black, Other) and use the results to answer the same questions (in table form below). Then use the table to answer questions 30–34.

Linear Regression Results for Education by Socioeconomic Status by Race

STATISTIC	WHITE	BLACK	OTHER
Pearson's r			
Y-intercept			
Gain per year of education			
Significance level			

30. For which of the three groups is the correlation strongest?

31. Is the association positive or negative?

32. For which group does education produce the greatest gains in socioeconomic status?

33. For Whites, what percent of the variance in socioeconomic status is accounted for by education?

34. For Blacks, what percent of the variance in socioeconomic status is accounted for by education?

Now You Try It Answers

1: $SS_x = 4$; $SS_y = 58$; $SP = 15$; Pearson's $r = .98$

2:
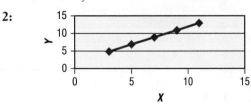

3: $\overline{X} = 14$, $\overline{Y} = 10$, y-intercept (a) = 1.6, slope

(b) = .6, when $x = 18$, $y = 12.12$

4: Pearson's $r = .673$, r square $= .454$, $t = -2.037$, Significant to the .10 level

Key Terms

Works Cited

Gerth, H. H., & Mills, C. W. (1958). *Max Weber: Essays in sociology.* New York: Galaxy.

Merton, R. (1968). *Social theory and social structure.* New York: Free Press.

National Opinion Research Center. (2006). *General Social Survey.* Chicago: Author.

Statistical Tables

TABLE A   *Percentage of Area under the Normal Curve*

Column a gives the distance in standard deviation units from the mean (z). Column b represents the percentage of area between the mean and a given z. Column c represents the percentage at or beyond a given z.

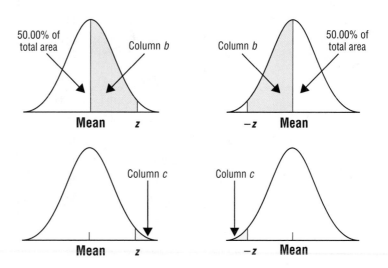

(Continued)

TABLE A *Continued*

(a) z	(b) AREA BETWEEN MEAN AND z	(c) AREA BEYOND z	(a) z	(b) AREA BETWEEN MEAN AND z	(c) AREA BEYOND z
.00	.00	50.00	.35	13.68	36.32
.01	.40	49.60	.36	14.06	35.94
.02	.80	49.20	.37	14.43	35.57
.03	1.20	48.80	.38	14.80	35.20
.04	1.60	48.40	.39	15.17	34.83
.05	1.99	48.01	.40	15.54	34.46
.06	2.39	47.61	.41	15.91	34.09
.07	2.79	47.21	.42	16.28	33.72
.08	3.19	46.81	.43	16.64	33.36
.09	3.59	46.41	.44	17.00	33.00
.10	3.98	46.02	.45	17.36	32.64
.11	4.38	45.62	.46	17.72	32.28
.12	4.78	45.22	.47	18.08	31.92
.13	5.17	44.83	.48	18.44	31.56
.14	5.57	44.43	.49	18.79	31.21
.15	5.96	44.04	.50	19.15	30.85
.16	6.36	43.64	.51	19.50	30.50
.17	6.75	43.25	.52	19.85	30.15
.18	7.14	42.86	.53	20.19	29.81
.19	7.53	42.47	.54	20.54	29.46
.20	7.93	42.07	.55	20.88	29.12
.21	8.32	41.68	.56	21.23	28.77
.22	8.71	41.29	.57	21.57	28.43
.23	9.10	40.90	.58	21.90	28.10
.24	9.48	40.52	.59	22.24	27.76
.25	9.87	40.13	.60	22.57	27.43
.26	10.26	39.74	.61	22.91	27.09
.27	10.64	39.36	.62	23.24	26.76
.28	11.03	38.97	.63	23.57	26.43
.29	11.41	38.59	.64	23.89	26.11
.30	11.79	38.21	.65	24.22	25.78
.31	12.17	37.83	.66	24.54	25.46
.32	12.55	37.45	.67	24.86	25.14
.33	12.93	37.07	.68	25.17	24.83
.34	13.31	36.69	.69	25.49	24.51

(Continued)

TABLE A *Continued*

(a) z	(b) AREA BETWEEN MEAN AND z	(c) AREA BEYOND z	(a) z	(b) AREA BETWEEN MEAN AND z	(c) AREA BEYOND z
.70	25.80	24.20	1.06	35.54	14.46
.71	26.11	23.89	1.07	35.77	14.23
.72	26.42	23.58	1.08	35.99	14.01
.73	26.73	23.27	1.09	36.21	13.79
.74	27.04	22.96	1.10	36.43	13.57
.75	27.34	22.66	1.11	36.65	13.35
.76	27.64	22.36	1.12	36.86	13.14
.77	27.94	22.06	1.13	37.08	12.92
.78	28.23	21.77	1.14	37.29	12.71
.79	28.52	21.48	1.15	37.49	12.51
.80	28.81	21.19	1.16	37.70	12.30
.81	29.10	20.90	1.17	37.90	12.10
.82	29.39	20.61	1.18	38.10	11.90
.83	29.67	20.33	1.19	38.30	11.70
.84	29.95	20.05	1.20	38.49	11.51
.85	30.23	19.77	1.21	38.69	11.31
.86	30.51	19.49	1.22	38.88	11.12
.87	30.78	19.22	1.23	39.07	10.93
.88	31.06	16.60	1.24	39.25	10.75
.89	31.33	16.35	1.25	39.44	10.56
.90	31.59	16.11	1.26	39.62	10.38
.91	31.86	15.87	1.27	39.80	10.20
.92	32.12	15.62	1.28	39.97	10.03
.93	32.38	15.39	1.29	40.15	9.85
.94	32.64	15.15	1.30	40.32	9.68
.95	32.89	14.92	1.31	40.49	9.51
.96	33.15	14.69	1.32	40.66	9.34
.97	33.40	14.46	1.33	40.82	9.18
.98	33.65	14.23	1.34	40.99	9.01
.99	33.89	14.01	1.35	41.15	8.85
1.00	34.13	13.79	1.36	41.31	8.69
1.01	34.38	13.57	1.37	41.47	8.53
1.02	34.61	13.35	1.38	41.62	8.38
1.03	34.85	13.14	1.39	41.77	8.23
1.04	35.08	12.92	1.40	41.92	8.08
1.05	35.31	12.71	1.41	42.07	7.93

(Continued)

TABLE A *Continued*

(a) z	(b) AREA BETWEEN MEAN AND z	(c) AREA BEYOND z	(a) z	(b) AREA BETWEEN MEAN AND z	(c) AREA BEYOND z
1.42	42.22	7.78	1.78	46.25	3.75
1.43	42.36	7.64	1.79	46.33	3.67
1.44	42.51	7.49	1.80	46.41	3.59
1.45	42.65	7.35	1.81	46.49	3.51
1.46	42.79	7.21	1.82	46.56	3.44
1.47	42.92	7.08	1.83	46.64	3.36
1.48	43.06	6.94	1.84	46.71	3.29
1.49	43.19	6.81	1.85	46.78	3.22
1.50	43.32	6.68	1.86	46.86	3.14
1.51	43.45	6.55	1.87	46.93	3.07
1.52	43.57	6.43	1.88	46.99	3.01
1.53	43.70	6.30	1.89	47.06	2.94
1.54	43.82	6.18	1.90	47.13	2.87
1.55	43.94	6.06	1.91	47.19	2.81
1.56	44.06	5.94	1.92	47.26	2.74
1.57	44.18	5.82	1.93	47.32	2.68
1.58	44.29	5.71	1.94	47.38	2.62
1.59	44.41	5.59	1.95	47.44	2.56
1.60	44.52	5.48	1.96	47.50	2.50
1.61	44.63	5.37	1.97	47.56	2.44
1.62	44.74	5.26	1.98	47.61	2.39
1.63	44.84	5.16	1.99	47.67	2.33
1.64	44.95	5.05	2.00	47.72	2.28
1.65	45.05	4.95	2.01	47.78	2.22
1.66	45.15	4.85	2.02	47.83	2.17
1.67	45.25	4.75	2.03	47.88	2.12
1.68	45.35	4.65	2.04	47.93	2.07
1.69	45.45	4.55	2.05	47.98	2.02
1.70	45.54	4.46	2.06	48.03	1.97
1.71	45.64	4.36	2.07	48.08	1.92
1.72	45.73	4.27	2.08	48.12	1.88
1.73	45.82	4.18	2.09	48.17	1.83
1.74	45.91	4.09	2.10	48.21	1.79
1.75	45.99	4.01	2.11	48.26	1.74
1.76	46.08	3.92	2.12	48.30	1.70
1.77	46.16	3.84	2.13	48.34	1.66

(*Continued*)

TABLE A *Continued*

(a) z	(b) AREA BETWEEN MEAN AND z	(c) AREA BEYOND z	(a) z	(b) AREA BETWEEN MEAN AND z	(c) AREA BEYOND z
2.14	48.38	1.62	2.50	49.38	.62
2.15	48.42	1.58	2.51	49.40	.60
2.16	48.46	1.54	2.52	49.41	.59
2.17	48.50	1.50	2.53	49.43	.57
2.18	48.54	1.46	2.54	49.45	.55
2.19	48.57	1.43	2.55	49.46	.54
2.20	48.61	1.39	2.56	49.48	.52
2.21	48.64	1.36	2.57	49.49	.51
2.22	48.68	1.32	2.58	49.51	.49
2.23	48.71	1.29	2.59	49.52	.48
2.24	48.75	1.25	2.60	49.53	.47
2.25	48.78	1.22	2.61	49.55	.45
2.26	48.81	1.19	2.62	49.56	.44
2.27	48.84	1.16	2.63	49.57	.43
2.28	48.87	1.13	2.64	49.59	.41
2.29	48.90	1.10	2.65	49.60	.40
2.30	48.93	1.07	2.66	49.61	.39
2.31	48.96	1.04	2.67	49.62	.38
2.32	48.98	1.02	2.68	49.63	.37
2.33	49.01	.99	2.69	49.64	.36
2.34	49.04	.96	2.70	49.65	.35
2.35	49.06	.94	2.71	49.66	.34
2.36	49.09	.91	2.72	49.67	.33
2.37	49.11	.89	2.73	49.68	.32
2.38	49.13	.87	2.74	49.69	.31
2.39	49.16	.84	2.75	49.70	.30
2.40	49.18	.82	2.76	49.71	.29
2.41	49.20	.80	2.77	49.72	.28
2.42	49.22	.78	2.78	49.73	.27
2.43	49.25	.75	2.79	49.74	.26
2.44	49.27	.73	2.80	49.74	.26
2.45	49.29	.71	2.81	49.75	.25
2.46	49.31	.69	2.82	49.76	.24
2.47	49.32	.68	2.83	49.77	.23
2.48	49.34	.66	2.84	49.77	.23
2.49	49.36	.64	2.85	49.78	.22

(Continued)

TABLE A *Continued*

(a) z	(b) AREA BETWEEN MEAN AND z	(c) AREA BEYOND z	(a) z	(b) AREA BETWEEN MEAN AND z	(c) AREA BEYOND z
2.86	49.79	.21	3.11	49.91	.09
2.87	49.79	.21	3.12	49.91	.09
2.88	49.80	.20	3.13	49.91	.09
2.89	49.81	.19	3.14	49.92	.08
2.90	49.81	.19	3.15	49.92	.08
2.91	49.82	.18	3.16	49.92	.08
2.92	49.82	.18	3.17	49.92	.08
2.93	49.83	.17	3.18	49.93	.07
2.94	49.84	.16	3.19	49.93	.07
2.95	49.84	.16	3.20	49.93	.07
2.96	49.85	.15	3.21	49.93	.07
2.97	49.85	.15	3.22	49.94	.06
2.98	49.86	.14	3.23	49.94	.06
2.99	49.86	.14	3.24	49.94	.06
3.00	49.87	.13	3.25	49.94	.06
3.01	49.87	.13	3.30	49.95	.05
3.02	49.87	.13	3.35	49.96	.04
3.03	49.88	.12	3.40	49.97	.03
3.04	49.88	.12	3.45	49.97	.03
3.05	49.89	.11	3.50	49.98	.02
3.06	49.89	.11	3.60	49.98	.02
3.07	49.89	.11	3.70	49.99	.01
3.08	49.90	.10	3.80	49.99	.01
3.09	49.90	.10	3.90	49.995	.005
3.10	49.90	.10	4.00	49.997	.003

Source: Table III from Fisher, R. A., & Yates, S. (1963). *Statistical tables for biological, agricultural, and medical research* (4th ed.). London: Longman.

TABLE B *Critical Values of t*

DEGREES OF FREEDOM (*df*)	LEVEL OF SIGNIFICANCE FOR ONE-TAILED TEST					
	.10	.05	.025	.01	.005	.0005
	LEVEL OF SIGNIFICANCE FOR TWO-TAILED TEST					
	.20	.10	.05	.02	.01	.001
1	3.078	6.314	12.706	31.821	63.657	636.619
2	1.886	2.920	4.303	6.965	9.925	31.598
3	1.638	2.353	3.182	4.541	5.841	12.941
4	1.533	2.132	2.776	3.747	4.604	8.610
5	1.476	2.015	2.571	3.365	4.032	6.859
6	1.440	1.943	2.447	3.143	3.707	5.959
7	1.415	1.895	2.365	2.998	3.499	5.405
8	1.397	1.860	2.306	2.896	3.355	5.041
9	1.383	1.833	2.262	2.821	3.250	4.781
10	1.372	1.812	2.228	2.764	3.169	4.587
11	1.363	1.796	2.201	2.718	3.106	4.437
12	1.356	1.782	2.179	2.681	3.055	4.318
13	1.350	1.771	2.160	2.650	3.012	4.221
14	1.345	1.761	2.145	2.624	2.977	4.140
15	1.341	1.753	2.131	2.602	2.947	4.073
16	1.337	1.746	2.120	2.583	2.921	4.015
17	1.333	1.740	2.110	2.567	2.898	3.965
18	1.330	1.734	2.101	2.552	2.878	3.922
19	1.328	1.729	2.093	2.539	2.861	3.883
20	1.325	1.725	2.086	2.528	2.845	3.850
21	1.323	1.721	2.080	2.518	2.831	3.819
22	1.321	1.717	2.074	2.508	2.819	3.792
23	1.319	1.714	2.069	2.500	2.807	3.767
24	1.318	1.711	2.064	2.492	2.797	3.745
25	1.316	1.708	2.060	2.485	2.787	3.725
26	1.315	1.706	2.056	2.479	2.779	3.707
27	1.314	1.703	2.052	2.473	2.771	3.690
28	1.313	1.701	2.048	2.467	2.763	3.674
29	1.311	1.699	2.045	2.462	2.756	3.659
30	1.310	1.697	2.042	2.457	2.750	3.646
40	1.303	1.684	2.021	2.423	2.704	3.551
60	1.296	1.671	2.000	2.390	2.660	3.460
120	1.289	1.658	1.980	2.358	2.617	3.373
∞	1.282	1.645	1.960	2.326	2.576	3.291

Source: Table III from Fisher, R. A., & Yates, S. (1974). *Statistical tables for biological, agricultural, and medical research* (6th ed.). London: Longman.

TABLE C *Critical Values of Chi-Square at the .05 and .01 Levels of Significance (α)*

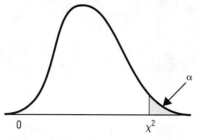

df	α .05	α .01	df	α .05	α .01
1	3.841	6.635	16	26.296	32.000
2	5.991	9.210	17	27.587	33.409
3	7.815	11.345	18	28.869	34.805
4	9.488	13.277	19	30.144	36.191
5	11.070	15.086	20	31.410	37.566
6	12.592	16.812	21	32.671	38.932
7	14.067	18.475	22	33.924	40.289
8	15.507	20.090	23	35.172	41.638
9	16.919	21.666	24	36.415	42.980
10	18.307	23.209	25	37.652	44.314
11	19.675	24.725	26	38.885	45.642
12	21.026	26.217	27	40.113	46.963
13	22.362	27.688	28	41.337	48.278
14	23.685	29.141	29	42.557	49.588
15	24.996	30.578	30	43.773	50.892

Source: Table IV from Fisher, R. A., & Yates, S. (1963). *Statistical tables for biological, agricultural, and medical research* (4th ed.). London: Longman.

TABLE D *Critical Values of F at the .05 Significance Level*

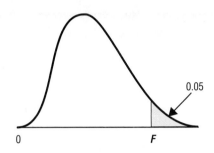

df FOR THE DENOMINATOR	df FOR THE NUMERATOR α = .05							
	1	2	3	4	5	6	8	12
1	161.4	199.5	215.7	224.6	230.2	234.0	238.9	243.9
2	18.51	19.00	19.16	19.25	19.30	19.33	19.37	19.41
3	10.13	9.55	9.28	9.12	9.01	8.94	8.84	8.74
4	7.71	6.94	6.59	6.39	6.26	6.16	6.04	5.91
5	6.61	5.79	5.41	5.19	5.05	4.95	4.82	4.68
6	5.99	5.14	4.76	4.53	4.39	4.28	4.15	4.00
7	5.59	4.74	4.35	4.12	3.97	3.87	3.73	3.57
8	5.32	4.46	4.07	3.84	3.69	3.58	3.44	3.28
9	5.12	4.26	3.86	3.63	3.48	3.37	3.23	3.07
10	4.96	4.10	3.71	3.48	3.33	3.22	3.07	2.91
11	4.84	3.98	3.59	3.36	3.20	3.09	2.95	2.79
12	4.75	3.88	3.49	3.26	3.11	3.00	2.85	2.69
13	4.67	3.80	3.41	3.18	3.02	2.92	2.77	2.60
14	4.60	3.74	3.34	3.11	2.96	2.85	2.70	2.53
15	4.54	3.68	3.29	3.06	2.90	2.79	2.64	2.48
16	4.49	3.63	3.24	3.01	2.85	2.74	2.59	2.42
17	4.45	3.59	3.20	2.96	2.81	2.70	2.55	2.38
18	4.41	3.55	3.16	2.93	2.77	2.66	2.51	2.34
19	4.38	3.52	3.13	2.90	2.74	2.63	2.48	2.31
20	4.35	3.49	3.10	2.87	2.71	2.60	2.45	2.28
21	4.32	3.47	3.07	2.84	2.68	2.57	2.42	2.25
22	4.30	3.44	3.05	2.82	2.66	2.55	2.40	2.23
23	4.28	3.42	3.03	2.80	2.64	2.53	2.38	2.20
24	4.26	3.40	3.01	2.78	2.62	2.51	2.36	2.18
25	4.24	3.38	2.99	2.76	2.60	2.49	2.34	2.16
26	4.22	3.37	2.98	2.74	2.59	2.47	2.32	2.15
27	4.21	3.35	2.96	2.73	2.57	2.46	2.30	2.13

(Continued)

TABLE D *Continued*

df FOR THE DENOMINATOR	*df* FOR THE NUMERATOR $\alpha = .05$							
	1	2	3	4	5	6	8	12
28	4.20	3.34	2.95	2.71	2.56	2.44	2.29	2.12
29	4.18	3.33	2.93	2.70	2.54	2.43	2.28	2.10
30	4.17	3.32	2.92	2.69	2.53	2.42	2.27	2.09
40	4.08	3.23	2.84	2.61	2.45	2.34	2.18	2.00
60	4.00	3.15	2.76	2.52	2.37	2.25	2.10	1.92
120	3.92	3.07	2.68	2.45	2.29	2.17	2.02	1.83
∞	3.84	2.99	2.60	2.37	2.21	2.09	1.94	1.75

TABLE E *Critical Values of F at the .01 Significance Level*

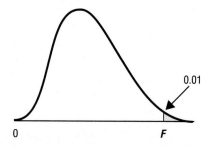

df FOR THE DENOMINATOR	*df* FOR THE NUMERATOR $\alpha = .01$							
	1	2	3	4	5	6	8	12
1	4052	4999	5403	5625	5764	5859	5981	6106
2	98.49	99.01	99.17	99.25	99.30	99.33	99.36	99.42
3	34.12	30.81	29.46	28.71	28.24	27.91	27.49	27.05
4	21.20	18.00	16.69	15.98	15.52	15.21	14.80	14.37
5	16.26	13.27	12.06	11.39	10.97	10.67	10.27	9.89
6	13.74	10.92	9.78	9.15	8.75	8.47	8.10	7.72
7	12.25	9.55	8.45	7.85	7.46	7.19	6.84	6.47
8	11.26	8.65	7.59	7.01	6.63	6.37	6.03	5.67
9	10.56	8.02	6.99	6.42	6.06	5.80	5.47	5.11
10	10.04	7.56	6.55	5.99	5.64	5.39	5.06	4.71
11	9.65	7.20	6.22	5.67	5.32	5.07	4.74	4.40
12	9.33	6.93	5.95	5.41	5.06	4.82	4.50	4.16
13	9.07	6.70	5.74	5.20	4.86	4.62	4.30	3.96
14	8.86	6.51	5.56	5.03	4.69	4.46	4.14	3.80

(Continued)

TABLE E *Continued*

df FOR THE DENOMINATOR	df FOR THE NUMERATOR α = .01							
	1	2	3	4	5	6	8	12
15	8.68	6.36	5.42	4.89	4.56	4.32	4.00	3.67
16	8.53	6.23	5.29	4.77	4.44	4.20	3.89	3.55
17	8.40	6.11	5.18	4.67	4.34	4.10	3.79	3.45
18	8.28	6.01	5.09	4.58	4.25	4.01	3.71	3.37
19	8.18	5.93	5.01	4.50	4.17	3.94	3.63	3.30
20	8.10	5.85	4.94	4.43	4.10	3.87	3.56	3.23
21	8.02	5.78	4.87	4.37	4.04	3.81	3.51	3.17
22	7.94	5.72	4.82	4.31	3.99	3.76	3.45	3.12
23	7.88	5.66	4.76	4.26	3.94	3.71	3.41	3.07
24	7.82	5.61	4.72	4.22	3.90	3.67	3.36	3.03
25	7.77	5.57	4.68	4.18	3.86	3.63	3.32	2.99
26	7.72	5.53	4.64	4.14	3.82	3.59	3.29	2.96
27	7.68	5.49	4.60	4.11	3.78	3.56	3.26	2.93
28	7.64	5.45	4.57	4.07	3.75	3.53	3.23	2.90
29	7.60	5.42	4.54	4.04	3.73	3.50	3.20	2.87
30	7.56	5.39	4.51	4.02	3.70	3.47	3.17	2.84
40	7.31	5.18	4.31	3.83	3.51	3.29	2.99	2.66
60	7.08	4.98	4.13	3.65	3.34	3.12	2.82	2.50
120	6.85	4.79	3.95	3.48	3.17	2.96	2.66	2.34
∞	6.64	4.60	3.78	3.32	3.02	2.80	2.51	2.18

Source: Table V from Fisher, R. A., & Yates, S. (1963). *Statistical tables for biological, agricultural, and medical research* (4th ed.). London: Longman.

Available Data Sets

Four databases are available with this text. Each database is a subset of the 2006 General Social Survey (GSS), which is conducted by the National Opinion Research Center (NORC). The 2006 GSS contains 5,084 variables and 4,510 cases. Out of this, 1,000 cases were randomly selected for inclusion in the four databases. Each of the four subset databases contains the same 1,000 respondents, identified by the variable name "ID."

Each of the four subsets contains roughly 40 variables. The first 17 variables are commonly used demographic variables in the social sciences and are identical in all four subsets. After the first 17 variables, the subset databases differ from one another. Subset A contains groups of variables that measure respondents' positions and attitudes on issues such as politics, government spending, and civil liberties. Subset B contains variables that tend to focus on religion and life satisfaction. Subset C contains variables that measure attitudes toward abortion, suicide, and gun ownership. Finally, Subset D contains variables that measure attitudes and behaviors dealing with sexual behavior.

All four of the subsets can be downloaded from the companion website for this course. Descriptions of the variables are shown below.

17 Variables Included in each of the Four Subsets

VARIABLE NAME	VARIABLE LABEL
id	RESPONDENT ID NUMBER
sex	RESPONDENT'S SEX
race	RACE OF RESPONDENT
age	AGE OF RESPONDENT
class	SUBJECTIVE CLASS IDENTIFICATION
realinc	FAMILY INCOME IN CONSTANT $
wrkstat	LABOR FORCE STATUS

(Continued)

17 Variables Included in each of the Four Subsets   Continued

VARIABLE NAME	VARIABLE LABEL
marital	MARITAL STATUS
agewed	AGE WHEN FIRST MARRIED
sibs	NUMBER OF BROTHERS AND SISTERS
childs	NUMBER OF CHILDREN
paeduc	HIGHEST YEAR SCHOOL COMPLETED, FATHER
degree	RS HIGHEST DEGREE
born	WAS R BORN IN THIS COUNTRY
income	TOTAL FAMILY INCOME
relig	RS RELIGIOUS PREFERENCE
partyid	RESPONDENT ID NUMBER

Subset A Variables (In Addition to the 17 Variables Listed Above)

VARIABLE NAME	VARIABLE LABEL
vote00	DID R VOTE IN 2000 ELECTION
pres00	VOTE FOR GORE, BUSH, NADER
vote04	DID R VOTE IN 2004 ELECTION
pres04	VOTE FOR KERRY, BUSH, NADER
polviews	THINK OF SELF AS LIBERAL OR CONSERVATIVE
natspac	SPACE EXPLORATION PROGRAM
natenvir	IMPROVING PROTECTING ENVIRONMENT
natheal	IMPROVING PROTECTING NATION'S HEALTH
natcity	SOLVING PROBLEMS OF BIG CITIES
natcrime	HALTING RISING CRIME RATE
natdrug	DEALING WITH DRUG ADDICTION
nateduc	IMPROVING NATION'S EDUCATION SYSTEM
natrace	IMPROVING THE CONDITIONS OF BLACKS
natarms	MILITARY, ARMAMENTS, AND DEFENSE
nataid	FOREIGN AID
natfare	WELFARE
natroad	HIGHWAYS AND BRIDGES
natsoc	SOCIAL SECURITY
natmass	MASS TRANSPORTATION
natpark	PARKS AND RECREATION
natchld	ASSISTANCE FOR CHILDCARE
natsci	SUPPORTING SCIENTIFIC RESEARCH

VARIABLE NAME	VARIABLE LABEL
eqwlth	SHOULD GOVT REDUCE INCOME DIFFERENCES
spkath	ALLOW ANTI-RELIGIONIST TO SPEAK
colath	ALLOW ANTI-RELIGIONIST TO TEACH
spksoc	ALLOW SOCIALIST TO SPEAK
colsoc	ALLOW SOCIALIST TO TEACH
spkrac	ALLOW RACIST TO SPEAK
colrac	ALLOW RACIST TO TEACH

Subset B Variables (In Addition to the 17 Variables Listed Above)

VARIABLE NAME	VARIABLE LABEL
cappun	FAVOR OR OPPOSE DEATH PENALTY FOR MURDER
gunlaw	FAVOR OR OPPOSE GUN PERMITS
grass	SHOULD MARIJUANA BE MADE LEGAL
fund	HOW FUNDAMENTALIST IS R CURRENTLY
attend	HOW OFTEN R ATTENDS RELIGIOUS SERVICES
reliten	STRENGTH OF AFFILIATION
postlife	BELIEF IN LIFE AFTER DEATH
pray	HOW OFTEN DOES R PRAY
prayer	BIBLE PRAYER IN PUBLIC SCHOOLS
bible	FEELINGS ABOUT THE BIBLE
affrmact	FAVOR PREFERENCE IN HIRING BLACKS
happy	GENERAL HAPPINESS
hapmar	HAPPINESS OF MARRIAGE
health	CONDITION OF HEALTH
life	IS LIFE EXCITING OR DULL
helpful	PEOPLE HELPFUL OR LOOKING OUT FOR SELVES
fair	PEOPLE FAIR OR TRY TO TAKE ADVANTAGE
trust	CAN PEOPLE BE TRUSTED
confinan	CONFIDENCE IN BANK'S FINANCIAL INSTITUTIONS
conbus	CONFIDENCE IN MAJOR COMPANIES
satfin	SATISFACTION WITH FINANCIAL SITUATION
getahead	OPINION OF HOW PEOPLE GET AHEAD

Subset C Variables (In Addition to the 17 Variables Listed Above)

VARIABLE NAME	VARIABLE LABEL
abdefect	STRONG CHANCE OF SERIOUS DEFECT
abnomore	MARRIED—WANTS NO MORE CHILDREN
abhlth	WOMAN'S HEALTH SERIOUSLY ENDANGERED
abpoor	LOW INCOME—CAN'T AFFORD MORE CHILDREN
abrape	PREGNANT AS RESULT OF RAPE
absingle	NOT MARRIED
abany	ABORTION IF WOMAN WANTS FOR ANY REASON
pillok	BIRTH CONTROL TO TEENAGERS 14–16
sexeduc	SEX EDUCATION IN PUBLIC SCHOOLS
divlaw	DIVORCE LAWS
premarsx	SEX BEFORE MARRIAGE
teensex	SEX BEFORE MARRIAGE—TEENS 14–16
xmarsex	SEX WITH PERSON OTHER THAN SPOUSE
homosex	HOMOSEXUAL SEX RELATIONS
pornlaw	FEELINGS ABOUT PORNOGRAPHY LAWS
xmovie	SEEN X-RATED MOVIE IN LAST YEAR
spanking	FAVOR SPANKING TO DISCIPLINE CHILD
letdie1	ALLOW INCURABLE PATIENTS TO DIE
suicide1	SUICIDE IF INCURABLE DISEASE
suicide2	SUICIDE IF BANKRUPT
suicide3	SUICIDE IF DISHONORED FAMILY
suicide4	SUICIDE IF TIRED OF LIVING
fear	AFRAID TO WALK AT NIGHT IN NEIGHBORHOOD
owngun	HAVE GUN IN HOME
pistol	PISTOL OR REVOLVER IN HOME
hunt	DOES R OR SPOUSE HUNT

Subset D Variables (In Addition to the 17 Variables Listed Above)

VARIABLE NAME	VARIABLE LABEL
partners	HOW MANY SEX PARTNERS R HAD IN LAST YEAR
matesex	WAS 1 OF R'S PARTNERS SPOUSE OR REGULAR
frndsex	R HAD SEX WITH FRIEND LAST YEAR
acqntsex	R HAD SEX WITH ACQUAINTANCE LAST YEAR
pikupsex	R HAD SEX WITH CASUAL DATE LAST YEAR

VARIABLE NAME	VARIABLE LABEL
paidsex	R HAD SEX FOR PAY LAST YEAR
othersex	R HAD SEX WITH SOME OTHER LAST YEAR
sexsex	SEX OF SEX PARTNERS IN LAST YEAR
sexfreq	FREQUENCY OF SEX DURING LAST YEAR
numwomen	NUMBER OF FEMALE SEX PARTNERS SINCE 18
nummen	NUMBER OF MALE SEX PARTNERS SINCE 18
evpaidsx	EVER HAVE SEX PAID FOR OR BEING PAID SINCE 18
evstray	HAVE SEX OTHER THAN SPOUSE WHILE MARRIED
condom	USED CONDOM LAST TIME
relatsex	RELATION TO LAST SEX PARTNER

Getting Started with SPSS for Windows

Introduction

This appendix is intended to assist you with the statistical techniques presented in your text: *Statistics and Data Analysis for Social Science,* by Eric Krieg. In this appendix, we introduce SPSS, the Statistical Package for the Social Sciences. SPSS is one of the most popular and widely available statistical software packages in the social sciences. In recent years, the name associated with the SPSS software package changed to PASW. Accordingly, SPSS and PASW are used interchangeably throughout this appendix.

This manual is written for *PASW Statistics* version 17.0.2 for Windows, but the instructions will work for most versions of this software. Throughout this appendix, you will learn how to use SPSS to perform a variety of the most popular and useful statistical procedures in the social sciences. The sections follow along with the chapters in your Krieg textbook. However, before we can get into those various statistical techniques, you must first become familiar with how to activate SPSS, the various SPSS windows, and the toolbar.

Activating SPSS

There are a couple of different ways to access SPSS in your Microsoft Windows operating system. The first is to locate the icon on the desktop. I have highlighted the PASW Statistics 17 icon in a white box in Figure C.1.

Your computer may have a similar icon with a different version number. Double-click on the icon to start SPSS. If you cannot find the SPSS or PASW icon on the desktop, you can activate SPSS via the **Start** menu. Click **Start** → **All Programs** → **SPSS Inc.** → **PASW Statistics 17** folder → **PASW Statistics 17.** Keep in mind that the names of your folders and the SPSS version number may be different.

When you double-click on the icon or click on **PASW Statistics 17** via the **Start** menu, you will first see the screen shown in Figure C.3.

Figure C.1 Windows Screen with PASW Statistics Icon

Figure C.2 Start → All Programs → SPSS Inc. → PASW Statistics 17 → PASW Statistics 17

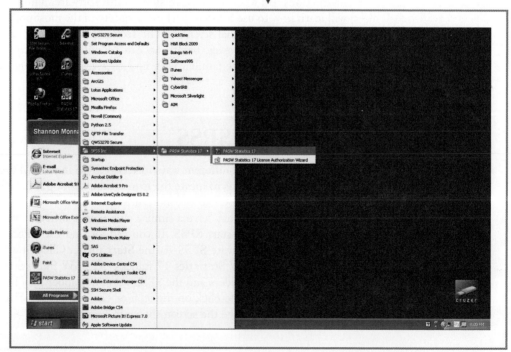

Figure C.3 **PASW Statistics Startup Box**

The **PASW Statistics** centered box will remain on your screen for a couple of seconds and then disappear. It will seem as if the program is not starting, but in actuality, the program is running behind the scenes. After several seconds, the startup screen shown in Figure C.4 will appear.

Figure C.4 **What Would You Like to Do?**

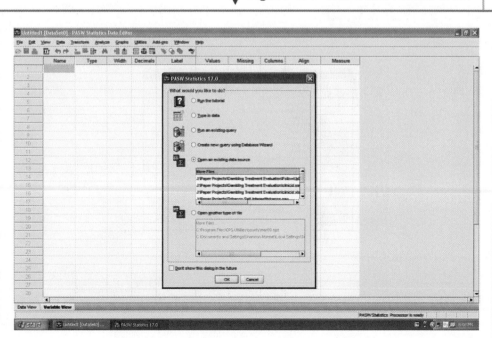

Opening Existing Data

If you are working with an existing dataset, choose the option to **Open an existing data source.** The **More Files…** option should already be highlighted. If you know where your data are saved, click **OK,** and SPSS will take you to your folders to choose your dataset, as shown in Figure C.5.

All SPSS datasets end with the extension, .sav. File selection for SPSS works much like any other Windows program. You simply locate where the file is saved, highlight the file (*gss06.sav* in the example shown in Figure C.6), and click **Open.**

Variable View

Once you click **Open,** the **PASW Statistics Data Editor** will open. By default, the dataset will typically open up in the **Variable View,** as shown in Figure C.7. The **Variable View** provides information about each variable in the dataset, including the variable name, the type of variable, the width (which represents the total number of character spaces the variable value can take up), the number of decimals allowed for each variable value, the variable label, the values of the variable, the values associated with missing information on each variable, columns, variable alignment, and the default level of measurement for each variable. A brief description of each column is below.

Figure C.5 **Locate Your Existing SPSS Dataset**

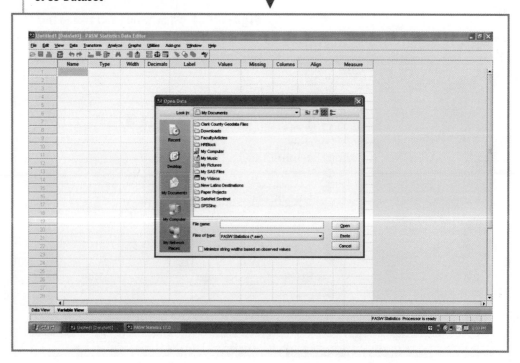

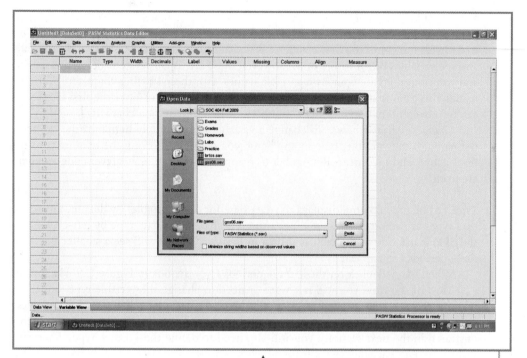

Figure C.6 Open Data

Figure C.7 Variable View

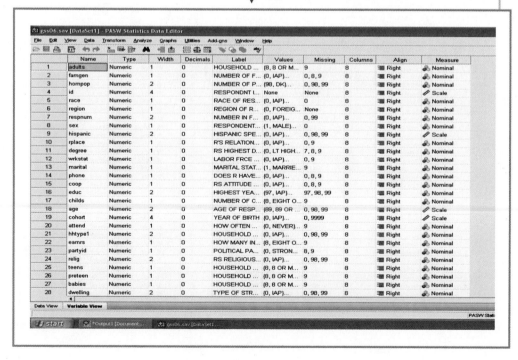

Name.   The name column displays the name of each variable. Variable names must be unique, cannot contain spaces, and must follow certain conventions. Names can be up to 64 bytes long, and the first character is typically a letter or the character @. You may also see variables begin with # or $. However, these are usually system-defined variables, and you cannot create your own variable names with these starting characters. Variable names also cannot start with a number. Subsequent characters (after the first character) can be any combination of letters, numbers, or nonpunctuation characters.

Change a variable name: To change a variable name, simply highlight the cell with the name of the variable, type in any name you choose following the naming conventions above, and hit **Enter.** Remember to record this change in whatever codebook you are using.

Type.   The type column displays the data type for each variable. By default, most new data types are assumed to be numeric. You can change the data type by left-clicking to the right-hand side of the cell, as shown in Figure C.8. You will see a smaller box with three periods (…) appear.

When you left-click on those three periods (…) the box in Figure C.9 will appear.

Most of the time you will not want or need to change the variable type, but there may be times when you are using a secondary dataset (data that you did not enter yourself) that has an inappropriate variable type. When you enter your own data (demonstrated in the next section), you will also need to define the variable type. There are eight different <u>Variable Types</u> from which to choose. For each variable, you will also need to define the <u>Width</u> and the number of <u>Decimal Places.</u> The eight variable types are defined below. More information on each is available via the SPSS Online Help Menu (**Help**).

Figure C.8 **Variable Type**

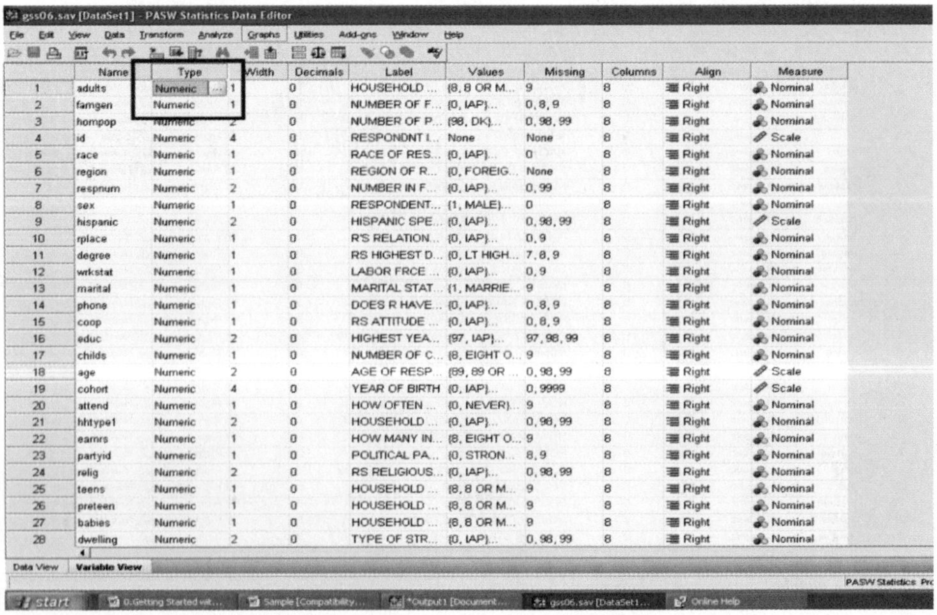

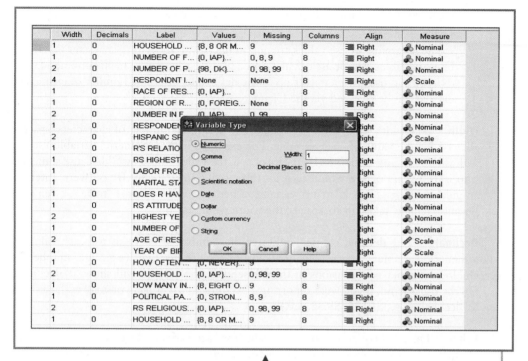

	Width	Decimals	Label	Values	Missing	Columns	Align	Measure
	1	0	HOUSEHOLD ...	{8, 8 OR M...	9	8	Right	Nominal
	1	0	NUMBER OF F...	{0, IAP}...	0, 8, 9	8	Right	Nominal
	2	0	NUMBER OF P...	{98, DK}...	0, 98, 99	8	Right	Nominal
	4	0	RESPONDNT I...	None	None	8	Right	Scale
	1	0	RACE OF RES...	{0, IAP}...	0	8	Right	Nominal
	1	0	REGION OF R...	{0, FOREIG...	None	8	Right	Nominal
	2	0	NUMBER IN F...	{0, IAP}	0, 99	8	Right	Nominal
	1	0	RESPONDEN...				Right	Nominal
	2	0	HISPANIC SF...				Right	Scale
	1	0	R'S RELATIO...				Right	Nominal
	1	0	RS HIGHEST...				Right	Nominal
	1	0	LABOR FRCE...				Right	Nominal
	1	0	MARITAL ST...				Right	Nominal
	1	0	DOES R HAV...				Right	Nominal
	1	0	RS ATTITUDE...				Right	Nominal
	2	0	HIGHEST YE...				Right	Nominal
	1	0	NUMBER OF...				Right	Nominal
	2	0	AGE OF RES...				Right	Scale
	4	0	YEAR OF BIF...				Right	Scale
	1	0	HOW OFTEN ...	{0, NEVER}...	9	8	Right	Nominal
	2	0	HOUSEHOLD ...	{0, IAP}...	0, 98, 99	8	Right	Nominal
	1	0	HOW MANY IN...	{8, EIGHT O...	9	8	Right	Nominal
	1	0	POLITICAL PA...	{0, STRON...	8, 9	8	Right	Nominal
	2	0	RS RELIGIOUS...	{0, IAP}...	0, 98, 99	8	Right	Nominal
	1	0	HOUSEHOLD ...	{8, 8 OR M...	9	8	Right	Nominal

Variable Type

- ⦿ Numeric
- ○ Comma
- ○ Dot
- ○ Scientific notation
- ○ Date
- ○ Dollar
- ○ Custom currency
- ○ String

Width: 1
Decimal Places: 0

[OK] [Cancel] [Help]

Figure C.9 Change Variable Type

Numeric: A variable whose values are numbers. Values are displayed in standard numeric format and can be any number of decimals, as long as you change the number of decimals in the <u>Decimal Places</u> box.

Comma: A numeric variable whose values are displayed with commas delimiting every three places and displayed with the period as a decimal delimiter. You will rarely use these types of variables in social science research.

Dot: A numeric variable whose values are displayed with periods delimiting every three places and with the comma as a decimal delimiter. You will rarely use these types of variables in social science research.

Scientific notation: A numeric variable whose values are displayed with an embedded E and a signed power-of-10 exponent. For example, 1.23E + 2.

Date: A numeric variable whose values are displayed in one of several different date formats. Once you click on the date circle, several options for calendar dates and time formats will appear. Simply choose the one you like and click the <u>OK</u> box.

Dollar: A number variable displayed with a leading dollar sign ($). You can enter dollar values with or without the leading dollar sign as long as the variable type is defined as a dollar type. Several dollar type options (commas, decimal spaces, etc.) are available once you click on the dollar circle. Choose the one you like and click the <u>OK</u> box.

Custom Currency: A numeric variable whose values are displayed in one of the custom currency formats that are defined via the <u>Currency tab</u> of the **Options dialog box.** Defined custom currency characters cannot be used in data entry but are displayed in the **Data Editor.** You will rarely see these types of variables in social science datasets.

String: A variable whose values are not numeric, but instead are character in nature. These variables cannot use calculations. This is also known as an alphanumeric variable and can use any character up to the defined length. The number of characters allowed can be changed via the Characters box.

Width. The width column informs you of the maximum number of characters (spaces) allowed for the value of each variable. For example, with a 'numeric' variable for *age* with values ranging from 0 to 100 years of age, the width would be '3' because someone who is 100 years of age would take up three spaces in the cell. If you were entering an individual's *gender* as a 'string' variable, a person could be either 'male' or 'female.' Because 'female' takes up six spaces, the width would be '6.'

Decimals. The decimal column indicates the number of decimals for each value of a numeric variable. For variables that do not require decimals (e.g., age, number of children, number of televisions in the household), the column will show '0' decimals. On the other hand, if you were reporting a person's hourly wage, you may wish to show '2' decimals (e.g., $10.25, $8.32, etc.).

Label. The label column displays the label for each variable. In Figure C.10, you can see that the label associated with the variable *adults* is 'Household Members 18 Yrs and Older.' You can change a variable label by simply clicking on the label's cell and typing in a new label. You can also widen the cell by hovering your cursor to the right of the cell and extending it.

Figure C.10 Variable Labels

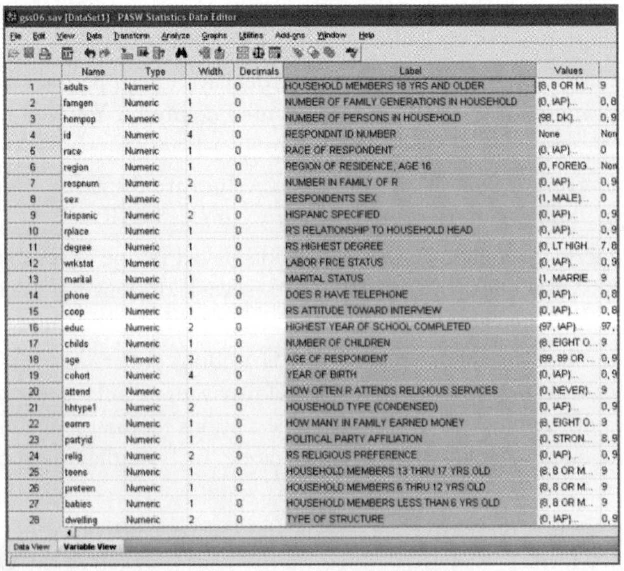

Values. Each variable has values. Most existing datasets have values already entered for your convenience. When this is not the case, you will need to locate the codebook associated with the dataset so that you know all of the different values associated with each variable. We will go through how to change and enter values a little later.

For now, you can examine the values associated with each variable by left-clicking the three periods (…) to the right of the **Values** cell for the variable of interest. In the example below, we are interested in examining the values associated with the variable *degree*.

We see that the label for the variable *degree* is 'Rs highest degree.' In the GSS dataset, R stands for 'respondent.' So, this variable represents the respondent's highest degree. Once we left-click to the right of the **Values** cell, the **Value Labels** screen appears, as shown in Figure C.12.

We can see that the value of '0' represents less than high school, '1' represents high school, '2' represents junior college, and so on.

If we were to scroll down a bit further, we would see values for this variable of '7,' '8,' and '9.' In these data, these values represent 'Inapplicable,' 'Don't Know,' and 'Not Answered.'

Missing. For the sake of data analysis, we would not treat these values the same as we would "valid" values of a variable. We would typically eliminate these cases from our analysis. In order to do so, we must identify these values as missing. In SPSS, values are identified as "missing" via the **Missing** column. Again, we simply left-click to the right of the cell and the **Missing Values** box appears. In this case, we see that the values of '7,' '8,' and '9' have been identified as "missing" for this variable *degree*.

Figure C.11 Variable Values

Left-click on the right side of the value cell

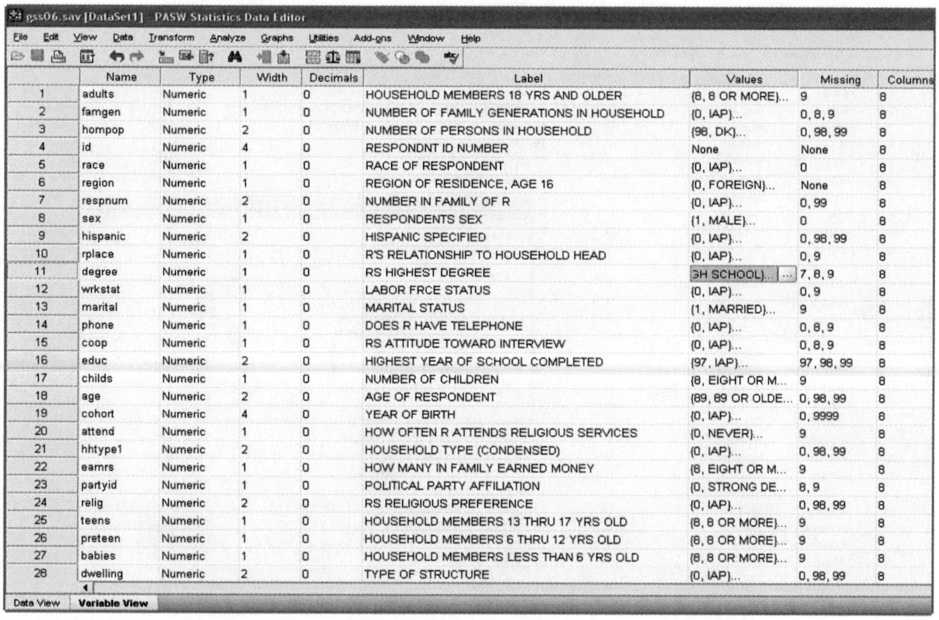

	Name	Type	Width	Decimals	Label	Values	Missing	Columns
1	adults	Numeric	1	0	HOUSEHOLD MEMBERS 18 YRS AND OLDER	{8, 8 OR MORE}...	9	8
2	famgen	Numeric	1	0	NUMBER OF FAMILY GENERATIONS IN HOUSEHOLD	{0, IAP}...	0, 8, 9	8
3	hompop	Numeric	2	0	NUMBER OF PERSONS IN HOUSEHOLD	{98, DK}...	0, 98, 99	8
4	id	Numeric	4	0	RESPONDNT ID NUMBER	None	None	8
5	race	Numeric	1	0	RACE OF RESPONDENT	{0, IAP}...	0	8
6	region	Numeric	1	0	REGION OF RESIDENCE, AGE 16	{0, FOREIGN}...	None	8
7	respnum	Numeric	2	0	NUMBER IN FAMILY OF R	{0, IAP}...	0, 99	8
8	sex	Numeric	1	0	RESPONDENTS SEX	{1, MALE}...	0	8
9	hispanic	Numeric	2	0	HISPANIC SPECIFIED	{0, IAP}...	0, 98, 99	8
10	rplace	Numeric	1	0	R'S RELATIONSHIP TO HOUSEHOLD HEAD	{0, IAP}...	0, 9	8
11	degree	Numeric	1	0	RS HIGHEST DEGREE	{GH SCHOOL} ...	7, 8, 9	8
12	wrkstat	Numeric	1	0	LABOR FRCE STATUS	{0, IAP}...	0, 9	8
13	marital	Numeric	1	0	MARITAL STATUS	{1, MARRIED}...	9	8
14	phone	Numeric	1	0	DOES R HAVE TELEPHONE	{0, IAP}...	0, 8, 9	8
15	coop	Numeric	1	0	RS ATTITUDE TOWARD INTERVIEW	{0, IAP}...	0, 8, 9	8
16	educ	Numeric	2	0	HIGHEST YEAR OF SCHOOL COMPLETED	{97, IAP}...	97, 98, 99	8
17	childs	Numeric	1	0	NUMBER OF CHILDREN	{8, EIGHT OR M...	9	8
18	age	Numeric	2	0	AGE OF RESPONDENT	{89, 89 OR OLDE...	0, 98, 99	8
19	cohort	Numeric	4	0	YEAR OF BIRTH	{0, IAP}...	0, 9999	8
20	attend	Numeric	1	0	HOW OFTEN R ATTENDS RELIGIOUS SERVICES	{0, NEVER}...	9	8
21	hhtype1	Numeric	2	0	HOUSEHOLD TYPE (CONDENSED)	{0, IAP}...	0, 98, 99	8
22	earnrs	Numeric	1	0	HOW MANY IN FAMILY EARNED MONEY	{8, EIGHT OR M...	9	8
23	partyid	Numeric	1	0	POLITICAL PARTY AFFILIATION	{0, STRONG DE...	8, 9	8
24	relig	Numeric	2	0	RS RELIGIOUS PREFERENCE	{0, IAP}...	0, 98, 99	8
25	teens	Numeric	1	0	HOUSEHOLD MEMBERS 13 THRU 17 YRS OLD	{8, 8 OR MORE}...	9	8
26	preteen	Numeric	1	0	HOUSEHOLD MEMBERS 6 THRU 12 YRS OLD	{8, 8 OR MORE}...	9	8
27	babies	Numeric	1	0	HOUSEHOLD MEMBERS LESS THAN 6 YRS OLD	{8, 8 OR MORE}...	9	8
28	dwelling	Numeric	2	0	TYPE OF STRUCTURE	{0, IAP}...	0, 98, 99	8

Data View   Variable View

Figure C.12 Value Labels

Figure C.13 Missing Value Labels

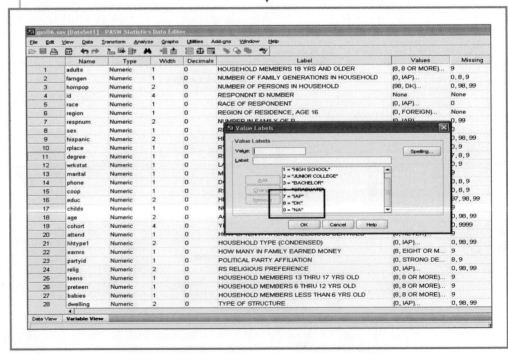

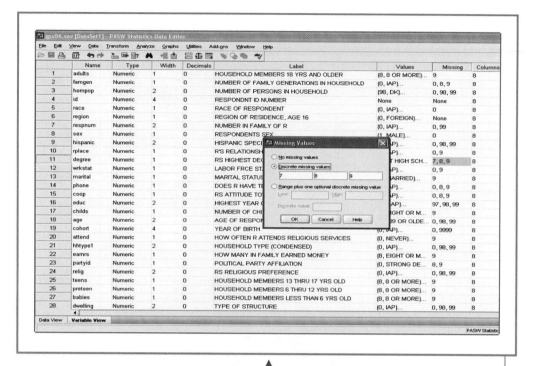

Figure C.14 Missing Values

Columns and Align: By default, the **Columns** cells will always display an '8,' and the **Align** cells will always display 'Right.' You should not change these settings.

Measure: The **Measure** column displays the level of measurement for each variable. There are three levels of measurement available in SPSS: scale, ordinal, and nominal. Scale is used for variables measured at the interval or ratio level of measurement, ordinal is used for ordinal (ranked categorical) variables, and nominal is used for nominal (unranked categorical) variables. But be careful! SPSS assigns levels of measurement by default, and they are often incorrect. It is your responsibility to know the level of measurement associated with each variable and change that measure in the **Measure** column if necessary. To change the measure in SPSS, left-click to the right of the cell and change the level in the drop-down menu, as shown in Figure C.16.

Data View

At the bottom left of the SPSS program, you will see a tab for **Data View.** Click on **Data View** to toggle to the SPSS data spreadsheet, as shown in Figure C.17. You will notice that the data view looks very much like an Excel data file.

In the data view, you will see numbered rows along the left side. These rows represent each case (i.e. respondent). There will be a row for each case in your dataset. All of the variables are displayed in the columns. Each case (row) will have a value entered for each variable (column). The value of each variable for each case is entered in a "cell." These are your data.

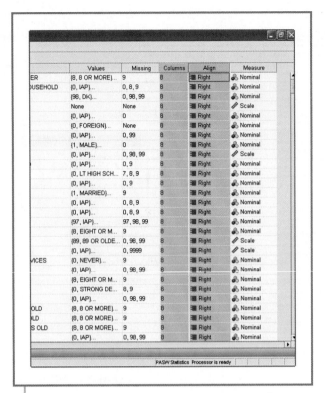

Figure C.15 Columns and Align Columns

Figure C.16 Level of Measurement

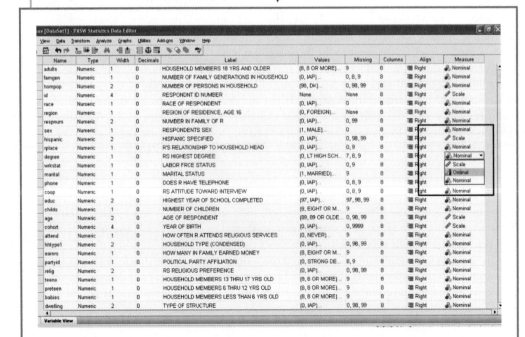

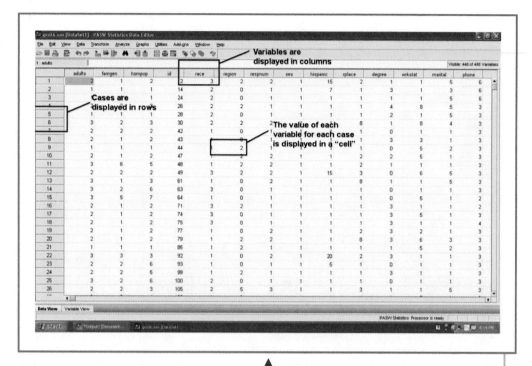

Figure C.17 Data View

Rows = cases
Columns = variables
Cells = values

Deleting Cases and Variables.   Generally, you will not want to delete cases or variables, but if a reason for deleting a case or variable arises, you can easily do this by right-clicking on the row or column associated with the case or variable and clicking on 'Clear.'

Menu Bar.   The menu bar appears at the top of the screen and will remain there no matter which window you work in. The menu bar for SPSS is very similar to other Windows programs. Clicking on any one of the functions opens up a drop-down menu. From these drop-down menus, you can access different procedures. We examine each of these menu options in detail later as we explore SPSS operations throughout this appendix.

From the **File** menu, you can open a new SPSS Data Editor or an existing dataset. You can also save your data if you have made any changes to it. Saving data in SPSS is similar to saving any other file. You must first be sure that you are in the Data Editor. Then you simply click **File** → **Save As** → locate the folder where you want to save your data → enter a name. The Save as Type should be *.sav. Then click **Save.**

Toolbar.   Below the menu bar is the toolbar. When you are in the **Data Editor,** you will see buttons that can be used to perform certain common functions needed to create and manage your dataset. This toolbar is displayed in Figure C.20.

These buttons are shortcuts for many of the most commonly used procedures in SPSS. The buttons in the toolbar are illustrated with icons that are indicative of the

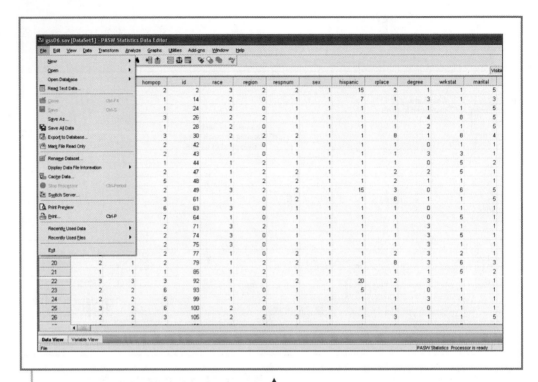

Figure C.18 File Menu Bar

Figure C.19 File → Save As → locate folder → name your dataset → Save

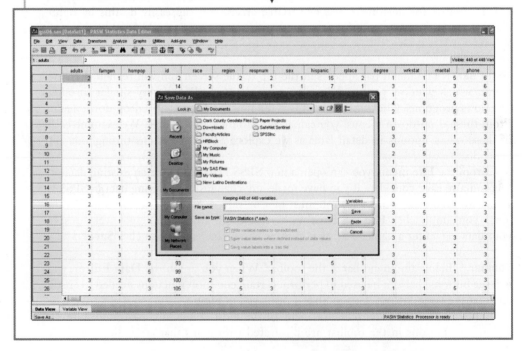

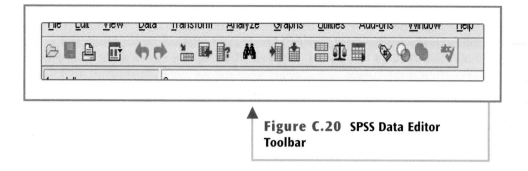

Figure C.20 **SPSS Data Editor Toolbar**

button's function. For example, the **Open File** function is illustrated with an open manila folder icon. The **Save** function is illustrated with a computer disk that will only light up if you have made changes to your data. The **Print** function is illustrated with an image of a printer. Only buttons that you may currently use will be shown in color. The other buttons will be muted. Take a few minutes to familiarize yourself with the functions of each button. We will use many of them throughout the manual as we explore the various functions of SPSS.

SPSS Output Viewer

When you open up any existing SPSS dataset or a new SPSS data editor window, the SPSS Output Viewer will also open, as shown in Figure C.21.

Figure C.21 **SPSS Output Viewer**

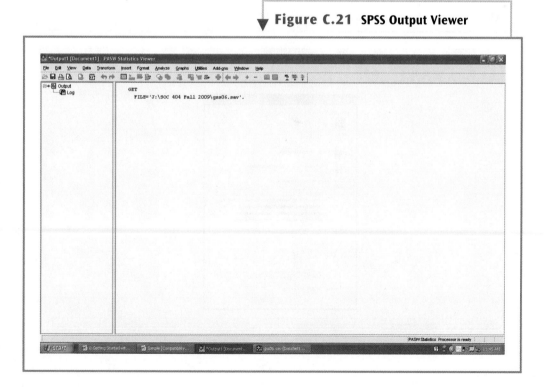

The SPSS **Output Viewer** records all of your procedures and the results of your statistical operations. When you first open up a dataset, the viewer will display the path name of those data. As you explore the various statistical procedures available to you, the output viewer will fill with results. The name of the output viewer will have an asterisk (*) next to it if there have been changes since the last time you saved it. To save the output, simply save as you would any word processing file in the same way we saved the data earlier. You can close the output viewer without saving it by simply clicking on the red **X** at the top right of the screen.

Entering Data and Defining Variables

There may be instances where you will need to enter your own data from a survey you have conducted or from some other source of data. You can open a blank <u>SPSS Data Editor</u> in a couple of different ways. The first is by opening SPSS via your desktop icon or **Windows Start Menu** as demonstrated earlier. When the "What would you like to do?" startup screen appears, just click **Cancel.**

Once you click Cancel, a blank **Data Editor** spreadsheet will open, typically in the **Data View.** If the Data Editor is not in **Data View,** go to the bottom left of the screen and click on **Data View.**

Alternatively, if you already have an existing dataset open like we did earlier, you can go up to the File menu and click **File → New → Data.**

Figure C.22 SPSS Startup Screen

Click Cancel to enter your own data

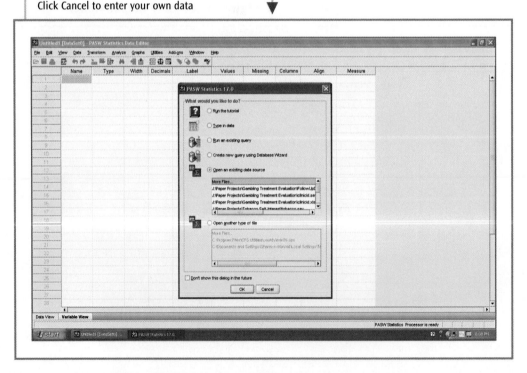

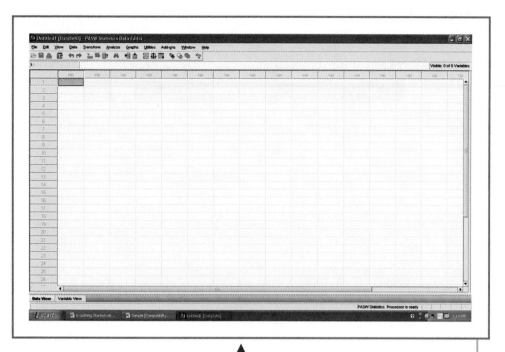

Figure C.23 Blank Data View Ready for Data Entry

Figure C.24 File → New → Data

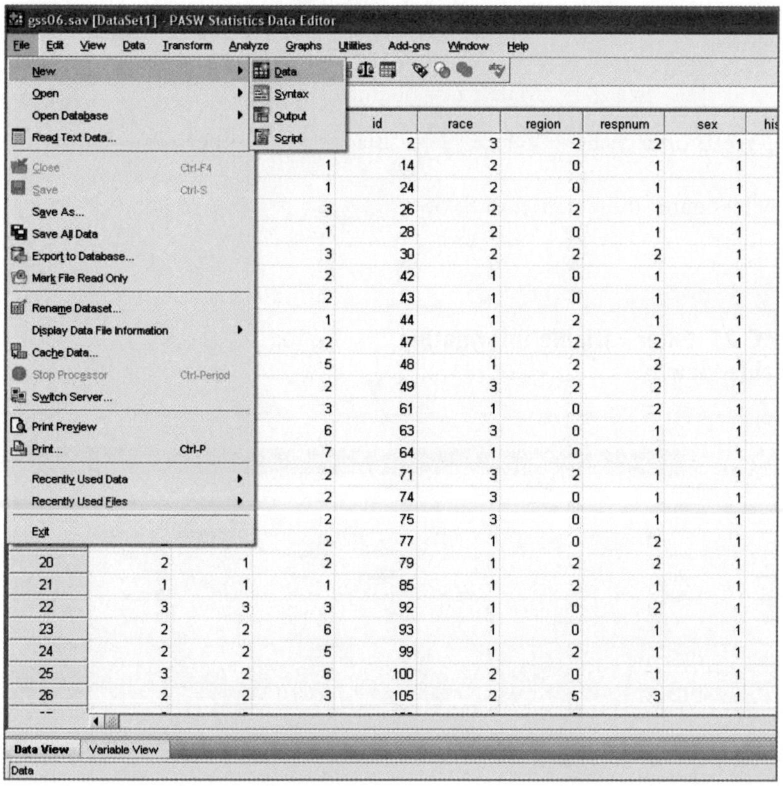

TABLE C.1 *Student Demographics and GPA*

ID	SEX	RACE/ETHNICITY	GPA
1	1	1	2.5
2	1	3	3.7
3	2	2	3.2
4	1	2	4.0
5	2	3	3.1
6	2	1	2.8
7	1	1	1.5
8	2	9	2.5
9	2	3	3.0
10	1	2	3.5

Before you can enter your data, you need to define the variable information. You can get to the **Variable View** by either clicking on the **Variable View** tab on the bottom left of the screen or by double-clicking on the 'var' cell in the first column. Once you are in **Variable View,** you will enter the name of your variable following the conventions outlined earlier, as well as all of the other information related to this variable (i.e., label, values, missing, etc.). To illustrate data entry in SPSS, take a look at the hypothetical student demographic and GPA data in Table C.1.

For the purposes of illustration, the value labels associated with *sex* and *race/ethnicity* are as follows:

Sex: 1 = 'Male'; 2 = 'Female'

Race/Ethnicity: 1 = 'White'; 2 = 'Black'; 3 = 'Other'; 9 = 'Refused'

Now let's enter these data into SPSS.

Figure C.25 Enter Variable Information in Variable View

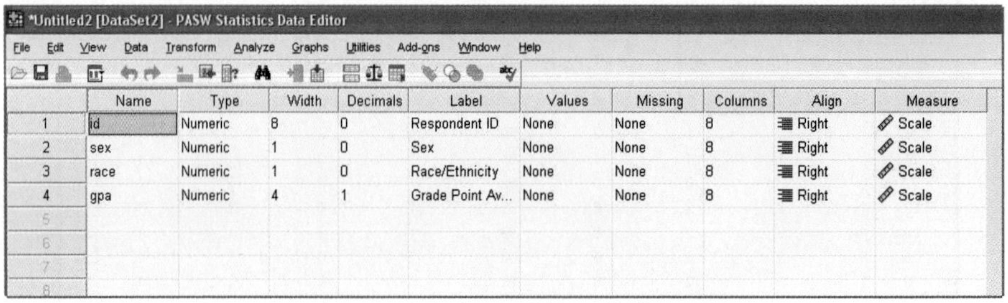

Defining Variables in Variable View

Once you are in **Variable View,** in the **Name** column, we would enter a name for each variable that is both efficient and clearly identifies the variable. In terms of **Type,** in this case, all of our variables are numeric. We can choose to keep the default **Width** of '8' for respondent ID. We know that *sex* and *race* have values that take up only one character (e.g., 1, 2, etc.). So, the **Width** for each of those is '1.' *GPA* takes up three characters (two numbers plus the decimal point). We then indicate that the *gpa* variable has one decimal point in the **Decimals** column. In the **Label** column, we would label each of our variables.

We must now enter information about the variable values and missing values. Left-click to the right of the **Values** cell for the appropriate variable, and the **Value Labels** box will appear. Simply enter the numeric value in the <u>Value</u> box and enter the value label in the <u>Label</u> box. Then you must click 'Add' in order for the change to take effect. Once you have added all of the value labels for the variable, click the <u>OK</u> button.

One of our respondents (respondent #8) refused to identify her race, so she has been coded as a '9' in our data spreadsheet above (Table C.1). When we identify value labels for race, we must be sure to include the value label for 'refused,' as well as identify the value associated with 'refused' ('9') as missing in the **Missing** column.

Finally, we need to identify the level of measurement associated with each variable. Respondent *id* and *gpa* are numeric interval level variables, so we chose 'Scale' for those two variables. *Sex* and *race* are categorical nominal variables, so we use the drop-down menu to choose 'Nominal,' as demonstrated in Figure C.29.

Once you have completed all of these steps, your final **Variable View** should look like Figure C.30.

Figure C.26 **Entering Variable Values**

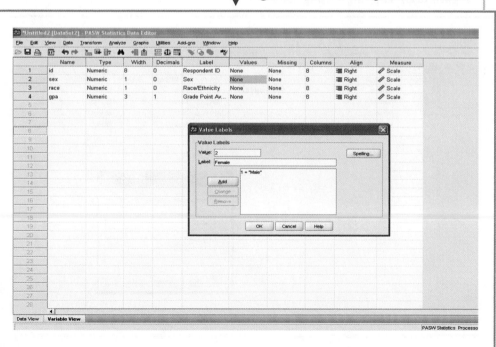

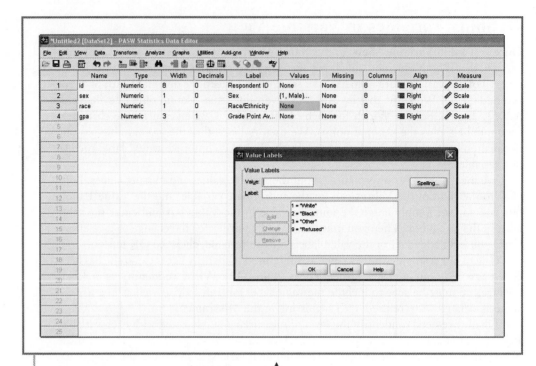

Figure C.27 **Entering Variable Values Continued**

Figure C.28 **Entering Missing Values**

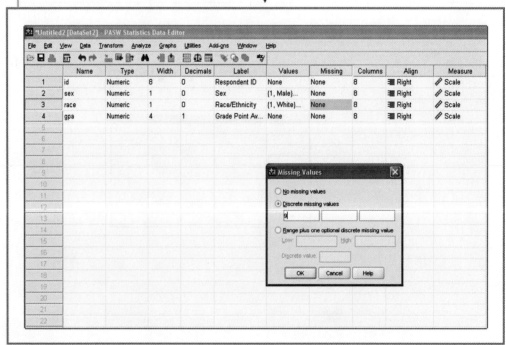

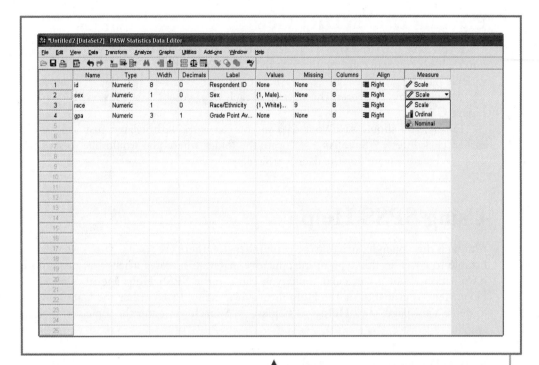

Figure C.29 Changing the Level of Measurement

Figure C.30 Final Variable View

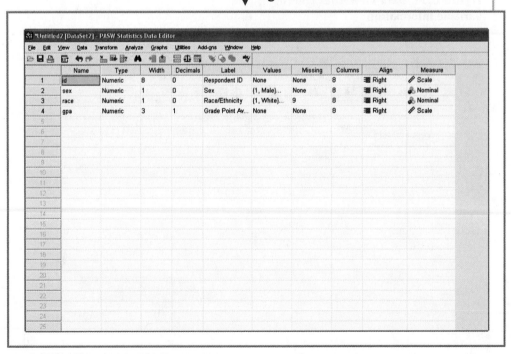

Entering Data in Data View

Once you have prepared your variables, you can go back to **Data View** to enter data into their appropriate cells. Notice that the first four columns are now labeled with our variable names.

After you have entered the data into each cell, your **Data View** will look like Figure C.32.

Finally, you should save your data so you can work with it later. Just like we did earlier, click **File** → **Save As** →. locate the folder where you would like to save the data → create a name for the data → **Save.**

Using SPSS Help

Although this appendix strives to be comprehensive, there are several things we will not be able to cover in this type of introductory material. In cases where you need more information about a particular topic, you can use the **SPSS Help Menu.** The SPSS Help Menu is available via the **Help** drop-down menu. From either the Data View or Variable View page, click **Help** → **Topics** → **Search** → enter the topic you wish to search.

SPSS Tutorials

If you need a review of any of the information presented in this appendix or would like further demonstrations of how to operate SPSS, you can also refer to the **SPSS Tutorial** that is available via the **Help** drop-down menu. This tutorial will walk you through all of the most useful and common operations in SPSS.

Figure C.31 **Data View After Entering Variable Information**

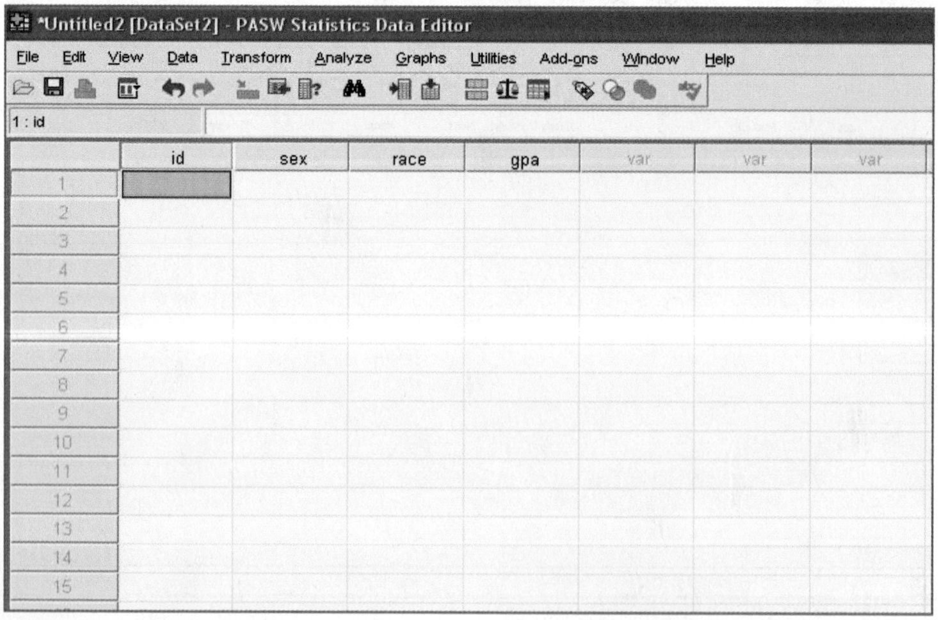

	id	sex	race	gpa
1	1	1	1	2.5
2	2	1	3	3.7
3	3	2	2	3.2
4	4	1	2	4.0
5	5	2	3	3.1
6	6	2	1	2.8
7	7	1	1	1.5
8	8	2	9	2.5
9	9	2	3	3.0
10	10	1	2	3.5

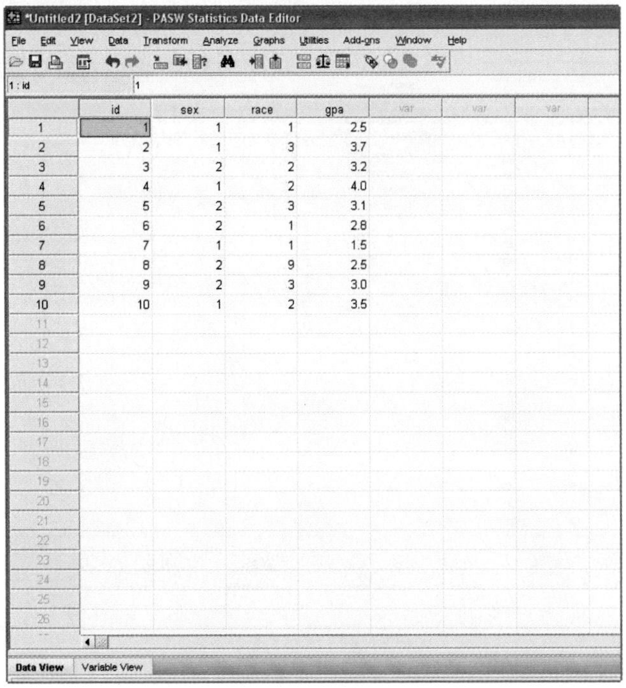

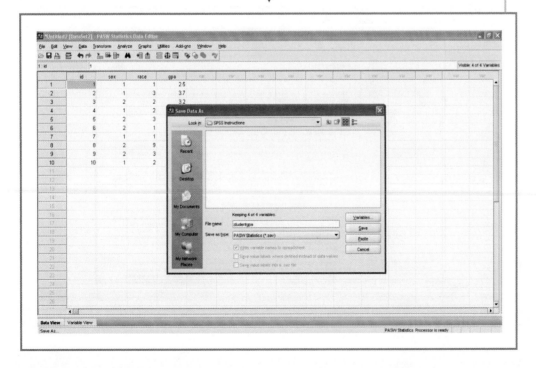

Figure C.32 Final Data View

Figure C.33 Save Your Data

File → Save As → locate folder → name your data → Save

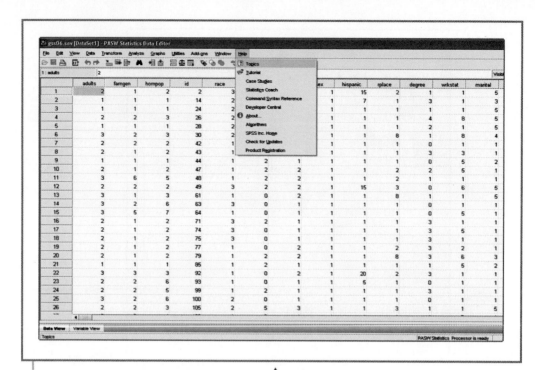

Figure C.34 SPSS Help Menu
Help → Topics

Figure C.35 Help Topics

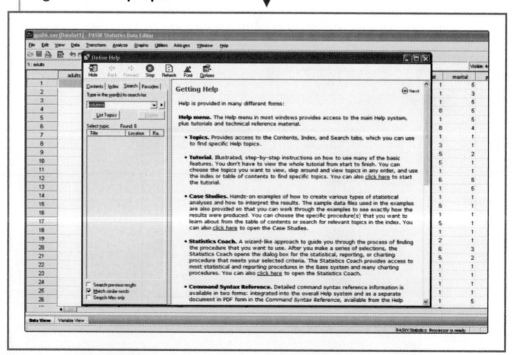

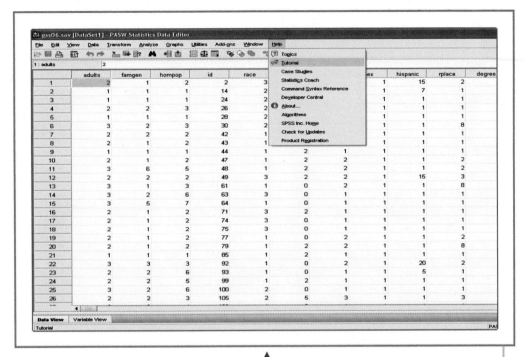

Figure C.36 SPSS Tutorials
Help → Tutorial

Figure C.37 SPSS Tutorial
Table of Contents

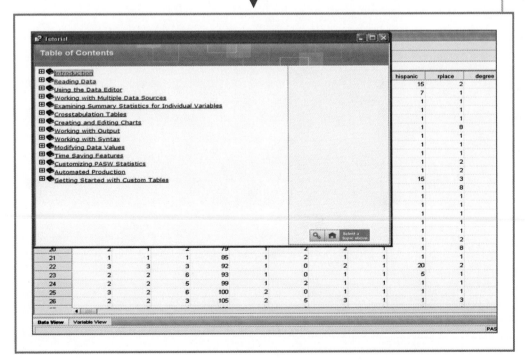

Answers to Odd-Numbered Chapter Exercises and Computer Exercises

Chapter 1

Exercises:

1. **A.** Academic achievement could be operationalized as an interval/ratio variable in which the value is equal to the respondent's GPA. ... 2.8, 2.9, 3.0, 3.1 ...

   B. Academic achievement could be operationalized as an ordinal variable as follows:
   Below Average
   Average
   Above Average

3. Proficiency in Spanish could be operationalized as follows:
   Beginner Intermediate Fluent

5. Collectively exhaustive refers to a condition that exists when each and every case can be placed into one of the attributes of a variable.

7. The attributes are not mutually exclusive.

9. Interval/ratio

11. Ordinal

13. Interval/ratio

15. Interval/ratio

17. Ordinal

Computer Exercises:

19. Nominal

21. Nominal

23. Nominal

25. Nominal

27. Ordinal

29. Ordinal

31. Nominal

33. Interval/ratio

35. Ordinal

37. Nominal

Chapter 2

Exercises:

1. 1492

3. 63.9

5. Nominal

7. .021

9. 24.35%

11. 84.35%

13. 4333

15. 27.2%

Computer Exercises:

17. Ordinal

19. 25

21. 40.0%

23. 2170

25. 16.3%

27. 12.0%

Chapter 3

Exercises:

1. 4

3. 4

5. 6

7. Working Full Time

9. NA

11. 21

13. Too little

15. NA

17. The median does not change.

19. Too little

21. NA

23. Yes, probably

25. 47

27. 47.14

Computer Exercises:

VARIABLE	MODE	MEDIAN	MEAN
29. Prestg80	51	43	44.17
31. Sibs	2	3	3.76
33. Gunlaw	Favor	NA	NA
35. Satjob	Very Satisfied	Mod. Satisfied	NA
37. Sei	63.5	42.2	49.41

QUESTION	MALES	FEMALES
39. What is the modal response for abany?	No	No
41. What is the modal response for fathers' highest degree (padeg)?	High School	High School
43. Which group has a higher mean response for socioeconomic index (sei)?	49.541	49.303

Chapter 4

Exercises:

1. 6

3. 1.5

5. 2.41

7. 3

9. 1.89

11. 12

13. 6.82

15. 15

17. 9.84

19. 2

21. 6

23. 2.15

25. 2

27. 2.45

29. 2

31. 1.39

33. 21

35. 5

37. 2.48

39. 21

41. 19.56

43. 3

45. 1.68

47. 1202

49. 17.8 and 27.8

Computer Exercises:

51. 16.894

53. 17.229

55. 19.5995

57. 19.3104

59. 10.68 and 87.92

Chapter 5

Exercises:

1. .111

3. .012

5. .118

7. .381

9. .280

11. .303

13. −1.25

15. −.25

17. 1.75

19. 2.5

21. .83

23. .35

25. Person #2 (New York)

27. .8264

29. .4443

Computer Exercises:

31. .556

33. .008

35. .460

37. .417

39. .290

41. .08

43. .86

45. 1.98

47. .441

49. .232

Chapter 6

Exercises:

1. .38

3. .12

5. .16

7. .03

9. .03

11. 25.61 to 26.39

13. 24.91 to 27.09

15. 3.95 to 4.05

17. 3.868 to 4.132

19. 76.9% to 87.1%

21. 77.7% to 86.3%

23. 10.3% to 25.7%

25. 13.6% to 22.4%

Computer Exercises:

27. 7.3913

29. 6.9832 to 7.7993

31. .30498

33. 6.8760

35. 6.3390 to 7.4130

37. .242

39. 46.49 to 47.79

41. .048

43. 13.20 to 13.39

45. 13.25 to 13.34

47. We can put more faith in wider confidence intervals (those with a greater range between the upper and lower bounds) because there is a greater probability the mean will fall between the upper and lower bounds. Therefore, the greater the percent of the confidence interval (99% as opposed to 95%), the greater the range between the bounds, and the greater the probability of the mean falling somewhere between them.

49. 0.004

51. 11.9% to 16.5%

Chapter 7

Exercises:

1. 1012

3. 106

5. 42.5%

7. 12.9%

9. 15.3%

11. 17

13. 83.3%

15. 21.7%

17. 259.4

19. 6.3

Computer Exercises:

21. 12

23. 14

25. 8

27. 15.0%

29. 50.0%

31. 30.0%

33. 90.0%

35. 55.0%

37. .371

39. .582

Chapter 8

Exercises:

1. Yes

3. The association is positive. As age increases, the likelihood of liking jazz music increases.

5. .273

7. .017

9. 0

11. .10

13. .76

15. .48

17. .36

Computer Exercises:

19. Phi = .032

21. V = .032

23. Phi = .071

25. V = .071

27. Phi = .251

29. V = .177

31. Phi = .112

33. V = .112

35. Phi = .147

37. V = .147

39. Gamma = .256

41. Gamma = −.052

43. Phi = .129

45. V = .091

47. Phi = .219

49. V = .219

51. Phi = .170

53. V = .120

Chapter 9

Exercises:

1. ANOVA is used to assess statistical significance when comparing means from two or more populations.

3. While ANOVA itself is not a measure of association, eta^2 is. Eta^2 is a ratio of the sum of squares between groups (SSB) to the total sum of squares (SST) and is based on a logic that is similar to gamma. Eta^2 can only be positive and is used as a measure of association when working with a categorical independent variable and an interval/ratio dependent variable.

5. 14

7. .67

9. Yes. Eta^2 is equal to .54, which indicates that 54% of the total variance in the number of parking tickets received is explained by Student Type. This is a very strong association.

11. Yes. Eta^2 is equal to .29, which indicates that 29% of the total variance in satisfaction with campus dining is explained by which dining hall students attend.

13. 78.571

15. 2.183

17. .20

19. Eta^2 indicates a weak association; however, because the significance level is .149, we cannot safely assume that this association is not the result of an error in our sample.

Computer Exercises:

21. 1,566,329.531

23. 371.344

25. .035

27. Although the results are highly significant, the association is extremely weak. Only 3.5% of the total variance in SEI is explained by political party affiliation.

29. 1,582,742.760

31. 373.376

33. .028

35. Although the results are highly significant, the association is extremely weak. Only 2.8% of the total variance in SEI is explained by race.

Chapter 10

Exercises:

1. A.

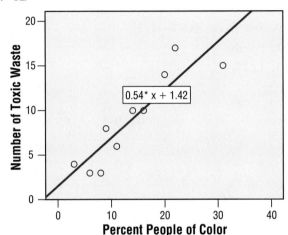

B. .901
C. 1.42, .54
D. 21.4
E. .8125; this means that 81.25% of the variance in the number of toxic waste sites is explained by the percent of the population that is people of color.
F. 5.89, Sig. = .001

3. A.

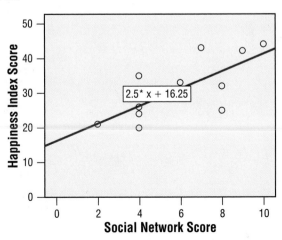

B. .724
C. 16.25; 2.5
D. 23.75
E. .525; this means that 52.5% of the total variance in the Happiness Index can be explained by the Social Network Index.
F. 3.32; Sig. = .01

5. A.

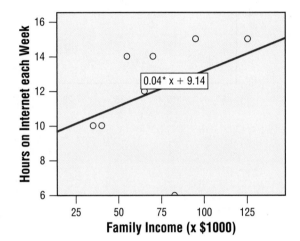

B. .378
C. 9.1, .04
D. 15.1
E. .143
F. 1.00, greater than .20 (not significant)

Computer Exercises:

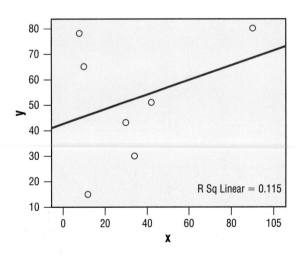

7. .458

9. .288

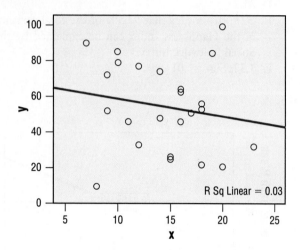

11. Yes. Negatively.

13. 3%

15. 47.07

17. Yes. Positively. r = .488

19. .219

21. 23.9%

23. .398

25. 3.17

27. 2.289

29. Yes. To the .000 level.

31. Positive

33. 32.1%

Index

Note: page numbers with f indicate figures; those with t indicate tables.

men, suicide rates among, 6–10,
7–8t
Merton, Robert, 324
"mind-blowing" statistics, 59
missing cases, 60–62
missing data, 38, 39t, 47
mode (Mo), 70
calculating measures of central tendency with grouped data and, 74
definition of, 68, 68t, 70, 72
distribution, 70
education and health, measures of
central tendency and, 80
interval/ratio variable, use of, 69, 69t
nominal variable, use of, 69, 69t
ordinal variable, use of, 69, 69t
raw data, calculating measures of
central tendency with, 72–73
symbol of, 68t
multiplication rule of probability,
141–43
independent events and, 141–42
multistage random sample, 169
mutually exclusive, 3, 16, 19

N

Naive consumers, 10
NASA, 167
National Environmental Policy
Act, 201
National Opinion Research Center
(NORC), 25, 79, 201, 349. *See
also* General Social Survey (GSS)
National Priorities List (NPL), 38, 43
National Survey of Student
Engagement (NSSE), 329–30
Newton, Sir Isaac, 4
Niagara Falls Homeowners Association
(NFHA), 36–37
95% confidence interval, 180
99% confidence interval, 180
No Child Left Behind Act, 24
nominal measures of association,
241–55
chi-square-based measures of,
241–49
contingency coefficient and,
246–47
Cramer's *V* and, 248–49
definition of, 241
lambda and, 249–55
phi and, 243–45
nominal variables, 3, 17–18, 19
example of, 25t

frequency tables for, 43–46
pie charts and, 21, 22f
use of, 69, 69t
nonparametric tests, 221
nonrandom sample, 169–70
definition of, 169
types of, 169
normal curve, 127
approximating, 128
probability and, 148–59, 148f
calculating, 152–54
randomness in, concept of, 149
z-scores, 149–51
standard (s) deviation and, 127–31,
128f, 129f
null hypothesis, 190–92, 217
number of degrees of freedom
among the subgroups (df_{within}), 277t
between groups ($df_{between}$), 277t
number of subgroups in the analysis
(N_k), 277t
numerator
frequencies and, 41
value of, in proportions, 40
numeric variable in SPSS, 361

O

observed frequencies, 217
Ocean's Eleven, 146
100-year flood line, 194
one-way chi-square, 218–23
for frequency table, 218–20
using SPSS for Windows, 221–23
operationalization, 13–14
opposite-direction pairs, 239t,
257, 260t
ordinal measures of association, 255–69
concept of ordered pairs and, 255–59
fundamentalism and, 260–62, 266–68
gamma and, 259–64
Somer's *d* and, 264–69
statistical uses and misuses of,
263–64
ordinal variables, 3, 18, 19
bar charts and, 22, 22f
example of, 26t
frequency tables for, 48–51
pie charts and, 21, 22f
use of, 69, 69t
outliers, 84
definition of, 68t, 83
effects of, 83–87
histogram of, 85f
skew as result of, 86

P

parameters, 166
PASW. *See* SPSS for Windows
Pataki, George, 277
Pearson's *r* (*r*)
calculating and interpreting, 311–19
formula for, 304t
squaring, 327
Pedagogy of the Oppressed (Freire), 126
per capita carbon dioxide emissions,
171–74
percent (%)
calculating, using Superfund site
data, 47
column, 42, 47, 54–55
cumulative, 36t, 42, 43, 47
definition of, 36t, 40
dispersion in, 166t
formula for, 36t, 40
frequency tables and, 40
valid, 42
percent column, 42, 47
in frequency tables, 54–55
percentiles
definition of, 137t, 159
formula for, 137t
using z-scores for finding, 159–60
phi (ϕ), 243–45
calculating, 243–45
definition of, 238t, 243
formula for, 238t, 244
pie charts, 21, 22f
politics of sampling, 167–69
population, 166
population proportion (π), 36t, 200t
population statistics
averages of, 69–70
education in United States,
distribution of, 106
position of median, 68t, 72–73
poverty in America, 305–7
predicted value of Y ($\hat{Y}$)
definition of, 305t
formula for, 305t
Principia (Newton), 4
probability. *See also* sampling; statistics
addition rule of, 141
college textbook expenses, 154–56
definition of, 136, 137t
disjoint events and, 141
formula for, 137t
frequency tables and, 143–48
fundamentals of, 139–43
human intelligence, measuring of, 137

Photo Credits

Key Symbols and Formulas

SYMBOL	MEANING OF SYMBOL	FORMULA
Standard Error of the Mean For Populations: $(\sigma_{\bar{x}})$ For Samples: $(s_{\bar{x}})$	A measure of variability in the sampling distribution of the mean.	For Population Data: $\sigma_{\bar{x}} = \dfrac{\sigma}{\sqrt{N}}$ For Sample Data: $s_{\bar{x}} = \dfrac{s}{\sqrt{N}}$
Dispersion in a Percentage	A measure of uniformity of responses.	$p(1 - p)$
Standard Error of the Proportion (Sp)	A measure of variability in a sampling distribution.	$Sp = \sqrt{\dfrac{p(1 - p)}{N}}$
Confidence Interval (CI)	A range of values in which the true population parameter is expected to fall.	95% CI for Proportion $= P \pm (1.96)s_p$ 95% CI for Mean $= \bar{X} \pm (1.96)s_i$
t ratio	A distribution that is used to determine probabilities when population parameters are unknown and estimated.	$t = \dfrac{\bar{X} - \mu}{s_{\bar{X}}}$
The Standard Error of the Difference Between Means $(S\bar{X}_1 - \bar{X}_2)$	A value that uses the standard deviations of two samples to estimate the difference between means.	$\sqrt{\left(\dfrac{N_1 S_1^2 + N_2 S_2^2}{N_1 + N_2 - 2}\right)\left(\dfrac{N_1 + N_2}{N_1 N_2}\right)}$
t test	A statistic used to determine the level of confidence at which the null hypothesis can be rejected.	$t = \dfrac{\bar{X}_1 - \bar{X}_2}{S_{\bar{X}_1 - \bar{X}_2}}$
Column %	Column Percent	$column \ \% = \dfrac{f}{N_{column}}(100)$
Row %	Row Percent	$row \ \% = \dfrac{f}{N_{row}}(100)$
χ^2	Chi-Square	$\chi^2 = \Sigma \dfrac{(f_o - f_e)^2}{f_e}$
df	Degrees of freedom for a frequency table	$df = \# \ rows - 1$
df	Degrees of freedom for a crosstabulation table	$df = (\# \ rows - 1)(\# \ columns - 1)$
alpha	Level of Statistical Significance	
Measures of Association	A group of descriptive statistics that indicate the strength of a relationship between two variables.	
Proportionate Reduction of Error	The degree to which our ability to predict outcomes in the dependent variable are influenced by the independent variable.	
Phi (ϕ)	A chi-square based measure of association used with 2 × 2 crosstabulation tables that contain at least one nominal variable.	$\phi = \sqrt{\dfrac{\chi^2}{N}}$
Contingency Coefficient (C)	A chi-square based measure of association used with crosstabulation tables that are square in shape and contain at least one nominal variable.	$C = \sqrt{\dfrac{\chi^2}{N + \chi^2}}$
Cramer's V (V)	A chi-square based measure of association used with crosstabulation tables that are rectangular in shape and contain at least one nominal variable.	$V = \sqrt{\dfrac{\chi^2}{N(k - 1)}}$
Lambda (λ)	A PRE measure of association used when at least one of the two variables in a crosstabulation table is nominal.	$\lambda = \dfrac{E_1 - E_2}{E_1}$
Gamma	A PRE measure of association based on the concept of concordant (same order) and discordant (opposite order) pairs that is used when both variables in a crosstabulation table are ordinal.	$G = \dfrac{S - O}{S + O}$